Images of the World

Not ideas, but material and ideal interests, directly govern men's conduct. Yet frequently the 'world images' that have been created by 'ideas' have, like switchmen, determined the tracks along which action has been pushed by the dynamic of interest. 'From what' and 'for what' one wished to be redeemed...depended upon one's image of the world.

Max Weber
The Social Psychology of the World Religions

Images of the World
Essays on Religion,
Secularism, and Culture

T.N. Madan

OXFORD
UNIVERSITY PRESS

OXFORD
UNIVERSITY PRESS

Oxford University Press is a department of the University of Oxford.
It furthers the University's objective of excellence in research, scholarship,
and education by publishing worldwide. Oxford is a registered trademark of
Oxford University Press in the UK and in certain other countries

Published in India by
Oxford University Press
22 Workspace, 2nd Floor, 1/22 Asaf Ali Road, New Delhi 110002, India

First published 2006
Oxford India Paperbacks 2008

ISBN-13: 978-0-19-569834-3
ISBN-10: 0-19-569834-7

Typeset in Lalit in 10/12
by Excellent Typesetters, Pitampura, Delhi 110 034
Printed in India by Manipal Technologies Limited, Manipal

For
Ayan with love

आ नो भद्राः क्रितवो यन्तु विश्वतः

Contents

Preface

Of the thirteen addresses and essays that comprise this volume, five were written (and published) between 1987 and 1998 and the rest, in the last five years (2000–5). Together they represent my continuing exploration of the significance of culture, religion, secularism, and ethnicity in social life in India and on occasion more generally. This is now an intellectual interest of more than twenty years, and has so far yielded, besides the compositions included here, many other papers and a book, *Modern Myths, Locked Minds: Secularism and Fundamentalism in India* (1997). Also, I have selected and edited two collections of readings, *Religion in India* (1991) and *India's Religions* (2004). All these publications together are a product of my reading and reflection and my own writings among them may be said to belong to the genre of discursive sociology.

Many years ago I published an article on a major domestic ritual of the Pandits of the Kashmir Valley, 'Herath: A religious ritual and its secular aspect' (1961), which was primarily based on fieldwork but also drew upon the textual tradition of the people. Without being wholly self-conscious about it then, I had already taken up a position on the productive dialectic of the religious and the secular in society and on the complementarity of the 'book' and 'field' views of Indian society. I should have by now published more on the religious life of the Pandits and the Muslims of the Valley but regrettably have not done so. In the meanwhile, Kashmir has passed through traumatic times since the late 1980s: the old social order comprising two religious communities living separately together has collapsed, and the old pluralist religious sensibilities too have been challenged.

Whereas Chapters 1 to 11 of this book deal with specific issues pertaining to religion, politics, and culture, Chapters 12 and 13 address broadly some issues in the comparative study of cultures and civilizations. Actually in all my studies of the above themes over the years, inter-cultural comparison has usually been present, if not as a central focus then as the backdrop. In this sense my work is also anthropological.

The chapters have been grouped into four, thematically akin, parts. A brief note introduces each part and the essays in it. I will refrain, therefore, from commenting on them here. I do, however, want to point out that a core idea that binds together the essays in this book is the understanding, supported by a vast body of historical and social science research, that despite ongoing secularization religion still occupies a significant place in the lives of most people in India, and that it exists not in isolation but in dynamic interaction with politics and the wider cultural settings. In the classical Hindu (Brahmanical) tradition, the pursuit of rational economic and political goals was deemed legitimate only if it was carried out within the framework of dharma. In the twentieth century, when nationalism (an idea borrowed from the West) came to occupy the political space, its linkages with religion took diverse forms, ranging from assertions of identity (nationalism is religion) to the explicit or implicit acknowledgement of religious identity as a useful instrument of political mobilization. Religion thus became, as Louis Dumont once put it succinctly, its own shadow: value became sign of distinction. Either way it remained in the centre of the political stage. Even a steadfast rationalist and agnostic such as Jawaharlal Nehru testified to its positive role alongside the negative in history, and eventually conceded that secularism in India would have to connote religious pluralism.

The wide scope and resilience of religion and the relationship of religion and politics remain in focus, directly or indirectly, throughout this book. Religion is seen here as a crucial element of culture, not an enclave within it. The objective has been to explore these relationships and to render explicit their implications. I have not held back from making value judgements, and made clear my lack of sympathy and support for homogenizing ideologies, whether religious or secular. Tolerance and pluralism, and through them a conception of multiple modernities, are surer guides to social harmony and a saner future, but one has to guard against entrapment in a runaway relativism. This is not easy but it is an imperative. I have argued in more than one publication that of the several possible ways in which pluralism may operate in a society, *participatory* pluralism—the recognition of one's incompleteness in the absence of the other—is perhaps the most constructive. And it may not be divorced from a grammar of values because it is based on deliberate choice making, not mere sentiment.

The fact that these essays were written over many years necessarily reflects sustained engagement with a number of issues. I have confined revision of the earlier papers (those published between 1987 and 1998) to minor verbal corrections. This does not mean that my views on the various issues under discussion have remained static: major revisions of argument would have obscured the fact that in some respects my views have indeed evolved, at times on further reflection and on certain points in response to the changing times in which we live. Letting the essays stand as originally written preserves the integrity of each composition. It has, however, resulted in some repetitiveness in my discussions of secularism and the current turmoil in the Kashmir Valley (subjects of the deepest concern to me) in the first two parts of the book. But my return to these themes after they have been first introduced occurs in discursive contexts that differ chapter to chapter. Chapters 5 and 11 are being published here for the first time. Both are attempts at participation in ongoing debates that have both academic and political aspects. Chapter 5 was actually begun as the introduction to the volume, but was shortened, and thereby given a sharper focus, and placed in Part One.

It may be noted here that the use of diacritical marks in the non-English words that occur in the text has been limited to the long vowels *ā*, *ī*, and *ū*. Whatever such words are included and printed in Roman in the *Concise Oxford English Dictionary* (11th edn, 2004) have generally been used here likewise, but with diacritical marks (for example, sannyāsī). The names of various corpuses of Indian literature are printed in Roman (for example, Upanishads), but particular titles have been italicized (for example, *Rāmāyana*).

The original place of publication of each address or essay is given in the initial footnote of each chapter. I am grateful to the copyright holders for their permission to reproduce the same here, in some cases in considerably revised form.

In studies such as these, one's indebtedness to the work of other, more accomplished scholars is of course immense; it is writ large on every page of this book. Acknowledgement of the encouragement of colleagues who read and criticized earlier drafts of the essays is made separately in each chapter. It is a joy to thank them all again. I owe the excellent index to Vandana Madan, my daughter. Finally, I am grateful to Rajesh Chatwal and Satya Narain for patiently converting over many years my hand written drafts into computer printouts. I have found working with them a pleasure.

New Delhi   T.N. Madan
31 May 2006

Part One

Religion and Secularism

The theme of the first chapter of the book is the persistence of religion in the modern world despite confident expectations to the contrary. The historic process of rationalization/secularization in Europe, which was at its peak at the beginning of the twentieth century, was believed to have the potential of becoming a world-wide force. Judging by the resurgence of religion as faith (religiousness) and as political ideology (religious mindedness) in its last two decades, the twentieth century indeed turned out to be (in Eric Hobsbawm's phrase) a short one. How did the expectations about the decline of religion arise, and why they have been not wholly fulfilled, are questions addressed in Chapter 1. In the circumstances, freedom of religion (more broadly, freedom of conscience) and religious pluralism in the setting of religious fundamentalism and intolerance, have acquired great salience in our times. The subject is discussed in the second chapter in comparative perspective with particular reference to the Indian situation.

Secularism (secularization as a universal *thesis* and not merely as a widespread *process*) has inevitably come under critical review, which does not mean, however, that it has been totally rejected, although particular forms of it, notably the Marxian view of religion, have turned out to be seriously flawed. Secularism is now seen as an ideology with varying connotations and fortunes that seem to go with cultural settings. Thus, laicism in France, the separation of the Church and the state in the USA, and secularism in India stand for different positions on the role of religion in public life, ranging from sustained efforts to banish it from the public square to affirmations of respect or equal regard for it. The relationship of secularism and religious fundamentalism, it is now recognized, is more complex than sheer antagonism would imply. Indeed, the excesses of the one feed the other. Paradoxically, for secularism to succeed, it has become apparent that religion itself needs to be taken seriously—that it can be a powerful resource in the struggle against religious fanaticism. These themes are developed in Chapters 3 and 4. The former is in the nature of a general statement and the latter focuses on India, where the Gandhian and Nehruvian perspectives frame the public discourse.

I may point out that 'Secularism in its place' (Chapter 3) is reproduced here exactly as it was first published in 1987. It has been anthologized a number of times, in full or in part, by various scholars, and has attracted considerable attention that has more often been critical than supportive. It has become, it seems, one of the essential readings on the theme of secularism for critics and supporters alike. Some arguments in it have perhaps needed elaboration, and some gross misrepresentations of it call for firm rebuttal. I have done this in Chapter 5. I would like to draw the reader's attention to the fact that Chapters 3, 4, and 5 were written at approximately ten year intervals, spanning a period of twenty years (1986–2005). Each essay is based on my understanding of the problem of secularism as I perceived it at the time of writing.

The last chapter also looks at the ongoing thinking on secularism, and points out that the limited and indeed insular Indian debate, which continues but does not move forward significantly, has not kept pace with developments in political theory elsewhere. A critical discussion of the issues involved is only too often clouded by rhetoric, and this is deplorable. What we need is clarity of thought, and not a confusion of it. I have tried to contribute to this process through this and the following parts of the book.

1

*Religion in the Modern World**

By the side of every religion is to be found a political opinion,
which is connected with it by affinity. If the human mind be left
to follow its own bent, it will regulate the temporal and spiritual
institutions of society in a uniform manner, and man will endeavour,
if I may so speak, to *harmonize* earth with heaven.

Alexis de Tocqueville
Democracy in America

A hypothetical world from which the sacred has been swept away
would admit of only two possibilities: vain fantasy that recognizes
itself as such, or immediate satisfaction which exhausts itself....
The conscience liberated from the sacred knows this, even if it
conceals it from itself.

Leszek Kolakowski
'The Revenge of the Sacred in Secular Culture',
Modernity on Endless Trial

Why is this phenomenon, so hastily called the 'return of religions',
so difficult to think? Why is it so surprising? Why does it particularly

* This essay is a revised and extended version of the spoken text of the
First M.N. Srinivas Memorial Lecture delivered at the National Institute
of Advanced Study (NIAS), Bangalore, on 9 January 2001, with the
Director, Roddam Narasimha, FRS, in the chair. I would like to place
on record my deep appreciation of the courtesies extended to me by
Professor Narasimha and his colleagues.

The present tense of the text is that of the time of its delivery, but
I have reworded it at places for the sake of better readability. A few
quotations, references, and footnotes also have been added (in 2005).
Personal tributes to Professor Srinivas with which the Lecture began and
ended have not been included here; they may be seen in the version
circulated by NIAS (Madan 2001).

astonish those who believed naively that an alternative opposed
Religion, on the one hand, and on the other, Reason, Enlightenment,
Science, Criticism (Marxist Criticism, Nietzschean Genealogy,
Freudian Psychoanalysis and their heritage), as though the one
could not but put an end to the other?

Jacques Derrida
'Faith and Knowledge', *Acts of Religion*

'The modern man', wrote Max Weber at the beginning of the
twentieth century, 'is in general, even with the best will, unable
to give religious ideas a significance for culture and national
character which they deserve' (1930: 183). How did this inability
emerge? And where do we stand today a hundred years after
Weber's seemingly enigmatic observation? These are the two
questions which I have briefly addressed in this essay dedicated
to the memory of the distinguished Indian sociologist M.N. Srinivas
(1916–99), who was deeply interested in studying and reflecting
on the place of religion in society (Madan 2000).

RELIGION AND MODERN SCIENCE IN THE WEST

To ask when and where the modern world had its birth is surely
an idle question, for modernity, as is now widely recognized,
has had many expressions and therefore many beginnings. I will
stay with the West in this part of the essay, thereby avoiding
entanglement with the definitional question, 'What is Religion?';
moreover, the confrontation between religion and modern science
began there. Let me note here, however, that when secularism
(alongside the concept of 'scientific temper') was adopted as the
ideology of the state in India (the Constitution of India, Preamble,
and Article 51A, h), it was explicitly defined as freedom of religion
for the citizen (Articles 25 to 30), and as the obligation of the
state to follow non-discriminatory policies towards the followers
of all religions (Article 15). The question of conflict between
religiousness and scientific temper was eschewed.

The West's own specific form of modernity, which has undeniably been one of the most powerful influences on the course of
social change (conceived comprehensively) in other parts of
the world, had its origin in the seventeenth century (if not earlier)[1]
in the 'spectacular triumphs of science' (Russell 1946: 547; see

also Russell 1961). The decline of the hold of religious beliefs over the minds of people was of course aided by the manifold distress generated by the Wars of Religion in Europe, particularly in the first half of the seventeenth century (Toynbee 1956: 180ff.; Dunn 1979).

The most representative philosopher of the Age of Reason, Immanuel Kant (1724–1804) wanted man to 'Dare to know [and have] the courage to use [his] own understanding', which was, according to him 'the motto of the Enlightenment'. Dependence on external authority was rejected, for it amounted to 'self-incurred immaturity' (Kant 1991: 54). He was, however, willing to compromise: 'religion within the limits of reason alone' was acceptable. Revelation was ruled out, and religion was in fact nothing more than pure morality, the 'knowledge of our duties as divine commands' (Cassirer 1981: 382). As for morality, Kant believed, its foundations wholly rested in practical reason, and traditional religion was redundant, and indeed a hindrance; to think otherwise would be delusional.

The spirit of the Enlightenment in France, going beyond Voltaire's combination of reason and deism (Ayer 1986: 109ff., 172), and in contrast to the German version, was uncompromisingly secularist. The ringing call of Denis Diderot (1713–84) to humanity was to 'Have the courage to free [itself] from the yoke of religion', so that one may regain one's humanity, be oneself (Cassirer 1968: 135). The total war which French Encyclopaedism began against religious faith in all its forms was reinforced by the Revolution (1789) with its strong anti-clericalism, opposition to religious institutions, and an ideological core which asserted, among other things, that everything concerning the human condition was in the end knowable and therefore changeable (Furet 1981: 25 et passim). Europe had come a long way since the time Descartes (1596–1650) had attempted to provide a rational proof of the existence of God, and Newton (1642–1727) had acknowledged a Supreme Intelligence that created both the world and its unchangeable laws.[2]

In the anarchic aftermath of the French Revolution, some perceptive social thinkers, such as Auguste Comte (1798–1857), who conceived of a positive science of society (grounded in empiricism and the belief in the perfectibility of institutions), and gave it the name of sociology, while sure that theological and metaphysical varieties of knowledge had had their day, still recognized the need for reformulated varieties of religion to hold together society, which stays in place not by any natural law but by morals and integrative symbols. Although intellectually obsolete, religion was socially necessary (Preus 1987: 109). Émile Durkheim (1881–1917), author of one of the greatest books ever written by a sociologist, *The Elementary Forms of Religious Life* (first published in French in 1912), believed that Comte's 'attempt to organize a religion using old historical memories' was doomed to fail. 'There are no immortal gospels', he added, 'and there is no reason to believe that humanity is incapable of conceiving new ones in the future' (1995: 429–30).

Durkheim was concerned with social order (or solidarity), the sociological problem par excellence, which he believed to be an outcome of assemblies of people and the rituals they perform together—somewhat like what is happening here just now![3]—but his conception of the social significance of religion was much broader. And in this broader conception I find a break with the dogmatism of the late nineteenth century of which Marx's views on the future of religion are of course the classic statement; on that more below.

According to Durkheim, religion was historically and everywhere the source of morality, law, science, and much else. And, as he put it, 'If religion gave birth to all that is essential in society, that is so because the idea of society is the soul of religion' (ibid.: 421). Durkheim's 'sociologism' has been criticized for its excess and exclusivism, but the deep insights into the nature of religious phenomena that he offered have, I think, largely stood the test of time. The fact that the processes of secularization had gradually seen such domains as art, law, and science move out of the ambit of religion did not basically alter Durkheim's vision of the importance of religion to the human condition in terms of what it does for it. 'Its true function', he asserted, ' is to make us act and help us live', not only routinely but, more significantly, in the face of 'the trials of existence' and in enabling us to be 'lifted above the human miseries' (ibid.: 419).

Durkheim further observed that 'insofar as religion is action and insofar as it is a means of making men live, science cannot possibly take its place', just as religion is not 'able to tell science what to do'. Science proceeds fragmentarily and slowly, 'but life—that cannot wait.' In the face of the ceaseless and indeed triumphal advance of science, however, religion itself had become 'an object of science!' Although religion seemed to him 'destined to transform itself rather than disappear', and although he saw 'something eternal in religion', Durkheim also noted that once 'the authority of science is established', religion must submit to the logic of science and substantively have its scope delimited (ibid.: 432–3). In his vision of the future, while secular education, civic morals, and professional ethics would help strengthen the bonds of social solidarity and provide new models of socialization and individual expression (Durkheim 1956, 1957), religious beliefs would not wholly disappear for 'they contain their own truth' (Durkheim 1995: 439).

Like every other European intellectual of his generation, Durkheim grew up in awareness of the writings of Karl Marx (1818–83), including his (Marx's) characterization of religion as socially determined 'false consciousness' that conceals the true nature of class-based society, and which must therefore be abolished in the interest of 'the real happiness' of people in general (Marx and Engels 1959: 262–3). Perhaps to ensure that his theory of the social origin of religion is not confused with the Marxian, Durkheim cautioned (without mentioning Marx by name) that 'collective consciousness' was not 'a mere epiphenomenon of its morphological base', and that his view of religion was not 'merely a refurbishment of historical materialism' (Durkheim 1995: 426).[4] It should also be noted here that the Marxian intervention represents, perhaps more powerfully than any other intellectual development, the transition from the eighteenth to the nineteenth century, from one kind of ethos to another, one that had a much broader social base. While the middle classes were reticent about their atheism (or secularism as it came to be called), the working classes embraced in their 'tens of thousands' (Chadwick 1975: 89). While the 'Enlightenment' had been 'of the few', 'Secularization' was 'of the many' (ibid.: 9).

More than Marx, perhaps, it was Charles Darwin (1809–82) and the social evolutionists who influenced thinking in the late nineteenth century about the end of the reign of religion in Western society. There were some thinkers, however, who felt deeply uncomfortable about the implications of this critical turn of the wheel of history. In the year of Darwin's death, and a year before

Marx's, Friedrich Nietzsche in his *Gay Science* spoke about the madman, who ran one morning into sunlit market place, with a lantern in his hand, and asked where he might find God. The atheists in the crowd made fun of him, suggesting God may be hiding, or he may have got lost, or perhaps he may have just gone away.

> The madman jumped in their midst and pierced them with his eyes. 'Whither is God?' he cried. 'I shall tell you. *We have killed him*—you and I. All of us are his murderers. But how did we do this? How could we drink up the sea? Who gave us the sponge to wipe away the entire horizon? What were we doing when we unchained this earth from its sun?... God is dead. God remains dead. What was holiest and most powerful of all that the world has yet owned has bled to death under our knives: who will wipe the blood off us?...' (Kauffman 1974: 960–7).

Astonished by what he had said, the listeners fell silent, hearing him say as he departed: 'I came too early, my time is not yet' (ibid.). The narrator of the parable, we may safely assume, is Nietzsche himself; and we know that in the last decade of his life he became insane. What engaged him all his life was not the expectation that the idea of God could be revived—in fact he considered traditional religions generally and Christianity in particular a blight—or the conviction that a new religion should be founded. In fact, Nietzsche's 'greatest and most persistent problem' was how to 'escape nihilism': if one affirms the presence of God, one denies the ultimate significance of the secular world; if one denies the idea of God, everything else is robbed of meaning and value (Kauffman 1947: 101). Either way, one ends up being a nihilist: there is no escape. It is arguable that Nietzsche's problem is indeed the predicament of modern man/woman, echoed in Ivan Karamazov's lament (in Dostoevsky's great novel), everything is permitted if God does not exist, nothing is sacred any more. The same idea has been recently reaffirmed succinctly by the political theorist William Connolly: 'contemporary carriers of the sacred and the secular often converge in thinking that only a god is worthy of reverence. The former invest reverence in god; the latter tend to invest it nowhere' (1995: 189).

The influence of Nietzsche's thought on Max Weber (1864–1920), a German sociologist who together with Durkheim is a founder of the sociology of religion, may not be exaggerated, but there is no denying the fact that these two German thinkers of great intensity shared a tragic view of the implications of the loss of faith. Weber described himself as 'absolutely unmusical religiously', but confessed that, on 'thorough self-examination' he found himself 'neither antireligious nor irreligious' (1975: 324); indeed he even felt tempted by mysticism as a means of recovering the meaningfulness of life (see Mitzman 1985: 218–19). And he was intellectually curious about its role in human affairs. Weber's principal interest was in the course and consequences of the historical process of rationalization in different cultural settings and the contribution (or lack of contribution) of different religions to it. Thus, while he believed that the Christian Puritan's anxiety about his salvation led him through a chain of unforeseen causality to the emergence of the spirit of capitalism in Europe, he regarded Indian religions (Hinduism, Buddhism) as the source of ethics 'which have abnegated the world, theoretically, practically, and to the greatest extent' (1948: 323). These are large and controversial theses and have been much discussed.

More relevant to the present discussion is Weber's vision of the nature of human existence in modern society, 'a world robbed of gods' (Weber 1948: 282). He saw no future for religion, which does not mean that he was overtly or covertly hostile to it. While the decline of mystery, magic and ritual, which he called the 'disenchantment of the world', was historically inevitable, he was also conscious of the fact that the long-term consequences of progressive rationalization were likely to entail heavy costs. He foresaw modern society overcome by a scientific-technological and manipulative world view and a consumerist lifestyle, deprived of legitimacy in terms of ultimate values and thus rendered meaningless. As he put it, 'the ultimate and the most sublime values have retreated from public life either into the transcendental realm of mystic life or into the brotherliness of direct and personal human relations' (ibid.: 155). The only values that a rationalized world knows are instrumental values and its conception of perfection is synonymous with efficiency. Expressing scepticism about science and its techniques being capable of leading modern man to happiness, Weber quoted Tolstoy to the effect that science is 'meaningless' because it does not answer the most important question of 'What shall we do and how shall we live?' Taking the example of 'modern medicine', and generalizing from it, he said in 1917:

> Whether life is worth living and when—this question is not asked by medicine. Natural science gives us an answer to the question of what we must do if we wish to master life technically. It leaves quite aside, or assumes for its purposes, whether we should and do wish to master life technically and whether it ultimately makes sense to do so (1948: 144).

Weber saw modern man trapped in an 'iron cage', faced with lack of 'spirit', 'nullity', and 'heartlessness', and engaged in the destructive 'sport' of 'machine production' that would be played out only when 'the last ton of fossil fuel' would have been burnt out (1930: 181–2).

In my reading of the classics of sociology, I know of few characterizations of modern life that are more insightful and prophetic and unsettling than the foregoing (and other related observations) by Weber. Questions of this kind continued to be asked throughout the twentieth century, and answers too have been provided. For example, it has been argued that questions of value cannot be decided 'intellectually', that they lie 'outside the realm of truth and falsehood', and 'what science cannot discover, man cannot know' (Russell 1961: 243). To bracket away questions of value in this manner is evidence, however, not of their worthlessness but of the limitations of the scientific method, of scientism. Similarly, the dismissal of such concerns as 'freedom' and 'dignity' as false (Skinner 1972) only exposes the weaknesses of a secularized consciousness and of crass behaviourism. All such scepticism notwithstanding, those secularists who have felt the need have sought to evolve a grammar of values to guide everyday life.

One of the well known such attempts was the *Humanist Manifesto* of the American Humanist Association issued in 1933. Prepared under the guidance of the famous philosopher John Dewey (who always made a distinction between formal religion and the religious attitude), it proclaimed that 'the nature of the universe depicted by modern science makes unacceptable any supernatural or cosmic guarantees of human values.' Further, it held, 'Man is at last becoming aware that he is responsible for the realization of the world of his dreams, that he has within himself the power of its achievement' (see Hitchcock 1982: 11). Needless to emphasize, what we have here is the old Enlightenment notion of the perfectibility of the human condition through human agency.

Forty years later, a second *Humanist Manifesto*, signed by distinguished scientists, philosophers and other intellectuals, reiterated: 'While there is much that we do not know, humans are responsible for what we are or will become. No deity will save us; we must save ourselves. We affirm that moral values derive from human experience. Ethics is *autonomous* and situational, needing no theological or ideological sanction' (ibid.: 13–14). A more positive attitude to ethics is discernible here. These manifestos were, in fact, identified by some proponents and critics as religious, although non-theistic (the term 'secular humanism' came into vogue only in the 1960s); they were grounded in empiricism, pragmatism, and relativism. A truly religious perspective does not, of course, have to be theistic, but it has to have a conception of ultimate values and some kind of a transcendent point of reference; the latter is ruled out from a secularist perspective. Even so, the defenders of the separation of the Church and the state in the USA were concerned that the teaching of the principles of secular humanism in state funded schools would amount to a breach of the First Amendment (regarding the non-establishment of a Church by the state), and they got a sympathetic hearing from the courts. Widespread religiousness in American society (something that Alexis de Tocqueville noticed and commented on in the middle of the nineteenth century) has been responsible, since the time of the colonies, for an attitude of wariness among both religious and secular people regarding the intentions of the state. Anxieties among the religious minded were deepened by the Darwinian and, later, Freudian challenges and had become manifest in, among other ways, the emergence of Christian fundamentalism early in the twentieth century (Marty 1986).

THE RISE OF COUNTER CULTURE

The two decades of the 1950s and 1960s were a kind of watershed in the West, marked by a resurgence of interest in the religious legitimation of human life, in a recoil, as it were, from the extremes of utilitarian individualism generally and the regulative mechanisms of the state. One of the remarkable reaffirmations of the religious perspective found expression in the inaugural address of John Kennedy as President of the USA in January 1961. He invoked god three times, but it is customary for American presidents to do so on ceremonial occasions. What is more noteworthy is that, while he pointed out that power had passed into the hands of a new youthful generation in his country, he also proclaimed: 'The rights of man come from not the generosity of the state but from the hand of God' (see Bellah 1976: 171). The master metaphor of 'the hand of God' was employed to stress that, while sovereignty rests with the people in a democracy, there is something higher than the verdict of the people, a higher criterion of legitimacy of the state than the reasons of the state that Machiavelli had nailed to the masthead of modern political thought.[5]

Kennedy's words were echoed by Martin Luther King Jr in his own celebrated 'I have a dream' speech at the 'March on Washington' in August 1963. He demanded freedom and justice for all Americans—'black men and white men, Jews and Gentiles, Protestants and Catholics'—on the ground that they were 'all God's children' (see Lewis 1970: 229). The religious inspiration of the Civil Rights Movement was no ordinary thing. Incidentally, the metaphor of the dream, of the dream convertible or converted into reality, might well have been borrowed by King from Mahatma Gandhi (ibid.: 210). I may recall here in passing that the cardinal principle of Gandhi's politics was that it should be rooted in morality and not in expediency, that the means were no less important than the ends. For him, the true goal of the vocation of politics was altruistic social service, a combination of, in Weber's words, 'an ethic of ultimate ends and an ethic of responsibility' (1948: 127).

Prominent politicians (like Kennedy and King) were not alone in reiterating the abiding place of religious values in public life; a wide range of scholars also came to be inclined in the same way. The 1960s saw the emergence of a highly complex 'counter culture' movement in the West spearheaded by the youth. At its centre lay a deep dissatisfaction with the basic assumptions of the Enlightenment and the resultant technocratic view of the world. It had a broad range of expressions including, at the one extreme, self-destructive and anti-social activities and, at the other, a turning towards the mystical and the spiritual. It was in this setting that Hare Krishna Consciousness (see Gelberg 1983), and Zen, too, took root on American university campuses. Those scholars who applied themselves to a serious study of the phenomena concluded that the quest of the youth was not 'how shall we know?', but 'how shall we live?' It was 'to discover ways to live from day to day that integrate the whole of our nature by way of yielding nobility of conduct, honest fellowship, and joy' (Roszak 1969: 233). One hears echoes here of Weber's concern about the importance of ultimate values and of Durkheim's observation that historically such values have come from the religious traditions of humanity. The fear that such rejections of rationalist world views could also open the way to a 'rhetoric of reaction' were not wholly misplaced. In short, there was a negative as well as a positive side to these developments, howsoever one may wish for a single judgement.

As the 1960s drew to their close, efforts were still on in some circles to reconcile the religious and secular points of view. Some Christian theologians argued that secularization must be welcomed for it would not have occurred unless God willed it (Cox 1965). At the same time, perceptive sociologists began to wonder whether the 'desiccation' of modern culture, which was 'what secularization [had] often meant, might begin to be reversed', and religion as 'an imaginative statement about the truth of the totality of human experience' reinstated (Bellah 1976: 244). The return of the sacred to the secular world seemed a genuine possibility.

There were other things happening, too, and other perceptions of the prevailing social reality. Thus, Robert Bellah, a distinguished American sociologist (from whose work I have already quoted), pointed out that shared historical experience of a people may generate values and principles that enshrine, as it were, a kind of consensus on national identity expressed in a religious idiom. The longing for celebratory togetherness that seems to be universal maybe fulfilled through ceremonies (such as the inauguration of the President at which it is customary to invoke the blessings of a non-denominational god on the American people), commemorations (Thanksgiving, Memorial Day) and holidays (the birthdays of national heroes like Abraham Lincoln and Martin Luther King Jr). The commonality thus conceived is the vision of a perfect society, a yearning for ultimate values, clearly differentiated from the teachings of the churches, but elaborated and institutionalized as what Bellah calls 'civil religion' (1976: 68–89).[6]

Actually he saw little scope for a complete rupture with the religious mode of thinking even among the votaries of secularism. He wrote: 'The notion of secularization is far from a simple empirical generalization. It is part of a theory of modern society, a theory that can almost be called a myth because it functions to create an emotionally coherent picture of reality. It is in this sense religious, not scientific at all' (ibid.: 237).

This was written in 1966 (Bellah 1976: 168 ff.). By the mid-seventies, Bellah was constrained by the manner in which events had unfolded in American society to lament over 'the broken covenant' (Bellah 1975), that is, the failure of the promise of the 1960s. Another decade on, he reported a shift in the locus of 'commitment' in American life from the collectivity (one another) to the self, alongside a transformation of 'religious self-understanding' in the direction of a narrow 'expressive individualism' ('my own religion') (Bellah 1985). A close reading of the writings of Robert Bellah reveals the contrary ways in which the religious life of middle class Americans evolved over a generation. Once again, the moral of the story is that a unilateral view of the march of history is a mirage—that religion neither stays nor disappears, or that its revival is neither all good nor all bad.

RETURN OF RELIGION TO THE PUBLIC ARENA

To look beyond the USA, what had seemed marginal phenomena for quite some time forced their way to the centre of the stage in many parts of the world as the 1970s drew to their close. Not that the processes of secularization were wholly reversed—far from that—but alongside them, and in some respects in opposition to them, there was a resurgence of religion in public life, particularly in the political arena. The year 1979 was marked by a number of major events of such resurgence, the most remarkable of which were, of course, the Iranian and Nicaraguan revolutions. The same year Pope John Paul II, head of the world's largest Christian church, travelled to Mexico at a time when a new movement of the 1960s called 'Liberation Theology', which sought to combine Christianity and Marxism–Leninism, had spread among local Christian communities in a number of Latin American countries. Later that year the Pope also travelled to Poland, lending the support of the Catholic Church there to the Solidarity Movement in its struggle against the communist state. In India, it was around this time that Sikh fundamentalism made its appearance as a political force, followed in the mid-1980s by a retreat into traditional Islamic civil law by sections of the Muslim community, on the one hand, and an aggressive assertiveness by a number of Hindu organizations, in support of a Hindutva-based national culture, on the other (see Madan 1997). As José Casanova puts it, apropos Europe and the Americas:

> What was new and unexpected in the 1980s was not the emergence of new 'religious movements,' 'religious experimentation' and 'new religious consciousness'—all phenomena which caught the imagination of social scientists and the public in the 1960s and 1970s—but rather the revitalization and assumption of public roles by precisely those religious traditions which both theories of secularization and cyclical theories of religious revival had assumed were becoming ever more marginal and irrelevant in the modern world (1994: 5).

In Iran it was the Shia clerics, led by the fundamentalist Ayatollah Khomeini, who wrested from liberals and Marxists the leadership of the gathering storm against the campaign for rapid industrialization (funded by rising oil revenues) and modernization that the Shah's regime had sought to impose on society from above. Calling the bloody end of the regime a 'sacred', 'one hundred per cent Islamic' movement, the Ayatollah, as the spiritual guide of the Islamic Republic of Iran, claimed inspiration from the example of the early Islamic governance inaugurated by the Prophet Muhammad himself. He proclaimed the end of the era of Westernization (which some Iranian intellectuals had characterized as *gharbzadegi*, 'being stricken by the West'), and its replacement by 'the culture of the Quran' and—a radical innovation—the vesting of the ultimate authority in relation to the state and the society in the hands of the clerics (*faqih*, jurists). The book *Fundamentals of Islamic Thought* (1985), authored by Khomeini's protege Ayatollah Mutahhari, which served as the manifesto of the revolution, is a strong challenge to modern, secular, scientific discourse and world view (see also Amuzegar 1991). The Iranian revolution, which, according to Eric Hobsbawm, 'will enter history as one of the major social revolutions of the twentieth century' (1994: 453), showed no mercy towards those it considered the enemies of the Islamic way of life. It replaced terror by terror and shed blood to avenge the blood of those it considered martyrs. To commemorate the latter, a fountain was erected in a public square in Tehran: lit up at night, the water looked red like blood.

If the symbol of the Iranian Revolution was the fountain of 'blood'—surely an awesome sight—the legitimizing ideology of the Sandinista revolution, which overthrew the police state in Nicaragua, and the subsequent reconstruction of society, was 'Liberation Theology' (Lancaster 1988). Essentially a form of praxis, it was evolved by theologians who worked together with the poor and with political workers at the grass roots level, the so-called 'base communities'. The dispossessed were the 'flock' in their care and keeping. The higher rungs of the Church were not involved in this interaction and were even opposed to it. Gustavo Gutierrez, who elaborated the notion of liberation theology in the 1970s, wrote of the 'eruption of the poor' into the history of Latin America, not as some kind of a secular revolt of the masses but as 'an expression of the presence of God within the tumult of real human history' (Cox 1984: 140). The Sandinista leadership originally looked upon the 'popular church' at the community level in purely pragmatic terms (even as the liberals and Marxists had looked upon Shia clerics in Iran), but eventually the relationship between the guerilla strategies of Sandino, Marxism, and Christianity become an organic one, making it difficult to separate politics from religion. Christianity became 'the master plan around which other plans and blueprints were organized' (Lancaster 1988: 57). Looking back at these developments twenty years later, Jay Demerath observed that the significance of what happened in Poland and under the auspices of the Latin American Church lies in that 'neither the religious nor the political agendas could have succeeded without the other', brought together in each case 'in a brilliantly conceived alliance' (2002: 177).

The Polish story of the political role of the Christian Church is of another kind. Poland found itself a predominantly Catholic country at the end of the Second World War with a Church that had a long record of standing up for the people (Casanova 1994: chapter 4). The communist state was an imposition from Moscow, engineered through a planted Workers' Party. Its objective was to abolish religious faith, allegedly a form of false consciousness, and to end the threat to the state from institutionalized religion. The Church was engaged in a battle of survival from 1948 to 1956.

The people's discontent boiled over in what came to be known as the 'bread and God' uprising of October 1956 ('the Polish October'). Thereafter the Church opened out to espouse the human and civil rights of agricultural and other workers. It presented itself not merely as the nourisher of the Christians, but also as the protector of Polish culture and the nation's keeper. In doing so, the Church acknowledged the legitimacy of material wants within a framework of morality, and the values of religious freedom and freedom of conscience (after Vatican II). It even associated itself with the Workers Defence Committee in 1976. All this led the way to the national resistance and Solidarity movements which gained mass support, legitimacy, and international visibility through their association with the Roman Catholic Church, and eventually to the collapse of the dictatorial state. The role of the Church since then has been rather controversial: it has taken an anti-pluralist stand in relation to other Christians (notably Greek Catholics). It is not quite as vocal in support of popular discontent as before, and seems to have become 'an instrument in the aggressive assertion of national identity' (Hann 2000: 17).

If the 1980s were marked by the emergence of religious fundamentalist movements around the world, grounded in scripturalism, questing for political power, intolerant of dissent, and often violent (Marty and Appleby 1991, 1995), the last decade of the century saw the collapse of the communist empire and the eclipse of the most rigorously worked out secularist ideology of society and philosophy of history that have ever existed.

Revolutions, whether accompanied by terror or more benign in nature, are of course big news, and they are not all lies. It is not they alone, however, that have rendered religion visible again in our time. There is much evidence of the tenacity, even vibrancy, of publicly observed private religious faith, not only in countries that have been known for the religiosity of their peoples—the examples of India and the USA come readily to mind—but even in those that were not so inclined in the past, such as Japan. The return of the sacred in China and Russia only testifies to the coming into the open of what was formerly suppressed. Ironically, the accoutrements of modern society itself—economic well-being of increasing proportions of national populations; quick, comfortable and affordable travel; ready information and easy communication; etc.—facilitate the practice of religion.

I remember hearing a lecture by the late A.L. Basham, distinguished historian, at the Indian Institute of Advanced Study, Shimla, in 1973, in which he remarked that the emergence of the cult of Santoshi Ma as a new goddess in the Hindu pantheon bore witness to the vitality of some religious traditions. One hears little about this cult nowadays, but yet another goddess, by no means new, Vaishno Devi, draws pilgrims in their hundreds of thousands to her mountain cave near Jammu from all parts of India virtually throughout the year. Many of them come to bargain with their goddess for mundane favours, pledging gratitude for gift. In Kashmir, militancy and the risk of violence and even death has not deterred devotees, in very large numbers, again from all over the country, to make the annual pilgrimage to the Amarnath cave. In fact, sporadic attacks and casualties have occurred. The fact that the government, the biggest employer of people in the country, and other corporate employers, periodically offer paid holidays to their personnel, has resulted in the combination of religiosity and recreation. Pilgrimages within countries and across countries are attracting larger numbers of devotees than ever before.

While the multitudes move, millions watch them on their television screens, fulfilled through vicarious participation, or simply entertained by the spectacle. The midnight Christmas mass in St Peter's Square in Rome is watched by millions of Christians and non-Christians the world over. The same is true of the annual Haj pilgrimage to Mecca in which Muslims from all over the world participate. The Mahakumbha *mela* at Prayag this winter[7] has been named by the media 'the greatest show on earth'; it, too, is being read and heard about and watched worldwide. By the time it is over more than twenty-five million people will have visited Prayag, including pilgrims hoping to wash off their sins, tourists seeking amusement, merchants making money, and media persons producing sensational news.[8]

Pilgrimages alone do not testify to the vitality of the religious life among urbanized educated Indians. Religious leaders are today more visible as the promoters of modern (medical, technical, other) education and providers of integrated modern health care (for instance at Sathya Sai Baba's institutional complex at Puttaparthi) than as holy preceptors, and as religious leaders, they command larger following as instructors of practical yoga and the 'art of living' (Sri Sri Ravishankar) than of esoteric doctrines and arcane rituals. The religiousness of these contemporary gurus is open rather than secret; it is for anyone who is interested (irrespective of caste and creed) and not for the select few. Their use of the written and spoken word (books, magazines, cassette tapes, CDs) and of the print and electronic media to propagate their teachings and publicize their activities is modern (technically and managerially efficient). The line that formally divides the religious from the secular is increasingly becoming blurred everyday for anyone to speak sensibly of their mutual exclusiveness.

Look at it in whichever way we may, religion survives in the world at the beginning of the twenty-first century, belying the expectations of those modern rational men and women of a hundred years ago—and in fact of most of the twentieth century—who were convinced that its days were coming to their end. It not only survives as private faith but has also re-emerged as public religion (Casanova 1994), and as an ideology of domination (Nandy 1990). Both violence (religious terrorism) and peaceful social endeavours (as for example of civil society groups) give it salience. Religion persists in one form or another, but is not the constitutive principle of society anywhere: the economy and the polity are its rivals. Their mutual antagonism produces the 'oscillation of secularization and sacralization' that marks our times (Demerath 2002: 211). It is a sign of the times that a scholarly work published in the last year of the twentieth century bears the title *Why Gods Persist* (1999). The author, Robert Hinde, biologist and psychologist, characterizing his approach as 'scientific', 'examines why so many religions continue to persist at a time when the answers they provide to the basic questions of life are unacceptable to many in the modern world', and turns to 'basic human propensities' for answers (ibid.: 206).

Needless to emphasize, a reasonable answer to this and similar questions does not have to be—indeed it should not be—in exclusively religious or secular terms. The 'totalizing propensity of reason to absolutize the tension between sacred and profane realms...into irreconcilable contradictions' (Seligman 2000: 132) has been the bane of discussions of the place of religion in the modern world.[9] But a 'theo-ethical equilibrium'—'a kind of integration between a religious outlook and secularly grounded moral or political principles'—is now coming to be considered 'achievable' (Audi 2000: 212–13). This is a long way from the earlier certitude (whether stated in Marxian or Weberian terms) about the fateful transformation of religious into secular culture. Indeed, it has been suggested that it is not all that unlikely that future historians 'will look back on the period from roughly 1750 to 2050 as a brief three-hundred-year secular parenthesis in a history of humanity that has always been religious' (Seligman: ibid.). One is reminded of Tocqueville's observation that 'Unbelief is an accident, and faith is the only permanent state of mankind' rooted as it is in 'human nature' (de Tocqueville 1976: I, 310). I do not have the space here to examine these arguments in any detail. I have referred to them only to point out that, currently, there is considerable evidence of serious rethinking of the place of religion in modern society.

SRINIVAS ON RELIGION AND SOCIETY

Let me add a clarification. If I have spoken about the persistence of religion in modern society, I have neither meant to suggest that religions have not changed in response to the challenges of secularization, nor wanted to recommend that religious conceptualizations of the limitations of modernity be uncritically accepted. Even less have I wanted to suggest that we all become religious, whatever that means.[10] I do not believe that ethically commanding directives issue from the social sciences generally any more than they do from the natural sciences. I know that the notion of a value-free social science is not defensible in all contexts and situations: for instance we have seen a fruitful coming together of ethics and economics in recent times (see Sen 1994). But I do believe that, while sociologists should study the value preferences of people, and spell out their likely consequences, they may not, as sociologists, recommend any selections. Such choices may truly be made by one only on the basis of moral or political convictions that are personal even when they are shared (see pp. 311–13 below).

In an article published in the *Times of India* on 9 July 1993, M.N. Srinivas wrote about our troubled times, marked by run-away gadgetry, frenetic consumption, and conflicts of various kinds, through which India was then (and is now) passing. He observed:

It is in this overall context that the need for a new philosophy and social ethic becomes urgent and imperative. And that philosophy cannot be secular humanism. It has to be firmly rooted in God as creator and protector and the sustainer of human societies. The fraternity of all human beings cutting across divisions of race, ethnicity, caste, class, religion and gender follows logically from the idea of God as creator. The idea of human free will is [present] in all religions, and it provides the basis for individual liberty without which there can be no true democracy.

Many sociologists were taken aback by Srinivas's rejection of secular humanism and by his plea for a God-centred fellowship of human beings. Sociology is after all a child of the European Enlightenment. Several years later (in 1998), he told me that he had learnt from more than one source that his article had evoked sharp criticism from some of the ablest of his professional colleagues. But he had no complaints, he said, nor had the criticism made him change his opinion. What he had written were his considered views, indeed his convictions, and he regarded it as his duty to make them known.

Just as Srinivas pursued his sociological studies in the most rigorous manner, and tried to state his conclusions without presuppositions or prejudice, he had similarly given expression to his personal convictions regarding the place of religion in human life without fear or compromise. Nowhere in the article, it should be noted, did he invoke sociological authority for his views, but it may not be denied that many among the reading public knew of his tall stature as a sociologist. He took the risks of misunderstanding and disapproval, guided by his conscience, *ātma tushti*, alone.

A study of Srinivas's writings on religion and related themes reveals an interesting parallelism between their course and the changing role of religion in Indian society in our times. Srinivas's first major work, *Religion and Society among the Coorgs of South India*, published in 1952, was almost immediately recognized in India and abroad as an outstanding contribution. Indeed it has since acquired the status of a modern classic in social anthropological literature. Its principal strength lay in a clearly articulated theoretical framework that focused on the role of social institutions in the maintenance of solidarity in society. Known as 'functionalism', he had come to appreciate its merits at Oxford University where he wrote a doctoral dissertation under the guidance mainly of A.R. Radcliffe-Brown. It was this work that was published as the book mentioned above. Such a view of religion, not as true or false, but as, functional or dysfunctional, was derived from Radcliffe-Brown's rather narrow exegesis of Durkheim's theory of religion, which was concerned, as I have earlier indicated, with more than the problem of social order. In a sensitive autobiographical essay Srinivas (1973) confessed that, on reflection, he had realized that functionalism tended to be overly neat, leaving no loose threads to be tied, narrow, and even dogmatic.

The Coorg book was not, however, concerned with social order as a static condition. The wide influence that the book achieved was a result of Srinivas's analysis of the inner dynamics of caste-based society. He showed that the very logic of stratification, which entails unequal distribution of social prestige and politico-economic power, generates the hope that something can be done to achieve that is denied to those ranked low. For instance, they can try to imitate the lifestyle of the privileged groups, and this indeed, Srinivas showed was happening among the Coorgs and everywhere else in Hindu society. He called this process Sanskritization (1952: 30–1 et passim).

Coinciding with the publication of the Coorg book in 1952, India began its career as a parliamentary democracy based on universal adult suffrage. The first assembly and parliamentary elections under the new Constitution were held that year. Srinivas was one of the first social scientists to note that caste, which had for millennia provided the social framework for the operation of Hindu religious beliefs, was being transformed into an instrument of politics. Although it was his interest in religion that originally led him to study caste, the changing character of caste now attracted him to focus on its political dimensions at the micro as well as macro levels. He wrote about caste disputes and dominance at the village level and examined the problems of nation-building as well. Religion and Hinduism as objects of study stayed in his mind throughout his professional life, although he wrote less on them than on other subjects. The newspaper article from which I quoted above bears witness to his deep engagement with the role of religion in the modern world. In several conversations I had with him during the last years of his life (in Bangalore and New Delhi), he told me that a legitimate concern about the resurgence of religious fanaticism in India had regrettably led to an uncritically negative attitude in certain circles to the deeper role of religion in human society. In fact, he had wanted to organize an international seminar on the subject but his unexpected death in 1999 precluded this from happening (see Chapter 11 below).

CONCLUDING REMARKS

I began this essay with two questions. First, how was it that enlightened intellectual opinion in the West had by the beginning of the twentieth century come to the definite conclusion that religion belonged with the left over debris of human history, that it had no future in the modern world. And, secondly, I asked what the prospect for religion actually looked like at the beginning of the twenty-first century. The decline of religion, I have briefly tried to show here, was a peculiarly Western development. The historical *process* of secularization, which had created separate domains of the sacred and secular in Western society, confining the former to the privacy of human lives, had been subsequently presented as a *thesis* of historical inevitability, that is, a precondition of modernity everywhere. Eurocentrism was as much of a blind spot of Weber's vision as Marx's. He wanted to believe, as he put it, that 'in Western civilization, and in Western civilization only', certain 'cultural phenomena' had 'appeared' which lay 'in the line of development having universal significance and value' (1930: 13). Weber wrote this in the context specifically of the rise of the spirit of capitalism to which the 'Protestant ethic' had by his reasoning made a critical contribution. His thesis could be extended to other cultural developments, such as secularization, and so it has been, without due regard for the cultural specificities of non-Western societies. Moreover, the closing decades of the twentieth century have exposed the flawed character of the universalist thesis, even in respect of the West itself. The secularists, whether liberals or Marxists, consider this a 'bizarre' reversal of history (Hobsbawm 1994: 202), but, as I have tried to show, that is a one-sided judgement. Religion survives in the modern world as much for good as for evil.[11] Alexis de Tocqueville may have been after all more prescient than many of his contemporaries and successors when he anticipated that humanity would endeavour to '*harmonize* earth with heaven' (1976: I, 300).

NOTES

1. Earlier beginnings too have been mentioned. Thus, Kolakowski (1990: 95) writes of 'the increasingly powerful advance of the distinction between secular reason and faith' from the eleventh century onward, following 'the emergence of cities and urban civilization' and 'the emergence of intellectuals'.

2. England did not quite participate in the European Enlightenment but David Hume (1711–76) must be mentioned for his stern opposition to all established religions through his critique of the notion of natural religion. It has been suggested that if Europe imagined the Enlightenment, America realized it (Commager 1978), but I do not have to go into that thesis here.

3. The reference is to the delivery of this memorial lecture.

4. I might add in passing that Marx's secular doctrine that installed dialectical materialism as the engine of change in human history, can itself be regarded as 'religious' insofar as, first, the problem of human existence lay at its core, and, secondly, it offered a confident way out of it by overcoming the constraints of the prevailing socio-economic situation (see, e.g. MacIntyre 1968).

5. Eleven days after this lecture was delivered, George W. Bush was sworn in as the forty-third President of the USA. His inaugural address went beyond the usual invocations of God and contained elements of Christian faith, which was a departure from convention, and in a pluralist vein mentioned other religions too: 'Church and charity, synagogue and mosque, lend our communities their humanity, and they will have an honoured place in our plans and in our laws.' This is a position far removed from secular humanism and is virtually the same as the *sarva dharma samabhava* (equal respect for all religions) of Indian secularism. But this is dangerous: politicians may claim to know the mind of God. This tendency was strongly visible throughout the first Bush presidency, particularly after the fateful events of 9/11. Christian theology has never been more powerfully entrenched in the corridors of power in Washington as it is now (i.e. in 2005) at the commencement of Bush's second term.

6. An American scholar of comparative religion, Gerald Larson, has suggested that, as in America, 'a Gandhian-Nehruvian Indic civil religion...exists in India alongside the various particular religious traditions. It is marked by national celebrations (Independence Day, Republic Day), and birthday holidays commemorating, besides the founders of religions, Mahatma Gandhi (see Larson 1995: 202–3). This judgement is, I think, premature. Official and urban Indias are as yet marginal phenomena.

7. The reference is to the winter of 2001. See note 1 above.

8. As this book goes to press, the funeral of Pope John Paul II (on 7 April 2005) has been described as the biggest such event in history, attended by seventy heads of state or government, representatives of fourteen religions, and about two million people, and watched worldwide by more than a billion TV viewers. This phenomenal event powerfully represents the enthronement of religion in spectacle and politics in contemporary times. More people knew of this Pope for his role in the ending of the Soviet Empire than those who admired him for his efforts at inter-religious reconciliation. Despite the reluctance to name Christianity as a major element of the cultural heritage of Europe in the Preamble to the draft constitution of European Union, the President of the European Commission publicly (and somewhat dubiously) claimed Pope John Paul II as 'the father of the Union'.

9. Jayant Narlikar, the distinguished astrophysicist writes:

    ...It is necessary to recognize that religion and science fulfil complementary urges of the human mind. The problems come when there is a trespass of the area of either one by the other. Thus, scientists should avoid passing value judgements on religious thoughts without appreciating their very different contexts. And religious thinkers should not try to look for post-facto justification for their thoughts in the findings of science (2000: 285).

10. Cp.: 'Religious faith comes by grace, not by will. Religion cannot be called to heel, like a dog, to suit human convenience' (Toynbee 1961: 95).

11. The darker side of religion today threatens at the very heart of the Western world: it is not a malady of the East alone. One third of the American electorate, according to a recent Gallup poll, believe that the Bible is literally true, that God will provide for everyone, so one need not worry about excessive population or environmental degradation. Indeed, such people believe that the worse things seem, the sooner Christ, the redeemer, will return.

    If the Americans are judged outlandish in any case, what about the British? Nearly three quarters of them declared themselves Christian in the 2001 census. The question is, who claims their loyalty? The Religious Right will do so everywhere, in America, Britain, and India, if the secularists do not realize that many, if not most people of faith are reasonable people with forward looking attitudes and the very same social sympathies that the secularists espouse. It is salutary to recall that the British Labour Party owed more to Methodism than it did to Marx.

References

Ayer, A.J. 1986. *Voltaire*. New York: Random House.

Amuzegar, Jehangir. 1991. *The Dynamics of the Iranian Revolution*. Albany, NY: State University of New York Press.

Audi, Robert. 2000. *Religious Commitment and Secular Reason*. Cambridge: Cambridge University Press.

Bellah, Robert. 1975. *The Broken Covenant: American Civil Religion in a Time of Trial*. New York: Seabury Press.

————. 1976. *Beyond Belief: Essays on Religion in a Post-Traditional World*. New York: Harper & Row.

———— et al. 1985. *Habits of the Heart: Individualism and Commitment in American Life*. Berkeley: University of California Press.

Casanova, José. 1994. *Public Religions and the Modern World*. Chicago: University of Chicago Press.

Cassirer, Ernst. 1968. *The Philosophy of the Enlightenment*. Princeton, N.J.: Princeton University Press.

————. 1981. *Kant's Life and Thought*. New Haven, CN.: Yale University Press.

Chadwick, Owen. 1975. *The Secularization of the European Mind*. Cambridge: Cambridge University Press.

Commager, Henry S. 1978. *The Age of Reason*. New York: Anchor Books.

Connolly, William F. 1995. *The Ethos of Pluralization*. Minneapolis: University of Minnesota Press.

Cox, Harvey. 1965. *The Secular City: Secularization and Urbanization in Theological Perspective*. New York: Macmillan.

————. 1984. *Religion in the Secular City*. New York: Simon and Schuster.

Demerath III, N.J. 2002. *Crossing the Gods: World Religions and Worldly Politics*. New Brunswick: Rutgers University Press.

Derrida, Jacques. 2002. *Acts of Religion*. Gil Anidjar (trs.). New York: Routledge.

de Tocqueville, Alexis [1835] 1976. *Democracy in America*. Vols I & II. The Henry Reeve Text. New York: Alfred A. Knopf.

Dunn, Richard S. 1979. *The Age of Religious Wars (1559–1715)*. New York: Norton.

Durkheim, Émile. 1956. *Education and Sociology*. S.D. Fox (trs.). Glencoe, Ill.: The Free Press.

————. 1957. *Professional Ethics and Civil Morals*. C. Brookfield (trs.). London: Routledge and Kegan Paul.

————. 1995. *The Elementary Forms of Religious Life*. Karen E. Fields (trs.). New York: The Free Press.

Furet, Francois. 1981. *Interpreting the French Revolution*. Cambridge: Cambridge University Press.

Gelberg, Steven J. (ed.). 1983. *Hare Krishna, Hare Krishna*. New York: Grove Press Inc.

Hann, Chris. 2000. 'Problems with the (de) privatization of religion'. *Anthropology Today* 16, 6, pp. 14–20.

Hinde, Robert. 1999. *Why Gods Persist: A Scientific Approach to Religion*. London: Routledge.

Hitchcock, James. 1982. *What is Secular Humanism*. Ann Arbor, MI.: Servant Books.

Hobsbawm, Eric. 1994. *Age of Extremes: The Short Twentieth Century*. London: Michael Joseph.

Hume, David. 1957. *Natural History of Religion*. H.E. Root (ed.). Stanford CA.: Stanford University Press.

Kant, Immanuel. 1991. *Political Writings*, 2nd edn. Hans Reiss (ed.), H.B. Nisbet (trs.). Cambridge: Cambridge University Press.

Kauffman, Walter. 1974. *Nietzsche: Philosopher, Psychologist, Antichrist*. Princeton, NJ: Princeton University Press.

Kolakowski, Leszek. [1973] 1990. 'The revenge of the sacred in secular culture'. In *Modernity on Endless Trial*. Chicago: University of Chicago Press.

————. [1973] 1990. 'The illusion of demythologization'. In *Modernity on Endless Trial*. Chicago: University of Chicago Press.

Lancaster, Roger. 1988. *Thanks to God and the Revolution: Popular Religion and Class Consciousness in the New Nicaragua*. New York: Columbia University Press.

Larson, Gerald J. 1995. *India's Agony over Religion*. Albany, NY.: State University of New York Press.

Lewis, David L. 1970. *Martin Luther King*. London: Allen Lane, The Penguin Press.

MacIntyre, Alasdair. 1968. *Marxism and Christianity*. Notre Dame: University of Notre Dame Press.

Madan, T.N. 1997. *Modern Myths, Locked Minds: Secularism and Fundamentalism in India*. New Delhi: Oxford University Press.

————. 2000. 'M.N. Srinivas, 1916–99: A Memoir'. *Indian Social Science Review* 2:2: 373–88.

————. 2001. *Religion in the Modern World*. First M.N. Srinivas Memorial Lecture. Bangalore: National Institute of Advanced Studies.

Marty, Martin E. 1986. *Modern American Religion: 1893–1919*. Chicago: University of Chicago Press.

Marty, Martin E. and R. Scott Appleby (eds). 1991. *Fundamentalism Observed*. Chicago: University of Chicago Press.

————. 1995. *Fundamentalism Comprehended*. Chicago: University of Chicago Press.

Marx, Karl and Friedrich Engels. 1959. *Basic Writings on Politics and Philosophy*. Lewis S. Feuer (ed.). New York: Doubleday.

Mitzman, Arthur. 1985. *The Iron Cage: An Historical Interpretation of Max Weber*. London: Transaction.

Mutahhari, Murtaza. 1985. *Fundamentals of Islamic Thought: God, Man and the Universe*. R. Campbell (trs.). Berkeley, CA.: Mizan Press.

Nandy, Ashis. [1990] 2001. 'The politics of secularism and the recovery of religious tolerance'. In *Time Warps: The Insistent Politics of Silent and Evasive Pasts*. New Delhi: Permanent Black.

Narlikar, Jayant. 2000. 'Science and religion: Approach towards a synthesis'. *Creeds of Our Times*. Delhi: Full Circle.

Preus, Samuel R. 1987. *Explaining Religion*. New Haven, CN.: Yale University Press.

Roszak, Theodore. 1969. *The Making of a Counter Culture*. New York: Doubleday.

Russell, Bertrand. 1946. *History of Western Philosophy*. London: Allen and Unwin.

————. 1961. *Religion and Science*. London: Oxford University Press.

Seligman, Adam B. 2000. *Modernity's Wager: Authority, the Self and Transcendence*. Princeton, NJ.: Princeton University Press.

Sen, Amartya. 1994. *On Ethics and Economics*. Oxford: Basil Blackwell.

Skinner, B.F. 1972. *Beyond Freedom and Dignity*. New York: Alfred Knopf.

Srinivas, M.N. 1952. *Religion and Society among the Coorgs of South India*. Oxford: Clarendon Press.

————. 1973. 'Itineraries of an Indian social anthropologist'. *International Social Science Journal* 25, 1–2, pp. 129–48.

————. 1993. 'Towards a new philosophy.' New Delhi: the *Times of India*, ed. page, 9 July.

————. 2002. *Collected Essays*. New Delhi: Oxford University Press.

Toynbee, Arnold. 1956. *An Historian's Approach to Religion*. London: Oxford University Press.

————. 1961. *A Study of History. Voll XII. Reconsiderations*. London: Oxford University Press.

Weber, Marriane. 1975. *Max Weber: A Biography*. New York: John Wiley.

Weber, Max. 1930. *The Spirit of Capitalism and the Protestant Ethic*. London: Allen and Unwin.

————. 1948. *From Max Weber: Essays in Sociology*. H.H. Gerth and C. Wright Mills (trs. and eds). London: Routledge and Kegan Paul.

————. 1958. *The Religion of India*. Hans Gerth and Don Martindale (trs. and eds). Glencoe: Ill.: The Free Press.

2

*Freedom of Religion**

> Be it therefore enacted by the General Assembly [of the state of
> Virginia], that no man shall be compelled to frequent or support
> any religious worship, place, or ministry whatsoever, nor shall be
> enforced, restrained, molested, or burdened in his body or goods,
> nor shall otherwise suffer on account of his religious opinions or
> belief; but that all men shall be free to profess, and by argument
> to maintain, their opinion in matters of religion, and that the same
> shall in nowise diminish, enlarge, or affect their civil capacities.
>
> Thomas Jefferson

Perspectives

As a formal concept, freedom of religion is a modern idea, not
more than three centuries old, and Western in origin. And it is a
contemporary concern everywhere in our human rights conscious
days. The major religious traditions of the world cannot truly be
considered supportive of it. As we know them today, if these

* Reproduced with minor verbal changes from *Economic and Political
Weekly*, 15 March 2003, pp. 1034–41. It was originally delivered as the
First Shankar Sahai Srivastava Memorial Lecture under the auspices of
the Uttar Pradesh Samaj Shastra Parishad at the University of Lucknow
on 8 February 2002. Professor Srivastava (1928–2001) was one of the
leading criminologists of the country and had been a Professor at Kashi
Vidyapeeth. And he was a dear friend.

The present text owes a great deal to discussions with Sudhir Chandra
(Delhi) who kindly provided me with the text of the governmental
response of 1840 to the Bombay memorialists quoted in this address.
I am also grateful to Mark Haberlein (University of Freiburg) for
critical comments on an earlier version. Thanks are due to Professor
Rajeshwar Prasad who invited me to give the Lecture.

traditions entertain the idea of religious pluralism it is more a concession to empirical reality rather than a matter of orthodoxy. In other words, toleration in the context of the diversity of religious faiths is a historical development in some traditions; and has scriptural sanction in others. Scriptures do not, however, always speak unambiguously; besides, whatever is in the scripture, or in the cultural tradition generally, may not also be for good or bad a matter of social practice.

Let me illustrate the foregoing observations, discussing very briefly the case of Christianity. I choose this particular religious tradition because freedom of religion although not one of its gifts was shaped in its ambience.

Obviously, we must begin with Christianity's relationship with Judaism, and this is complex. Everyone knows that the Old Testament is the Hebrew Bible, a product of early Jewish society. The New Testament comprises the four gospels and other short works concerning the life and teachings of Jesus of Nazareth. He was a Jewish prophet, but considered a foe by the Jewish priesthood that was wholly intolerant of dissent, and was betrayed by a Jew. The Roman governor condemned him to die on the cross, but it was really the Jews who crucified him. They thus came to be stigmatized as his murderers. Discrimination against them was justified on the ground that they refused to acknowledge him as the Son of God. But Christian theologians (notably St Augustine) also argued that Jews have an important role as witnesses to God's covenant with his people and as keepers of the Hebrew tradition. Moreover, in Christian eschatology, conversion of the Jews is a necessary precondition of Christ's second coming. Anyhow, the persecution of Jews was an essential element of the history of medieval Christian churches. Christian anti-Judaism is distinct from modern anti-Semitism, which emerged as a rationalist and racial ideology in the late eighteenth century, and survived into the twentieth century. The former serves, however, as the setting for the latter. As we know, the attitude of the Roman Catholic Church during the dark days of the Holocaust in the 1930s and 1940s was marked more by silence than protest.

The attitude of the Christian churches to Islam, the third Abrahamic religion, is no more tolerant. Jerusalem, which was considered a holy city by Jews, Christians, and Muslims alike, came under the control of expansionist Islam in the middle of the seventh century AD. The realization of the Christian goal of its 'liberation' had to wait three-and-a-half centuries. This happened in the last year of the eleventh century on the successful conclusion of the First Crusade launched by Pope Urban II. The pursuit of Crusades to expel Islam from Christian lands was later taken over by European kings (such as those of Spain and Portugal). In course of time, the Crusades lost their force owing to changing religio-political circumstances. The idea of the incompatibility of Christian and Islamic world views is not, however, dead (see, for example, Huntington 1996).

Apart from the tensions that have prevailed between Christianity and the two other Abrahamic religions, there have been strains within the Christian fold itself from early times onward. The big schism represented by the Reformation early in the sixteenth century, and the subsequent, calamitous religious wars (1500–1650) between the Catholics and Protestants made toleration among the Christian nations of Europe imperative, for the alternative could only have been mutual destruction. The principle that the prince could choose the religion of his state (*cuius regio cius religio*) was established as early as 1555 in the religious peace of Augsburg, and reiterated in the Treaty of Westphalia in 1648, which acknowledged this imperative and gave legitimacy to territorial churches headed by monarchs. Henry VIII of England (once ironically acclaimed by the Pope as the Defender of Faith when he sided with the latter against the Lutheran 'heresies') had already shown the way when he broke with Rome in 1533. It was Elizabeth I, however, who consolidated the policy of peace and compromise between 1559 and 1563 (Dunn 1979). The spirit of the peace settlements of the sixteenth and seventeenth centuries was, however, one of intoleration. The Calvinist Theodore Beza put it succinctly when he called religious liberty 'a most diabolical dogma because it means that every one should be left to go to hell in his own way' (Bainton 1956: 211).

The Reformation is of interest here for another crucial reason. By denying the legitimacy of an intermediary role of the Church between the true believer and God, and by placing the responsibility for redemption on the individual himself or herself, Martin Luther and John Calvin opened the way, although not directly— they shrank away from the consequences of their own argument for the priesthood of all believers—for the freedom of religion as a human right to be eventually promoted by public opinion and guaranteed by an impartial (although not necessarily secular) state (see Bainton 1956; Troeltsch 1981). This is the modern Western idea that I mentioned at the very beginning.

But it was not the Reformation alone that placed the individual defined by his moral dignity and responsibility at the centre of the stage, as it were; the Enlightenment during the seventeenth and eighteenth centuries also challenged the individual, defined by his or her reason and rights, to take charge of his or her own fate (see Cassirer 1968). The religious and secular impulses converged in this regard, although not always and everywhere harmoniously.

Toleration was also developed into a philosophical position, most notably by John Locke (in the late 1680s), who called it the chief characteristic of the true church. For him, religious liberty was a natural right that the state (in effect limited parliamentary government) should protect, and he rejected the notion of the divine right of kings to exercise absolute paternal power. He stressed the reasonableness of men (repudiating the Hobbesean notion of passions) as the guarantee of perfect freedom and peace. He recognized in his later writings the functional difference between the church and the state, relating them hierarchically by arguing for the encompassing of the positive laws of civil society by divine law. It is remarkable that in his *Letters Concerning Toleration* he attacked those who believed in the use of force for the promotion of Christianity, and he included non-Christian religions (Judaism and Islam) within the ambit of toleration (see Mabbott 1973).

A most significant development in this context was the French Revolution (1789), which was aggressively anti-clerical in action and republican and secular in aspiration. The Constitution of 1791 had for its preface 'The Declaration of the Rights of Man'. Besides the secular rights of liberty, property, security, and resistance to oppression, the freedom of religious expression also was endorsed and declared to be entitled to state protection. For decades to come in the nineteenth century the Declaration inspired European liberals enormously. The French Constitution (1958) today echoes many of its ideals. Thus, Article 2 proclaims: 'France is an indivisible, secular, democratic, and social Republic. It ensures the equality of all citizens before the law, without distinction as to origin, race, or religion. It respects all beliefs.' The declaration of 1791 owed some of its core ideas to certain recent American developments to which I now turn.

As already noted, the Peace of 1648 (at the end of the Thirty Years War) had led to the establishment of territorial churches in central and western Europe. These were dependent upon royal patronage in whatever they did, whether traditionalist or reformist in character. This did not mean that all the people of a country were either Catholics or Protestants. Innovation and resistance both made sure that religious tensions remained alive. Many of the 'pilgrim fathers' who founded the colonies in North America were not merely seeking fortunes, but also escaping from state control of religion, if not religious persecution, in their native lands.

Thus, large numbers of people from among the Anabaptists of Germany, the Netherlands, and neighbouring countries were among the early migrants to go to America. The Anabaptists were a radical Protestant group who strongly opposed state control over religious belief and practice. Migrants from the British Isles, particularly England, constituted the majority of the settlers. They were driven, year after year, to leave their homes in large numbers, and seek the hospitable shores of America, by the religious passions, political turmoils, and social and economic problems that had become endemic in England in the opening decades of the seventeenth century. The great majority of them in New England were Puritans, but they also included Episcopalians owing allegiance to the Church of England and the Anglican Communion. The Puritans (Calvinist Congregationalists), who arrived in what is now the Massachusetts Bay in 1628, initially wished to realize their own vision of the 'Godly Commonwealth', which really means that they were basically lacking in toleration. Catholics and Quakers found no place in their colony. In fact, the first hundred years of American colonial history were disfigured by much inter-denominational intolerance. The beginnings of toleration also were, however, made early enough. Among the first colonizers who broadly embraced religious freedom were Roger Williams, founder of the colony of Rhode Island, expelled from Massachusetts for his liberal views, and the Quaker William Penn, who established the colony of Pennsylvania, although even he recognized none but the monothesists as deserving of toleration!

Coming to 1776, we read in the historic Declaration of Independence, which was drafted by Thomas Jefferson, that 'governments are instituted among men', so that the 'inalienable Rights' of 'Life, Liberty and the Pursuit of Happiness' may be secured. While the 'just powers' of governments were said to be derived from 'the consent of the governed', the rights of the latter were 'endowed by their Creator'. The concept of freedom of religion was given precise definition by Jefferson, in the Virginia Act for Establishing Religious Freedom (1786): 'no man shall be compelled to frequent or support any religious worship, place, or ministry whatsoever', and 'all men shall be free to profess, and by argument to maintain, their opinions in matters of religion'. Simultaneously, James Madison, who succeeded Jefferson as president, wrote in 1785 (in a tract entitled 'Memorial and Remonstrance against Religious Assessments'):

> We maintain therefore that in matters of Religion, no man's right is abridged by the institution of Civil society, and that Religion is wholly exempt from its cognizance. True it is, that no other rule exists, by which any question which may divide a society can be ultimately determined, but the will of the majority; but it is also true that the majority may trespass on the right of the minority.

The contemporary relevance of Madison's formulation of more than two centuries ago need hardly be emphasized.

The framers of the American constitution in 1787 were god-fearing people who prayed for divine guidance, but they did not deviate from the foregoing principles of the sovereignty of people and religious liberty. The new government was established in 1789 and only two years later the celebrated First Amendment was adopted by the Congress. It enunciated the principles that have guided countries like India in the second half of the twentieth century as they framed their own constitutions. It said, among other things, that the 'Congress shall make no law respecting an establishment of religion, or prohibiting the free exercise thereof'. In the famous words of Jefferson (in a letter to the Danbury Baptists in 1802), 'a wall of separation between the Church and the state' was thus put in place. (Incidentally, it was in the Paris home of Jefferson, who was ambassador in France, that the French Declaration of the Rights of Man was discussed privately before its adoption in 1791. His opinion on the issue of freedom of religion must have been quite influential.)

The interpretation of the notion of the separation of church and state is an ongoing process and cannot but be of deep interest to us in India. It comprises two ideas: one, non-interference, that is, the state or, more precisely the government, shall not promulgate a state religion; and two, entitlement, that is, the citizen has the inalienable right to follow a religion of his or her own choice.

Now, is free exercise of religion an 'equality right' or a 'liberty right'? An American Supreme Court ruling of 1990, which upheld the Oregon state ban on the use of the drug peyote in certain American Indian rituals, affirmed the 'equality right' interpretation. A privilege that is not equally available to all was judged to be discriminatory and therefore unconstitutional. Following public protests, Congress passed the Religious Restoration Act three years later, upholding the 'liberty right' view as the correct one. In India too we seem to vacillate between the two interpretations, but usually lean towards the 'liberty right' view, recognizing the legitimacy of distinctive religious beliefs and social practices of the various communities. Neither view, it may be emphasized, opens the way for direct state support to religious activity.

I should dwell just a little longer on the comparative perspective before I turn to the predicaments of the Indian situation. The Universal Declaration of Human Rights adopted by the UN General Assembly in 1948 (the vote was 48: 0 with the six Soviet bloc countries, Saudi Arabia, and South Africa abstaining) has a number of provisions directly or indirectly concerning freedom of religion. It is obvious that the Declaration represented the consensus of opinion among the Christian countries/secular states of the West, which constituted the majority of the membership of the UN at that time.

While Article 2 of the Declaration guarantees all the rights set forth in it without any distinction on the ground of religion and such other attributes as race and colour, it is Article 18 which specifically focuses on the freedom of religion. It reads as follows:

> Everyone has the right to freedom of thought, conscience and religion; this right includes freedom to change his religion or belief, and freedom, either alone or in community with others and in public or private, to manifest his religion or belief in teaching, practice, worship and observance.

This statement, explicit as well as comprehensive, has served as a guide for the freedom of religion enactments around the world. It is a moot point, however, whether 'teaching' only refers to the transmission of religious beliefs and practices within the community of believers, or also includes propagation of one's faith across religious boundaries.

PREDICAMENTS OF THE INDIAN SITUATION

One of the countries that voted in favour of the Universal Declaration of Human Rights adopted by the UN General Assembly in 1948 was India, which had become a member of the United Nations soon after the attainment of independence in 1947. The Constituent Assembly was already at work under the shadow of the partition of the subcontinent on the basis of religious difference—the 'two nations' theory of the Indian Muslim League—and the accompanying widespread communal riots and mass migrations. The country had seen the ugly face of religious identity, but it was not at all ready to turn its back on religion. The framers of the Constitution did not write the words 'secular' or 'secularism' into it despite the efforts of one member (K.T. Shah) to have this done. But it also did not accept the suggestion of another member (H.V. Kamath) to open the document with an invocation of God. Words apart, the spirit of the Constitution certainly breathed the ideal of freedom of religion. It was only in 1976, during the 'Emergency' regime of Prime Minister Indira Gandhi, that the word 'secular' was introduced into the Preamble of the Constitution by the 42nd Amendment. It was thus that India came to be characterized as a 'Sovereign, Socialist, Secular, Democratic Republic'. The precise sense in which the word secular is used is clarified by the corresponding term *pantha nirpeksha* (denominationally neutral) in the Hindi version of the document.[1]

Article 15 of the Indian Constitution prohibits discrimination on grounds of religion, caste, sex, or place of birth; Article 16 guarantees equality of opportunity in matters of public employment irrespective of one's religious identity; and Article 17 abolished the practice of untouchability. Articles 25 to 30 deal specifically with the freedom of religion. Leaving aside for the moment the explanatory notes and qualifications, which are important, these Articles guarantee the following fundamental (unalterable) rights: 'Freedom of conscience and free profession, practice and propagation of religion' (Article 25); 'Freedom to manage religious affairs', which includes the right 'to establish and maintain institutions for religious and charitable purposes' (Article 26); 'Freedom as to payment of taxes for promotion of any particular religion' (Article 27); 'Freedom as to attendance at religious instruction or religious worship in certain educational institutions', with the clarification that 'No religious instruction shall be provided in any educational institution wholly maintained out of State funds' (Article 28); 'Protection of interests of minorities' (Article 29); and the 'Right of minorities to establish and administer educational institutions' (Article 30).

It seems to me that Article 25 focuses on the most basic of the various rights defined in the full set and merits further comment. But before I do so, three clarifications need to be made. First, Article 13 declared 'void' any existing laws that might be judged to be 'inconsistent with or in derogation of the fundamental rights' listed in Part III of the Constitution (Articles 12–35).

Secondly, all the freedoms and rights conferred by Articles 25–30 were made 'subject to public order, morality and health'. Not only that: they are to be exercised in a manner that is progressive in spirit. Clause 2(b) of Article 25 provides for state intervention within the framework of the said Article to promote 'social welfare and reform', and to throw open 'Hindu religious institutions of a public character to all classes and sections of Hindus'. (Explanation II attached to sub-clause (b) clarifies that the category Hindu shall for purposes of this clause include Sikhs, Jains, and Buddhists. I will not go here into the tricky but important question whether such categorization limits in any way the freedom of religion of these latter communities. I think it does.) Read together, Articles 25 and 26 place public interest above the claims of freedom of religion. In this respect, 'the Constitution *is*', in Marc Galanter's words, 'a charter for the reform of Hinduism' (1989: 247).

Moreover, since all the fundamental rights must be read together, nothing may be claimed in terms of freedom of religion that would deny or abridge any other fundamental right. Thus, human sacrifice cannot be claimed as essential to any community's religious practice since Article 21 guarantees 'protection of life and personal liberty'. Similarly, the dedication of any girl or woman to a temple deity (as a devadasi, for example), who is then compelled to engage in sexual intercourse with specified men, cannot be claimed as a religious right as it would violate Article 23, which prohibits 'traffic in human beings'.

Thirdly, although there is no specific prohibition of the establishment of a religion by the state, the spirit of the Constitution, specifically of Article 15, and, after the 42nd Amendment, the Preamble also entail the prohibition.

Thus understood, Article 25 focuses on the entitlements within defined limits. There never has been any doubt or controversy about the connotation of either the phrase 'freedom of conscience', or of the rights to profess and practice a religion of one's choice. It is the right to propagate one's religion that has become a bone of contention. This right was written into the Constitution on the insistence of the Christian members of the Constituent Assembly. Under the Government of India Act of 1935, the right of representation of religious minorities (Muslims, Sikhs, Indian Christians) had been secured through separate electorates and the reservation of seats in the provincial and central legislatures. Such measures had come to be seen by the leadership and the mass following of the Indian National Congress as the imperial stratagem of 'divide and rule' and were, therefore, considered highly mischievous. They had paved the way for the enunciation of 'the two nation theory' by the Indian Muslim League, which, as already noted, eventually became the basis of the partition of the country on the basis of religious identity.

Understandably, the framers of the Constitution wanted to completely do away with what they generally regarded as divisive statutory measures. Separate electorates were discarded forthwith, but reservation survived, notwithstanding the doubts of forward looking leaders like Jawaharlal Nehru, who warned in the Constituent Assembly (on 26 May 1949) that the 'cost' would be 'isolating and keeping away' the minorities from the mainstream. The Christian members not only wanted quotas for their representation to be retained, they also insisted on the right of conversion as an essential element of their faith, which they therefore wanted to be included under fundamental rights. From the Christian point of view the right to change one's religion was the litmus test of the freedom of religion.[2]

Historical Background

Let me go back in time to sketch a background to this contention. It is well known that conversion has been the principal means by which the Christian faith was established in India two thousand years ago. Those who arrived from abroad and made converts, and those who came specifically to make converts, never came in hordes, and they did not have the support of the state. Indeed, the chaplains of the East India Company were, from the mid-eighteenth century onwards, primarily required to meet the religious and spiritual needs of the British, but the objective of spreading the Christian faith was not wholly ignored. After somewhat uncertain beginnings, reflecting conflicting aims, a policy of non-interference was firmly put in place in 1862 through an order made at Bombay. According to it there was to be 'no compulsory conversion, no interference with native habits, and no cow killing in Hindu quarters' (Smith 1963: 66). Pressures at home (in England) to permit missionary work in India continued, however, and eventually bore fruit in 1813, at the time of the renewal of the charter of the East India Company, when the British Parliament allowed the same.

Second generation problems, notably the loss of rights of inheritance following conversion, now made their appearance. A regulation in the Bengal Code of 1832 attended to this problem. Further clarifications were made as and when the need arose. In 1840, responding to a memorial from Hindus and Parsis, asking for restraints on missionaries and for the imposition of disabilities of the kind that the 1832 regulation had removed, the government pleaded its inability to do so in the name of its policy of 'strict neutrality', in protection of 'the rights of civil and personal liberty', and in compliance with 'the principles laid down by the British Parliament'. All these steps led to the enactment of the Caste Disabilities Removal Act of 1850, applicable to all of British India, which prevented any disadvantages or disabilities resulting from the change of religion. Orthodox Hindu opinion unsuccessfully protested that this was indeed interference in their religious usages, delinking religious obligations and property rights that had traditionally gone together (Smith 1963: 70). As far as I have been able to find out, this was the first use of the notion of 'freedom of religion' in the legislative discourse of modern India. And the Christian leadership has held firmly to it.

Just a year before the deliberations of the Constituent Assembly commenced late in 1946, a joint committee of the Catholic Union of India and the All India Council of Indian Christians formally asked that 'the free profession, practice and propagation of religion' should be guaranteed in free India (see Kim 2002: chapter 3). Other Christian bodies also put forward the same demand. Needless to say, many others including sections of the Hindu leadership were opposed to such demands: there had been much disquiet in its ranks in the past regarding the activities of missionaries, particularly among the poorer lower castes and tribal peoples. It was strongly felt, among other leaders by Gandhi, that missionaries were taking undue advantage of the poverty and illiteracy of the masses. The resentment caused by covert and overt official support to the missionaries in the Punjab had led to the emergence of a powerful counter movement from the newly formed Arya Samaj in the late nineteenth century.

The Issue of Conversion

This, then, was the historical background to the debates in the Constituent Assembly. One may add that the Karachi session of the Indian National Congress (1931) also had affirmed the principles of religious liberty and the secular state. Limitations of space preclude further details, but let me highlight a couple of points. Two sub-committees, set up in January 1947, stated their views on conversion and, expectedly, they were not of the same opinion. While the Sub-Committee on Fundamental Rights recommended that 'conversions from one religion to another brought about by coercion or undue influence' should not be recognized by law, the Minorities Sub-Committee, which had a number of Christians as members, insisted on legal sanction for the propagation of faith and conversion. The first Sub-Committee asked that persons under the age of eighteen must not be made to profess a religion other than that in which they were born. The second clarified that, in the interests of family solidarity, if the parents change religion, their minor children too must be converted. And so it went on and on until February 1948, when the revised draft Constitution, prepared by a committee under B.R. Ambedkar's chairmanship, was submitted. In it the right to propagate as well as to profess and practice the religion of one's choice was recognized. There was no caveat about minors.

The controversy did not, however, die down. Eventually, some highly respected and articulate Hindu members of the Constituent Assembly put their weight behind the acceptance of the wording in the draft. The right to convert, it was pointed out, would surely not be employed in a divisive manner by the Indian Christians, who had generally been with the mainstream during the national movement. Moreover, the right would be available to every community that believes in propagation, such as the Arya Samaj. And so Article 25, as we know it today, became part of the fundamental rights chapter of the Constitution of India.

Rajeev Dhavan, a jurist, has written about 'the seamy side' of constitution making in India inasmuch as bargains and compromises were made continuously (Dhavan 2001: 309). Thus it has been suggested by a number of commentators that it was in anticipation of the Christian members giving up the reservation of seats in legislative bodies that the Hindu members eventually came round to supporting the notion of propagation as an element of the freedom of religion.

Post-1950 Developments

Deep-seated and old doubts do not disappear suddenly, and constitutions are not sealed books; they are open to amendment and interpretation. As already stated, the fundamental rights enshrined in the Indian Constitution cannot be amended, but their interpretation is and will remain an on-going process. It is thus that the question whether the right to propagate one's religion, in fulfilment of the constitutional endorsement of the freedom of religion, entails the right to convert without any limitation, continues to arouse controversy even today.

In the years following independence, the work of Christian missionaries, who included foreigners, continued to be the target of suspicion, particularly in areas such as Madhya Pradesh and Orissa, which had large tribal populations, and where strict anti-conversion laws of some of the erstwhile 'native' states had lapsed following the integration of these states into the Indian Union. The government of Madhya Pradesh took the lead and set up a committee (one of its members was a Christian) to inquire into the activities of missionaries in the state. Its work was opposed by various Christian bodies, and not in Madhya Pradesh alone.

The committee's report focused on, among other things, the inflow of money from abroad, which raised in many minds concerns about foreign interference in Indian affairs. The social service and charitable activities of the missionaries in the areas of education and health came under a cloud insofar as these were seen linked to the objective of conversion. The findings and recommendations of the committee caused widespread anger among Christians. Nevertheless, they became the basis of new legislation on the issue of freedom of religion in Orissa (1967) and Madhya Pradesh (1968). The latter state modelled its legislation on the former's. Ten years later (in 1978), the Arunachal Pradesh Legislature also placed on the state statute book a Freedom of Religion Act to prohibit conversions from 'indigenous faiths' to 'any other faith or religion by use of force or inducement or by fraudulent means'. Since 'nature worshippers' as well as Buddhists and Vaishnavas were identified as followers of indigenous faiths, the prohibition affected the proselytizing activities of the Christian missionaries alone.

The basic premise of the Orissa Freedom of Religion Act (1967) is that: 'Conversion in its very process involves an act of undermining another faith. This process becomes all the more objectionable when this is brought about by recourse to methods like force, fraud, material inducement and exploitation of one's poverty, simplicity and ignorance.' Pursuantly, these Acts, while accepting that 'propagation' was allowed by the Constitution, placed various restrictions on the same in the very specific context of conversion. Both Acts were challenged: while the Orissa High Court ruled that the Orissa Act was *ultra vires* of the Constitution, the Madhya Pradesh High Court upheld similar legislation of that state. Eventually, the matter was taken to the Supreme Court, which gave its verdict in January 1977, agreeing with the Madhya Pradesh High Court. Chief Justice A.N. Ray ruled that 'what is freedom for one, is freedom for the other, in equal measure, and there can, therefore, be no such thing as a fundamental right to convert another person to one's own religion', because doing so 'would impinge on the "freedom of conscience" guaranteed to all the citizens of the country alike' (AIR, Supreme Court, 1977: 908–12).

The foregoing crucial and much quoted opinion is unfortunately not clearly worded, and is too literalist in its reading of the Constitution. It took away, according to its critics, the right to propagate one's religion. The right of propagation without the right of carrying it to its logical conclusion of the right to convert was considered empty. According to H.M. Seervai, 'To propagate is not to impart knowledge and to spread it more widely, but to produce intellectual and moral conviction leading to action, namely to adopt that religion' (1978: 1287). The propagation for 'edification' argument of Justice B.K. Mukherjee of the Supreme Court (AIR, Supreme Court 1954: 391) sounds rather simple minded today. Seervai's appears to be the more practicable interpretation, but it does not invalidate the implication of Justice Ray's argument that freedom of religion is exercised in the act of conversion only when it is the voluntary decision of an individual without the intervention of another person, notwithstanding the latter's goodwill and good faith (no pun is intended here).

An intractable problem that persists in this context is how to determine with absolute certainty that a particular act of conversion is voluntary or not, that it is fair and not fraudulent, sincere and not contrived. As Gandhi used to say, no one but God knows a man's heart. The criteria laid down in the various pieces of legislation are not wholly feasible. The latest attempt in this direction, the Tamil Nadu Prevention of Forcible Conversion of Religion Act (2002), goes well beyond the Madhya Pradesh and Orissa Acts to render conversions, particularly of or by the Dalits, virtually impossible. This is so because of the stringent reporting obligations imposed upon the converts and the converted, the discretionary powers conferred upon law enforcement officers, and the provision of fines and imprisonment for those who may be judged to have violated the law.[3]

It seems that the time is now opportune to argue forcefully that the best guardian of freedom of religion, and the most effective guarantor that unfair conversions, particularly on a collective basis, shall not take place, will be not the state but civil society, or, better still, the two in association. Vigilant public opinion expressed in institutionalized ways, acting as a monitor rather than a substitute, should be preferable to executive authority, particularly if this is to be exercised by the lower rungs of the bureaucracy and magistracy. (One is here reminded of John Locke's recommendation that religious belief should be beyond the reach of civil government.) This is at the moment only an idea: it will need serious effort to work it out, particularly if communal dissensions are acute as they are now. Also to be kept in mind is the issue of the role of the secular state in other contexts.[4]

THE ROLE OF THE SECULAR STATE

Secularism, understood as the attitude of mutual toleration among the religious communities comprising the nation, and of neutrality or non-discrimination on the part of the state in its dealings with the citizens, irrespective of their religious identity, apparently protects freedom of religion. Two problems must be addressed, however. First, is the secular state neutral through engagement, that is by being respectful towards all religions (*sarva dharma samabhāv*), or through disengagement, that is by erecting a wall, as it were, between itself and the religious life of the citizens? Secondly, what is involved in a community's conception of the profession and practice of its religion.

On the basis of the Constitution itself, the Indian state has remained engaged from the very beginning with the religious life of its citizens and, what is more, in disparate ways. What I have in mind is, first, clause 2 of Article 25, which empowers the state to regulate or restrict various kinds of secular activities (economic, political, etc.) that may be associated with religious practice. Article 31A also provides for the acquisition of estates and their management in public interest. One of the best known instances of this is the Dargah Khwajah Saheb Act of 1955 of the Indian Parliament that empowered the state to oversee the management of the famous Muslim Sufi shrine at Ajmer. A recent example was the takeover of the management of the Vaishno Devi temple complex in the state of Jammu and Kashmir (while the state was under President's rule) on the ground of mismanagement by the trust that had the responsibility for running its affairs. The same principle was invoked to bring the affairs of Vishvanath Temple at Varanasi under the control of a board (see Dhavan 2001: 315). Besides, there is provision in the Constitution for state support to religious activity. Article 290A provides for annual payments to certain Devaswom Funds for the use of Hindu temples in Kerala and Tamil Nadu, on the ground that these temples and shrines were the beneficiaries of state patronage before the integration of the states of Travancore and Cochin into the Indian Union.[5]

Further, since the all-important Article 25 holds the state responsible for ensuring the maintenance of 'public order, morality and health', while granting citizens the freedom of religion, it is arguable that the resources of the state should be drawn upon in a big way for the foregoing purposes on such occasions as the periodic, multitudinous Hindu Kumbh *mela*s at Haridwar and elsewhere. Similar administrative back-up (including deployment of law and order and public health personnel) is provided on an appropriate scale whenever and wherever people gather in large numbers for religious performances. Even financial support may be provided, as is done, for instance, in the case of Haj pilgrims whose travel to Saudi Arabia by sea or air is subsidized by the state, costing the government currently several hundred crores of rupees annually. Government largess has enabled some major places of worship, such as the Jagannath temple complex at Puri, to undertake repairs, restoration or reconstruction. On the very day on which the Babri mosque was demolished by Hindu hooligans in 1992, Prime Minister P.V. Narasimha Rao announced that it would be rebuilt, presumably by the government. That this did not happen is another matter. Limitations of space preclude further examples, but I trust it is clear that the practice of the Indian state in relation to the religious life of the people has not been exactly what would be expected from a secular state if the French or the American state were to be regarded as the model, or if Gandhi's conception of the secular state had been adhered to. He emphatically denied any role whatsoever to the state in the religious affairs of the people. Moreover, he argued, that if a community depends 'partly or wholly on state aid' for 'the existence of its religion', then 'it does not have any religion worth the name' (Iyer 1986: 287).

Apart from the involvement of the legislative and executive branches of the government in religious affairs, the judiciary too has entered into such controversial areas—veritable minefields—as the definition of the essentials of religious identity, belief, and practice. This has happened on many occasions. As, for instance, when P.B. Gajendragadkar, Chief Justice of the Supreme Court, ordered in 1966 that temples of the Satsangi community be thrown open to the (so-called) untouchables. Or when Justice Y.V. Chandrachud, again the Chief Justice of the same court, pronounced in 1985 in favour of respondent Shah Bano, a divorced

Muslim woman, granting her the enhanced monthly maintenance that the Madhya Pradesh High Court had ordered her husband, the complainant in the Supreme Court, to pay her, rejecting his interpretation of the issues involved, which had been supported by the All-India Muslim Personal Law Board. In both cases the reformist justices could well be said to have been motivated by considerations of fair play and justice, but their pronouncements were seen by those affected—the small sect of Satsangis, who unsuccessfully asserted that they were not Hindus and therefore not obliged to allow Hindus of any caste whatsoever into their temples, in the one case, and by millions of Muslims, in the other—as grave interference in the practice of their rights as religious minorities. Given Article 17 of the Constitution, which forbids the practice of untouchability in any form, and their small numbers and character as a local community, the Satsangis did not have a chance of having things their own way.

The case of the Muslims was significantly different and so not because of numbers alone. Muslim public opinion was widely and rapidly aroused on the ground that the interpretation of Shariat-based Muslim personal law was outside the jurisdiction of secular courts. Further, any alteration or abridgement of the provisions of this law was regarded as unwarranted interference that amounted to restriction of the freedom of religion. Keen to calm down the angered Muslim public opinion, the Union government, which was in 1986 in the hands of the Congress, a Muslim vote-dependent political party, enacted through the Parliament the Muslim Women (Protection of Rights on Divorce) Act. This excluded divorced Muslim women from the purview of the relevant provisions (Section 125) of the Criminal Procedure Code, that would have been helpful to them, and limited the liability of the husband in respect of his former spouse. The protection of the rights of such women was to be in terms of traditional Muslim personal law. (Incidentally, not all the Muslim communities of India had in past followed the Shariat in respect of personal law; in fact, some of them had even followed Hindu personal laws. All this changed in 1937, during British Raj, when the Shariat Act made Shariat-based personal laws applicable to all Muslims of the subcontinent.)

This brings me to the second problem mentioned above, namely the possibility of conflict between the obligation of the secular state to ensure freedom of religion and a community's own definition of the essence of religious belief and practice. The constitutional background to it is provided by the tension between the freedom of religion as a fundamental right (Article 25) and the directive principle of state policy *vide* Article 44, which requires the state to 'endeavour to secure for the citizens a uniform civil code' throughout India. On this issue, Chief Justice Chandrachud had observed (in the Shah Bano case judgement) that, regrettably, this Article had remained 'a dead letter' (AIR, Supreme Court 1985: 954), under the belief that it was for the Muslim community to take the initiative in this matter. This is what many leaders of public opinion and scholars of law believe even today, sixteen years after the justice's *obiter dicta*.

At this point we need to turn briefly to Hindu personal law based on the *dharmashāstra*, which the Hindus, like the Muslims, have considered a part of their religious tradition. Nevertheless, the Government of India under the leadership of Jawaharlal Nehru went ahead within a year of independence, although not as speedily and comprehensively as it wanted, to enact a number of progressive laws in respect of marriage and divorce (1955), adoption and maintenance (1956), minority and guardianship (1956), succession and inheritance (1956), etc. (see Derrett 1978). These broke away from the shāstric tradition and represented the initial steps in the direction of, first, the liberalization and secularization of Hindu personal law and, second, the formulation of a uniform civil code. Articles 25(2)(b) and 44 are relevant in this context.

As is well known, there was much opposition to the proposed legislation from conservative Hindu leaders, including the first President of India himself (Rajendra Prasad), but the progressive elements prevailed ultimately. Since the mid-1950s, however, there has been no further progress towards the secularization of personal laws. In fact, Muslim leadership has come to consider it as an attempt to impose amended Hindu personal laws on the non-Muslims. Another viewpoint holds that the burden of the movement towards a uniform civil code will fall less heavily on the Hindus, in respect of whom a beginning was made in the 1950s, than on the other communities who have remained static. In the event, the feeling has grown that the Hindu right wing exploits the issue of the uniform civil code to embarrass Muslims. A way out of the impasse, it has been suggested by a Harvard law professor, might be to begin with less controversial issues than personal laws, such as religious and charitable endowments (Mansfield 2001: 93). It is also high time that reformist Muslim opinions are expressed openly and with conviction.[6]

The foregoing discussion of the implications of the right to propagate one's religion, and of the framing of a uniform civil code, highlights, I trust, the intricacies of securing the freedom of religion in a vast country such as India, marked by religious pluralism, the intertwining of the religious and the social, and the politicization of religious identities. The road ahead is long and hazardous.

CONCLUDING REMARKS

To conclude, let me return to where I began. I said that the concept of freedom of religion is a modern idea. It is so both chronologically and normatively. It is a gift of the modern state that is not necessarily itself formally secular, but operates in the social setting of widespread secularization. (The case of the United Kingdom readily comes to mind.) The radical break with traditional ideas about the place of religion in social life in the West went hand in hand with the secularization of institutions (as well as of attitudes) throughout the nineteenth century. Religion 'retreated from public life', as Max Weber put it, 'into the transcendental realm of mystic life or into the brotherliness of direct and personal relations'. This was what Weber called the 'disenchantment of the world' (1948: 155). Freedom of religion or, more broadly freedom of conscience, is an aspect of the liberal ideology of individualism, which, following the collapse of the communist alternative, is in today's world an ideal to strive for everywhere. Understandably, it is conceived broadly enough to include the freedom to profess no religion at all.

Needless to emphasize, the notion of freedom of religion could not be reasonably expected to spring from within a religious tradition. As I indicated earlier, the most that may be expected from such traditions is the idea of toleration between religions and, perhaps, some degree of freedom of choice within the confines of a particular tradition. The latter possibility is best illustrated by the denominational splits that came in Europe in the wake of the Protestant Reformation, dividing Christians into

Lutherans, Calvinists, Presbyterians, Anglicans, Puritans, and others. Within the amorphous Hindu religious tradition, which is a congeries rather than a single tradition, a plurality of belief and practice has long been recognized, as I said earlier, as the cultural dimension of the caste system.

The freedom to move from one religion to another is altogether a different matter. No spokesperson for a religious tradition would sound credible if he or she were to say that, not only are its followers free to embrace another religion, which they of course are, but also that doing so is right or commendable. They could only be called apostates and regarded as misguided if not morally degenerate. Within the value framework of a proselytizing religion, such an attitude of toleration would be irrational and self-defeating.

As for non-proselytizing religions, notably Hinduism, its most vocal modern exponent, Vivekananda, was emphatic in holding the view that anyone who went 'out of the Hindu pale [was] not only a man less, but an enemy more' (Punj 2002: 25). Indeed, Vivekananda considered it his mission to 'awaken' India so that it could conquer (not merely convert) the world spiritually. In his own eye his message was of universal scope: it was unfortunate that the Hindus should have at some point of time acquired the notion of the *mleccha*, the uncultured outsider. Moreover, he considered it absurd that Christian missionaries should want to preach to the Hindus, since Hinduism acknowledged reverence for all religions and was therefore the superior faith. Using their own idiom, he called Vedanta 'the wonderful voice of God' (Basu 2002: 56).

While seeking to unite Hindus as one national community (or nation), and thereby eroding internal pluralism, Vivekananda relocated toleration in the domain of inter-religious relations. At the same time, he hierarchized plurality in a manner that placed Vedanta at the very apex of the religious heritage of humankind as its highest expression and future possibility.

Dayananda found the 'freedom' of a Hindu to convert to Christianity or Islam to be only serfdom, and set out to define the procedure (purification or *shuddhi*) to reclaim the trapped individuals. And Gandhi argued with absolute conviction that, while the idea of free choice of religion by the individual should be an inalienable right, the effort to convert or reclaim him or her could only come from someone who is an alien to the true essence of religion. 'If conversion is the work of God', he asked with characteristic directness, 'why should that work be taken away from him?' (Sudhir Chandra 2002: 284). For himself, he was content to be called a *sanātanī* Hindu and, at the same time, a multi-religious person: it apparently did not require any radical transformation of the tradition to believe (and behave) thus (see Jordens 1998).

If Hinduism too, in its own manner, does not entertain the idea of freedom of religion, what is the record of the pre-modern state in this regard in the long history of India? The illustrious name of Ashoka readily comes to one's mind, but what we know from his edicts is his exhortation of toleration, mutual respect, and concord, rather than of state support for freedom of choice of religion (Rock Edict XII; see Thapar 1961: 225). Nor did he call upon people to embrace any particular religion. Allowing for the much greater complexity in matters of religion in Akbar's time, we have to say that the latter emperor's personal catholicity of mind and search for religious syncretism was unique in the annals of world history (see Sharma 1962). Moreover, he did go further than Ashoka in terms of action by the state to protect the rights of citizens (it was the non-Muslims who were the relevant category) to pursue their religions freely. By his own actions he provided symbolic support for religious pluralism at the cost of the charge of apostasy levelled against him by the *ulama*. What is more, he did not impose the syncretic *dīn-i-Ilāhī* on his subjects, and it had few takers. It is noteworthy here that throughout the centuries of Muslim rule, non-Muslims could choose to remain outside the Islamic fold, although at a certain cost. And most of them chose to do so.

Under British colonial rule, as noted above, the policy of non-interference of its earlier period was abandoned early in the nineteenth century, ironically in the name of religious liberty. Thereafter, the association between the government and the Church was close, more openly so in some places, and at certain points of time, than at others. The alleged religious 'causes' of the 1857 uprising did, however, result in an emphatic restatement of the official policy of the neutrality of the state. The royal proclamation of 1858, on the occasion of the assumption of the responsibility of the governance of British India by the British sovereign, declared that 'none be any wise favoured, none molested or disquieted, by reason of their religious faith or observances'; 'all interference with the religious belief or worship' of any 'subjects' was strictly prohibited. But the same proclamation also affirmed at the outset 'the Truth of Christianity' (Smith 1963: 71–2). By implication whatever was in conflict with it was not true.

In short, freedom of religion as a fundamental right as we find it in the Indian Constitution owes more to modern Western models, particularly the American, and to the Universal Declaration of Human Rights, than to India's religious traditions or the practices of pre-modern Indian states (Hindu or Muslim). The 'doublespeak' policies of the colonial regime may, however, be credited with holding forth the *principle* of the religious neutrality of the state. The absence of firm cultural and historical roots of the idea of freedom of religion, as it is understood today, is perhaps made good by the fact that some Hindu religious reformers of the nineteenth and twentieth centuries, notably Vivekananda and Gandhi, have been powerful voices in support of religious toleration.

Freedom of religion is, however, seriously threatened today by the ideology of cultural nationalism (Hindutva) espoused by Hindu right-wing political and cultural bodies, which would like to require non-Hindus to acknowledge the primacy of various upper caste religious beliefs, symbols, and practices as central to a national culture of India. Through the route of an ostensibly non-political national culture, the cause of Hindu political domination (majoritarianism) is indirectly served, but no one is fooled by this masquerade. Freedom of religion is also given narrow or excessively combative interpretations by certain leaders of the minority communities, which are more likely to hurt everyone in the long run rather than promote the common good. 'In this situation', writes the noted journalist B.G. Verghese, 'Muslim Indians must not shrink back into the ghetto or opt out after Gujarat. The community must bestir itself to modernize, reform, compete and change. Christians too must reject the carryover of caste that disfigures the Church and admonish revivalist and so-called charismatic preachers who revile other faiths while propagating their own' (2002: 55). Similarly, the distinguished jurist Fali Nariman publicly advised Muslims that letting the Hindus build a temple at what they regard as Rama's *janmabhumi* 'would not be an act of surrender, but an act of statesmanship—

for the greater good of the greater number (of Muslims)' (2003). Genuine toleration is a two-way street.

Resistances to the freedom of religion come in different idioms and are not peculiar to India: they occur in one form or another elsewhere too. For example, in the USA, where interpretations of the First Amendment continue to be made, notably by the Supreme Court, which is divided between conservatives and progressives among the justices; in China, where Marxist perspectives on religion still influence state policy; in Israel with its unique Zionist tradition that privileges Judaism; or among the Muslim nations that, inter-country variations notwithstanding, are committed to Islam as the most perfect, straight, path to salvation. Freedom of religion may, therefore, be said to be an ideal that is *complex* (given the wide variety of historical backgrounds), *controversial* (given not only the prevailing religious discords but also serious and unsettled philosophical doubts: does freedom of religion imply that all religions are of equal merit?), and *contemporary* or *relatively recent*. From the *longue durée* perspective of world history, freedom of religion is a young idea with a somewhat uncertain future. It is an idea on trial, as it were, and should be examined carefully so that it may be strengthened. It is an idea worthy of all the intellectual vigour and moral courage that we can muster.

NOTES

1. It is arguable that the 42nd Amendment is bad in law. How could even duly elected parliamentarians claim in 1976, as they did, that it is what they wrote into the Constitution (through the amendment), rather than the original text of the Preamble, which is what the 'people of India', speaking through the Constituent Assembly, gave unto themselves in 1949? Seervai (1978: 276) calls it 'patently false'.
2. For further discussion of the Constitution, see Chs 3 and 4 below.
3. Soon afterwards the Gujarat government also enacted similar legislation. But the Tamil Nadu Act was repealed through an ordinance in 2004. The Chief Minister of the state explained that, although the Act was intended to promoted 'comunal harmony', it was eventually repealed to allay misgivings among the religious minorities.
4. Iqbal Ansari, a former professor of Aligarh Muslim University, has advocated 'evolving a code of ethics by all preachers—including

Hindus involved in 'reclaiming' non-Hindus to its fold—not to combine charitable work with proselytization especially among weak and vulnerable sections like the tribals' (2003).

5. The dilemmas of the involvement/non-involvement of the state in the religious affairs of the people were evident throughout the colonial period. Thus, at first the East India Company took over the responsibility for temple protection in South India from the rulers it displaced. The Directors of the Company, however, ordered disengagement in 1863 (Religious Endowments Act), and the responsibility for temple management was vested in local management committees.

6. Martha Nussbaum holds a contrary point of view: 'I would argue that it was a mistake all along to exempt personal laws from the scrutiny of Fundamental Rights.... To allow compromise here is to allow compromises with the very foundations of citizenship and the equal dignity of citizens' (2004: 45–6). Purely at the level of theoretical argument, Nussbaum is right, but the constraints of social reality may not be easily brushed aside.

REFERENCES

Ansari, Iqbal. 2003. 'Converse on conversion', *Hindustan Times* (New Delhi), 10 June 2003, Ed. page.

Bainton, Ronald H. 1956. *The Reformation of the Sixteenth Century*. Boston: Beacon Press.

Basu, Shamita. 2002. *Religious Revivalism as Nationalist Discourse*. New Delhi: Oxford University Press.

Cassirer, Ernest. 1968. *The Philosophy of the Enlightenment*. Princeton, N.J.: Princeton University Press.

Derrett, J.D.M. 1978. *The Death of a Marriage Law*. New Delhi: Vikas.

Dhavan, Rajeev. 2001. 'The road to Xanadu: India's quest for secularism.' In Gerald J. Larson (ed.). *Religion and Personal Law in Secular India*. New Delhi: Social Science Press.

Dunn, Richard S. 1979. *The Age of Religious Wars 1559–1715*. New York: Norton.

Galanter, Marc. 1989. *Law and Society in India*. New Delhi: Oxford University Press.

Greene, Everts B. 1941. *Religion and the State: The Making and Testing of an American Tradition*. New York: New York University Press.

Huntington, Samuel. 1996. *The Clash of Civilizations and the Remaking of World Order*. New York: Touchstone.

Iyer, Raghavan (ed.). 1986. *The Moral and Political Writings of Mahatma Gandhi.Vol. I: Civilization, Politics and Religion*. New Delhi: Oxford University Press.

Jones, Kenneth W. 1976. *Arya Dharm: Hindu Consciousness in Nineteenth Century Punjab*. New Delhi: Manohar.

Jordens, J.T.F. 1998. *Gandhi's Religion*. London: Macmillan.

Kim, Sebastian C.H. 2003. *In Search of Identity: Debates on Religious Conversion in India*. New Delhi: Oxford University Press.

Mabbott, J.D. 1973. *John Locke*. London: Macmillan.

Madan, T.N. 2003. 'Freedom of Religion'. *Economic and Political Weekly* 15: 1034–41.

Mansfield, John H. 2001. 'Religious and charitable endowments and a uniform civil code'. In Gerald J. Larson (ed.). *Religion and Personal Law in Secular India*. New Delhi: Social Science Press.

Nariman, Fali. 2003. 'Giving isn't giving in', *Hindustan Times*, 14 August.

Nussbaum, Martha. 2004. 'On equal conditions.' In M. Hasan (ed.). *Will Secular India Survive?* New Delhi: Imprint One.

Punj, Balbir K. 2002. 'The Hindu soul in search of its body'. *Outlook*, 30 September.

Seervai, H.M. 1978. *Constitutional Law of India*. 4th edn. Vol. 1. Bombay: N.M. Tripathi.

Sharma, Sri Ram. 1962. *The Religious Policy of the Mughal Emperors*. Bombay: Asia.

Smith, Donald E. 1963. *India as a Secular State*. Bombay: Oxford University Press.

Sudhir Chandra. 2002. 'An unresolved dilemma: Gandhi on religious conversion'. In Sudhir Chandra, *Continuing Dilemmas: Understanding Social Consciousness*. New Delhi: Tulika.

Thapar, Romila. 1961. *Asoka and the Decline of the Mauryas*. London: Oxford University Press.

Troeltsch, Ernst. 1981. *The Social Teaching of the Christian Churches*. Vol. 2. Chicago: University of Chicago Press.

Verghese, B.G. 2002. 'India's forgotten gospel of fraternity'. *Outlook*, 18 November.

Weber, Max. 1948. *From Max Weber: Essays in Sociology*. London: Routledge and Kegan Paul.

3

*Secularism in its Place**

The paper was delivered at a moment when the idea of secularism, entrenched in the Indian Constitution by legislators who had experienced the chaos of communal conflict in 1946–7, is again being raised. The secular settlement, elaborated in the shadow of partition, deprived the politicization of religious identities of legitimacy. But this settlement has weakened. Contrary to the expectations of a rationalist social science, economic growth and the breakdown of previously settled relations among local communities and classes have led to the revival of religious identities and to their expression in public and conflictual forms. These circumstances have led to a vigorous debate about how to understand and how to address the new conflicts.

The debate follows, to an extent, earlier channels of argument elaborated in the nationalist era. Jawaharlal Nehru's secularism rested on the notion that religion is an erroneous view of the cosmos that will yield to more rational understanding as scientific thinking and economic growth advance. This position entails the construction of an edifice of public law that is applicable to all persons and an edifice of politics that recognizes individual, not

* This is the text, as originally published in *The Journal of Asian Studies* 46, 4 (November 1987), pp. 747–59, of the Fulbright Fortieth Anniversary Distinguished Fellow's Lecture delivered at the President's panel at the meeting of the Association of Asian Studies in Boston in April 1987. The AAS President, Professor Susanne Rudolph, wrote a prefatory note, an excerpt from which is reproduced here in lieu of an epigraph.

I am grateful to Alan Babb, Ainslee Embree, Ashis Nandy, Susan Pharr, and Stanley Tambiah, and above all to Lloyd and Susanne Rudolph, for their comments on the original spoken text.

Almost everyone who has written about secularism in India since the publication of this essay has referred to it, but not always appreciatively. For some of the criticisms and my responses to them, see Chapter 5 below.

group, identities. Mohandas Gandhi's secularism rested on the notions that all religions are true, that they give meaning to the moral life, and that Indian society can be built on a community of religious communities. The policy implications of this position are more responsive to group identities. Although Professor Madan's argument does not rest on the same ontological premises as Gandhi's, his position is closer to Gandhi's than to Nehru's. He argues where religion persists as a powerful element in personal identity, secular policy cannot build on a rationalist avoidance of religious community but must take it into account.

Susanne Hoeber Rudolph

By asking me to speak to you here this evening, you have done me an honour, and I am grateful for it. I also know that you expect me to say something worthy of discussion: of my ability to do so I am doubtful, but I will try. You will have to show me great indulgence, for the theme I have chosen, namely the prospects of secularism in India, is not only of immense significance but also very complex, and the time at my disposal is very limited. I will take a great deal for granted and plunge straight into my subject.

We live in a world which we call modern or which we wish to be modern. Modernity is generally regarded as both a practical necessity and a moral imperative, a fact and a value. When I say this I am not using the word 'modern' in one of those many trivial senses which I trust we have by now left behind us. Thus, by modernity I do not mean a complete break with tradition. Being modern means larger and deeper things: for example, the enlargement of human freedom and the enhancement of the range of choices open to a people in respect of things that matter, including their present and future lifestyles. This means being in charge of oneself. And this, you will recognize, is one of the connotations of the process of secularization.

You will recall that the word 'secularization' was first used in 1648, at the end of the Thirty Years' War in Europe, to refer to the transfer of church properties to the exclusive control of the princes. What was a matter-of-fact statement then became later, after the French Revolution, a value statement as well: on 2 November 1789, Talleyrand announced to the French National Assembly that all ecclesiastical goods were at the disposal of the nation, as indeed they should have been. Still later, when George Jacob Holyoake coined the term 'secularism' in 1851, and led a rationalist movement of protest in England, secularization was built into the ideology of progress. Secularization, though nowhere more than a fragmentary and incomplete process, has ever since retained a positive connotation.

As you know, 'secularization' is nowadays generally employed to refer to, in the words of Peter Berger, 'the process by which sectors of society and culture are removed from the domination of religious institutions and symbols' (1973: 113). While the inner logic of the economic sector perhaps makes it the most convenient arena for secularization, other sectors, notably the political, have been found to be less amenable to it. It is in relation to the latter that the ideology of secularism acquires the most salience.

Now, I submit that in the prevailing circumstances secularism in South Asia as a generally shared credo of life is impossible, as a basis for state action impracticable, and as a blueprint for the foreseeable future impotent. It is impossible as a credo of life because the great majority of the people of South Asia are in their own eyes active adherents of some religious faith. It is impracticable as a basis for state action either because Buddhism and Islam have been declared state or state-protected religions, or because the stance of religious neutrality or equidistance is difficult to maintain since religious minorities do not share the majority's view of what this entails for the state. And it is impotent as a blueprint for the future because, by its very nature, it is incapable of countering religious fundamentalism and fanaticism.

Secularism is the dream of a minority which wants to shape the majority in its own image, which wants to impose its will upon history but lacks the power to do so under a democratically organized polity. In an open society the state will reflect the character of the society. Secularism therefore is a social myth which draws a cover over the failure of this minority to separate politics from religion in the society in which its members live. From the point of view of the majority, 'secularism' is a vacuous word, a phantom concept, for such people do not know whether it is desirable to privatize religion, and if it is, how this may be done, unless they be Protestant Christians, but not if they are Buddhists, Hindus, Muslims, or Sikhs. For the secularist minority to stigmatize the majority as primordially oriented and to preach secularism to the latter as the law of human existence is moral arrogance and worse—I say 'worse' since in our times politics

takes precedence over ethics—political folly. It is both these—
moral arrogance and political folly—because it fails to recognize
the immense importance of religion in the lives of the people of
South Asia. I will not raise here the issue of the definition of
religion: suffice it to say that for these peoples their religion
establishes their place in society and bestows meaning on their
life, more than any other social or cultural factor.

Unable to raise the veil of its illusions, the modernist minority
in India today is beset with deep anxieties about the future of
secularism in the country and in South Asia generally. Appeals
are made day in and day out to foster a modern scientific temper,
of which Jawaharlal Nehru is invoked as a principal exponent.
Books are written and an unending round of seminars held on the
true nature and significance of communalism and how to combat
it. In fact, there is much talk these days in the highest political
quarters about the need for stern legislative and executive measures to check the rising and menacing tide of majority and
minority fundamentalism and revivalism, and this even as the
so-called Hindu society continues splintering.

An astonishing (or should one say impressive?) consensus
among Indian Muslims about preserving the sharia, or 'holy
law', against what they consider the legislative onslaught of a
godless state, but others call the indispensability of a common
civil law as a foundation of the modern state, was witnessed in
1986 in connection with the rights of Muslim divorced women
(the Shah Bano case, see pp. 45–7 above). This has now been
followed by the biggest-ever public protest by Muslims since
independence forty years ago, held at New Delhi on 30 March
1987, to demand full possession of a sixteenth-century mosque
in the city of Ayodhya in north India, which was built after
Babar's invasion at what Hindus believe to have been the
birthplace of god-incarnate Rama. The whole country held its
breath, fearful of a counter demonstration of strength by the
Hindus: it took place but luckily there was no major communal
flare-up. Meanwhile, Sikh and Hindu fundamentalists continue
to face one another in Punjab, and innocent people are killed
every day by Sikh terrorists. Social analysts draw attention to the
contradiction between the undoubted though slow spread of
secularization in everyday life, on the one hand, and the unmis-
takable rise of fundamentalism, on the other. But surely these

phenomena are only apparently contradictory, for in truth it is the marginalization of religious faith, which is what secularization is, that permits the perversion of religion. There are no fundamentalists or revivalists in traditional society.

The point to stress, then, is that, despite ongoing processes of secularization and deliberate efforts to promote it, secularism as a widely shared world view has failed to make headway in India. Obviously what exists empirically but not also ideologically exists only weakly. The hopes about the prospects of secularism raised by social scientists in the years soon after independence—recall the well-known books by Donald Eugene Smith (1963) and Rajni Kothari (1970)—have been belied, notwithstanding the general acceptability of their view of 'Hinduism' as a broadly tolerant religion. Acute observers of the sociocultural and political scenes contend that signs of a weakening secularism are in evidence, particularly among the Hindus. Religious books, a recent newspaper report said, continue to outsell all the others in India and, one can be sure, in all the other South Asian countries. Religious pilgrimages attract larger and even larger congregations counted in millions. Buildings of religious worship or prayer dot the urban landscape. New Delhi has many new Hindu temples and Sikh gurudwaras, and its most recent modern structure is the Bahai temple facing the old Kalkaji (Hindu) temple, thrown open to worshippers of all faiths late last year. God-men and gurus sit in seminars and roam the streets, and American 'Hare Krishnas' take the initiative in organizing an annual *ratha yātrā* (chariot festival).

While society seethes with these and other expressions of a vibrant religiosity, the feeble character of the Indian policy of state secularism is exposed. At best, Indian secularism has been an inadequately defined 'attitude' (it cannot be called a philosophy of life except when one is discussing the thought of someone like Mahatma Gandhi or Maulana Azad) of 'goodwill towards all religions', *sarvadharma sadbhāva*; in a narrower formulation it has been a negative or defensive policy of religious neutrality (*dharma nirpekshata*) on the part of the state. In either formulation, Indian secularism achieves the opposite of its stated intentions; it trivializes religious difference as well as the notion of the unity of religions. And it really fails to provide guidance for viable political action, for it is not a rooted, full-blooded, and well-thought-out Weltanschauung, it is only a stratagem. It has been so self-confessedly for fundamentalist organizations such as the Muslim Jamat-i-Islami (see Mushir-ul-Haq 1972: 11–12). I would like to suggest that it was also so for Jawaharlal Nehru, but let me not anticipate: I will have more to say about Nehru's secularism in a short while. Just now, let me dwell a little longer on the infirmity of secularism.

Now, what exactly does the failure of secularism mean? For one thing, it underscores the failure of the society and the state to bring under control the divisive forces which resulted in the partition of the subcontinent in 1947. Though forty years have passed and the Midnight's Children are at the threshold of middle age, tempers continue to rage, and occasionally (perhaps too frequently) blood even flows in some places, as a result of the mutual hostility between the followers of different religions.

What produces this hostility? Surely not religious faith itself, for even religious traditions which take an uncompromising view of 'non-believers' (that is, the followers of other religions) speak with multiple tongues and pregnant ambiguity. The *Qur'ān*, for example, proclaims that there should be no coercion in the matter of faith (2: 256). Even an agnostic such as Nehru acknowledged this before the burden of running a secular state fell on his aging shoulders. As long ago as 1936 he said, 'The communal problem is not a religious problem, it has nothing to do with religion' (1972–82, 7: 82). It was not religious difference as such but its exploitation by calculating politicians for the achievement of secular ends which had produced the communal divide.

It is perhaps one of the tragedies of the twentieth century that a man who had at the beginning of his political career wanted above all to bridge religious differences should have in the end contributed to widening them. As is well-known, the young Muhammad Ali Jinnah was a non-practising Muslim in private life and a secularist in public, but later on he (like many others, Hindus and Sikhs as well as Muslims) played with the fire of communal frenzy. Inevitably, perhaps, he became a victim of his own political success, of, as Ayesha Jalal puts it, 'an unthinking mob, fired by blood lust, fear and greed' (1985: 216). I should think he too realized this, for, without any loss of time, four days before the formal inauguration of Pakistan, he called upon his people to 'bury the hatchet' and make common citizenship, not communal identity, the basis of the new state (see Sharif ul Mujahid 1981:

247). And within a month he reiterated: 'You may belong to any religion, or caste, or creed—that has nothing to do with the business of the state' (Jinnah 1947–8: 8). How close to Nehru he was, and, though he pulled himself far apart for the achievement of his political goals, he obviously remained a secularist.

* * *

Tolerance is indeed a value enshrined in all the great religions of humanity, but let me not underplay the historical roots of communal antagonism in South Asia. I am not wholly convinced when our Marxist colleagues argue that communalism is a result of the distortions in the economic base of our societies produced by the colonial mode of production and that the 'communal question was a petty bourgeois question par excellence' (Bipan Chandra 1984: 40). The importance of these distortions may not be minimized, but these analysts should know that South Asia's major religious traditions—Buddhism, Hinduism, Islam, and Sikhism—are totalizing in character, claiming all of a follower's life, so that religion is constitutive of society. In the given pluralist situation, both tolerance and intolerance are expressions of exclusivism. When I say that South Asia's religious traditions are 'totalizing', I am not trying to argue that they do not recognize the distinction between the terms 'religious' and 'secular'. We know that in their distinctive ways all four traditions make this distinction. I wish I had the time to elaborate on this theme, but then there is perhaps no need to do so here. What needs to be stressed, however, is that these religions have the same view of the relationship between the categories of the 'religious' and the 'secular'.

My studies convince me that in Buddhism, Hinduism, Islam, and Sikhism this relationship is hierarchical (in the sense in which Louis Dumont uses this term). Thus, though Buddhism may well be considered as the one South Asian religious tradition which, by denying supernatural beings any significant role in human life, has the most secularist potential, yet this would be an oversimplified view of it. What is important is not only what Émile Durkheim so clearly perceived, namely the central importance of the category of the 'sacred' in Buddhism, but also (and more significantly in the present context) the fact, so well documented for us by Stanley Tambiah (1976) that the *bhikkhu*, or the world renouncer, is superior to the *chakkavatti*, or the world conqueror, and that neither exists by himself. Similarly, in every Sikh gurudwara the sacred sword is placed for veneration at a lower level than the holy book, the *Granth Sahab*, which is the repository of the Word (*shabad*), despite the fact that, for the Sikhs, the sword too symbolizes the divinity or, more accurately, the inseparability of the spiritual and secular functions.

I trust you will allow me to speak at a little greater length about Hinduism and Islam. I would have liked not to go all the way back to the *Rig Veda* of three thousand years ago, were it not for the fact that it presents explicitly, employing a fascinating simile, the hierarchical relationship between spiritual authority and temporal power. It would seem that originally the two functions were differentiated, but they were later deliberately brought together, for the regnum (*kshatra*) could not subsist on its own without the sacerdotium (*brahma*) which provided its principle of legitimacy. Says the king to the priest: 'Turn thou unto me so that we may unite...I assign to you the precedence; quickened by thee I shall perform deeds' (see Coomaraswamy 1978: 8). The very word used for the priest, *purohita*, points to precedence. What is more, the priest and the king are united, as husband is to wife, and they must speak with one voice. This is what Dumont would call hierarchical dyarchy or complementarity. Even if one were to look upon the king and the *purohita* as dissociated (rather than united) and thus contend that kingship had become secularized (see Dumont 1980: 293), the hierarchical relation between the two functions survives and is even emphasized. The discrete realms of interest and power (*artha*) are opposed to and yet encompassed by dharma.

Let me move on to the *Kautilya Arthashāstra* (? fourth century BC/AD), which has been said often enough to present an amoral theory of political power. Such a reading is, however, contestable. What I find more acceptable is the view that the *Arthashāstra* teaches that the rational pursuit of economic and political ends (*artha*) must be carried out in fulfillment and not violation of dharma. More broadly, '*artha* must be pursued in the framework of *kāma*, *dharma* and *moksha*...the principle remains that *artha* to be truly *artha* must be part of a larger totality, individual and social' (Shah 1982: 72; see also pp. 268–71 below).

I might add here parenthetically that in traditional Brahmanical political thought, cultural pluralism within the state was accepted and the king was the protector of everybody's dharma: being *that* was *his dharma*. Only in very exceptional circumstances, apprehending disorder, might the king have used his authority to abrogate certain customs or usages (see Lingat 1973: 226). Hence, the idea of a state religion was not entertained.

I will say no more about the ancient period but only observe that some of these traditional ideas have reverberated in the practice of Hindu kings and their subjects all the way down the corridors of time into the twentieth century (see Mayer 1982). Even today, these ideas are relevant in the context of the only surviving Hindu monarchy of the world, Nepal, where the king is considered an incarnation of God and yet has to be consecrated by the Brahman royal priest.

In our own times it was, of course, Mahatma Gandhi who restated the traditional point of view in the changed context of the twentieth century, emphasizing the inseparability of religion and politics and the superiority of the former over the latter. 'For me', he said, 'every, the tiniest, activity is governed by what I consider to be my religion' (see Iyer 1986: 391). And, more specifically, there is the well-known early statement that 'those who say that religion has nothing to do with politics do not know what religion means' (Gandhi 1940: 383). For Gandhi, religion was the source of absolute value and hence constitutive of social life; politics was the arena of public interest; without the former the latter would become debased. While it was the obligation of the state to ensure that every religion was free to develop according to its own genius, no religion which depended upon state support deserved to survive. In other words, the inseparability of religion and politics in the Indian context, and generally, was for Gandhi fundamentally a distinct issue from the separation of the state from the church in Christendom. When he did advocate that 'religion and state should be separate', he clarified that this was to limit the role of the state to 'secular welfare' and to allow it no admittance into the religious life of the people (see Iyer 1986: 395). Clearly the hierarchical relationship is irreversible.

Let me now turn briefly to Islam. Traditionally Islam postulates a single chain of command in the political domain: God-Prophet-caliph-king. God Almighty is the ever-active sovereign of His universe, which is governed by His will. In his own life Muhammad symbolized the unity of faith (*dīn*) and the material world (*dawla*). His successors (*khalīfa*) were the guardians on whose authority the kings ruled. They (the kings) were but the shadow of God on earth, holding power as a trust and answerable to their Maker on the Day of Judgement like everybody else. In India, Ziya-ud-Din Barni, an outstanding medieval (mid-fourteenth century) theologian and political commentator, wrote of religion and temporal government, of prophets and kings, as twin brothers, but without leaving the reader in any doubt about whom he placed first (see de Bary 1970: 459–60).

In the twentieth century, Muhammad Iqbal occupies a very special place as an interpreter of Islam in South Asia. Rejecting the secularist programme of Turkish Nationalists, he wrote: 'In Islam the spiritual and the temporal are not two distinct domains, and the nature of an act, however secular in its import, is determined by the attitude of mind with which the agent does it.... In Islam it is the same reality, which appears as Church looked at from one point of view and State from another' (1980: 154). Iqbal further explains: 'The ultimate Reality, according to the Quran, is spiritual, and its life consists in its temporal activity. The spirit finds its opportunities in the natural, the material, the secular. All that is secular is therefore sacred in the roots of its being.... There is no such thing as a profane world.... All is holy ground' (ibid.: 155). In short, to use the idiom adopted by me, the secular is encompassed by the sacred.

An autonomous ideology of secularism is ruled out. This is how Fazlur Rahman (a most distinguished South Asian scholar writing on such subjects today) puts it: 'Secularism destroys the sanctity and universality (transcendence) of all moral values' (1982: 15). If secularism is to be eschewed, so is neo-revivalism to be avoided for its 'intellectual bankruptcy' (ibid.: 137). Rahman argues that a modern life need not be detached from religious faith and should indeed be informed by it, or else Muslims may well lose their very humanity.

This excursus into South Asia's major religious traditions was important for me to make the point that the search for secular elements in the cultural traditions of this region is a futile exercise, for it is not these but an ideology of secularism that is absent and is resisted. What is important, therefore, is the relationship between the categories, and this is unmistakably hierarchical, the religious encompassing the secular. Louis Dumont recently reminded us that the doctrine of the subordination of the power of the kings to the authority of the priests, enunciated by Pope Gelasius around the end of the fifth century, perhaps represents 'simply the logical formula for the relation between the two functions' (1983: 15). Indeed, the world's great religious traditions do seem to speak on this vital issue with one voice. Or they did until the Reformation made a major departure in this regard within the Christian tradition.

Scholars from Max Weber and Ernst Troeltsch to Peter Berger and Louis Dumont have in their different ways pointed to the essential linkages among Protestantism, individualism, and secularization. You all know well Max Weber's poignant statement that 'the fate of our times is characterized by rationalization and intellectualization and, above all, by the "disenchantment of the world." Precisely the ultimate and most sublime values have retreated from public life either into the transcendental realm of mystic life or into the brotherliness of direct and personal relations' (see Gerth and Mills 1948: 155). Or, to put it in Peter Berger's succinct summing up, 'Protestantism cut the umbilical cord between heaven and earth' (1973: 118).

This is not the occasion to go into the details of the well-grounded idea that secularization is a gift of Christianity to mankind, but it is important for my present concern to note that the privatization of religion, through the assumption by the individual of the responsibility for his or her own salvation without the intervention of the Church, is very much a late Christian idea. The general secularization of life in the West after the Reformation is significantly, though only partly, an unintended consequence of this religious idea. Luther was indeed a man of his times, a tragic medieval figure, who ushered in a modern age that he would hardly approve of.

But let us not stray too far. How does all this bear upon my present theme, namely the prospects of secularism in India? I put it to you for your consideration that the idea of secularism, a gift of Christianity, has been built into Western social theorists' paradigms of modernization, and since these paradigms are believed to have universal applicability, the elements, which converged historically—that is in a unique manner—to constitute modern life in Europe in the sixteenth and the following three centuries, have come to be presented as the requirements of modernization elsewhere, and this must be questioned. Paradoxically, the uniqueness of the history of modern Europe lies, we are asked to believe, in its generalizability.

To put what I have just said in other words, secularism as an ideology has emerged from the dialectic of modern science and Protestantism, not from a simple repudiation of religion and the rise of rationalism. Even the Enlightenment—its English and German versions in particular—was not against religion as such but against revealed religion or a transcendental justification for religion. Voltaire's 'dying' declaration was of faith in God and detestation of 'superstition'. Models of modernization, however, prescribe the transfer of secularism to non-Western societies without regard for the character of their religious traditions or for the gifts that these might have to offer. Such transfers are themselves phenomena of the modern secularized world: in traditional or tradition-haunted societies they can only mean conversion and the loss of one's culture, and, if you like, the loss of one's soul. Even in already modern or modernizing societies, unless cultural transfers are made meaningful for the people, they appear as stray behaviouristic traits and attitudinal postures. This means that what is called for is translation; mere transfer will not do.

But translations are not easily achieved. As Bankim Chandra Chatterji (that towering late nineteenth century Indian intellectual) put it, 'You can translate a word by a word, but behind the word is an idea, the thing which the word denotes, and this idea you cannot translate, if it does not exist among the people in whose language you are translating' (see Chatterjee 1986: 61). It is imperative, then, that a people must themselves render their historical experience meaningful: others may not do this for them. Borrowed ideas, unless internalized, do not have the power to bestow on us the gift and grace of living.

In this regard, I should like to point out that once a cultural definition of a phenomenon or of a relationship (say, between religion and politics, or society and the state) has crystallized, it follows that subsequent formulations of it, whether endogenous or exogenous, can only be *re*-definitions. Traditions posit memory. Given the fact of the unequal social distribution of knowledge and the unequal impress of social change, it is not at all surprising that some elements of tradition should survive better and longer among the ordinary people, who may not think about it but live it, and others among the intellectuals.

In short, the transferability of the idea of secularism to the countries of South Asia is beset with many difficulties and should not be taken for granted. Secularism must be put in its place: which is not a question of rejecting it but of finding the proper means for its expression. In multi-religious societies, such as those of South Asia, it should be realized that secularism may not be restricted to rationalism, that it is compatible with faith, and that rationalism (as understood in the West) is not the sole motive force of a modern state. What the institutional implications of such a position are is an important question and needs to be worked out.

* * *

I am afraid I have already spoken enough to invite the charge of being some kind of a cultural determinist, which I am not. I am aware of the part that creative individuals and dominant minorities play in changing and shaping the course of history. As a student of cultural anthropology, I know that even in the simplest of settings cultures, ways of life, are not merely reproduced but are also resisted and changed, more in some places and times and less in others, more successfully by some individuals or groups than by others. In this connection, I must now return to Jawaharlal Nehru as the typical modern Indian intellectual.

It has been argued well by many scholars that while Gandhi put his faith in the reformed, ethically refined individual, in creating a better if not ideal society, Nehru considered the shaping of suitable institutions as the best means to achieve the same goal. And of all the modern institutions it was the state which he believed would be the principal engine of social change. Hegel, you will remember, said that the Hindus were a people and did not constitute a state: this judgement (and similar others) have informed Western social science thinking about India, expressed recently, for instance, in the contrast between primordial bonds and civic ties made by Edward Shils and Clifford Geertz, and by others.

Nehru, like many other modern Indians, imbibed the same point of view and obviously wanted to remove the deficiency. The Nehruvian state was first and foremost democratic, but in an economically poor and culturally diverse country it could hardly be truly democratic without being socialist and secularist. I am not here concerned with the course of democracy and socialism in India, but I must make some observations about the difficulties encountered by the secular state established under the Constitution.

I will not enter into the controversy whether the Indian state is at all secular in the sense in which, say, the American state is, or that it is only jurisdictionalist (see Luthera 1964). We do not, of course, have a wall of separation in India, for there is no church to wall off, but only the notion of neutrality, or equidistance between the state and the religious identity of the people. What makes this idea important is that not only Nehru but all Indians who consider themselves patriotic and modern, nationalist and rationalist, subscribe to it. What makes it impotent is that it is a purely negative strategy. And as you know, in the history of mankind, nothing positive has ever been built on denials or negations alone.

An examination of Nehru's writings and speeches brings out very clearly his conviction that religion is a hindrance to 'the tendency to change and progress inherent in human society', and that 'the belief in a supernatural agency which ordains everything has led to a certain irresponsibility on the social plane, and emotion and sentimentality have taken the place of reasoned thought and inquiry' (Nehru 1961: 543). Religion, he confessed candidly, did not 'attract' him for 'behind it lay a method of approach to life's problems which was certainly not that of science' (ibid.: 26). But, then, he did not worry too much about religion or its political expression, namely communalism, because he passionately believed that these epiphenomena would 'vanish at the touch of reality' (1980: 469). Hence his insistence that, quoting from a 1931 speech, 'the real thing to my mind is the economic factor. If we lay stress on this and divert public attention to it we shall find automatically that religious differences recede into the background and a common bond unites different groups. The economic bond is stronger than the national one' (1972–82, 5: 203).

Nehru insisted that his conclusions were not speculative but based on practical experience. Many years later, after mature reflection, he wrote that once the national state came into being it would be economic problems that would acquire salience; there might be 'class conflicts' but not 'religious conflicts, except insofar as religion itself expressed some vested interest' (1961: 406). It is not, therefore, at all surprising that until the very end Nehru was puzzled and pained by Muslim separatism and was deeply distrustful of politicians who exploited religion for political purposes; and yet he was contemptuous of those who took the religious question seriously. Not for him Iqbal's insistence that the cultural question was as important as the economic (see Malik 1963: 253). The irony of it is that Iqbal too considered himself a socialist!

In the end, that is in 1947, Nehru knew that the battle at hand, though not perhaps the war, had been lost, that the peoples of the subcontinent were not yet advanced enough to share his view of secular politics and the secular state. A retreat was inescapable, but it was not a defeat. Sorrowfully he wrote in 1961, just three years before his death: 'We talk about a secular state in India. It is perhaps not very easy even to find a good word in Hindi for "secular". Some people think it means something opposed to religion. That obviously is not correct.... It is a state which honours all faiths equally and gives them equal opportunities' (see Gopal 1980: 330).

Having thus described Indian secularism, he proceeded in line with his own earlier thinking on the subject: 'Our constitution lays down that we are a secular state, but it must be admitted that this is not wholly reflected in our mass living and thinking. In a country like England, the state is...allied to one particular religion.... Nevertheless, the state and the people there function in a largely secular way. Society, therefore, in England is more advanced in this respect than in India, even though our constitution may be in this matter more advanced' (ibid.: 330–1). It is obvious that Nehru had not given up his trust of the secularization process, that his view of religion remained unchanged.

What is noteworthy, therefore, is Nehru's refusal (or failure) to use the coercive powers of the state in hastening this process. In this regard he invites comparison with Lenin and Ataturk, and, if you allow dictatorship, suffers by it. I do not have the time to discuss in any detail this instructively fascinating comparison or pose the question as to the conditions under which a part (state) may dictate to the whole (society), but let me say a few words about it, very briefly.

Take Lenin's position. Continuing the Feuerbach–Marx, line he asserted that the religious question must not be advanced to 'the first place where it does not belong at all' (see Dube and Basilov 1983: 173). To match this by action, he played an active and direct part in the formulation of the 1918 decree on 'the separation of the church from the state and of the school from the church'. While every citizen was in principle free to profess any religion, or none at all, he could not actively propagate it; what is more, the educational function of the Communist Party ensured that 'senseless ideas' arising from a false consciousness would be countered.

Similarly, Ataturk, proceeded by one deliberate step after another, beginning with the abolition of the Caliphate in 1924, of the religious orders in 1925, of sharia courts in 1926, and of Islam as the state religion in 1928. The process of secularization was continued thereafter, and the changes effected were enforced strictly, with Kemal himself often setting the example in even minor points of detail (see Lewis 1968: 239–93).

Contrast the internal coherence and sense of urgency of these two experiments with the uncertainties of the 1949 Indian Constitution, which sought to establish a secular state (Article 15) in a society which it allowed and even encouraged to be communally divided (Articles 25–30). Under the rubric of 'freedom of religion', it allowed citizens not only the profession and practice of their respective religions but also their propagation. Besides, it allowed the establishment of educational institutions along community lines. A direct reference to secularism had to wait until 1976, when it was introduced into the preamble of the Constitution by the 42nd Amendment.

It must be admitted here that the pluralistic situation which Nehru and the other framers of the Constitution faced was immensely more complex than anything that Lenin, and far less Ataturk, faced; yet the fact remains that Nehru did not use his undoubted hold over the people as a leader of the freedom movement and his vast authority as the head of government to bring communal tendencies under strict control. It is often said that he was too much of a liberal and a cultured aristocrat to think of strong-arm methods; I think he was also too optimistic about the decline of the hold of religion on the minds of people. He did not seem to take into consideration the fact that the ideology of secularism enhances the power of the state by making it a protector of all religious communities and an arbiter in their conflicts.

No wonder, then, that secularism as an alien cultural ideology, which lacks the strong support of the state, has failed to make the desired headway in India. What have done so are, apparently and by general agreement, Hindu revivalism and Muslim and Sikh fundamentalism. This brings me to the last of the observations I want to make, and I will also do this briefly.

* * *

Contrary to what may be presumed, it is not religious zealots alone who contribute to fundamentalism or fanaticism, which are a misunderstanding of religion, reducing it to mere political bickering, but also the secularists who deny the very legitimacy of religion in human life and society and provoke a reaction. This latter realization has been slow in coming to Indian intellectuals, but there are some signs of change in this regard. It is thus that old, familiar questions begin to be reformulated. The principal question of this address could be considered to be not whether Indian society will eventually become secularized as Nehru believed it would, but rather in what sense it should become so and by what means. The limitations of secular humanism (so-called) and the falsity of the hope of secularists—namely, that all will be well with us if only scientific temper becomes generalized—need to be recognized. Secularized man can confront fundamentalism and revivalism no more than he may empathize with religion.

Maybe religion is not a fake as Marx asserted; maybe there is something eternal about it as Durkheim maintained. Perhaps men of religion such as Mahatma Gandhi would be our best teachers on the proper relation between religion and politics—values and interests—underlining not only the possibilities of inter-religious understanding, which is not the same as an emaciated notion of mutual tolerance or respect, but also opening out avenues of a spiritually justified limitation of the role of religious institutions and symbols in certain areas of contemporary life. The creeping process of secularization, however, slowly erodes the ground on which such men might stand. As Ashis Nandy puts it, 'There is now a peculiar double-bind in Indian politics: the ills of religion have found political expression but the strengths of it have not been available for checking corruption and violence in public life' (1985: 17). My question is, Is everything lost irretrievably?

I must conclude; but I really have no conclusions to offer, no solutions to suggest. Let me hasten to say, however, that I am not advocating the establishment of a Hindu state in India—not at all. It simply will not work. Should you think that I have been sceptical about the claims that are made for secularism, scientific temper, etc., and that I have suggested a contextualized rethinking of these fuzzy ideas, you would be quite right. You would also be right in concluding that I have suggested that the only way secularism in South Asia, understood as inter-religious understanding, may succeed would be for us to take both religion and secularism seriously, and not reject the former as superstition and reduce the latter to a mask for communalism or mere expediency. Secularism would have to imply that those who profess no religion have a place in society equal to that of others, not higher or lower.

Should you think further that the scepticism to which I have given expression has been easy to come by, cultivate, and accept, you would not be, I am afraid, quite right. Secularism has been the fond hope of many people of my generation in South Asia. But, then, that is my personal problem, and therefore let me say no more about it. I will end simply by recalling the following words of the young Karl Marx, spoken, of course, in a very different context: 'Ideas which have conquered our minds...to which reason has welded our conscience, are chains from which we cannot break away without breaking our hearts; they are demons which man can vanquish only by submitting to them' (see Lowith 1982: 23).

REFERENCES

Berger, Peter L. 1973. *The Social Reality of Religion*. London: Allen Lane.
Bipan Chandra. 1984. *Communalism in Modern India*. New Delhi: Vikas.
Chatterjee, Partha. 1986. *Nationalist Thought and the Colonial World*. Delhi: Oxford University Press.

Coomaraswamy, Ananda. 1978. *Spiritual Authority and Temporal Power in the Indian Theory of Government*. New Delhi: Munshiram Manoharlal.

de Bary, Theodore (ed.). 1970. *The Sources of Indian Tradition*, Vol. 1. New York: Columbia University Press.

Dube, S.C. and V.N. Basilov (eds). 1983. *Secularisation in Multi-Religious Societies*. New Delhi: Concept.

Dumont, Louis. 1980. *Homo Hierarchicus: The Caste System and Its Implications*. Chicago: University of Chicago Press.

————. 1983. 'A Modified View of Our Origins: The Christian Beginnings of Modern Individualism.' *Contributions to Indian Sociology*, n.s. 17: 1–26.

Gandhi, M.K. 1940. *An Autobiography or the Story of My Experiments with Truth*. Ahmedabad: Navjivan.

Gerth, H.H. and C.W. Mills (trs. & eds). 1948. *From Max Weber: Essays in Sociology*. London: Routledge and Kegan Paul.

Gopal, S. (ed.). 1980. *Jawaharlal Nehru: An Anthology*. Delhi: Oxford University Press.

Iqbal, Muhammad. 1980. *The Reconstruction of Religious Thought in Islam*. Delhi: New Taj Office.

Iyer, Raghavan (ed.). 1986. *The Moral and Political Writings of Mahatma Gandhi*. Vol. 1: *Civilization, Politics, and Religion*. Oxford: Clarendon Press.

Jalal, Ayesha. 1985. *The Sole Spokesman: Jinnah, Muslim League, and the Demand for Pakistan*. Cambridge: Cambridge University Press.

Jinnah, M.A. 1947–8. *Speeches as Governor-General of Pakistan*. Karachi: Pakistan Publications.

Kothari, Rajni. 1970. *Politics in India*. New Delhi: Orient Longman.

Lewis, Bernard. 1968. *The Emergence of Modern Turkey*. London: Oxford University Press.

Lingat, Robert. 1973. *The Classical Law of India*. Berkeley and Los Angeles: University of California Press.

Lowith, Karl. 1982. *Max Weber and Karl Marx*. H. Fantel (trs.). London: Allen and Unwin.

Luthera, V.P. 1964. *The Concept of the Secular State and India*. Calcutta: Oxford University Press.

Malik, H. 1963. *Moslem Nationalism in India and Pakistan*. Washington, D.C.: Public Affairs Press.

Mayer, A.C. 1982. 'Perceptions of Princely Rule: Perspectives from a Biography'. *Contributions to Indian Sociology*, n.s. 15: 127–54.

Mushir-ul-Haq. 1972. *Islam in Secular India*. Simla: Indian Institute of Advanced Study.

Nandy, Ashis. 1985. 'An Anti-Secularist Manifesto'. *Seminar* 314: 14–24.

Nehru, Jawaharlal. 1961. *The Discovery of India*. Bombay: Asia.

Nehru, Jawaharlal. 1972–82. *Selected Works of Jawaharlal Nehru*. New Delhi: Orient Longman.

————. 1980. *An Autobiography*. Delhi: Oxford University Press.

Rahman, Fazlur. 1982. *Islam and Modernity*. Chicago: University of Chicago Press.

Shah, K.J. 1982. 'Of Artha and the *Arthaśāstra*'. *Contribution to Indian Sociology*, n.s. 15: 55–73.

Sharif ul Mujahid. 1981. *Quad-i-Azam Jinnah*. Karachi: Quad-i-Azam Academy.

Smith, Donald Eugene. 1963. *India as a Secular State*. Bombay: Oxford University Press.

Tambiah, S.J. 1976. *World Conqueror and World Renouncer*. Cambridge: Cambridge University Press.

4

Secularism in India
*Predicaments and Prospects**

India will be a land of many faiths, equally honoured and respected,
but of one national outlook.

Jawaharlal Nehru, 24 January 1948

'When I use a word', Humpty Dumpty said, in rather a scornful
tone, 'it means just what I choose it to mean—neither more nor
less.'

'The question is', said Alice, 'whether you can make words
means so many different things.'

'The question is', said Humpty Dumpty, 'which is to be
master—that's all.'

Lewis Carroll, Through the Looking Glass

INTRODUCTION

In the present essay, I will explore the nature of Indian secularism
and discuss the difficulties into which it has run. This is a large
undertaking and could well be the theme of a book rather than
of a chapter in one. The most that I can hope to do here is to pose
some critical questions and make suggestions for rethinking the
answers.

Three basic assumptions are implicit in the apprehensions
about Indian secularism having run into difficulties. There is,

* Originally delivered as the Fourth (1991) Caparo Annual Lecture at the
University of Hull (UK) and published in *Modern Asian Studies* 27, 3 (1993)
667–97. The present revised version is reproduced here from my book
Modern Myths, Locked Minds: Secularism and Fundamentalism in India (1997),
chapter 8.

first, the assumption that secularism as an anti-religious or, at any rate, non-religious ideology has universal applicability, but that it has culturally specific expressions. This is how many intellectuals consider it permissible to speak of *Indian* secularism. In other words, secularism is not Indian ideology, but there is an Indian ideology of secularism. The *general* ideology of secularism, it is asserted, has been historically validated by the experience and achievements of the so-called modern societies of the West in the last four hundred years, and it should have succeeded in India too. Secondly, it is assumed that secularism will be welcomed by all right-thinking persons, for it shows the way to the making of rational plans for social reconstruction and state action, placing ultimate faith in the adequacy of human agency. Finally, there is the assumption that, with appropriate corrective measures, ideological secularism can still be made to succeed in India, notwithstanding all the faltering of the last five decades.

All three assumptions, I think, should be subjected to critical scrutiny, without conflating on-going processes of secularization with the ideology of secularism. The virtues claimed for ideological secularism are not unquestionable, nor does it provide answers to all questions about life and living. It has not been a complete success anywhere, and we do not know of any wholly secularized societies. Our times are witness to both secularization and fundamentalism. There are obvious limits to what the theoretical and experimental sciences can enable human beings to know; and there are even more obvious limits to what technology and the bureaucratic organization of work can enable us to do. These limits are the limits of the historic process of 'rationalization', valorized in the ideology of secularism, even in the West, which is said to bring to the non-Western countries intimations of their future as modernizing societies.

I have discussed elsewhere (Madan 1997) the emergence of the ideology of secularism in the West in the seventeenth century. Some later developments, including most significantly the rise of religious fundamentalism, were also noted. I drew pointed attention to the Christian setting and, indeed, described secularism as an outcome of the dialectic of the Enlightenment and Protestantism. Finally, I mentioned the distinctiveness of the religious traditions of India including Islam. Three major traditions—Sikhism, Islam, and Hinduism—were discussed at considerable length. I devoted a chapter to Hindu revivalism, with a critical summary of Gandhi's conception of Hinduism and his ideal of inter-religious harmony. Here I take up his views on secularism as a backdrop for a discussion of Jawaharlal Nehru's ideology of secularism, which is the main theme of this essay.

A GANDHIAN PERSPECTIVE

Secularism in India is a multivocal word: what it means depends upon who uses the word and in what context. There is, therefore, no single or straight answer to the question as to why secularism in India has run into difficulties. Let me then attempt to present two possible answers which are based on my understanding of Mahatma Gandhi's and Jawaharlal Nehru's views on the relationship of religion, politics, and the state. Needless to emphasize, I do not pretend that my answers are what Gandhi and Nehru themselves would have said had they been alive today.

Obviously, we must begin with Mahatma Gandhi because he is often referred to as the spiritual father of Indian secularism. He has even been inaccurately and unjustly called a secularist. If the essence of all varieties of secularism is the demarcation of boundaries between the sacred and secular domains per se, then Gandhi would have had no use for any such ideology. Its success would have been a moral disaster. His vision, as has been noted so often, was holistic, with religion as its constitutive principle— as the source of value for judging the worth of all worldly goals and actions. Religion here means, above all, altruism (*sevādharma*), self-assurance arising from inner conviction (*ātma tushti*), and the putting of one's faith in the saving grace of God (*Rāma nāma*).

'For me', Gandhi observed, 'every, the tiniest, activity is governed by what I consider my religion' (Iyer 1986: 391). Like religious pietists generally, he believed that God permeates every fibre, nook and corner of human experience. This for him was a timeless principle and yet he was very sensitive to the conditions and demands of particular times and places, in conformity with the *kala-desha* (time-place) sensitivity of Indian classical tradition. 'Every age', Gandhi wrote, 'is known to have its predominant mode of spiritual effort best suited for the attainment of *moksha*.... In this age, only political *sannyasīs* can fulfil and adorn the ideal of *sannyāsa*.' Consequently, 'No Indian who aspires to follow the

way of true religion can afford to remain aloof from politics'
(Parekh 1989a: 100). Gandhian politics, in short, were inseparable
from religion. He wrote in 1940:

> I cannot conceive politics as divorced from religion. Indeed religion
> should pervade every one of our actions. Here, religion does not mean
> sectarianism. It means a belief in ordered moral government of the
> universe. It is not less, because it is unseen. This religion transcends
> Hinduism, Islam, Christianity, etc. It does not supersede them. It
> harmonises them and gives them reality (Mohan Rao 1968: 34–5).

Now, Bhikhu Parekh asserts in an insightful and thought-provoking
discussion of Gandhi's political philosophy that, 'there was hardly
a Hindu religious category and practice to which [Gandhi] did
not give a worldly and secular content'. In other words, 'Gandhi
secularized Hinduism as much as it was possible to do *within* a
spiritual framework' (ibid.: 109). The emphasis upon the word
'within' is Parekh's and it is of crucial importance. It signifies that
the relationship of the sacred and the secular—of dharma and
artha, or religion and politics—is 'hierarchical' (in the Dumontian
sense): the latter category is opposed to the former but also
encompassed by it. Did Gandhi, then, secularize religion or did
he sacralize politics? Both positions have strong adherents. I
would rather side with Margaret Chatterji's judgement that
'Gandhi seems almost a secularist', but judged by his handling of
concrete issues, notably the communal (Hindu–Muslim) problem,
he 'was not secularist, if by this we mean an attempt to prune
away all religious considerations from political matters' (1983:
85).

Gandhi was very careful with his use of words and so must
we be in attempting to construct an answer to our question on the
basis of first principles such as the above. Politics were sacralized
by Gandhi, they became the dharma of the age (*yugadharma*) and,
consequently—*not* contradictorily—the state was devalorized, for
its constitutive principle is power or coercion. In his conception
of the moral or perfect society, Gandhi emphasized that its
enduring basis can only be the moral calibre of the individuals
who constitute it. He extended the principle to the relationship
of the citizen to the state. As Parekh puts it, 'For Gandhi it was
the citizen's sense of moral responsibility for his actions that
ultimately determined the character of the state' (1989a: 124). In

itself, the state, in Gandhian reckoning, is amoral, impersonal, distant, coercive, and even violent. Although Gandhi's views on the modern state became less negative over time, he never warmed up to this institution. In Parekh's summing up, 'It took him a long time to appreciate its moral, regenerative and redistributive role and even then his acceptance of it remained half-hearted and unintegrated into his general perspective' (ibid.: 204). Gandhi did not set much store by Western liberal democracy either, considering it to be rooted in individual selfishness and a materialist conception of the good life (Parekh 1989b: 74).

A Gandhian, it seems to me, would have to say that secularism has run into difficulties in India because the modern state is too much with us, and intrudes into areas of life where it has no business even to peep. That state is best which governs the least. The ideal to strive for is that of morally sensitive individuals actively promoting civil society. Talking with a Christian missionary in September 1946, Gandhi said: 'If I were a dictator, religion and state would be separate. I swear by my religion, I will die for it. But it is my personal affair. The state has nothing to do with it. The state would look after your secular welfare, health, communications, foreign relations, currency and so on, but not your or my religion. That is everybody's personal concern!' (Iyer 1986: 395). A year later, soon after independence and a few months before his death, he said: 'The state should undoubtedly be secular. Everyone in it should be entitled to profess his religion without let or hindrance, so long as the citizen obeys the common law of the land' (Bose 1948: 256). But he was totally against the idea of a state religion or state support for any religion. 'A society or group', he said, 'which depends partly or wholly on state aid for the existence of its religion, does not deserve or, better still, does not have any religion worth the name' (ibid.: 287).

To the extent to which Indian secularism, even though it stands for equal respect for all religious faiths (*sarva dharma samabhāva*), is a state ideology, enshrined in the Constitution in which it is linked to the materialist ideology of socialism, and to the extent to which it has nothing to say about the individual except in terms of his or her rights, it is from the Gandhian perspective a hedonistic ideology, and bound to fail. In Judith Brown's excellent summing up, 'In Gandhi's eyes men and women were human in virtue of their capacity for religious vision.... [If] this was stifled by the individual or by political and economic structures then people were degraded and dehumanized. This was so strong and striking an attack on secular materialism as could be made' (1992: 392).

A Gandhian critique of secularism in terms of ultimate values and individual responsibility is in some respects similar to Max Weber's concern with the problem of value. What Gandhi and Weber are saying is that a secularized world is inherently unstable because it elevates to the realm of ultimate values the only values it knows and these are instrumental values. 'Natural science', Weber said, 'gives us an answer to the question of what we must do if we wish to master life technically. It leaves quite aside, or assumes for its purposes, whether we should and do wish to master life technically and whether it ultimately makes sense to do so' (1948: 144).

NEHRU ON RELIGION, POLITICS, AND SECULARISM

Gandhian remedies are believed by modernist Indians to be far-fetched and impractical, if not obscurantist. The fact that he was not a systematic thinker, attaching greater importance to action (*ācāra*) and experience (*anubhava*) than to formal thought (*vicāra*), does not make the task of examining the contemporary relevance of Gandhi's views any easier.[1] In any case, there was hardly anyone among the leaders of independent India who could be said to want to build on the basis of Gandhi's political and economic philosophy. In relation to the character of the new state, Sardar Patel (the powerful Deputy Prime Minister) and Rajendra Prasad (the first President) were no closer to Gandhi than was Nehru (the first Prime Minister, 1947–64), which does not mean that their notions of a strong state were identical. It is perhaps ironic that Gandhi's public designation of Nehru as his political heir added strength to and bestowed legitimacy on Nehru's own independent position as a national leader. Let us then turn to Jawaharlal Nehru for a diagnosis of the malady that has afflicted Indian secularism. Before we proceed let us look again at the words 'religion' and 'secularism' in the context of Nehru's views, abiding by the good advice that we must pay a word extra when we make it do a lot of work!

By intellectual preference, Nehru's concept of secularism was the same that I wrote about earlier (see Chapter 3 above) in the context of the Enlightenment. He was against institutional religion, ritual, and mysticism and did not consider himself a religious person. He was not, however, uninterested in spiritual matters. Any impressions of his boyhood experiences of Brahmanical belief and ritual were erased by the powerful impact of his father's personality and, later, by his reading of the works of Karl Marx, Bertrand Russell, and other similar thinkers.[2] Nehru's study of world history and his encounters with the Indian masses in the 1920s and 1930s made him feel very negative about the role of religion in human affairs and he looked forward to a secularized society. He was an agnostic who subscribed to a rationalist, and even a historicist, world view.

Gandhi's religiosity, to put it mildly, puzzled and annoyed Nehru. It caused him to write (in his autobiography) one of his clearest and most mature statements on the subject of religion. Referring to the anguish that the news of Gandhi's fast (in September 1932) on the subject of separate electorates (in Nehru's judgement 'a side political issue') had caused him while he was in prison, Nehru wrote: 'I felt angry with him at his religious and sentimental approach to a political question, and his frequent references to God in connection with it.' He further observed (1980: 374):

India is supposed to be a religious country above everything else.... [And yet] I have frequently condemned [religion] and wished to make a clean sweep of it. Almost always it seemed to stand for blind belief and reaction, dogma and bigotry, superstition and exploitation, and the preservation of vested interests. And yet I knew well that there was something else in it, something which supplied a deeper inner craving of human beings.

Indian religiosity had been on Nehru's mind for quite some time, though he refused to be unduly worried about it. It was more a nuisance than a real problem. In 1928 he had declared: 'If religion, or rather what is called religion, in India continues to interfere with everything, then it will not be a mere question of divorcing it from politics, but of divorcing it from life itself' (Nehru 1972: 233). The Gandhian imperative of religion as the guide to all, even 'the tiniest', activities was not what Nehru believed in. As for the Gandhian notion of divine grace, Nehru considered the idea of 'a personal god' 'very odd' (1961: 28). Like all modern intellectuals he had implicit confidence in the processes of secularization.

Proclaiming this confidence in his presidential address to the Lahore (1929) session of the Congress, he said:

> I have no love for bigotry and dogmatism in religion, and I am glad that they are weakening. Nor do I love communalism in any shape or form.... I know that the time is coming soon when these labels and appellations will have little meaning and when our struggle will be on the economic basis (1973a: 188).

Two years later—in fact again and again during the next two decades—he reaffirmed the primacy of the economic factor: 'the real thing to my mind is the economic factor. If we lay stress on this and divert public attention to it we shall find automatically that religious differences recede into the background and a common bond unites different groups. *The economic bond is stronger than even the national one*' (1973b: 203, emphasis added). These concluding words underlined Nehru's secular position and his socialist convictions.

Given this position, it is no wonder that Nehru was dismissive about the Hindu–Muslim problem: 'the question does not exist at all for us', he declared (ibid.: 282). When he did acknowledge the seriousness of communalism, he looked upon it as an expression of class interests. In 1928 he said: 'It may be a giant today, but it has feet of clay.... It is really the creation of our educated classes in search of office and employment' (Akbar 1988: 217). Later, and more thoughtfully, he said in his presidential address at the Lucknow (1936) Congress: 'First of all the Congress always put independence first and other questions, including the communal one, second, and refused to allow any other of those questions to take the pride of place'. He added: 'I am afraid I cannot get excited over the communal issue, important as it is temporarily. It is after all a side issue, and it can have no real importance in the larger scheme of things' (1975: 190).

The same train of thought was given considered expression in *The Discovery of India* (written in prison during 1944). Nehru wrote (1961: 543):

> The belief in a super-natural agency which ordains everything has led to a certain irresponsibility on the social plane, and emotion and sentimentality have taken the place of reasoned thought and inquiry. Religion, though it has undoubtedly brought comfort to innumerable human beings and stabilized society by its values, has checked the tendency to change and progress inherent in human society.

He confessed candidly in the same work, that religion did not 'attract' him for 'behind it lay a method of approach to life's problems which was certainly not that of science' (ibid.: 26). Just three years before he became the Prime Minister of India, Nehru looked forward to the future and exhorted Indians that they face life 'with the temper and approach of science allied to philosophy and with reverence for all that lies beyond' (ibid. 547).

Out of prison in 1945, Nehru faced a rapidly changing political situation and, much to his chagrin, the 'side issue' moved fast to occupy the centre of the stage. He was disbelieving and appalled. 'To think in terms of Pakistan when the modern trend is towards the establishment of a world federation is like thinking in terms of bows and arrows as weapons of war in the age of the atomic bomb' (1981: 187). The viceroy, Lord Wavell, recorded in his journal on 14th July 1945, 'the theme of [Nehru's] discourse was that...[Pakistan was] a narrow medieval conception; and that the eventual cleavage when India's freedom was secured would be between classes rather than communities, between poor and rich, between peasant and landlord, between labourer and employer' (Wavell 1977: 155–6). India's freedom was secured two years later, but the country was partitioned on the basis of religion.

I have quoted fairly extensively from Nehru's writings, statements, and speeches to highlight the consistency of his thinking over two decades and more. It is obvious that the decisive element in this thinking was, at the broadest level, an Enlightenment view of religion, which was against revelation and dogmatism rather than religion as such, if it did not offend against reason, and, more specifically, the Marxian position on religion, though considerably diluted. It is thus that we find Nehru attacks the bigotry and dogmatism of religion, but acknowledges that religion stands for higher things of life too. He wrote of the comfort that religion had brought to innumerable people and did not dismiss the phenomenon as 'the opium of the people' as Marx had done.

But the idea of economic issues having precedence over even the question of independence from colonial rule is in accordance with the Marxian position. As is well known, in their discussion of the role of ideologies, Marx and Engels observed in *The German Ideology* that any attempt to understand an epoch of history in terms of political and religious issues is to 'share the illusion of the epoch' (Marx and Engels 1959: 259). Similarly, Engels in his graveside summary of Marx's thought had said that Marx had 'discovered the simple fact, hitherto concealed by an overgrowth of ideology, that mankind must first of all eat and drink, have shelter and clothing, before it can pursue politics, science, religion, art, etc.' (Acton 1955: 143). Actually, Marx believed that religion had already been dissolved by the circumstances prevailing in Europe in his own time (Marx and Engels 1959: 260). And Lenin had affirmed that even while the socialists must fight against religion, doing so did 'not mean that the religious question must be pushed into the foreground where it does not belong' (n.d.: 16). Nehru acknowledged his indebtedness to the teachings of Marx and Lenin in his autobiography, *The Discovery of India* and elsewhere; but he was too much of a liberal to be called a copybook Marxist.

In short, Nehru's position on religion, religious conflict, and the significance of the processes of secularization was what would be called rationalist and modern, whether one sees it derived from Marxian or Lockean roots. It was also idealist in the sense that it reflected more the ideals of the European Enlightenment than the hard facts of society, culture, and politics in India. The latter generated compulsions at variance with these ideals. It is remarkable that it was Nehru who in the same year, 1931, in which he gave the hopeful message of the recession of religious differences (quoted above) persuaded the All-India Congress Committee (at its Karachi session) to insert in the resolution on fundamental rights 'Freedom of conscience and of the profession and practice of any religion' (see Nehru 1973a: 512). Further, all citizens of free India would be equal before the law, irrespective of religious (and other similar) differences, and the state would observe neutrality with regard to all religions (*dharma nirpekshatā*). 'This', Nehru's biographer S. Gopal tells us, 'was the first breakdown, in concrete terms, of the concept of secularism in the Indian context and formed the basis of the [relevant] articles in the constitution many years later' (1987: 12).

The Constitution did not, however, contain the word 'secularism' anywhere, and 'secular' only once, but that too to denote an aspect of religious practice.[3] The addition of the words 'secular' and 'socialist' to the description of India as a 'sovereign republic' in the Preamble of the Constitution came through the 42nd

Amendment in 1976 (during Indira Gandhi's Emergency rule).[4] It is important to note that the Hindi version of the Constitution uses *panth nirpeksha*, 'neutral in relation to religious denominations' (that is, non-sectarian) as the equivalent for 'secular'. Was specific reference to secularism considered unnecessary earlier, when the Constitution was being framed (1946–9)? Or was it too controversial? Perhaps both; which exactly would depend upon whose views one has in mind.[5] The transcript of the debate in the Constituent Assembly reveals that there was considerable difference of opinion on the right of propagation of one's religion, in addition to its profession and practice, but it was ultimately approved. The following statement by the well-known Congressman, H.V. Kamath, perhaps represented the general feeling of the members of the house (Constituent Assembly of India Debates, 6 December 1948: 825):

> The State represents all the people who live in its territories, and, therefore it cannot afford to identify itself with any particular section of the population.... We have certainly declared that India should be a secular State. But...a secular state is neither a Godless State nor an irreligious, nor an anti-religious, state.

Already, one can see, the notion of the secular state, and of secularism, as known in the West, were being enveloped here in ambiguity, meaning what one wished the terms to mean.

More about the Constitution below. Let me first recall how Nehru, having seen his confidence in the primacy of the economic over the religious factor proven premature, if not wholly misplaced, looked to the future after partition and independence. Not long after these cataclysmic events he posed the key question (in 1949): 'Do we believe in a national state which includes people of all religions and shades of opinion and is essentially a secular state, or do we believe in the religious, theocratic conception of the state?' His answer was unequivocal: 'we shall proceed on secular and national lines' (Nehru 1987: 26). This then became the guiding principle that animated the Constitution (then on the anvil) and became the basis of state policy in all relevant areas of action. The great Indian experiment of nation building, or national integration, had thus entered its most crucial phase.

It, however, suffered from a critical infirmity. Given Nehru's lifelong aversion to religion as practised by common people—the so-called popular religion—he could not have suddenly begun to see virtues in it. Moreover, within the Western liberal tradition, the modern state had emerged as secular in the specific sense that the maintenance of the 'true faith', or any faith, was none of its concerns (see Skinner 1978: 352) Nehru's definition of the secular state in terms of religious pluralism (quoted above) was, it seems obvious to me, a compromise, a strategy to deal with an awkward problem, namely the all-pervasive influence of religion in society, that would not go away. Nehru had made such compromises more than once in his political career: on one historic occasion (the 1936 presidential address to the Congress) he had called them 'temporary expedients of a transition rather than as solutions of our vital problems' (1975: 182). Like his attitude to khādī (hand-spun and hand-woven cloth) defined thus on that occasion, his attitude to religious pluralism was, it seems to me, an arrangement *ad interim*, a strategy rather than a surrender.

It was not an ideological commitment to religion or spirituality comparable to, for instance, Sarvepalli Radhakrishnan's, who thought that it would be 'strange that our government should be a secular one while our culture is rooted in spiritual values'. 'Secularism', Radhakrishnan believed, had to be given a new, *appropriate*, definition 'here' (in India), namely 'stress on the universality of spiritual values which may be attained in a variety of ways' (1956: vii–viii). Constitutionally, this translates as the principle of (to use a term from the legal discourse in the USA) 'non-preferentialism' between different religions rather than 'neutrality' between spirituality and materialism or religion and agnosticism. And Nehru was a self-proclaimed agnostic.

The paradox of Indian secularism lies not only in that religious pluralism is meaningless in the absence of a positive attitude to religion, but equally significantly in that the idiom of its articulation is trapped in a double-bind. Nehru wrote that ideas like 'socialism' and (I should think) 'secularism' must be communicated to the people in 'the language of the mind and the heart...the language which grows from a complex of associations of past history and culture and present environment' (1975: 182). Needless to add, this would not easily have been the language of India's westernized educated elite, whom Gandhi had called 'hard hearted'.

Eleven years after independence, and eight years after the adoption of the Constitution, Nehru was visited by André Malraux in Delhi and asked what his greatest problem had been during his years of power. Nehru replied, 'Creating a just state by just means', and, after a pause, 'Perhaps, too, creating a secular state in a religious society' (Malraux 1968: 145). I detect a sense of dismay in Nehru's observations on the subject in his later years. Sorrowfully, he wrote in 1961, just three years before his death (Gopal 1980: 330–1):

> We talk about a secular state in India. It is perhaps not very easy even to find a good word in Hindi for 'secular'. Some people think it means something opposed to religion. That obviously is not correct.... It is a state which honours all faiths equally and gives them equal opportunities.

Having written this, he proceeded more in line with his earlier thinking on the subject:

> Our Constitution lays down that we are a secular state, but it must be admitted that this is not wholly reflected in our mass living and thinking. In a country like England, the state is...allied to one particular religion.... Nevertheless, the state and the people there function in a largely secular way. *Society, therefore, in England is more advanced in this respect than in India*, even though our Constitution may be in this matter more advanced (ibid., emphasis added).

It is clear from this that Nehru had not given up this trust of the processes of secularization and of the secularization thesis. The chasm between him, on the one hand, and Gandhi and Radhakrishnan, on the other, was deep. For Gandhi religious pluralism entailed inter-religious understanding and mutual respect: it was the strength of Indian society while communal politics tied to statism would be its bane. For Nehru, however, religiosity and the attendant conflicts were the badge of social backwardness. Secularism in the sense of neutrality as state policy was a strategy to cope with a difficult situation. And the state was potentially a very important instrument of public welfare and social advancement, very much on the lines J.S. Mill and other liberals had advocated.[6] I am puzzled by those intellectuals who speak of a hyphenated Gandhi–Nehru view of secularism or, for that matter, of development. It is high time we accepted the authoritative verdict of B.R. Nanda, biographer of both Gandhi and Nehru: 'The working partnership of Nehru and Gandhi lasted till the end, but their philosophies of life never really converged' (1974: 103).

A Nehruvian answer to the question why secularism has run into difficulties in India would, then, be that the people are not yet ready for it. It requires a level of general education that is yet beyond them, and a liberal outlook on life and scientific temper which unfortunately they lack. I will not discuss here the larger and more complex issue of the lack of a sense of Indian history. Not only did Nehru consider such a sense vital to the cultivation of the spirit of nationalism, he also stressed the importance of comparison: this is obvious from his historical reflections. His reading of Indian history (Nehru 1946) has come under attack recently for allegedly being tainted by a soft Hindutva ideology (see, for example, Abdullah 1993: 74). This is absurd, for Ashoka and Akbar receive the highest honour from him, and neither was a Hindu. Religious intolerance has, meanwhile, intensified in recent years and fundamentalisms of various names and hues stalk the land today. The question that strikes one is that, if Nehru understood what India's problem in this regard was, why did he not strive harder than he did to remove the obstacles that stood in the way of a modern, secular, society? One can never be sure, but I could venture a reasonable guess.

In the early years after independence Nehru remained firmly wedded to the belief that state-sponsored economic growth was the key to social development. Hence, in his eyes, dams and factories were India's new temples.[7] In believing so in the 1950s he was in excellent company. Confessional statements by economists on the 'sins' of a narrow concept of the contents of the growth basket and of the quantitative approach to development were not to come before another decade would pass. By the time this approach to development ran into a crisis Nehru was a sick man and he died soon afterwards in 1964. He had bet on what had then seemed a sure winner, but after a good early run, it turned out to be a lame horse. The most serious failure of the 1950s from the point of view of the present discussion was the shocking neglect of investment in health and of radical educational reform. Gunnar Myrdal (1968) was one of the early critics of the Nehruvian experiment to draw pointed attention to this failure. More broadly, and more fundamentally, there was a dangerous dependence on the state. As Edward Said subtly puts it, 'Nehru's accomplishment was to take the Indian nation as liberated from modernity by Gandhi and deposit it entirely within the concept of the state' (1993: 262).[8]

SECULARISM AND THE CONSTITUTION

As an aspect of his basic approach Nehru also put his faith in the Constitution and the legislative process, and this turned out to be a case of excess rather than neglect. I have already referred to some of the features of the Constitution bearing upon the contemporary crisis of secularism. There are other problems too to which I now turn briefly. I am not a jurist any more than I am an economist, but I find certain unresolved tensions in the Constitution. An examination of Articles 13 to 17, 19, 23, 25 to 30 (all from Part III dealing with 'Fundamental Rights'), and of Articles 44, 48, and 51 (from Part IV on 'Directive Principles') brings these out clearly. Thus, Articles 25 to 30, which are the most crucial in this regard, guarantee 'freedom of conscience and free profession, practice and propagation of religion' (25), 'freedom to manage religious affairs' (26), 'freedom as to payment of taxes for promotion of any particular religion' (27), and 'freedom as to attendance at religious instruction or religious worship in certain educational institutions' (2). They protect the 'interests of minorities' (29), including their 'right . . . to establish and administer educational institutions' (30). Article 44 directs that 'the State shall endeavour to secure for the citizens a uniform civil code throughout the territory of India'. The way things have proceeded reveals the contradiction between Articles 25 to 30 and Article 44. The jurists may well argue that Directive Principles do not have the same force as Fundamental Rights and, therefore, the question of contradiction does not arise. It would be undeniable, however, that the former have contributed enormously to the strengthening of inward-looking, communal feelings and attitudes, and obstructed the spread of modern, secular education and attitudes among the cultural minorities.

It is not at all surprising that the state has so far failed to implement the constitutional directive of evolving a uniform civil code. The resistance has come principally from Muslims, some of whose leaders claim that their social life cannot be governed by any laws other than the sharia. It may be recalled that the Constituent Assembly had, by a resolution in 1948, rejected the contention that Muslim personal law was inseparable from Islam and, therefore, protected against legislative interference. The British had greater success in this regard as the Criminal Procedure Code that they enacted—it is still largely in force in India, but has been modified in Pakistan—overrode traditional laws and conventions.

The framers of the Constitution, it seems to me, overlooked the possibility that in a democratic polity the state may reflect the character of the society, and that a communally divided society and a secular state could be mutually contradictory. On the one hand, there is the danger of majoritarianism and, on the other, that of vesting the religious minorities with a kind of veto power. In other words, there is a tension here that must be resolved deliberately; it will not go away by itself. One is reminded of Karl Marx's perceptive observation, in his tract on 'The Jewish Question', that 'the emancipation of the state from religion is not the emancipation of the real man from religion' (1975: 146–74); needless to add, the real man he spoke of is the socially situated person.

There are other contradictions in the Constitution that bear upon the present discussion. I mentioned Articles 17 and 48. The former was a triumph for what Gandhi would have called moral reason: it abolished the practice of untouchability 'in any form'. This was intended to promote the cause of the so-called low caste Hindus, who had been exploited and humiliated by upper caste Hindus for as long as any one could remember, actually for centuries. But Article 48 represented a concession to high caste sentiment, 'prohibiting the slaughter of cows and calves and other milch and draught cattle', though the reason given is a secular one, namely the organization of 'agriculture and animal husbandry on modern scientific lines'. The record of the debate on this issue in the Constituent Assembly reveals that Nehru had to threaten resignation in order to have this ban given a secular character. The Hindu lobby, which had the informal patronage of the President, Rajendra Prasad, had wanted a general ban, and Nehru none of it. As early as 1923, when he was the mayor of Allahabad, he had persuaded the Municipal Board to reject a proposal to prohibit cow slaughter (see Gopal 1987: 24). It may be argued that the ban on cow slaughter is no more Brahmanical than Article 47, which includes a directive about prohibition on the consumption of intoxicants, is Islamic. This would be legal quibbling, for we know the strong sentiment against cow slaughter, generated among Hindus generally during the last one hundred years, to be a politically explosive issue.

It is noteworthy that, in the furtherance of the objectives of a secularized society and the establishment of a secular state, Nehru showed a much greater willingness to oppose what he considered reactionary elements among the Hindus than among the other communities. This was best illustrated by his stand on the Hindu Code Bill. The Hindu Marriage Act, 1955, the Hindu Succession Act, 1956, and the Hindu Adoption and Maintenance Act, 1956, were enacted by the Parliament, despite opposition by conservative Hindu leaders, including President Prasad, mainly because of Nehru's insistence. I agree with Bhikhu Parekh's insightful observation that:

> Nehru's state acted as, and claimed all the rights of a *Hindu* state in its relation to the Hindus...because he and his colleagues were and thought of themselves as Hindus...they [thus] both dared take liberties with the Hindus and *dared not* take them with respect to the Muslims and even Sikhs (1991: 42).

THE MAJORITY–MINORITY CONUNDRUM

Nehru's firm stand apparently contrasts with the vacillating attitude of the Rajiv Gandhi government, which rushed through Parliament the Muslim Women (Protection of Rights) Act in 1986, to nullify the Supreme Court's verdict in the Shah Bano case upholding the legal liability of a Muslim male to provide maintenance support for the wife he divorces. The new law was a concession to the conservative Muslim lobby according to which Muslim society is subject to sharia everywhere and for all time (see Baxi 1992: 95 and Sathe 1991: 39–59). But there is a sense in which Rajiv Gandhi was simply continuing with the Congress legacy of providing special treatment and protection to religious minorities in accordance with their own wishes. This had been endorsed by both Gandhi and Nehru before independence, and represented 'the benign elder brother' attitude. In any case, the

1986 happenings could hardly be cited as the best way of using the legislative process as an instrument of secularization. This is particularly regrettable in view of the directives incorporated in Article 44 ('to secure for citizens a uniform civil code') and in Article 51 (by Amendment in 1976) 'to promote scientific temper' (51-A[a]). One could, however, well argue that these additions to Article 51 are so vague and trite that those responsible for their inclusion in the Constitution could hardly have been serious about them.

Why did Nehru treat Hindus and Muslims differently? And why have successive governments at the Centre since Nehru's death in 1964 often done so? Should not non-discrimination between different religious communities be one of the first principles of the policies of a secular state? The answer, it seems to me, lies largely in the fact that, as observed earlier, non-discrimination may not be sufficient to meet the requirements of the situation. The anxieties and sensitivities of the minorities must be recognized. But where does the state draw the line? There is no easy answer to this question. Consequently, the majority–minority conundrum has become an almost insoluble problem. In a democratic polity being in a majority betokens public approval and signifies legitimate electoral success for the group concerned. Such majorities represent interest groups and ideological positions. In Thomas Jefferson's celebrated phrase, 'the will of the majority' is 'the Natural law of every society' and 'the only sure guardian of the rights of man' (Cunningham Jr 1991: 133). The legitimacy of majority rule disappears, it must be stressed, if it takes away or abridges the rights of the minorities or, for that matter, of the individual. It becomes tyranny. Nobody should be in a majority or out of it, because of ascribed, or near-ascribed, attributes of race, gender, language or religion. Majorities so defined are rightly judged to be unfair winners in political games.

A questionable assumption, however, underlies the existence of majorities of this kind, namely that they are internally undifferentiated in terms of social customs, economic interests, and political loyalties, and are, therefore, able to appear and even act as monoliths, as it were. No religious community of India—the Hindus least of all—is, however, internally undifferentiated. So much so, indeed that, as a sociologist, I find little warrant for using the word 'community' in referring to the Hindus. But politically motivated Hindus have learnt the immense usefulness of the term and non-Hindus never let go of it, whether in reference to themselves or the threatening Hindus. The majority–minority differentiation in religious terms has thus become an integral part of Indian political rhetoric: it is the language of communalism rather than liberalism.

We need to go back a little in time to appreciate how things have come to such a pass. It is perhaps ironic that primordially defined majorities and minorities entered the Indian political idiom in the context of granting representation to people in local self-governance. The conceptualization of the people of India as quantitatively defined tribes, castes, and religious communities was made possible by yet another instrument of modern governance, namely the periodic census, begun in 1872 and made into a decennial exercise from 1881 onward. The best known critics of the introduction of Western liberal notions of elective representation in the 1880s, when the viceroy, Lord Ripon, brought forward his Local Self-Government Bill (1883), were Sayyid Ahmad Khan and Amir Ali, who maintained that such a measure would be unsuitable to a heterogeneous society such as the Indian, characterized as it was by not only differences of race and religion, caste and creed, but also of numbers. Speaking in Lucknow on 28 December 1887, Sayyid Ahmad presented his thesis of Hindus and Muslims as 'two different nations'. The Muslim, he declared, would come under Hindu domination because of their fewer numbers: 'It would be like a game of dice, in which one man had four dice and the other one' (Akbar 1988: 46–7). Arguments were backed by action: for instance, the influential ulama of the newly founded seminary at Deoband (in north India) issued fatwas discouraging social and economic contacts between Muslims and Hindus (see Madan 1997: chapter 4). The notion of a Muslim minority, threatened by a socially mobile and politically assertive Hindu majority was thus born. It accorded well with the official British perception of India as a country of discordant religious communities, castes, and tribes.

Moreover, several historians have argued that, at the core of the Muslim opposition to Western-style political representation lay several religious and political convictions. Thus, Muslims are said to be ever conscious of belonging to a divinely constituted religious brotherhood, entitled to wield political power over non-Muslims by virtue of their moral superiority. In India, in the late nineteenth century, they also considered themselves—at least the descendants of immigrants and the aristocrats among them did so—the legatees of the Mughal empire. Indeed, M.A. Jinnah himself said in 1942 that 'if the British hand over power to the Muslims, they will be making full amends to [those] from whom they have taken it' (Nanda 1974: 177). Finally, the political domain is seen by Muslims as the arena par excellence for the expression of religious values, and not a domain apart (see Shaikh 1989).

Unable to stop the idea of representative government, even in its most limited form, in the tracks, Sayyid Ahmad put forward the notion of 'separate electorates', based on religious identity, towards the end of the nineteenth century. The idea of 'weightage' also was mooted in course of time to overcome the disadvantage of numbers. The new principle that came to dominate the thinking of certain sections of Muslim political leadership in the twentieth century was that of 'parity'. This notion was finally embraced by Jinnah in the crucial final years leading to partition and independence in 1947. Had the principle of parity at the federal level been conceded, treating Muslims on par with Hindus, and providing safeguards for the others, some historians believe, partition may have been avoided (see Jalal 1985). In its absence, emphasis upon the character of Muslims as a 'minority', or as a separate 'nation', depending upon the context was Jinnah's trump card.[9]

Addressing the All-India Muslim League in Lahore in 1940 at the Lahore session, which later adopted the separate Muslim states resolution, Jinnah echoing Sayyid Ahmad's 'game of dice' argument, ridiculed Gandhi's protestations of brotherly feelings towards non-Hindus and Jinnah himself: 'The only difference is this, that brother Gandhi has three votes and I have only one vote' (Wolpert 1988: 181). This was, of course, a reference to the arithmetic of Hindu and Muslim populations in the 1941 census.

A decade later, the Constitution of India acknowledged the concept of minorities, but did not define it precisely, leaving a good deal to be inferred. Thus, Articles 29 and 30 specifically refer to the rights (in fact, Fundamental Rights) of 'minorities' to conserve their languages, scripts and cultures, have free access to state-aided educational institutions, and to establish and administer their own educational institutions. Although it seems perverse to me to place an interpretation on these constitutional provisions to the effect that *only* the minorities have such rights, mischievous politicians have not been reluctant to cite them as evidence of 'minorityism'. The forthright views of B.R. Ambedkar, hailed as 'the father of the Indian Constitution', do not exactly help in removing such doubts. The minorities, he said in the Constituent Assembly, 'have loyally accepted the rule of the majority which is basically a communal majority and not a political majority. It is for the majority to realize its duty not to discriminate against minorities. Whether the minorities will continue or will vanish must depend upon this habit of the majority. The moment the majority loses the habit of discrimination against the minority, the minorities can have no ground to exist' (CAD, vol. 7, I: 39). The majority and the minorities thus stood defined, though in a somewhat Humpty Dumpty fashion.

Without any regard for the social reality of the multiplicity of economic interests and political opinion among Hindus as well as Muslims and Sikhs, *imagined* majorities and minorities were said by these political leaders to be pitted against each other in a life-and-death struggle. For Jinnah, who claimed to be 'the sole spokesman' on behalf of the Muslims, the Congress was a Hindu organization and Maulana Azad its 'show-boy' President; Gandhi was merely the leader of the Hindu 'community', an opinion which he reiterated in his condolence message on Gandhi's death, ignoring the circumstances of the assassination. And for Ambedkar, Gandhi was an usurper who unjustly claimed to speak on behalf of low-caste Hindus.

Not everybody, however, agreed, then or later, with such views of dominant and dominated majorities and minorities. Frank Anthony, at that time the acknowledged leader of the Anglo-Indians, repudiated, on the floor of the Constituent Assembly itself, the allegation that the minorities were being deprived of their rights and otherwise oppressed. On the contrary, he said, the minorities had made demands that were not tenable (see CAD, vol. 8: 333–8; 346–9). But he did not abandon the concepts of majority and minority. V.V. John, a distinguished Indian intellectual who happened to be a Christian, and many others like him, have done precisely this, and asked for the protection of *human rights* rather than minority rights. According to him, the leaders of the minority communities practice 'selective secularism' and demand from Hindus what they do not themselves practice.[10] One ingenious argument in this regard is that minority communalism is a half-way house to secularism (Baig 1967: 164–80).

It will be recalled that, after partition, the Muslim fundamentalist organization, Jamat-i-Islami (Hind), through a series of pronouncements, accepted 'in the present circumstances', which meant conditionally, 'the secular form of government', but rejected secularism as an ideology. It described its decision quite explicitly as one dictated by 'utilitarian expediency'. Many other Muslim organizations and leaders took up the same position (see Mushir-ul-Haq 1972: 6–21). Similarly, fundamentalist Sikh leadership used to say that the Sikh religious tradition does not permit the separation of religion and politics and that, unless this right is recognized, the state in India is not truly secular but under Hindu domination. Some of them have, of course, since opted for the demand for an autonomous theocratic Sikh state (see Madan 1997: chapter 3).

The notion of minority status as privilege is of course a gross exaggeration, but many governmental actions based on political expediency have given it currency. How far people will go in the abuse of this idea was well illustrated by the successful effort of the Ramakrishna Mission members in Calcutta to get themselves recognized by a court of law as a non-Hindu minority (see Smith 1993). This decision was, however, set aside by the Supreme Court in July 1995. Meanwhile the Hindu–Muslim problem which had eased, more than somewhat, in the years following independence has become salient again. While the aggressive elements among the leaders of the so-called minorities raise cries of alarm that India is fast degenerating into a Hindu country, their counterparts among the Hindus cry foul and accuse the government of 'minorityism'. Addressing the 1923 session of the Congress at Delhi, its President, Maulana Abul Kalam Azad, had observed about the then prevailing political differences and slogans: '"Save the Hindu from Muslims", says one group, "Save Islam from Hinduism", says another. When the order of the day is, "Protect Hindus" and "Protect Muslims", who cares about protecting the nation?' That was said eighty odd years ago, but could have been said today.

Within this overall framework of majority–minority politics, there are variations and ramifications. Thus the violent student agitation of 1990 against reservations (vide Articles 330 and 332 of the Constitution) being sought to be raised to the level of nearly 50 per cent was the protest of a minority—those classified neither as Scheduled Caste or Scheduled Tribe nor as 'other backward classes'—against a majority of allegedly uniformly non-privileged people, although many among them were by no means economically deprived. Limitations of space do not allow me to discuss the thorny issue of reservations, which deserves detailed discussion (see Béteille 1992). But I should point out that, although the exploitation of certain castes and communities at the hands of others over the centuries down to this day, cannot be denied, the idea of reservation quotas—notwithstanding the fact that it was intended to be a temporary protective measure for thirty years only (Article 334)—does not fit well with the idea of secularism, understood as non-discriminatory state policy, particularly if it threatens to become a permanent vested interest. The hope that compensatory discrimination will transform communal groups into 'components of a pluralistic society in which invidious hierarchy is discarded while diversity is accommodated' (Galanter 1984: 561) in a kind of 'principled eclecticism' (ibid.: 567) is far from being realized.

Ironically, Nehru anticipated the danger. Speaking on the subject of reservation in the Constituent Assembly, he warned (Nehru 1991: 54):

> I would like you to consider this business, whether it is reservation or any other kind of safeguard for the minorities objectively. There is some point in having a safeguard of this type…when there is autocratic or foreign rule. As soon as you get…political democracy, then this kind of reservation, instead of helping the party to be safeguarded or aided, is likely to turn against it….[In] a democracy…it is the will of the majority that will prevail….Frankly, I would like…[to] put an end to such reservations as there still remain.

Nehru was obviously thinking of the 'majority' in the Jeffersonian sense, which is of course inseparable from individual rights.

Another critical issue for Indian secularism that I will only mention, but not discuss at any length, is the problem of the Kashmir Valley.[11] Through Article 370, the Constitution gave to

Jammu and Kashmir a special status, making it impossible for the Parliament to make laws for this state without the concurrence of its legislature in respect of subjects other than those mentioned in the Instrument of Accession or corresponding to them. This too was intended as a temporary measure, as the future of the state had become an international dispute by India's appeal for UN intervention to end Pakistani aggression. This specific legal context was soon overgrown by political considerations: the Kashmir Valley with its Muslim majority was vital to secular India's interests as a token of the repudiation of the two-nation theory which was the basis of Pakistan.

Since Sheikh Muhammad Abdullah, the acknowledged leader of the majority of Kashmir Muslims, had explicitly rejected this theory, the position of Indian leadership did not then seem unreasonable (see Abdullah 1993). But with the passage of time, Kashmiri Muslims came to be seen as hostages, and a special status was needed for retaining the state within the Union for still newer considerations. Article 370 is now said to protect 'Kashmiriyat' or Kashmiri identity. Why Kashmiri identity needs special protection any more than, say, Bengali or Tamil identity is difficult to understand, unless it is taken to mean Kashmiri *Muslim* identity and brought under the rubric of minority rights and privileges.

Although the state was ruled between 1947 and 1990 by a succession of elected governments, headed by Muslim chief ministers, they have not been of like mind regarding the nature of the state's relation with the Union (see Abdullah 1993; Qasim 1992). Administrative inefficiency and political corruption in the state have been matched by the machinations of the Union government. Although the representation of Muslims in the bureaucracy and the professions and the overall economic situation had improved considerably, yet a secessionist movement erupted there in the mid-1980s. It turned violent in 1989. Well-trained and heavily armed militants, supported by Pakistani authorities, are being fought by the security forces and there is blood-letting on both sides. Innocent people of all communities are caught in the crossfire, literally and figuratively, and suffer. What the turbulent elements are asking for is, in effect, another partition, and this fans the fires of Hindu reaction elsewhere in the country, resulting in such politically bizarre happenings as the 'unity march' (*ektā yātrā*) of the Bharatiya Janata Party president, Murli Manohar Joshi, in January 1992.

In the Valley itself, the Hindus were a 3 per cent minority of about 200,000 people, several thousand of whom have been reportedly killed or critically injured, and many of whose homes or properties have been plundered or burnt. Most of them have fled their homes and live in refugee camps in Jammu and Delhi, or with relatives, outside the Valley. They are another example of a non-privileged minority. Not only Hindus, but those Muslims too, who do not seem to be in full agreement, are the targets of fundamentalists and secessionists. In fact, about three times as many Muslims as Hindus are reported to have been killed.

The silence of Muslim political leadership in India about the happenings in Kashmir underscores the tragic fact that all is not well with Indian secularism.[12] For Jawaharlal Nehru, Kashmir had been India's answer to communalism, the shining token of her secularism. He had been encouraged in this belief by the leaders of the Muslim masses of Kashmir, including the tallest of them all, Sheikh Abdullah. Today Abdullah's is not a universally honoured name in the Valley and his grave has to be guarded by police to prevent its desecration by his own people. He had led these people in a liberation struggle that had been conspicuously socialist and secular in its ideological stance and action programmes, and had been actively supported by Nehru (see Abdullah 1993).

The militant secessionism of Kashmiri Muslims is more inspired by religious and ethnic (Muslim-Kashmiri) considerations than by pure Islamic fundamentalism, but the influence of the latter (particularly after the Iranian Revolution) is not absent. There have been clashes between Islamic fundamentalists and devout Kashmir Muslims because the former regard the relic and saint worshipping, and *urs* celebrating, Kashmiri Muslims as imperfectly Islamized (see Khan 1994). Whatever is judged to be the character of Kashmiri separatism, it is perfectly clear that it is against pan-Indian secular nationalism (see Varshney 1992). It is not going to be easy, therefore, to accommodate Kashmiri nationalism within the Indian state without imposing a very severe strain upon Indian secularism. A restatement of Kashmiri aspirations in terms of cultural pluralism and administrative decentralization of which a national state would be seen as the guarantor is not yet in sight (at the beginning of 1995).

Kashmir alone is not a cause of the crisis of Indian secularism. The destruction of the Babri mosque in Ayodhya in December 1992 by right-wing Hindu extremists, including prominently the so-called RSS family (*sangh parivār*), was an unprecedented and crippling blow to Indian secularism. The events leading upto the demolition are well-known (see Gopal 1991; Srivastava 1991). There was a widespread sense of foreboding;[13] yet the Indian state, at the state and national levels, became an accomplice, through acts of omission and commission, in this act of betrayal of both traditional cultural pluralism and modern secularism. As Prime Minister P.V. Narasimha Rao put it, the demolition posed a 'grave threat' to 'the institutions, principles and ideals on which the constitutional structure of [the Indian] republic has been built' (see Larson 1995: 273). The communal riots that followed (in January 1993) in different parts of the country, particularly the cities of Bombay and Surat, far away from Ayodhya, were widely described as anti-Muslim pogroms. Subsequently, Bombay has also to witness retailatory bombings by Muslim gangsters and their accomplices. These events revealed as nothing else until then the fragility of Indian secularism.

In the two years since then (1993–5), a semblance of communal peace has returned to the country, even Punjab seems to be well set on the road to recovery, but Kashmir continues to be in turmoil. State legislative assembly elections, involving more than half of the total country-wide electorate, have produced both defeats and victories for the Bharatiya Janata Party, but it is not clear whether its success has been due to its Hindutva appeal. It is noteworthy that in Uttar Pradesh, the home state of the Babri mosque, and in Bihar, caste solidarity rather than religious identity has won at the hustings. It would be very short sighted to consider casteist politicians as the soldiers of Indian secularism simply because in certain situations they establish alliances with Muslims against upper caste Hindus. The most dangerous portent is the coming to power of the ultra-chauvinistic Shiv Sena, in coalition with the BJP, in Maharashtra. Nothing is more inimical to the spirit of Indian secularism (cultural pluralism in society and a non-discriminatory state) than the vituperations of the Sena chief, Bal Thackeray, against non-Maharashtrians and those Muslims whom he considers anti-national. The end of the crisis of Indian secularism is not yet in sight.

CONCLUDING REMARKS

I began this essay by recalling that secularism as an explicitly formulated ideology was born of the dialectic of religion and science, and was not simply an anti-religious ideology, though many intellectuals have desired and even believed it to be so. There is much rethinking these days about the standard accounts of the Enlightenment, and the misleading preoccupation with what Stephen Toulmin (1990) calls its 'sunny side', to the neglect of its dogmatism and of the narrowing of rational debate by seventeenth-century scientists. Attention has also been drawn to the fact that the notion of the self-emancipation of humankind, which lies at the very core of the secularization thesis also implies the sacralization of the secular. Such reconsiderations are bound to affect our appreciation of secularism also, for it was, as already pointed out, partly an expression of the Enlightenment.

It is important to recognize that one of the major reasons for the rise of religious fundamentalism all over the world today is the excesses of ideological secularism, and its emergence as dogma, or a religion, just as Karl Marx, Max Weber, and some other social theorists had anticipated. By subverting religion as generally understood, secularism sets off a reaction in the form of fundamentalism, which usually is a perversion of religion, and has less to do with the purity of faith and more with the acquisition of political power.[14] The temple and the mosque lovers of today's India are, first and foremost, power-hungry politicians. In their hands, religion no longer is concerned with value, but only with instrumentalism; that is, religion is a means among others for the achievement of whatever goals are adopted.

If secularism is not essentially anti-religious, but only against revelation and unreason, Indian secularism with its ideal of respect for all religions would be much less so. Why then did Nehru complain to Malraux that it was difficult to establish a secular state in a religious country such as India? Elsewhere in my writings, I have attempted an answer to this question, which could hardly have been Nehru's own answer, too, though it does perhaps come within recognizable distance of a Gandhian position. My main argument is that neither India's indigenous religious traditions nor Islam recognize the sacred–secular dichotomy in the manner Christianity does so and, therefore, the modern processes of secularization (in the sense of expanding human control over human lives) proceed in India without the support of an ideology that people in general may warm up to, such as one legitimized by religion. What exists empirically, but not also ideologically, exists but weakly (see Madan 1987 and 1997). The conclusion is not that the secular state should be jettisoned, or, more absurdly, all Indians should become Christians, but that special efforts are needed to give it clear definition, work out its relation to civil society, and reinforce it ideologically.

More generally, one recognizes that, as Louis Dumont (1994: 6, 14–15) has argued, the alternatives available in situations of civilizational contact are not limited to mutual exclusion or unilateral surrender. Most often a 'synthesis' takes place; of what kind is the key question. Such syntheses have a universalistic potential; they characterize not only particular cultural spaces but many also enter into 'the world culture of the time'. Hence the immense importance of what happens in India.

India is not entirely lacking in its own resources to cope with the processes of secularization in the midst of much religiosity and to find support for its evolving notion of secularism as inter-religious understanding. What I have in mind is not so much the medieval religious syncretism—there are differences of opinion about both its significance and recoverability[15]—as the fact that none of India's indigenous religions has been considered by its traditional thinkers a revealed religion in the sense in which the Abrahamic religions are so. The call recently given by certain intellectuals to 'Semitize' Hinduism bears witness to the lack of confidence that assails the innermost spirit of Hindutva. The Indic religious traditions are more or less open to questioning from within and reformulation through interpretation. Also, they have been subject to considerable pressure from outside, producing a flexibility of attitudes if not always religious liberality. In the not too distant past, Gandhi showed that reinterpretation through questioning and receptiveness to outside influences was still possible.

For these resources to be turned into strength we have to substitute a clearly defined religious pluralism for a narrow secularism and also to further explore India's cultural traditions for suitable ideas. The Indic religions share crucial metaphysical presuppositions about 'being', 'knowing', and 'value', contribute significantly to the over-all cultural ambience of the country, and provide the foundation for regional composite cultures. Their followers share many attitudes and have many social practices in common. Islam and Christianity are non-indigenous in origin, but can hardly be considered alien today. It may not be denied that there are significant theological, metaphysical, cognitive, and ethical differences between Indic and classical Islamic world-views. But differences alone do not characterize their relationship. Considerable ethnographic and historical evidence bears witness to cultural exchanges, shared value-orientations, and compatible lifestyles evolved over the centuries (see Chapter 8 below and Bayly 1989).[16] The task of socio-cultural reconciliation is daunting but not beyond reach.

At the same time, we have to recognize, first, the limitations of an ambiguous concept of pluralism and, then, the real dangers of Hindu communalism and the insensitivity of the Hindus generally to the feelings of those who consider themselves non-Hindus. It has been noted that these non-Hindus are treated as permanent outsiders if they happen to be Christians or Muslims, or are denied a sense of separate identity if they are 'tribals' or Sikhs (see Oommen 1990: 11). Gandhi no less than Nehru was conscious of the greater harm that majority communalism might do in India though neither could be said to have approved of minority communalism. As Ashis Nandy (1980: 70–98) has insightfully argued, Gandhi was the sterner foe of Hindu communalism and paid for it with his life.

If India is to be saved from religious discord reinforced by fundamentalist tendencies present in all three traditions, and the resultant political divisiveness, we need rigorous rethinking and concerted action. What is at stake is the very survival of the Indian state. Social backwardness in the form of a weakly developed sense of civic ties—the bond of responsible citizenship—that would moderate if not replace the divisive primordial loyalties of religion, language, and caste, is indeed a very severe handicap. Nehru saw this clearly and articulated it forcefully. What he did not see well was that when the state is made to take on too much out of the ambition and hubris of those who take charge of it, they run the risk of making it totalitarian or seeing it fall flat on its face. The emergency regime of Indira Gandhi (1975–7) revealed the limitations and the heavy costs of the totalitarian option in a large, internally diverse, and politically conscious country, such as India. The events that have unfolded since then have shown that the state in India has become increasingly ineffective (sometimes by choice) in coping with caste and communal violence, just as its achievements in bringing about social and economic development have been meagre and uneven.

It may be argued that Nehru failed to realize fully the importance of the symbolism of the sacred in a secular society. His reference to the dams and factories of modern India as 'temples' (noted above) showed his awareness of the symbolic value of the sacred, but, perhaps, he remained content with too little. The example of the USA may be cited to underscore the importance of the aura of the sacred. An American president may not be at all personally religious, yet he must publicly acknowledge the religious foundations of American society. It is not any particular religion or church that is valorized, but the embodiment of the historical and spiritual experience of the American people, called 'civil religion' by Robert Bellah (1970) and others. The presence of civil religion, it has been suggested, has made the separation of the Church and the state successful in the USA.

The situation in India is significantly different, however, because of the prevailing religious plurality, which turns into antagonism only too readily. Moreover, the partition of India in the name of religious and cultural differences made the secular nationalists recoil from the idea of associating the state with religion, which in the circumstances could only have meant Hinduism. Contrary to what some scholars have suggested optimistically (see Larson 1995), there are no signs of an Indian civil religion taking shape.[17] The late twentieth century is, perhaps, too late in the day for such a development. Nehru proceeded only as far as he did because he was very much a creature of his times. In short, even when we recognize clearly the problems we face, and envisage possible solutions, the passage from thought to action is fraught with serious difficulties. The future of India as a civic society, and the character of its polity in the years to come, are as yet far from settled issues. All those who cherish the values of democracy and cultural pluralism—of human freedom and dignity—can hardly afford to be complacent.

NOTES

1. I owe this framework for the interpretation of traditional Indian thought to the late K.J. Shah. It is a great pity that Shah died (in 1994) without bringing together his original reflections, some of them unpublished, on Gandhi.
2. Nehru grew up in a divided home. He recalled in his autobiography that, when he was a child, religion seemed to be a 'woman's affair' that his father and other men in the house 'refused to take seriously' (1980: 8). B.R. Nanda has written of Jawaharlal's mother's 'attachment' to the Hindu scriptures, pūjās, orthodox rituals and pilgrimages (1962: 41). As for his father, Nanda describes him as 'a product of the late Victorian "free thinking" rationalism, which was learning to dispense with divine explanations of the working of the universe and to pin faith in the human intellect and on science to lead mankind along vistas of progress' (ibid.: 43).

    Henny Sender (1988) describes the composite culture of the Kashmiri Pandit community of the United Provinces, of which the Nehrus were distinguished members, and the personal unorthodoxy of Motilal Nehru. She also quotes from the senior Nehru's presidential address to the Congress at Calcutta (1928): '[The] association [of religion] with politics has been to the good of neither. Religion has been degraded and politics has sunk into the mire. Complete divorce of one from the other is the only remedy' (ibid.: 295). Jawaharlal's political world, too, like his home, was a divided one, with Gandhi taking the place of his mother, as it were, and insisting on the validity and indispensability of religious values. Gandhi's influence, however, never succeeded in erasing the earlier and deeper influence of Motilal. Incidentally, it has been recorded that the senior Nehru used to tease both his wife and Gandhi about their religiosity (see Nanda 1962: 41; Akbar 1988: 229).
3. While Article 25 of the Constitution grants 'Freedom of conscience and free profession, practice and propagation of religion' as a fundamental right to the citizens of India, its sub-clause 2(a) makes room for 'regulating or restricting any economic, financial, political or other secular activity which may be associated with religious practice'. The Hindi version of the Constitution uses *laukika*, literally 'worldly, for 'secular'.
4. A further amendment to specify the secular and democratic character of the state, and to define the word 'secular' (in Article 366)

was passed in 1978 by the newly elected Lok Sabha but failed to receive the approval of the Rajya Sabha where the Congress party had a two-thirds majority. It is ironical that the same party proposed in 1993 to amend the Constitution to include in it a definition of secularism as the state policy of equal respect for all religions.

5. A prominent member of the Constituent Assembly, K.T. Shah, tried, through two amendments to the Draft Constitution, to have India declared a secular state, specifying that it would have nothing to do with any religion, creed or faith. According to the first of these amendments India would have been described as a 'Secular Federal Socialist Union of States'. B.R. Ambedkar, who was piloting the draft, rejected both amendments on the ground that it was not advisable to prescribe a particular form of social organization for future generations. On another occasion he denied that the Indian state was secular because he wanted it to have the right of intervention in religious matters in the same manner as in secular affairs. It may be added here that another vocal member, H.V. Kamath, proposed that the Preamble to the Constitution begin with the words 'In the name of God'; this too was found unacceptable by the majority of the members present, because such an invocation would not be in consonance with the secular spirit of the Constitution. The consensus of opinion among the members was that the reference to 'liberty of thought, expression, belief, faith and worship' in the Preamble was comprehensive enough to cover all reasonable points of view. Subsequently, after the Kesavananda Bharati case of 1973, the Preamble came to be formally recognized as an essential part of the Constitution, proclaiming its philosophy, and secularism as one of its 'basic' (that is unalterable) features.

6. 'In many parts of the world, the people can do nothing for themselves which requires large means and combined actions; all such things are left undone, unless done by the state': John Stuart Mill, *Principles of Political Economy*, II, pp. 602–3, quoted in de Schweinitz, Jr 1983: 125.

7. Thus, in 1953, Nehru described the laying of the foundation stone of the Nagarjuna Sagar dam by himself as a 'sacred ceremony' and called the dam itself 'a temple dedicated to the humanity of India'.

8. Said's judgement is based on Partha Chatterjee's insightful analysis of what the latter calls 'the moment of arrival' in Indian nationalist thought. According to it: 'Once established, this state will stand above the narrow interests of groups and classes in society, take an overall view of the matter and, in accordance with the best scientific procedures, plan and direct the economic processes in order to create enough social wealth to ensure welfare and justice to all' (Chatterjee 1986: 133). Hindsight is a chastening perspective, and

we know today the limitations of the socially aware but historically mistaken view of the state that Nehru and others of his generation embraced. To repeat, they expected too much of the state, and not in the economic domain alone.

9. It is noteworthy that, alongside of the characterization of the Muslims as a minority, there have also been repeated denials of its appropriateness. Thus, Abul Kalam Azad wrote in the very first volume of *Al-Hilal* (1912) that the preoccupation with their status as a minority was 'the root' of the Muslims' problem: 'members of brotherhood of four hundred million believers in the unity of God are afraid of two hundred and twenty million idol worshippers of India'. He exhorted them: 'You must realize your position among the peoples of the world. Like God himself, look at everyone from a lofty position' (Douglas 1988: 144). Similarly, Rahmat Ali, to whom we owe the word Pakistan, denounced the idea of Muslims being considered a minority, and believed that it had been invented by the Hindus to ensure their domination over the Muslims (Malik 1963: 245–6). And Jinnah himself denied the relevance of minority status (merely a demographic fact) when he stressed the principle of parity between Hindus and Muslims in the political arena in recognition of what he regarded as the significant facts of history.

10. From notes taken by the author at a lecture given by Professor John in New Delhi on 28 November 1979.

11. The following discussion, written in 1995, has partly been overtaken by later events, notably in Gujarat. See also Chapters 6 and 7 below.

12. Syed Shahabuddin, a prominent Muslim leader and parliamentarian (formerly a member of the elite Foreign Service), clarified in a letter to the Editor, the *Times of India*, New Delhi, 30 August 1994:
    'On militancy in Kashmir they [Indian Muslims or, as the author prefers, Muslim Indians] have been largely silent primarily because the Government of India has treated Kashmir as a law and order problem and there has been massive and indiscriminate use of force against our own citizens in Kashmir. Muslims face a moral dilemma of speaking out on both aspects and being misunderstood.'

13. Anticipating damage to the mosque, I wrote just a week before the demolition (Madan 1992):
    'Today's purveyors of *hindutva*, who speak of righting old wrongs, and do not believe that a mosque, which may have been built after demolishing a temple on the site four and a half centuries ago, deserves to exist as a place of Muslim worship, may or may not succeed in bringing it down. They have certainly diminished the very cultural tradition they seek to protect by making it appear intolerant.... It is said that the Babri Masjid is a symbol of oppression and must go. Did the great Hindu temples that were a symbol

of the oppression of the so-called low castes have to go? Or, for that matter, the palaces of British Raj?'

14. While philosophers do not seem to find this distinction difficult to accept, some sociologists reject it as sophistry (see Bailey 1991). I would like to recall here an observation by Wittgenstein that echoes Gandhi's views closely. Gandhi wrote: 'Religion is outraged when an outrage is perpetrated in its name' (1961: 47). And this is what Wittgenstein noted: 'Religion as madness is a madness springing from irreligiousness' (1984: 13e).

15. For a richly documented account, see Roy 1983. A sceptical assessment will be found in Ahmad 1964.

16. The character of Muslim society in India has been the subject of an important debate in recent years. While some scholars (mainly anthropologists and sociologists) have focused on local level accommodations and adjustments, emphasizing cultural borrowing between Hindus and Muslims and survivals of pre-Islamic beliefs and customs among the latter, others (mainly historians) have asserted that Muslim communities in South Asia have been subject to the efforts of their religious leaders to attain perfection as practising believers. The relations of these Muslims with their cultural environment have been marked, it is said, more by 'tension' than 'equilibrium' (see, e.g., Ahmad 1964, 1967, Ahmad 1978, Das 1984, Madan 1995, Robinson 1983, and Roy 1983). The current salience of fundamentalism itself bears witness to the accommodations and adjustments mentioned above.

17. Larson is of the opinion that the Indian secular state is 'basically Neo-Hindu' in origin, and has generated a 'Gandhian–Nehruvian Indic civil religion', the 'cognitive base or belief system' of which is 'the loose conglomeration of Neo-Hindu notions and liberal-democratic-cum-socialist ideas'. He detects in the contemporary Indian rhetoric of 'secular' traditions of tolerance, non-violence', etc., and in the pride in 'the Indic heritage', echoes of the rhetoric about the 'American way of life', 'the religion of the Republic', and 'the promised land'. He concludes: 'In both instances one is dealing with much more than rhetoric or a political idiom with a religious tint. One is also dealing with the religious idiom of an institutionalized civil religion' (ibid.: 202–3).

I know of no other interpretation of the same kind and am not sure that the comparison is wholly defensible. The Biblical heritage in America is far more internally harmonious than the Indo-Islamic legacy. Moreover, the one-half century after partition, itself a divisive act, that has been witness to many kinds of inter-community conflicts (based on religion, language, caste, etc.), is much too short a period for the shaping of significant common aspirations and expressive national symbols and rituals. Larson reads more into the ceremonies associated with the independence and Republic days—particularly those held in Delhi—and in the observance of a multitude of religious holidays. The strength of the state in the USA is matched by the strength of the civil society (Alexis de Tocqueville noticed this more than a century and a half ago); in India we can only speak of a double weakness—of the state and of civil society.

REFERENCES

Abdullah, Sheikh M. 1993. *Flames of the Chinar: An Autobiography.* New Delhi: Viking.

Acton, H.B. 1955. *The Illusion of the Epoch: Marxism-Leninism as a Philosophical Creed.* London: Cohen and West.

Ahmad, Aziz. 1964. *Studies in Islamic Culture in the Indian Environment.* Oxford: Clarendon Press.

———. 1967. *Islamic Modernism in India and Pakistan 1857–1964.* London: Oxford University Press.

Ahmad, Imtiaz (ed.). 1978. *Caste and Social Stratification among Muslims in India.* 2nd edn. New Delhi: Manohar.

Akbar, M.J. 1988. *Nehru: The Making of India.* London: Viking.

Baig, M.R.A. 1967. *In Different Saddles.* New Delhi: Vikas.

Bailey, F.G. 1991. 'Religion and religiosity: Ideas and their use'. *Contributions to Indian Sociology* 25, 2: 211–32.

Baxi, Upendra. 1992. 'Secularism: real or pseudo'. In M.M. Sankhder (ed.), *Secularism in India,* New Delhi: Deep and Deep.

Bayly, Susan. 1989. *Saints, Goddesses and Kings: Muslims and Christians in South Indian Society, 1700–1900.* Cambridge: Cambridge University Press.

Bellah, Robert N. 1970. *Beyond Belief: Essays on Religion in a Post-traditional World.* New York: Harper & Row.

Béteille, André. 1992. *The Backward Classes in Contemporary India.* New Delhi: Oxford University Press.

Bose, N.K. (ed.). 1948. *Selections from Gandhi.* Ahmedabad: Navjivan.

Brown, Judith M. 1992. *Gandhi: Prisoner of Hope.* New Delhi: Oxford University Press.

CAD, 1948–49. *Constituent Assembly of India Debates,* Vols 7 and 8, India Official Reports. New Delhi: Lok Sabha Secretariat.

Chatterjee, Margaret. 1983. *Gandhi's Religious Thought.* London: Macmillan.

Chatterjee, Partha. 1986. *Nationalist Thought and the Colonial World: A Derivative Discourse?* New Delhi: Oxford University Press.

Cunningham, J.D. 1955 [1916]. *A History of the Sikhs.* Delhi: S. Chand & Co.

Cunningham Jr, Noble E. 1991. *In Pursuit of Reason: The Life of Thomas Jefferson.* New Delhi: Affiliated East-West Press.

Das, Veena. 1984. 'For a folk theology and theological anthropology of Islam'. *Contributions to Indian sociology* (n.s.), 18, 2: 292–305.

Douglas, Ian Handerson. 1988. *Abul Kalam Azad: An Intellectual and Religious Biography*, Gail Minault and Christian Troll (eds). New Delhi: Oxford University Press.

Dumont, Louis. 1994. *German Ideology: From France to Germany and Back.* Chicago: University of Chicago Press.

Gallanter, Marc. 1984. *Competing Equalities.* Berkeley: University of California Press.

Gopal, Sarvepalli. (ed.). 1980. *Jawaharlal Nehru: An Anthology.* New Delhi: Oxford University Press.

————. 1987. *Nehru and Secularism.* Occasional Papers, No. 42 (mimeo). New Delhi: Nehru Memorial Museum and Library.

————. (ed.). 1991. *Anatomy of a Confrontation: The Babri Masjid-Ram Janmabhumi Issue.* New Delhi: Viking.

Iyer, Raghavan. 1986. *The Moral and Political Writings of Mahatma Gandhi. Vol. I: Civilization, Politics, and Religion.* Oxford: Clarendon Press.

Jalal, Ayesha. 1985. *The Sole Spokesman: Jinnah, the Muslim League and the Demand for Pakistan.* Cambridge: Cambridge University Press.

Khan, M. Ishaq. 1994. *Kashmir's Transition to Islam: The Role of Muslim Rishis.* New Delhi: Manohar.

Larson, Gerald James. 1995. *India's Agony over Religion.* Albany: State University of New York Press.

Lenin, Vladimir Ivanovich. (n.d.), *Religion.* Calcutta: Burmon Publishing House.

Madan, T.N. 1987. 'Secularism in its place'. *The Journal of Asian Studies*, 46, 4: 747–59.

————. 1989. 'Religion in India'. *Daedalus*, 118: 115–46.

————. 1992. 'Menace of intolerance: National interests get short shift'. *Times of India* (New Delhi), 30 November.

————. 1994. 'Secularism and the intellectuals'. *Economic and Political Weekly*, 19: 1095–6.

————. 1995. 'From orthodoxy to fundamentalism: A thousand years of Islam in South Asia'. In Martin E. Marty and R. Scott Appleby (eds), *Fundamentalisms Comprehended.* Chicago: University of Chicago Press.

————. 1997. *Modern Myths, Locked Minds: Secularism and Fundamentalism in India.* New Delhi: Oxford University Press.

Malik, Hafeez. 1963. *Moslem Nationalism in India and Pakistan.* Washington: DC: Public Affairs Press.

Malraux André. 1968. *Antimemoirs.* London: Hamish Hamilton.

Marx, Karl. 1975. 'On the Jewish question.' In Karl Marx and Friedrich Engels, *Collected Works.* Vol. 3. Moscow: Progress Publishers.

Marx, Karl and Friedrich Engels. 1959. *Basic Writings on Politics and Philosophy*. Lewis S. Feuer (ed.). New York: Doubleday, Anchor.

Mohan Rao, U.S. 1968. *The Message of Mahatma Gandhi*. New Delhi: Government of India Press.

Mushir-ul-Haq. 1972. *Islam in Secular India*. Shimla: Indian Institute of Advanced Study.

Myrdal, Gunnar. 1968. *Asian Drama*. 3 vols. New York: Pantheon.

Nanda, B.R. 1962. *The Nehrus—Motilal and Jawaharlal*. London: Allen & Unwin.

————. 1974. *Gokhale, Gandhi and the Nehrus: Studies in Indian Nationalism*. London: Allen & Unwin.

Nandy, Ashis. 1980. *At the Edge of Psychology: Essays in Politics and Culture*. New Delhi: Oxford University Press.

Nehru, Jawaharlal. 1946. *The Discovery of India*. Calcutta: The Signet Press.

————. 1961 [1946]. *The Discovery of India*. Bombay: Asia Publishing House.

————. 1972. *Selected Works of Jawaharlal Nehru* [SWJN], Vol. 3. New Delhi: Orient Longman.

————. 1973a. *SWJN*, Vol. 4, New Delhi: Orient Longman.

————. 1973b. *SWJN*, Vol. 5, New Delhi: Orient Longman.

————. 1975. *SWJN*, Vol. 7, New Delhi: Orient Longman.

————. 1980. [1936]. *An Autobiography*. Delhi: Oxford University Press.

————. 1981. *SWJN*, Vol. 14, New Delhi: Orient Longman.

————. 1987. *SWJN*, Second Series, Vol. 5. New Delhi: Jawaharlal Nehru Memorial Fund.

————. 1991. *SWJN*, Second Series, Vol. 11, New Delhi: Jawaharlal Nehru Memorial Fund.

Oommen, T.K. 1990. *State and Society in India: Studies in Nation-building*. New Delhi: Sage.

Parekh, Bhikhu. 1989a. *Gandhi's Political Philosophy*. London: Macmillan.

————. 1989b. *Colonialism, Tradition and Reform: An Analysis of Gandhi's Political Discourse*. New Delhi: Sage.

————. 1991. 'Nehru and the national philosophy of India'. *Economic and Political Weekly* 5–12 January, 26, 1: 35–48.

Qasim, Syed Mir. 1992. *My Life and Times*. New Delhi: Allied.

Radhakrishnan, S. 1956. Foreword in S. Abid Hossain, *The National Culture of India*. Bombay: Jaico.

Robinson, Francis. 1983. 'Islam and Muslim society in South Asia'. *Contributions to Indian Sociology* (n.s.) 17: 185–203.

Roy, Asim. 1983. *The Islamic Syncretistic Tradition in Bengal*. Princeton, N.J.: Princeton University Press.

Said, Edward W. 1993. *Culture and Imperialism*. London: Chatto and Windus.

Sathe, S.P. 1991. 'Secularism, law and the constitution of India'. In M.S. Gore (ed.). *Secularism in India*, Allahabad: Vidya Prakashan.

Schweinitz Jr, Karl de. 1983. *The Rise and Fall of British India: Imperialism as Inequality*. London: Methuen.

Sender, Henny. 1988. *The Kashmiri Pandits: A Study of Cultural Choice in North India*. New Delhi: Oxford University Press.

Shaikh, Farzana, 1989. *Community and Consensus in Islam: Muslim Representation in Colonial India, 1860–1947*. Cambridge: Cambridge University Press.

Skinner, Quentin. 1978. *The Foundation of Modern Political Thought: The Age of Reformation*. Cambridge: Cambridge University Press.

Smith, Brian. 1993. 'How not to be a Hindu: The case of the Ramakrishna Mission'. In Robert D. Baird (ed.). *Religion and Law in Independent India*. New Delhi: Manohar.

Smith, Donald Eugene. 1963. *India as a Secular State*. Bombay: Oxford University Press.

Srivastava, Sushil. 1991. *The Disputed Mosque: A Historical Inquiry*. New Delhi: Vistaar.

Toulmin, Stephen. 1990. *Cosmopolis: The Hidden Agenda of Modernity*. New York: The Free Press.

Varshney, Ashuthosh. 1992. 'Three compromised nationalisms: Why Kashmir has been a problem'. In Raju G.C. Thomas (ed.). *Perspective on Kashmir: The Roots of Conflict in South Asia*. Boulder: Westview Press.

Wavell, A.P. 1977. *The Viceroy's Journal*. Penderel Moon (ed.). New Delhi: Oxford University Press.

Weber, Max. 1948. *From Max Weber: Essays in Sociology*. H.H. Gerth and C.W. Mills (trs. and eds). London: Routledge and Kegan Paul.

Wittgenstein, Ludwig. 1984. *Culture and Value*. Chicago: University of Chicago Press.

Wolpert, Stanley. 1988. *Jinnah of Pakistan*. New Delhi: Oxford University Press.

5

Secularism Revisited
Doctrine of Destiny or Political Ideology?*

[Feuerbach's] work consists in the dissolution of the religious world into its secular basis. He overlooks the fact that after completing this work, the chief thing still remains to be done. For the fact that the secular foundation detaches itself from itself and establishes itself in the clouds as an independent realm is really to be explained by the self-cleavage and self-contradictoriness of this secular basis.

Karl Marx
'Theses on Feuerbach'

The historical modus vivendi of secularism, while seeking to chasten religious dogmatism, embodies unacknowledged elements of immodesty in itself. The very intensity of the struggle it wages against religious intolerance may induce blind spots with respect to itself.

William Connolly
Why I am not a Secularist

* * *

Alongside democracy, federalism, and socialism, secularism was one of the foundational principles on which the leaders of the new state of independent India set out in the middle of the twentieth century to create an economically developed and socially just society. Democracy was of course the legacy of the freedom

* Written in early 2005 as an exercise in summing up and moving forward, this essay is being published here for the first time. It draws some materials from my earlier writings.

movement and the animating spirit of the Constitution adopted in 1949; it found prominent mention in its Preamble. The federal structure of the state—an imperative in view of the large size and huge population of the country and its regional diversities—was also laid out in great detail in the Constitution. Socialism and secularism did not find direct mention despite the efforts of many members to have them written into it. B.R. Ambedkar, the presiding deity as it were of the drafting committee, considered it unwise to constitutionally bind the future generations to a socio-economic agenda that may have to be changed with the passage of time (see pp. 84–5 and 106 above).

As for secularism, the liberty of 'belief, faith and worship', inscribed in the Preamble and spelled out in a member of clauses in the chapter on fundamental rights (see Chapter 2 above), was obviously considered adequate enough for the word secularism also to be mentioned in the Constitution. Fearful of the mutual hostility of religious communities (which had led to the partition of the subcontinent) though India's leaders were, and committed to a modern rational outlook on national life, secularism in its original sense of the ideology of those committed to bringing about the decline of religion in human affairs (see Madan 1997: chapter 1), obviously was considered inappropriate in the Indian cultural setting. Widely respected and influential intellectuals actually said so. I have already cited the view of Radhakrishnan (see p. 86 above) that what India needed to do was to evolve its own concept of secularism. The effort to do so began straightaway and we do indeed now have our own definition of the term, although the same is not followed consistently; nor has it yet entered into sociological literature generally or such widely consulted dictionaries as the *Concise Oxford English Dictionary*, which now abounds with Indian words.

Indian secularism has come to have both a focused meaning and also a wider connotation. Interestingly, Jawaharlal Nehru brought them together in an early statement. In a letter to the chief ministers in 1952, he observed that the word 'secular' meant more than the 'free play of religions': it also conveyed 'the idea of social and political equality'. Thus, he did not consider 'a caste ridden society…properly secular'. He concluded: 'we must always keep the ideal of the unity of India and of the political and social equality of her people, to whatever group, religion or province they might belong' (see Austin 1999: 557f.). As is well known, Nehru was not happy about caste-based reservations in civil services and legislatures. It is indeed ironical that today's 'secular forces' (so called) are headed by, among others, mutually antagonistic caste leaders for whom secularism and casteism are not at all contradictory as Nehru correctly perceived them to be. The 'wretched national agonizing about secularism' about which Shashi Tharoor (2003: 3) has written simply does not go away.

* * *

There are two bodies of reflection and writing on Indian secularism understood as the freedom of conscience (or religion) of the individual, and as the commitment of the state to protect this freedom and to ensure that religious identity in no way interferes with citizenship rights. There is a multi-vocal public discourse carried on by politicians, journalists, and lawyers and judges; and there is an academic discourse. In my reading of these two discourses, the former is, of course, much older and therefore the original discourse; the latter is generally reactive and hesitant to break new ground. Of late it has begun to seem even insular, somewhat cut off from discussions on secularization and secularism (actually the former term is used to refer to both the *process* and to the *thesis* that the process is linear and universal, and the latter term is not equally in vogue) among political and social theorists in the West.

In the public or political discourse, the secularist position (or what could be called so) first made its appearance as nationalist rhetoric towards the end of the nineteenth century. Its precise context was the efforts of the leaders of the newly founded Indian National Congress to secure participation of the Muslims in its activities and programmes. As I have already pointed out elsewhere (Madan 1997: 267ff.), a Muslim leader from Bombay, Badruddin Tyabji, in his presidential address to the Congress in 1887, hoped that there was nothing in the mutual relations of the various religious communities that would make anyone of them refrain from joining the others to obtain from the British 'general' administrative reforms and civic rights 'for the common benefit' of all people. The principal opponent of this point of view was

Sayyid Ahmad Khan, one of the most prominent public figures of north India and an energetic promoter of modern education among the Muslims. Through an exchange of letters in 1888, these two distinguished Muslims may be said to have opened the secularism debate of modern India, although they did not use the term 'secularism'. Tyabji argued that community and national interests were both equally legitmate and they were non-antagonistic; Khan insisted on the priority of the former and questioned the validity of the latter in India where the Hindus outnumbered Muslims three to one. In Tyabji's judgement, Muslim interests would be best served by linking them to general interests, and not by pursuing a separatist strategy.

From the nationalist Muslim point of view, secularism (read nationalism) could be an encompassing or a residual concept: general interests could be so stated as to include community interests; or community interests even when granted primacy still would leave a residual space for common interests. Muhammad Ali Jinnah, a follower of Tyabji and a Congressman who later also became a Muslim League leader, put the secularist position succinctly when he famously rebuked one of his protégés (and clients), the Raja of Mahumdabad, who showed increasing consciousness of his Muslim identity, that he was 'an Indian first and then a Muslim' (Wolpert 1985: 79). Actually, as far as I have been able to find out, Jinnah was one of the first public figures of modern India to speak of the 'affairs of our common secular existence'. He did this in his presidential address to the Indian Muslim League in 1916, when he was also one of the leading lights of the Congress.[1]

It is not my intention here to undertake a survey of usages: I only want to draw attention to three noteworthy conceptions of secularism discernible in the public discourse during the years of the national movement. The first has been noted above. The second we owe to Mahatma Gandhi. His support in 1920 to the Khilafat movement in India, which campaigned for the grant of sufficient temporal powers to the defeated Sultan of Turkey, so that he might discharge his duties as the *khalīfa* of the Muslims (that included notably the protection of the major holy places of Islam worldwide), appeared to be paradoxical from a nationalist (secular) point of view. He defended his decision in terms of his moral obligation (dharma) to forge bonds of 'friendship' between

Hindus and Muslims and thereby promote 'internal peace' in the country (see Brown 1992: 142). He placed the burden of winning Muslim participation in national affairs on the shoulders of Hindus, the majority community. For him, this too was an issue of moral obligation; his critics considered it a policy of appeasement. But he firmly denied that there was any element of bargaining in his politics (see Nanda 1989: 223f.). If secularism in the context of the 1920s was the cultivation of common interests, even when these interests were apparently not secular, like the Muslim demand for the protection of the *khalifa* and the Hindu demand for the protection of the cow, then the Gandhian version of it was a morally grounded social contract of mutual benefit, which also served higher national interests through a reconciliation of the two communities.[2] But Gandhi was not a secularist; he was very much a religious person. Given his absolute stand that good ends do not justify bad means, his approach cannot really be considered (as some critics have done) a compromise with communalism for the furtherance of national goals. That his actions contributed to the communalization of politics can only be called 'an unintended consequence'.

The third conception of secularism was characteristic of the thinking of Jawaharlal Nehru (and has already been discussed in Chapters 3 and 4). It came closest to the Western conception of secularism as agnosticism and rationalism. Nehru was actually more concerned with exposing the economic foundations of Muslim separatism and the negative ideology of communalism than with the elaboration of a positive ideology of secularism. The word (or its cognates) do not occur in either his autobiography (1936) or *The Discovery of India* (1946). He did, however, write about the secular state in *Glimpses of World History* (1942: 706) in the specific context of Kemalist Turkey.

These formulations, made in the context of the movement for independence rooted in the ideology of nationalism, are now of no more than historical interest. As already noted, Jinnah eventually promoted the thesis of incompatibility of cultural values and secular interests of the two major 'nations' of the subcontinent (Hindus and Muslims) that became the basis for partition, and swept away Gandhi's politico-moral endeavour to build a social contract between the religious communities. Nehru's modernist thesis about the primacy of secular interests, and the irrelevance (if not unreal character) of the religious factor in public life, to which he adhered until the very last years of the freedom movement, also fell by the way.

After independence, the focus shifted to the making of the state, and secularism, so called, derived from Western sources, but not wholly faithful to them, was presented as its ideology. The limited appeal of the liberal or Marxist notions of secularism among the people generally convinced Nehru and other leaders that in India, 'a religious country' (as he called it, see p. 81 above), secularism would have to mean, at least in the foreseeable future, that the state would honour all faiths without discrimination (*sarva dharma samabhava*), and that it would provide equal opportunities to all citizens. This position was, of course, in consonance with Gandhi's pluralist perspective on inter-religious understanding. It is this which has become the state ideology, and has now been for quite a while the basis of virtually all discussions of Indian secularism, whether in the public arena or the academe.

In the post-Nehruvian period, the characterization of the current pluralist ideology as 'pseudo-secularism' by the intellectuals of the Hindu right, because of its emphasis on minority rights, allegedly denies Hindus the advantage of numbers that an unqualified policy of equal treatment would give them, is a clever political ploy to further the agenda of majoritarianism. Hence, they bring forward the charge of appeasement of the minorities, which does, however, stick on some political parties. Untrustworthy minorities are a creation of diffident and mistrusting minds that pick up aberrant cases of espionage, sabotage, terrorism, etc., as evidence of a general malaise.

* * *

At the dawn of independence, the ideal of the secular state was enshrined in the Constitution, which became operative in 1950. The earliest scholarly discussions that attracted attention were by political scientists and focused on the character of the new state. In a thoughtful doctoral dissertation written in the late 1950s, Luthera argued that, in the prevailing socio-cultural and political milieus, the Indian state would have to be 'jurisdictionalist', and that this was what the Constitution had provided. Under jurisdictionalism, he explained, the state guarantees freedom of conscience and worship to all citizens and treats them equally otherwise too. Moreover, it assumes a supervisory and vigilant role towards religious institutions (Luthera 1964: 21–3 et passim). In short, Luthera did not consider a secular state of the Western type (based on the separation of the church and the state) feasible in India. He did not, however, entertain any doubts about the viability of the kind of state provided for in the Constitution.

Whatever its deficiencies, the Luthera thesis highlighted some significantly specific and fairly explicit features of the Indian Constitution. Its publication in 1964 was preceded by a year by Donald Eugene Smith's *India as a Secular State*, (1963) which instantaneously and deservedly achieved the status of a premier authoritative work on the subject. Smith's answer to the question whether India was a secular state was a qualified 'yes'. He maintained that one could be cautiously optimistic but not absolutely sure about the future of secularism. 'The forces of Hindu communalism' were the potential threat that would have to be watched carefully, for there was 'much that could go wrong' (1963: 493–501). Needless to emphasize, this was a very perceptive observation, almost a premonition.

These early reservations and warnings received less attention than they deserved. The 1950s and early 1960s, upto Nehru's passing in 1964, were the years of high hope, and even heady enthusiasm, for the votaries of the ideologies of secularism and socialism. When anxieties began to emerge, and later in the 1970s to thicken, these concerned the slow pace of secularization and the recurrence of communal conflict rather than the suitability or viability of received ideas and institutions. A widely discussed public document, voicing serious concern about 'the accelerating pace of retreat from reason' and 'the decay of rationality', was 'A statement on scientific temper', issued in 1981 by a galaxy of intellectuals (see Bhaduri et al. 1981). It called for the fostering of 'scientific temper' (the phrase was attributed to Jawaharlal Nehru) and the recognition of science and technology as 'viable instruments of social transformation'. It drew a spirited retort from the cultural psychologist Ashis Nandy in the form of a 'Counter-statement on humanistic temper' (1981), in which he focused attention on the role of science in 'the institutionalization of suffering' and promotion of modern 'superstitions' and 'authoritarianism'.

Subsequently, Nandy published a radical critique of ideological secularism, under the provocative title of an 'An anti-secularist manifesto' (1985), pointing out that the Indian national movement had stressed that religious tolerance may be derived from an attitude of respectfulness toward all religions, and did not have to depend upon the devaluation of religion. If secularism 'is not to become a reformist sect within modernity, [it] must respect and build upon the faiths and visions that have refused to adapt to the modern worldview' (ibid.: 2). It is not people of faith, Nandy added, but religious zealots and secularists who are respectively against religious tolerance and religion itself. He argued that religious violence becomes unmanageable when its foundation is secular logic and political calculation rather than orthodox religious passion. An increase in the 'pathologies of religion' was, however, only a part of the full story. There was also a turning back to traditional ('non-secular') ideas of religious tolerance (Nandy 2001: 161–88).

Nandy's assertations did not come as a surprise to those Indian scholars familiar with Western sociological literature on secularization; unfortunately not many are, even now. After all, the high noon of the secularization thesis was in the 1970s (see Glasner 1977), and the thesis about its 'self-limiting' nature was being increasingly argued in the 1980s: the process of secularization generates its own reversal through religious revival. The Iranian Revolution of 1978–9 was the best known example of this phenomenon. Nandy's polemical style and occasional carelessness (for example, the opening sentence of his 1985 article—'Gandhi said once in a while that he was secular' [sic]—evoked hostile reactions that have been frenetic and have expanded their scope to excoriate the work of several other scholars who engaged in serious examination of the infirmities of the concept of secularism.

In one of his most recent essays, Nandy writes that the twilight of the certitudes of dogmatic secularism may already be upon us, that the 'concept' [ideology] 'has begun to deliver less and less' (2003: 67). He reiterates his well-known earlier position that tradition had its own ways of dealing effectively with bigotry and communal conflict, which in any case never flared into the kind of large scale riots that defaced the Indian landscape in the twentieth century. But these ways have been eroded by an aggressive secularism just as traditional systems of medicine have been displaced by modern (allopathic) medicine. Nandy thinks that secularism survives today because it serves the 'interests of the hegemonic state (cherished equally by self-styled secularists as well as those they call communalists, by the Congress no less than by the Bharatiya Janata Party) and of those who serve this state' (ibid.: 70–5). In spite of its sweeping character there is much weight in this argument.

I have followed, over the years, Nandy's writings on the theme of religious tolerance, and am in sympathy with the main thrust of his arguments. I agree that, paradoxical though it may seem, religion itself can perhaps still be a resource in the fight against religious bigotry. I also agree that modernity (including secularism), being hegemonic in character, narrows rather than enlarges the domain of significant choice-making, but it surely is not all bad. I do not also agree with all the claims Nandy makes on behalf of abstract religion as against historical religions. He tends to idealize tradition, and does not recognize the enormous philosophical doubts and practical difficulties that will attend any serious attempt at the recovery of religious tolerance in a measure that proves adequate in today's circumstances. It is not only the place of religion in public life that has been challenged, so much else also has changed, including the scale and technology of violence. Our times are not of the local riot of the *lathi* and the knife, they are of the terror symbolized by 9/11.

Let me hasten to add, I am not against such critiques of modernity by intellectuals and civil society groups, and indeed support them. I only want to stress that the cultivation of the pluralist attitude, and of religious tolerance in particular, is not going to be easy. Considering, for instance, the lack of success of the three-language formula, because most Indians are reluctant to seriously learn a second Indian language, what are the chances of religious-minded people in this country taking a genuine interest in faiths other than their own? Is religious tolerance possible unless it is based on engagement and dialogue rather than indifference or avoidance? And what about the secularists? Moreover, historical memories of the pasts of India as shaped by, among other things, the century-old debate about secular and religious nationalisms, have tended to be divisive rather than cohesive.

* * *

Starting off from a different point of departure than Nandy's, I have presented a critique of ideological secularism in several essays, some of which have been collected in Part One of the present volume, and in a book (Madan 1997). One of the early such writings was an address (Madan 1987, Chapter 3 above) in which I emphasized, first, the origin of secularism in the dialectic of Protestant Christianity and the Englightenment and, second, its incompatibility with India's major religious traditions. Consequently, I expressed scepticism about an easy passage of the Western ideology of secularism to India, and stressed the importance of taking religion seriously. The intention was to warn against complacency in both thought and action, to sound a wake-up call. Such is the zeal of the missionaries of secularism that my essay was promptly judged to be heretical and I, along with Nandy, was called 'anti-secularist', a term that he had of course used to describe himself (Nandy 2001: 67). Thanks to the furore, 'Secularism in its place' has enjoyed a long life!

The strategy of the critics has been (i) partial or out of context quotation, (ii) disregard of such of my arguments as clearly contradict the critics' assertions, (iii) insertion of words into my text that are not there, and (iv) attribution of motives. It is with much hesitation that I have decided to address this problem here, more because of its general bearing on scholarly practice than personal significance. In doing so I have drawn on two earlier responses (Madan 1994 and 2003a).

It may be noted that at the beginning of my address I had presented my diagnosis of the infirmities of secularism in South Asia 'in the prevailing circumstances' as a world view, as a political ideology, and as a societal blueprint (see p. 57 above). Several critics have quoted the statement in question in abridged form, implicitly dis-regarding the qualification in respect of *'prevailing circumstances'* and leaving out the clarification of the terms of the diagnosis (see, for example, Baxi 1992 and Béteille 1994)[3]. Thus, I had clarified that secularism was, in my opinion, 'impossible as a credo of life *because* the great majority of the people of South Asia are in their own eyes active adherents of some religious faith' (ibid.).

It will be seen that what occurs in my text primarily as a statement of the facts on the ground at a particular time, and only secondarily as my interpretation of them, appears, because of partial quotation, as an acerbic ideological attack on secularism. Now, I do have my reservations about this Enlightenment ideology, more so about the received wisdom regarding it, and so have many other scholars about the Enlightenment itself (see, for example, Toulmin 1990). The statement in question was intended to state some of them and to draw attention to their implications for the Indian political experiment. It was not a plea for the abandonment of the secular state. To draw attention to the limitations of the original ideology of secularism and its Indian version does not necessarily imply that one totally rejects the ideologies or the institutions that embody them. Critiques may well result in strengthening the institutions concerned if the necessary corrective or reinforcing measures, practical as well as ideological, are carefully put in place. I am sceptical about the easy confidence of secularists regarding unproblematic adaptation.

Apropos my stress on the positive significance of religion, Béteille observes: 'What causes the most anxiety to secular intellectuals is a conception of religion which demands that every aspect of every individual's life be brought under religious scrutiny and control' (ibid.: 562 fn 2). He refers to it as the 'totalizing aims' of religion, more demanding in some cases than in others. The crucial question is, he writes, 'how much space will be allowed within society by doctrinaire religion for the growth of secular ideas and institutions' (ibid.: 564) . I agree that this is a key question and, as Béteille acknowledges, it applies, mutatis mutandis, to all doctrinaire ideologies, religious as well as secular.

I would like to emphasize here, since I perhaps overstated the holistic character of traditional religions, that I do not read the Hindu tradition as absolutely totalistic, denying the existence of what may be called secular elements, but rather as a case of a hierarchical relation between the religious and the secular (or the encompassing of the contrary). Although I use the language made familiar by Louis Dumont, the idea of encompassment itself may be derived from the key concept of *purushārtha*, or the triple goals of human endeavour (dharma, *artha*, *kāma*) as presented in the classical texts, notably, the *Arthashāstra* and the *Manusmriti*. Moreover, the traditional view of the hierarchical relationship of the sacerdotal and the royal functions is relevant to the extent that the Hindu tradition does not provide us with a dualistic view of the kind that Christianity does. The Christian distinction between what is due to God and what to Caesar is widely held to have contributed to the success of the modern ideology of secularism in the West, which restated it as the separation of the Church and the state.

This does not mean that Indians have first to be converted to Christianity before they may be expected to appreciate the virtues of the political ideology of secularism (see p. 102 above). It only draws attention to the need for greater efforts on the part of Indian intellectuals to elaborate the notion of secularism in a context-sensitive manner, drawing upon India's pluralist traditions as well as the Western ideology of liberalism. There is sufficient historical and ethnographical evidence that it is the masses of this country, Hindus and Muslims alike, who are comfortable with religious pluralism, and indeed practise it in one form or another. The traditional elite, from whom the great majority of today's intellectuals are descended, generally disapproved of such pluralism as the superstitious ways of the masses.

Not only have Indian intellectuals to make greater efforts to clarify the notion of secularism and distinguish between different connotations of the term; they also have to devise the most effective ways of communication, carrying the people with them, although not in the manner of the politicians. Unless they do this, the intellectuals will succeed only in convincing one another. Secularism has to be rescued from the prevailing semantic conflation, but this should not mean the imposition of one particular meaning on it, and it has to be made into a national ethos. Despite some ongoing efforts, the task of clarification is not yet complete; it will take time.

Let me now turn briefly to the two other devices of critics mentioned above. Sunil Khilnani (a political scientist) writes that the argument underlying 'Secularism in its place' leads to the conclusion that 'the religious preferences of the majority rule the state' (1999: 180). This inference completely ignores a clear affirmation at the end of the address, that I was 'not advocating the establishment of a Hindu State in India, not at all' (p. 72 above). Further, I had 'suggested that the only way secularism in South Asia, understood as interreligious understanding, may succeed would be for us to take both religion and secularism seriously' (ibid.), thus anticipating much later formulations, such as Martin Marty's (2003) notion of a 'religio-secular world'.

Khilnani does not tell his readers, for whom he provides a list of essential readings and graciously includes my *Modern Myths, Locked Minds: Secularism and Fundamentalism in India* (1997) under the topic of secularism, that I explicitly reject majoritarianism in that book (p. 251).

Another critic, P.C. Chatterji (a moral philosopher), had already concluded that my address advocated Hindu rule in a shamefaced manner. He wrote (1995: 111):

> Prof. Madan has argued that religion confers order and meaning on the lives of the vast majority of the people who in India are Hindus. It is moral arrogance on the part of the secularists, because they are a minority, to preach to the majority to change their religious beliefs. The argument points to the conclusion that India should transform itself into a Hindu state.

Somehow mindful of the fact that I had rejected the idea of a Hindu state, Chatterji decided to read my mind: 'was he simply shying away from this conclusion because such a view might not be popular with an American audience?' (ibid.).

Needless to remind the reader of the present book that the impugned address nowhere identifies the majority of the people of India as Hindus: what it does say is that the great majority of the people of South Asia are believers in 'some religious faith'. Blatant distortion could not go further; so the knowledgeable author inferred that my fear of my audience made me hide my true intentions. This is simply outrageous ! But then there are two more critics (a geographer and an economist) who also let free rein to their imagination: 'Madan seems to be arguing that secularism *should* not work in India because it is a foreign ideology' (Corbridge and Harriss 2001: 197, original emphasis). I refer my readers to the essays in Parts One, Two, and Three of this book and to *Modern Myths, Locked Minds* (particularly pp. 272–9), to know what my position is, notwithstanding what it '*seems to be*' to some fanciful authors.

Finally, I may mention the case where I was credited with a statement that does not exist in 'Secularism in its place'. The second part of one of the concluding sentences was that the principal question that faced us was 'not whether Indian society would eventually become secularized...*but rather in what sense it should become so and by what means*' (p. 71, new emphasis).

This appeared as follows in a book by a historian: 'but rather whether it is desirable that it should' (Hasan 1997: 134). Following my protest, the distortion was acknowledged by the author as an inadvertence; the necessary correction was made in a subsequent edition of the book.

The foregoing is, I believe, enough to indicate the nature and extent of misunderstanding or misrepresentation of an admittedly condensed text of 1987; it was given as a lecture in limited time. Most of my critics seem to have read nothing else that I have written on the subject, disregarding the fact that no scholar's thinking on a controversial contemporary issue of both intellectual and public importance is not normally frozen, unless of course he or she has what I have called a locked mind.[4]

There is one critic though, Achin Vanaik (1997: 153–62 et passim), who has indeed read quite a few things that I have written, more than may have seemed directly relevant, but it is 'Secularism in its place' that is used by him too as a guide to my other work. The problem of my condensed text crops up again in his reading of it. How can I, he asks, maintain simultaneously that, first, the ideology of secularism has not made much progress in India despite the effort of a secularist minority to impose it upon the majority, and, secondly, the state has not done enough to promote it? The argument is simple: that the ideology has been met with opposition or indifference is a fact; that the state has relied excessively on the constitutional (legislative and judicial) route is also a fact. The role of the educational process and of civil society, for instance, has not received enough attention. As M.N. Roy succinctly put it once, secularism is an ethos, it cannot be enacted.

It should be noted here that not all readers seem to have had problems understanding what I have written, although they do not agree with all of it. Rajeev Bhargava (1998) and Asim Roy (2005) are excellent examples. Bhargava even correctly reads the title of the 1987 address: 'putting "Secularism in its place" must mean finding for modern secularism an appropriate means of expression in its specific Indian setting' (ibid.: 524). That indeed is it. Writing nearly twenty years after the address was composed, Roy (ibid.: 13–16) is able to look back from a balanced perspective and puts his finger on not only what I said but also on that which the critics got wrong.

As I have said above, the issues of misunderstanding and illegitimate inference are important because they obstruct certain lines of inquiry that some of us tried to open in the 1980s. Not long after Nandy's and my early essays, Partha Chatterjee, a political theorist, also sought to clear the conceptual confusion and carry the discussion forward. Ignoring significant differences in the scope and style of these interventions the uncritical critics slapped the label of anti-secularists on us to reiterate their own dogmatic positions. I must briefly recall here Chatterjee's seminal contribution to the debate on secularism (Chatterjee 1994/1998).

* * *

Partha Chatterjee's point of departure was 'the political challenge of Hindu majoritarianism', particularly I presume in the wake of the Ramjanmabhumi agitation of the late 1980s and the subsequent demolition of the Babri Masjid at Ayodhya in 1992. 'The majoritarianism of the Hindu right,' he wrote perceptively, 'is perfectly at peace with the institutional procedures of the "western" or "modern state"' (1998: 346). The question that arose therefore was, 'Is the defence of secularism an appropriate ground for meeting the challenge of the Hindu right? Or should it be fought where the attack is being made, i.e. should the response be a defense of the duty of the democratic state to ensure policies of religious toleration' (ibid.: 348)? The short history of the secular state in India, which derived its basic principles of liberty, equality, and neutrality from the West had revealed the anomalies into which it had run in the Indian historical and cultural setting.

The crucial issue that had emerged from the muddling was the articulation of the best means of protecting the right of a minority to live as a minority. Chatterjee's carefully argued answer was 'toleration...premised on autonomy and respect for persons' was the reasonable course to follow in the Indian situation, so that the minorities can 'resist homogenization from outside and push for democratization from inside' (ibid.: 375, 378). Chatterjee's constructive intervention in the debate did indeed seek to move 'beyond secularism' after pointing out the difficulties in which the secular state in India had become enmeshed. But almost as he had expected, Chatterjee too had to face resistance, but the wall had surely begun to show some cracks.

Writing about the same time as Chatterjee, economist Amartya Sen (1998) drew attention to a new 'intellectual scepticism', underscored the 'incompleteness of secularism, and the need to go beyond', and regretted the 'reluctance' of 'secularist intellectuals in India' to address the issues that had been presented by critics such as Varshney (1993), Nandy and myself, and later others. In a well organized but rapid review of the various critiques, he concluded that in an 'integrally pluralist society' secularism as the 'symmetric political treatment of different religious communities' (ibid.: 484) was an imperative. In fact, the pluralist social structure of the country had long had the cultural backdrop of toleration (ibid.: 478). That, such open mindedness notwithstanding, Sen chooses to call himself an 'unreformed secularist' is, I believe, a matter of personal preference. The important thing is that he emphasized the need for discussion, which is what I also have stressed all along.

Another political theorist, Rajeev Bhargava, presented a defence of secularism which included a significant clarification of the concept and a constructive critique of 'the Madan–Nandy thesis' (Bhargava 1994, 1998). I accept his contention that 'Secularism in its place' suffers from a certain conflation of two distinct notions of secularism (the ethical and the political, as he calls them). My essay did mention the Enlightenment and Indian versions of secularism, the one calling for the privatization of religion and the other advocating the state policy of acknowledgement of the presence (even legitimacy) of religion in public life and the symmetric treatment of their followers. My criticism of the former was read by many critics as my rejection of the latter. Actually, this misunderstanding should not have occurred (even Bhargava did not get me right on this point) because I had explicitly written that in South Asia we need to take both religion and secularism seriously. It should hardly be necessary in our time to have to say that, as many scholars, including Durkheim and Weber among the sociologists (see Chapter 1 above), have long acknowledged, religion and science do not pertain to the same areas of human life and, therefore, there is no essential conflict between them.

Bhargava's thesis of two secularisms is an important contribution and should be pursued seriously. According to him:

Ethical Secularism…seeks the separation of religion from politics by virtue of the contribution it makes to the realization of some ultimate ideal. The second type of secularism, I shall call, Political Secularism because, rather than contribute to the realization of some external comprehensive set of ultimate ideals, the separation of religion from politics, on this view, merely makes for a more livable polity (1998: 492).

It is clear that, although narrower in scope, political secularism is not less important than ethical secularism. In its absence the larger enterprise of providing space for the pursuit of ethical secularism itself may be jeopardized. Political secularism does not challenge the legitimacy of ultimate goals, whether these be said to flow from religion or ethical secularism; it only excludes them from the political arena and the larger public square, or neutralizes them by treating different religions and ethical traditions symmetrically (the celebratory *sarva dharma samabhava* of India).

The problem that remains is how to render a society 'guided by principles of political secularism…in the long run…a viable community' (ibid.: 508). Obviously, Bhargava holds the view (and I agree with it) that societies do not live on stratagems alone, even though politics may be a matter of, in F.G. Bailey's (1969) famous phrase, 'strategems and spoils'. Politics do not constitute human life in its entirety as (to borrow Weber's deeply insightful words of almost a century ago) 'every one of us who is not spiritually dead must realize'. It follows that 'an ethic of ultimate ends and an ethic of responsibility are not absolute contrasts but rather supplements' (1948: 127). Considerations of ethical secularism, or of religion, may be postponed, they must not be shelved.

As for the relationship of ethical secularism and religion, Bhargava detects the existence of 'quite irreconcilable conflict', although he says in an aside that this may not be true of all versions of ethical secularism (1998: 495). This is a complex issue with definitional and substantive dimensions, and calls for a fuller and more nuanced discussion than he provides. One would have to convincingly argue that the principle of ethical secularism (or secular humanism), such as respect for human life, liberty, and dignity, is necessarily absent from religious ethics. I am sure Bhargava does not want to take such a position, for he agrees with Nandy and me that 'the resources of religious tolerance', derived from the religious traditions (I presume), must be deployed to confront bigotry and social conservatism. Indeed, he considers such deployment, alongside 'a strong defence of minority rights' and the consolidation of 'whatever space of the common good [that] already exists' [ibid.: 542], as a kind of minimum definition of Indian secularism. I find this agreeable. I do think, however, that the issue of the determination of the minority status of a community is not addressed adequately by him.[5]

I again agree with Bhargava, political secularism is more than 'a good fallback strategy', it may be 'the only available way to prevent a community from falling apart' (ibid.: 511). And if that political community happens to be multi-religious like the Indian, the secular state may have to intervene in the areas of life of the citizenry that are seen by them to belong to the domain of religion, so long as this is done in a non-discriminatory (which does not necessarily mean identical) manner. In the language of the Indian Constitution, for example, 'The state shall endeavour to secure for the citizens a uniform [not *common*] civil code throughout the territory of India' (Article 44). Moreover, the state shall have to ensure 'a strong defence of minority rights' (Bhargava 1998: 542), the justification for which I have argued earlier, juxtaposing 'Hindu insensitivity to the feelings of those who consider themselves non-Hindu' with the valid 'anxieties and sensitivities of the minorities' (see pp. 92 and 103 above).

In Chapter 4 above, I have discussed at some length and in historical perspective the majority–minority conundrum. It lies at the very core of the contemporary debate on Indian secularism. In *Beyond Secularism* (1999), Neera Chandhoke, yet another political theorist, argues rigorously for the rights of religious minorities. She writes that formal equality is the justificatory principle of Indian secularism and the foundation of the secular state's policy of non-discrimination. But formal equality in a setting of demographic and socio-economic inequalities is a recipe for the perpetuation of inequalities. The policy of *sarva dharma samabhāva*, unexceptionable in itself, is of little use if minorities are victims of systematic neglect on the part of the state, and unable to mobilize the necessary resources to hold their own against the assertiveness of the majority. What is called for, therefore, Chandhoke maintains, is a corrective policy based on the notion of substantive equality, so that the minorities may be compensated for the conditions of political and economic deprivation that cannot reasonably be said to be their own creation, and enabled to preserve their cultural heritage. The state should therefore be required to put in place 'supportive structures', which are exclusive to the minorities, to enable them to survive without loss of cultural identity and prosper like anybody else.

'The idea of shifting ground from secularism to equality', Chandhoke observes, 'is not meant to devalue the concept', but to strengthen it and, indeed, to help it to realize the goal of equality. 'Secularism alone cannot do this; for in its present form, it has simply exhausted its potential. We will have to go beyond secularism to look for ways in which relationships between communities can be arranged in a just and fair manner' (ibid.: 95–6). The notion of tolerance too is inadequate: she develops at length a holistic framework for achieving the stated goal on the basis of interwoven patterns of democracy, equality, and rights. The last category is in some ways the most crucial and also complex as there is inherent in it a tension arising from the fact that the rights of the individual do not always coincide with that of the community. Chandhoke comes out on the side of the individual characterizing the rights of the community as 'conditional'.

The supportive structures that Chandhoke mentions were in principle written into the Constitution as, for instance, when, under Articles 29 and 30, the minorities were given the fundamental (inalienable) right to establish their own educational institutions. But more can be done as, for instance, in promoting minority languages and literatures and other artistic and creative activities. She goes quite far in developing this argument, and runs the risk of being criticized for making recommendations that would perpetuate communal identities and also not be quite workable. Thus, how could the state prevent the Parsis from dying out through intermarriage, or a tribal community from disappearing through gradual absorption into the surrounding caste-based Hindu society or willing conversion to Christianity?

Mukul Kesavan, a historian, in a short polemical work, argues that Chandhoke's recommendations could be 'dangerous' as they would allow majoritarian Hindus to 'substantiate' their 'fantastical claim' that 'the Indian state is perversely against India's majority community'. The cost of substantive equality, such as advocated by Chandhoke, would be 'unacceptably high'. Reversing her argument, he advises 'modesty' and settles for 'procedural equality, not preferential rights based on minority status' (2001: 22). To the best of my knowledge, this important and urgent argument has made no progress. It is regrettable that interventions in the secularism debate often end up as occasional forays for lack of collective engagement with them. Often even their authors do not pursue them.

Kesavan's charge against India's intellectuals and the state is that, in their hands, secularism has been 'often shrunk to one of its functions, minority protection'. He derides their attitude as an 'all-are-welcome' doctrine of 'behalfism'. 'Secularism in independent India soon became patronage when it was practised by the State and gallantry when it was practiced by the secular' and by 'chivalrous' Hindus (ibid.: 10–11). When then did it become 'passé'? He of course mentions the rise of Hindu chauvinism. More interestingly, he suggests that being secular was for the Nehruvian elite 'a hegemonic style—it was fashionable': 'it wasn't a political stance [firm stand, ideological commitment ?].... And styles change' (ibid.: 28–30). That is true, but whatsoever it may have been for the elite generally, secularism for Nehru was surely a matter of both substance and style. This line of inquiry also is worth pursuing.

What is to be done? Some obvious things, Kesavan thinks. For instance, the Indian state should endeavour 'to establish restraining norms' that enable it 'to work credibly for all its constituents' (ibid.: 118). Secular coalitions of various kinds have been successful and therefore hold considerable promise. Of his other recommendations I am less sure, because I do not always know what he means. Is he recommending reservations for Muslims when he contends that reservations for Dalits (and, I guess, OBCs) are a reservation for Hindus? If so, would not this mean those same separate electorates that were a prelude to partition? 'Secular common sense', I fear, is an elusive idea; it could even be dangerous.

The debate on Indian secularism has continued and the doubts about simplistic expositions of complex notions have deepened. In an innovative turn of phrase, the sociologist Dipankar Gupta has asserted that the old rhetoric of secularism, 'hoping for a change of heart to come along' (2002: 4618), has not worked, nor for that matter has the notion of tolerance. What is called for, he

says, is 'intolerant secularism', which in effect is a call to the
Indian state to discharge its responsibility to govern—to exercise
its authority—firmly and impartially, and guarantee 'the
inalienable rights of citizen' and 'the due process of law, in the
context of communal violence' (ibid.: 4619). Gupta has not (as far
as I know) developed this thesis in any subsequent publication
of note. One would have agreed with this without any reservations,
but after the Gujarat carnage of 2002, which provided the stimulus
for his intervention, one can no longer be sure that a blatantly
partisan government will not bend the institutions of the state to
serve communal and party objectives rather than protect and
promote the interests of the citizenry. There is urgent need to
keep the state itself under watch lest 'the war of all against
all' should be unleashed under its umbrella. Who will be the
watchdog? Civil society—comprising voluntary associations,
giving expression to general concerns, providing the means for
collective (not necessarily communitarian) action, and mediating
between citizens and primary groups—on the one hand, and the
state, on the other.[6]

There is considerable and welcome interest today in the nature
and scope of civil society's initiatives. Issues like the constitution
of civil society (are religious institutions and organizations in, as
in Europe, or out?), and its relations with the state (adversarial,
complementary, regulatory), are being debated. By definition
civil society is heterogeneous: it thrives in pluralist settings.
Throughout *Modern Myths, Locked Minds*, from the first epigraph
to the last paragraph, runs the conviction that participatory
pluralism, rather than a hegemonic and homogenizing secularism,
is what will serve India's interests best (see Madan 1999, 2005).
Some commentators, I might note, have recognized this critical
strand of my argument (see, for example, Joseph 1998: 167–8).
Needless to emphasize, pluralism is contextual, comes in several
kinds, and poses many intractable problems, of which cultural
relativism is one of the most debated.[7]

* * *

In an overview of the debate on secularism worldwide, Nikki
Keddie observes that 'India has produced perhaps the world's

largest contemporary body of publications debating the merits of secularism' (2003: 28). This, I presume must be true, but I have been struck by the fact that the preoccupation with India, while giving discussions some depth, has tended to make them insular (as I said at the beginning of this chapter). One major reason for this may be that secularism has acquired the character of a doctrine of redemption. It is not politicians and journalists only but social scientists also who have cryptically pronounced secularism as India's destiny (Béteille 1994). In the event, critical discussion has been stymied. Fresh thinking on broad theoretical issues has, in recent years, emanated more from where the original formulations came than, a few notable exceptions apart, from Indian scholars. Some of the discussion in the West is still working out the significance of the varieties (societal, organizational, individual) of secularism (see, for example, Dobbelaere 2002). Other writings, more radical in nature, have identified certain problems that should engage our attention in India. I do not, once again, intend to attempt a survey of contemporary literature, but would like to illustratively draw attention to some recent refreshingly radical formulations to which we have, I think, much to contribute.

The setting for these reformulations is provided by the events of the last quarter of the twentieth century, notably the Iranian and Nicaraguan Revolutions and the collapse of the secular communist state in Poland in the face of the Solidarity Movement which had the support of the Roman Catholic Church (see Chapter 1 above and Casanova 1994). The 1990s, already under the shadow of religious fundamentalisms virtually everywhere in the world (see Marty and Appleby 1991, 1995), were witness to the end, for all practical purposes, of the Marxist version of the ideology of secularism. Even the liberal version with its emphasis on the privatization of religious belief faced the challenge, whether acknowledged or not, of reconsidering the role of religion in public life. As Casanova put it, 'we are witnessing the "deprivatization" of religion in the modern world ... religions are here to stay, thus putting to rest one of the cherished dreams of the Enlightenment' (ibid.: 5–6). In other words, we must redefine the relationship of religion to the public square and more fundamentally to modernity itself.

One way of doing this seemingly is unproblematic, and best stated in Charles Taylor's words: 'A thoroughly post-Durkhemian society would be one in which our religious belonging would be unconnected to our national identity. It will certainly be one in which the gamut of religious allegiances will be wide and varied' (2003: 111–12). In other words, a complementary relationship of the secular (non-discriminatory) state and a religiously plural society is envisaged, such as we are familiar with in India. Doubts will persist whether citizens who actively affirm particular religious beliefs and adhere to the related religious practices will be truly neutral in their capacity as functionaries of the state. The only assurance can come from the strength of secular institutions that will restrain individual proclivities. But the usual problem of reification arises here.

Taylor has another formulation also: secularity should mean 'the disappearance of an ontic dependence on something higher', and its replacement by a strong presence of God in our political identity, just as God's presence survives in our personal life in which 'devotion' is immune to the inroads of disenchantment (in the Schiller-Weber sense of the term). It is obvious that Taylor's use of the phrase 'presence of God' is here to be construed in abstract non-denominational terms, as an awareness to which one bears witness in both one's private and public lives. The possibility of religion being a 'defining constituent in political identities' is, on this view, always present, 'virtually everywhere', but carries with it the risk of 'a reinvasion of the political identity by the confessional'. Taylor thinks this is precisely what has happened in India with the rise of the BJP (2004: 193–4). What is obviously indicated here is the possibility of alternative kinds of religiousness rather than the total displacement of religion from the public sphere; it is the view that 'religion occupies a different place, compatible with the sense that all social action takes place in profane time' (ibid.: 194). I am not sure whether the Taylorian project is to reconcile the two scenarios, or whether they are deemed to be already reconciled within a democratic framework, for 'the inescapability of secularism flows from the nature of the modern...democratic state'(Taylor 1998: 38).

With this last point—'no secularism; no democracy'—John Keane (2000: 5) is in strong disagreement. He questions the assumption that secularization 'promotes open-minded tolerance, itself a vital ingredient of a pluralist democracy' (ibid.: 6). Indeed,

Keane is in disagreement with the presumptuousness and prescriptiveness of the secularists who base their case about 'a fully secular world stripped of religious illusions and foundational certainties' on selective empirical evidence (ibid.: 8). On his showing, and indeed also on my reading of the relevant literature, this is a charge that sticks.

Echoing Marx's perceptive remarks about the self-contradictoriness of the secular basis of the religious world in the fourth thesis on Feuerbach (see the first epigraph of this chapter), without citing him, Keane questions the certitudes of secularists about the future, for these are, according to him, based on a wishful reading of the history of the West as a story of settled scores of the Judeo-Christian struggles for power. 'The victory of the forces favouring the "privatization" of religion within civil society may yet prove to be temporary and (considered as an episode in the complex history of religious politics) fleeting' (ibid.: 11). The reasons are several. Condensing Keane's argument, I will mention just two. First, if secularism (in its liberal version) guarantees freedom of conscience, it follows that it must provide spaces to citizens for freedom of religious association, just as there are spaces where religion is absent. Religious believers use their space to work for the 'rebirth of God'.

In other words, and as already noted, secularization is a self-limiting process that gives birth to religious revivalism or religious innovation—worldwide phenomena that may be illustrated as well from what has been happening in India as in the USA since the 1970s. In Keane's words, 'secularizing societies display a propensity to replace religiosity with existential uncertainty [and this] prompts the return of the sacred in everyday life' (ibid.: 12). One form (not the only one) of this return of 'religiousness' as such is that of, in the words of Clifford Geertz (2005), 'religious mindedness'—the replacement of 'everyday reflexive faith' by 'self-conscious, doctrinaire belief ' (ibid.: 9–10), which, I may add, readily becomes a public political ideology of dominance. Others more generally have called it fundamentalism.

It is, therefore, to Keane's last example about the self-contradictoriness of secularism that I want to draw particular attention, because it pinpoints a most dangerous possibility: namely 'the theoretical and practical affinity' of secularism with 'political despotism'. Keane writes:

For the principle of secularism, which 'represents a realization of crucial motifs of Christianity itself' (Benhoffer), is arguably founded upon a sublimated version of Christian belief that Christianity is 'the religion of religions' (Schleiermacher), and that Christianity is entitled to decide for non-Christian others what they can think or say or even whether they are capable of thinking and saying anything at all (ibid.: 14).

This is precisely what I had in mind when I said in 1987: 'For the secularist minority to stigmatize the majority as primordially oriented and to preach secularism to the latter as the law of human existence is moral arrogance and worse—I say worse since in our times politics take precedence over ethics—political folly' (pp. 57–8 above). The negative reaction to my plea for caution convinced me that the uncritical secularists too are fundamentalists and have locked minds (see Madan 1997).

The problem is that secularists generally do not acknowledge their 'immodesty' as William Connolly calls it (see the second epigraph of this chapter). His call to rework 'the secular problematic' has not, as far as I know, found many echoes in India. Doctrines of manifest destiny are, I believe, less demanding of intellectual effort than ideologies: the former are received, the latter have to be constructed and defended. The aphorism 'Secularism is India's destiny' calls for assent; the argument that in a religiously plural society the state must be secular (neutral) calls for theoretical elaboration and practical action. What is needed is that we first recognize that several secularisms walk the high street of the Indian political arena, and (as already noted earlier in this chapter) beyond this arena there is a domain of ethics and world views. These various ideologies then need to be brought to the negotiating table, as it were, within a truly pluralistic framework, not in the search for some single Truth, but in the quest for what Connolly calls a 'modus vivendi'. The first principle on which to base the discussion is 'the 'profound contestability' of everybody's 'fundamentals' in the sense that, while one may not give up one's own beliefs, one should extend the same courtesy to the others, thus 'decentering the political imagination of the ensconced contestants so that each becomes an honored participant in a pluralistic culture rather than the authoritative embodiment of it' (Connolly 1999: 6).

I have elsewhere (for example, Madan 1997: 279; 1999; 2005) called this 'participatory pluralism' and cited Gandhi as an exemplar of it. In a genuine dialogue one begins with honest concession that one could be wrong on some points just as one is right on others. 'Where' and 'how precisely' one is wrong has to be found, and for this one needs a like-minded interlocutor. Recognition of one's vulnerability—of the incompleteness of one's faith, as Gandhi would have had it—can be converted into a source of moral strength. If it is mutual, it could start a virtuous circle.

Connolly's discussion of 'the conceits of secularism' covers the ground incisively in respect of the Western intellectual traditions. But there is more to the world than the West, there is China for a notable instance. India's cultural ties with China, although 2000 years old, became attenuated in later times, but that is no reason why we should not enlarge our understanding of secularism by examining the Chinese version. Wang Gungwu (2003) has pointed out that the millennia old 'this-worldiness' of the Chinese did not originate in any conflict between the political and the sacerdotal, but rather that 'the secular outlook ensured that no church would be established to challenge political authority' (ibid.: 309). In a setting of warring polities, not of wars of religion, 'secularization of public affairs became the norm', and this was in consonance with 'Confucius' insistence that people should be concerned with this life and not speculate about the next' (ibid.: 313). Religion did not have to be privatized in China, it already was elsewhere. I am not concerned here with the implications of the secular ethic for the later history of China down to contemporary times which, Gungwu sketches succinctly: my interest rather is to draw attention to the preoccupation of the debate on secularism in India with the religious and political history of the West, and the imperative of enlarging one's mind by looking elsewhere too. If in the West the church and the state have had to be separated, and in China they never were together, one can argue that, in India dharma traditionally encompassed 'secular' activity including kingship. And, 'reverberations' of the relationship have been heard in contemporary times too (see Mayer 1982).

* * *

For a final comment I come back to India today. In the debate on secularism the 'academic field' reflects, I think, the 'power field', which may be characterized in terms of different sets of relations. One such characterization hinges on the interplay of demography, geography, history, and ideology.

The four-fifths majority of the Hindus (80.5 per cent) in the population of the country, and the considerable share at 13.4 per cent of the Muslims in it (between themselves the two religious 'communities' account for 94 per cent of the total, with Christians and Sikhs accounting for a little over 4 per cent in about equal measure), creates a severe lack of balance which generates fears of majoritarianism that are not wholly unrealistic. I might add in passing that among those counted at the 2001 census, less than 1 per cent were silent on the question of their religious identity. This is not merely a demographic datum; it is a sociological fact of immense political significance.

The geographical distribution of the Muslims, with only two states out of 35 having an absolute majority (Lakshadweep 95 per cent and Jammu and Kashmir 67 per cent) and three others having about one-fourth share in the population (Assam 31 per cent, West Bengal and Kerala 25 per cent each), reveals extreme spatial unevenness. Moreover, at the district and lower levels, there are many pockets of Muslim concentration (old or new) generating a sense of security among the residents, but renewed fears of Muslim separatism among the others. Parochial programmes of traditional (madrasa) education, resistence to social reform, exclusivist claims to historical monuments, etc., aggravate the situation.

History speaks in multiple voices. Hindu and Muslim readings of the past are often not the same. The demand for parity for the two communities, or for weightage, in employment and political representation in the years leading up to partition in disregard of the population statistics, but in recognition of the historical role of Muslims during the 'medieval' period, on the one hand, and negative readings of the same period by some Hindu historians and their empathetic readers, on the other, went a long way in creating both deep cleavage and distrust. Eventually the partition came to be seen on both sides as the result of a community consensus among the Muslims rather than the handiwork of a party (Muslim League) or its top leadership (see Shaikh 1989). As such, it was and is generally regarded as an achievement by Pakistani and Bangladeshi Muslims, and as the betrayal of Muslim interests by Indian Muslims (see Hasan 1997), and of larger national interests by many others. One might have thought all these differences now belonged to the past, but the unfortunate course of events that ultimately led to the demolition of the Babri Masjid and the Gujarat pogrom, from which the country has not yet recovered, revealed that this is not so. The situation has been complicated by the emergence of a militant separatist movement among Kashmiri Muslims in the late 1980s (see Chapters 6 and 7 below), some of whom claim to be the third nation of the subcontinent, and international terrorism, and by the upsurge of Hindutva.[8]

Finally, the ideological ambiguities of Indian secularism, which I have discussed above, have generated more heat than light. The facts of demographic and geographic distribution are virtually unalterable. But multiple readings of history and construction of accommodative, forward-looking, ideologies of nationhood and pluralism provide immense scope for human agency. Some years ago, as the movement for the European Union gathered support, one of France's leading intellectuals, Paul Ricoeur, and others like him, gave the call for overcoming the bitter legacies of the past through such means as the 'exchange of memories', 'promotion of plural readings of founding events', 'narrative hospitality', and above all, 'forgiveness' (Ricoeur 1992). If the West, which we like call materialist, can think in such terms (Ricoeur writes of 'spiritual density'), maybe Indian intellectuals also can do the same. And maybe secularism can yet be reworked as an ideology of participatory pluralism based on the values of dignity (equality of rights) and freedom of conscience, attentive to new situational exigencies and open to radical ways of conceptualizing and coping with them. The foregoing values (and others like them), it must be remembered, can become imperatives only within the normative frameworks of particular configurations of cultural life, and the social practices of particular communities.

As for the state, its policy, as I have argued in more than one place in this book, should have the twin objectives of, first, protecting everybody's freedom of conscience (as provided for in the Constitution) and, secondly, contrary to present practice, denying without exception financial assistance for the practice of religion. Let me recall, once again, Gandhi's admonition that a religion that depends on state support for its existence does not deserve to exist. Thus would the policy of uniform treatment of all religious communities (*sarva dharma samabhāva*) be truly implemented.

NOTES

1. In Chapter 3 above, I have described Jinnah as a public figure who began as a secularist and ended as one, and deviated from the nationalist to the communalist path only temporarily. This calls for correction, for it is a fact of history that Jinnah himself disowned his earlier political goal of self-governance for a united India, which he pursued for more than two decades (1910–34), when he became the principal exponent of the 'two nation theory' (Wells 2005). The formal bow to the secular state once the partition had been announced turned out to be just that (Wolpert ibid.: 339), if not worse, hypocrisy and opportunism. His closet comrades did not allow him to turn his back on the concept of an Islamic state of Pakistan. In any case, he was in 1947 a man on his death bed. When I wrote (in 1987) of Jinnah's secularist orientation, what I had in mind was that communalism was Jinnah's strategy to secure for Indian Muslims what he considered a fair deal in the context of their economic and political rights. He showed no interest in the quality of their religious life; as is well known, he himself was a non-practising Muslim. Jinnah may have begun as a secularist, and ended as one, but the genie could not be put back in the bottle!

2. For an insightful argument regarding a 'secular contract' between Muslim rulers and their Hindu subjects, which had been gradually evolved during the medieval period and continued thereafter, having been breached in the 1980s and eventually virtually destroyed when the Babri Masjid was demolished, see Gould 1999.

3. Upendra Baxi is a jurist and André Béteille, a sociologist. I cite them from among several other critics, who have likewise abridged my text, because of their eminence as scholars.

4. At least one of the critics considered it sufficient to discuss my essay because it seemed to him to be representative of the views that he disapproved. 'In this article I will mainly use Madan and that for one simple reason, his is a neatly argued out position cast in a rational mould' (Alam 1994: 36. n2). He of course focuses on what he calls 'Madan's anti-secularism'.

5. It is often suggested that the status of a community as a minority (or majority) should be determined by its demographic strength at the macro level, irrespective of regional or local variations. How problematic this is becomes immediately clear when we recall that

around the time militant secessionism arose in Kashmir (1989), Muslims of the Kashmir Valley accounted for 95 per cent of the population and the Hindus for 4 per cent.

6. Apropos the necessity of taking on the state in certain situations, an unusual contribution to the debate on secularism has come from a philosopher. Vinit Haksar (2001) suggests that the secularism of the Indian Constitution is accommodative, seeking to harmonize contradictory values of different religious traditions in the wholeness of a composite culture. To realize such an ideal in real life, however, is far from easy (as the experience of more than half a century attests). The obstacles are many and include the possibility of the state becoming biased in favour of the dominant community. In such a contingency, Haksar argues, a case can be made for 'extra-constitutional safeguards, such as civil disobedience [of the Gandhian kind] for the disadvantaged and marginalized' (ibid.: 102), and presumably the victimized also.

7. Lack of both space and competence forbid an engagement here with the jurisdical discourse. Discussions of the constitutional dimension of secularism are, of course, very important and the accumulated corpus is quite large. It is no less marked by ambiguities and controversies than the debates among social scientists. Certain judgements of the Supreme Court have propounded notions such as secularism being a part of 'the basic structure of the Constitution' without clarifying this fundamental notion. It reminds one of 'the original construction' of the American Constitution that conservative justices and politicians in the USA (the so-called 'orignalists') often invoke in defence of their agenda. Other judgements and obiter dicta of Indian Supreme Court justices, including one on the character of Hindutva, have produced clarifications as well as uncertainties and even dismay (see Crossman and Kapur 1999).

As for the recent contributions of the politicians and the media, these are undoubtedly important as indicators of shifting political alignments and chicanery. Political formulations like the National Democratic Alliance and the United Progressive Alliance, each claim to be the torch-bearers of 'true' secularism; the former call the latter the 'pseudo secularists'; and the latter reciprocate with the slur of 'communal forces'. It often descends to the level of puerility. While Sonia Gandhi lauds the pluralistic tolerance of Hinduism, and she and Atal Behari Vajpayee respectively extol the Shankaracharya of Kanchipuram as the 'symbol of unity' and the 'upholder of secularism' (this happened in June 2003 well before the Acharya's arrest in late 2004 on criminal charges, as yet unproven), George Fernandes neatly divides the people of India into the 'normal' and 'secularist' categories!

The media of course wield the time tested weapons of short shrift and the one-liner. One of the most respected journalists of India, Kuldip Nayar wrote recently: 'We in India...believed that there was a fuzzy area of overlap which went on expanding. That was secularism and the sense of tolerance and the spirit of accommodation that grew out of it was the glue that held us together' (2004: 64). In the face of such home-grown confidence, one can only plead guilty to the charge of scepticism.

8. Limitations of space preclude discussion of Hindutva in its current phase, following the establishment of the Vishwa Hindu Parishad in 1964 and the 1981 conversion of a Hindu Dalit community to Islam at Meenakshipuram (Tamil Nadu). I should like to note, however, that while Hindutva is undoubtedly an ideology of cultural homogenization and pursuantly of political domination, it is yet not strictly speaking a fundamentalist movement. I distrust the arbitrary use of the term 'fundamentalism' to characterize internally diverse religious movements and that too in the absence of a clear scripture–power dialectic (Madan 2003b).

References

Alam, Javeed. 1994. 'Tradition in India under interpretive stress; Interrogating its claims'. *Thesis Eleven* 39: 19–38.

Austin, Granville. 1999. *Working a Democratic Constitution: The Indian Experience*. New Delhi: Oxford University Press.

Bailey, F.G. 1969. *Stratagems and Spoils: A Social Anthropology of Politics*. Oxford: Basil Blackwell.

Baxi, Upendra. 1992. 'Secularism: Real and pseudo'. In M.M. Sankhdher (ed.). *Secularism in India*. New Delhi: Deep & Deep.

Béteille, André. 1994. 'Secularism and the intellectuals'. *Economic and Political Weekly* 29, 10: 560.

Bhaduri, Amit et al. 1981. 'A Statement on scientific temper'. *Mainstream* 25 July.

Bhargava, Rajeev. 1994. 'Giving secularism its due'. *Economic and Political Weekly* 9 July.

———. 1998. 'What is secularism for?' In Rajeev Bhargava (ed.). *Secularism and its Critics*. New Delhi: Oxford University Press.

Brown, Judith. 1992. *Gandhi: Prisoner of Hope*. New Haven: Yale University Press.

Casanova, José. 1994. *Public Religions in the Modern World*. Chicago: University of Chicago Press.

Chandhoke, Neera. 1999. *Beyond Secularism: The Rights of Religious Minorities*. New Delhi: Oxford University Press.

Chatterjee, Partha. (1994) 1998. Secularism and toleration. In Rajeev Bhargava (ed.). *Secularism and its Critics*. New Delhi: Oxford University Press.

Chatterjee, P.C. 1995. *Secular Values and Secular India*. New Delhi: Manohar.

Connolly, William. 1999. *Why I am not a Secularist*. Minneapolis: University of Minnesotta Press.

Corbridge, Stuart and John Harriss. 2000. *Reinventing India: Liberalisation, Hindu Nationalism and Popular Democracy*. New Delhi: Oxford University Press.

Crossman, Brenda and Ratna Kapur. 1999. *Secularism's Last Sigh: Hindutva and the Mis(rule) of Law*. New Delhi: Oxford University Press.

Dobbelaere, Karel. 2002. *Secularization: An Analysis at Three Levels*. Brussels: PIE-Peter Lang.

Geertz, Clifford. 2005. 'Shifting aims, moving targets: On the anthropology of religion'. *The Journal of the Royal Anthropological Institute* 11, 1: 1–16.

Gould, Harold A. 1999. 'The Babri Masjid and the secular contract'. In Veena Das et al. (eds). *Tradition, Pluralism and Identity: In Honour of T.N. Madan*. New Delhi: Sage.

Glasner, Peter.1977. *The Sociology of Secularization: A Critique of a Concept*. London: Routledge and Kegan Paul.

Gungwu, Wang. 2003. 'Secular China'. *China Report*, 39, 3: 305–21.

Gupta, Dipankar. 2002. 'Limits of tolerance'. *Economic and Political Weekly* 16 November: 4615–20.

Haksar, Vinit. 2001. *Rights, Communities and Disobedience: Liberalism and Gandhi*. New Delhi: Oxford University Press.

Hasan, Mushirul. 1997. *Legacy of a Divided Nation: India's Muslims since Independence*. New Delhi: Oxford University Press.

Joseph, Sarah. 1998. *Interrogating Culture: Critical Perspective on Contemporary Social Theory*: New Delhi: Sage.

Keane, John. 2000. 'Secularism?' In David Marguand and Ronald L. Nettler (eds). *Religion and Democracy*. Oxford: Blackwell.

Keddie, Nikki R. 2003. 'Secularism and its discontents'. *Daedalus* 132. 3: 14–30.

Kesavan, Mukul. 2001. *Secular Common Sense*. New Delhi: Penguin India.

Khilnani, Sunil. (1997) 1999. *The Idea of India*. New Delhi: Penguin India.

Luthera, V.P. 1964. *The Concept of the Secular State and India*. Calcutta: Oxford University Press.

Madan, T.N. 1987. 'Secularism in its place'. *Journal of Asian Studies* 46, 4: 747–59.

————. 1993. 'Whither Secularism in India?' *Modern Asian Studies* 27, 3: 667–97.

————. 1994. 'Secularism and the intellectuals'. *Economic and Political Weekly* 19: 1995–6.

Madan, T.N. 1997. *Modern Myths, Locked Minds: Secularism and Fundamentalism in India*. New Delhi: Oxford University Press.

————. 1999. 'Perspectives on pluralism'. *Seminar* 484: 18–23.

————. 2003a. Introduction to the fourth impression of Madan 1997, q.v.

————. 2003b. [On secularism & religion] The case of India. *Daedalus* 132, 3: 62–6.

————. 2005. 'Participatory Pluralism'. *The Telegraph* (Calcutta) 9 February.

Marty, Martin. 2003. 'Our religio-secular world'. *Daedalus* 132, 3: 42–8.

Marty, Martin E. and R. Scott Appleby (eds). 1991. *Fundamentalisms Observed*. Chicago: University of Chicago Press.

————. 1995. *Fundamentalisms Comprehended*. Chicago: University of Chicago Press.

Mayer, A.C. 1982. 'Perception of princely rule: perspective from a biography'. In T.N. Madan (ed.). *Way of Life: King, Householder, Renouncer*. New Delhi: Vikas.

Nanda, B.R. 1989. *Gandhi, Pan-Islamism, Imperialism and Nationalism*. New Delhi: Oxford University Press.

Nandy, Ashis 1981. 'Counter statement on humanistic temper'. *Mainstream* 10: 16–18.

————. 1985. 'An anti-secularist manifesto'. *Seminar* 314 (October) 1–12.

————. 2001. 'The politics of secularism and the recovery of religious tolerance'. In *Time Warps: The Insistent Politics of Silent and Evasive Pasts*. New Delhi: Permanent Black.

————. 2003. 'The twilight of certitudes: Secularism, Hindu nationalism and other masks of deculturation'. *The Romance of the State and the Fate of Dissent in the Tropics*. New Delhi: Oxford University Press.

Nayar, Kuldip. 2004. 'Abhor singularity'. *Outlook* 31 May.

Nehru, Jawaharlal. (1933) 1942. *Glimpses of World History*. New York: John Day.

————. 1936. *An Autobiography*. London: John Lane.

————. 1946. *The Discovery of India*. Calcutta: Signet Press.

Radhakrishnan, S. 1956. 'Foreword in Abid Hassain'. *The National Culture of India*. Bombay: Jaico.

Ricoeur, Paul. 1992. 'Quel éthos nouveau pour l'Europe'. In Peter Koslowski, *Imaginer l'Europe*. Paris: Editions de Cerf.

Roy, Asim. 2005. 'Introduction' in Mushirul Hasan and Asim Roy (eds). *Living Together Separately: Cultural India in History and Politics*. New Delhi: Oxford University Press.

Sen, Amartya. [1993] 1998. 'Secularism and its discontents'. In Rajeev Bhargava (ed.). *Secularism and its Discontents*. New Delhi: Oxford University Press.

Shaikh, Farzana, 1989. *Community and Consensus in Islam: Muslim Representation in Colonial India*. Cambridge: Cambridge University Press.

Smith, Donald Eugene. 1963. *India as a Secular State*. Bombay: Oxford University Press.

Taylor, Charles. 1998. 'Modes of secularism.' In Rajeev Bhargava (ed.). *Secularism and its Critics*. New Delhi: Oxford University Press.

————. 2003. *Varieties of Religion Today*. Cambridge: Harvard University Press.

————. 2004. *Modern Social Imaginaries*. Durham: Duke University Press.

Tharoor, Shashi. 2003. 'Interrogating Indianness'. *The Hindu Magazine* (New Delhi) 16 February: 3.

Toulmin, Stephen. 1990. *Cosmopolis: The Hidden Agenda of Modernity*. New York: The Free Press.

Vanaik, Achin. 1997. *Communalism Contested: Religion, Modernity and Secularization*. New Delhi: Vistaar.

Varshney, Ashutosh. 1993. 'Contested meanings: Indian national unity and the politics of anxiety', *Daedalus* 122.

Weber, Max. 1948. 'Politics as vocation'. In H.H. Gerth and C.W. Mills (trs. and eds). *From Max Weber: Essays in Sociology*. London: Routledge and Kegan Paul.

Wells, Ian Bryant. 2005. *Jinnah's Early Politics: Ambassador of Hindu-Muslim Unity*. New Delhi: Permanent Black.

Wolpert, Stanley. 1985. *Jinnah of Pakistan*. New Delhi: Oxford University Press.

Part Two

Religious and Secular Identities

The partition of the Indian subcontinent in 1947 was based on the dubious equation of the religious community with the nation, but the religious community itself was imagined more in terms of political and economic interests than religious values. Its proponents defended it as religious nationalism and were sceptical of the idea of territorial nationalism; for its opponents it stood for narrow communalism and the illegitimate abandonment of 'true' (European) style nationalism. The former looked upon religious identities as historically validated, primordial givens of the political situation in India. They were said to override the secular commonalities of class, regional culture, etc. Before long, however, the break-up of Pakistan in 1971, because of the suppression of another so-called primordial bond, that of language, and internal economic exploitation along regional (West Pakistan versus East Pakistan) and ethnic (Bengali versus Pathan and Punjabi) lines, made it clear that the content and strategies of ethnic self-assertion are flexible and redefinable in a pragmatic manner. The success or failure of an ethnic movement cannot be, therefore, accurately foretold. Flux and adjustment appear to be the essence of such situations, as the separatist movements in Punjab (in the 1980s) and Kashmir (in the 1990s) have revealed.

A brief comparison of the Bangladeshi, Punjabi, and Kashmiri cases is attempted in Chapter 6. I have tried to explore the combination of circumstances that persuaded Bangladeshis to switch identities (Bengali *Muslims* to Muslim *Bengalis)* and achieve their political goals, something that has eluded Punjabi Sikhs and Kashmiri Muslims. The situation in Kashmir is still open-ended. The next chapter is a fairly detailed, historically situated, discussion of the tragedy that has overtaken Kashmir in recent times. Whether presented in a religious or a secular idiom, what has happened in Kashmir is the attempt to replace cultural pluralism by an insular homogenizing ideology dressed up as jihad or freedom struggle. Some separatist ideologues speak of Kashmiris as the 'third nation' of the subcontinent which is ironical. The traditional pluralistic culture, which went hand in hand with both participation in common social arrangements and different perceptions of the same among the Valley's Hindu and Muslim peoples respectively, has been severely—perhaps irreparably—damaged. Chapter 7 ends on a note of cautious hope about future possibilities, which lie for the displaced Pandits outside their homeland rather than within it, but for Kashmiri Muslims *by their own choice* in the Valley only.

6

The Dialectic of Religion and Ethnicity in Bangladesh, Punjab, and Kashmir*

There will be time, there will be time
To prepare a face to meet the faces that you meet;
There will be time to murder and create…
And time yet for a hundred indecisions,
And for a hundred visions and revisions,
Before the taking of a toast and tea.

T.S. Eliot
'The Love Song of J. Alfred Prufrock,' *Prufrock*

INTRODUCTORY REMARKS

In the early 1950s, when I became a student of sociology and anthropology at the University of Lucknow, the term 'ethnic group' was used in India only restrictively and ethnicity not at all. Ethnic groups were also called tribes and defined by their physical and cultural features. Needless to add, ethnography was the outsider's description of these given 'realities' or 'objective facts' collected through intensive fieldwork. Max Weber had already suggested that the objective facts—so-called—of similarities of physical type or custom or both may only be subjective beliefs (see Weber

* Reproduced from *Ethnic and Racial Studies* 21, 5 (1998): 969–89 (www.tandf.co.uk). It was originally presented at an *ERS* conference in London in May 1997. I am grateful to Martin Bulmer, editor *ERS*, for his invitation to speak at the conference and for later publishing it. I am also grateful to Athena Leoussi for her interest and friendship. She reproduced the paper in a volume she edited jointly with S. Grosby, *Nationality and Nationalism, Vol. III: Area and Period Studies,* London: IB Tauris, 2004. Thanks are also due to Paul Brass for his comments on the first draft.

1968: I, 389–95), but this was not known to us then. The certainties afforded by the prevailing notions of social reality, and of a social science grounded in the mirror theory of knowledge, were comfortable and deemed unquestionable.

Today India seemingly abounds in ethnic groups—perhaps more in some parts of the country than in others—that are defenders of cultural pride and material interests in their own eyes, but enemies, often militant, in the eyes of their competitors, and insurgents in the law books of the state. Ethnicity—the term made its appearance only in the 1970s, bringing with it a dynamic conception of the ethnic group—fills the air, as it were, and signifies not only a state of being but also, and more importantly, strategies for action. Coping with ethnicity means its successful management by an ethnic group through 'identity games' to further its economic and political interests. By 'identity game' I mean the deliberate choice by an ethnic group of particular aspects of its cultural profile for highlighting in the expectation that doing so will yield the desired results in the given situation. If the situation changes, appropriate adjustments or fresh choices may be made. From the point of view of the state, to cope with ethnicity means to combat it in the interests of the status quo in the distribution of power.

Now, is the use of these terms a case merely of yielding to the temptation of words in vogue in the academe and the political arena? Or is there more to it than that? What do ethnic group and ethnicity enable us to say that tribe, caste, and community, and tribalism, casteism, and communalism, did not? This is the question I address here, not in the abstract, but through the examination, necessarily very brief, of three concrete cases.

To the best of my knowledge, the only major figure in the field of Indian studies who has commented on the current terminological preference that I have just mentioned is F.G. Bailey. In a recent work in which he discusses the 'domestication of ethnicity' in a village in Orissa, where he did fieldwork in the 1950s, Bailey (1996) writes that, while he then found the notion of caste adequate to analyse intercaste and caste–tribe relations of cooperation and conflict, he now realizes that this key term of Indian sociology is too heavily culture specific and, therefore, a more general term is needed to capture the broad significance of intergroup rivalry over claims to 'moral status' in society. Ethnicity defined culturally rather than racially is such a general concept and, when compared to race, also politically correct. I admire Bailey's forthrightness about political rectitude as much as I respect his concern for analytical rigour, but, for want of space, must confine myself here to the latter, that is, the conceptual issue.

Apparently, tribe, caste, and community (more precisely, religious community) conceived of as objective social facts, as 'things', seemed to suffice in the descriptive endeavours of the 1950s. Tribes remained largely in their remote habitats, but were not always peaceful. They were, of course, gradually being deprived of their culture and possessions (including the very precious forests) by outsiders, including entrepreneurs and government officials. Castes carried on their stable ways of life in networks of cooperation sanctified by tradition and religious values. The national movement led by the village-centred Gandhi had, however, planted seeds of doubt in the minds of political workers as well as numerous villagers about the morality of imputations of unequal moral worth and social status among different groups and strata comprising Indian society. Tribal turmoil and caste restiveness were, however, regarded as largely circumstantial, not inevitable.

In respect of communal conflict between Hindus and Muslims also, the emphasis in secular nationalist rhetoric was upon its fabricated character, blaming it almost exclusively on the 'divide and rule' policies of the colonial government. By contrast, the so-called communalist discourse conceptualized religious difference in immutable civilizational terms. Hindus and Muslims were projected as, not merely two religious communities, but as two ways of life that differed in fundamental perspectives as well as the details of everyday life. They were indeed said to be two nations, each awaiting the birth of its state.

The partition of the subcontinent on the basis of religious difference was followed in India by the setting up of a secular state, introduction of a community development programme premised on the notion of a plural village community, and adoption of a culture-preservative policy towards the tribes. These measures raised high the expectation that primordial identities would dissolve, yielding place to national unity based on the secular criterion of common nationhood. While the sagacious Edward Shils expressed doubts (in 1957) about uncritical contrasts and asserted that modern society too is 'held together' by 'an infinity' of personal attachments, moral obligations and primordial affinities alongside of a 'civil sense' (Shils 1975: 112), the sardonic Clifford Geertz, half a dozen years later, wrote of 'divided nations en route—*ex hypothesi*—to unity' (1973: 279). Borrowing E.M. Forster's mocking image, he wrote of India 'waddling in at this late hour to take her seat among the nations'. But, 'beset by virtually the entire range of primordial conflicts complexly superimposed one upon the other' (ibid.: 289), she was having to work hard, and her survival into the second decade of independence as a new state was for Geertz 'something of an Eastern mystery' (ibid.: 292). I fear the mystery has deepened since then and in more respects than one.

The uncertainties at the top (national) level in those days were matched by the dissolution of certainties at the bottom (local) level. When everybody thought that she or he knew what caste was all about, Edmund Leach (who else could it have been?) came along and threw a spanner in the works. 'What should we mean by caste'?, he asked (Leach 1960: 1–10). One of the contentious issues he commented on was that of competition between castes, that is, castes acting as political factions. When they do so—when castes acting as corporations compete for the same scarce resources (material wealth or moral worth)—they act, Leach asserted, 'in defiance of caste principles' (ibid.: 7).

The sociology of India was having its research agenda redefined by the changes that were taking place in the political and social arenas. From Alfred Kroeber's (1930) definition of caste as a subdivision of an ethnic unity (read religious community), we were moving in the direction of castes themselves becoming ethnic groups by acting as competitive corporations in pursuit of power. Louis Dumont was soon to call this the substantialization of caste: that is, 'the transition from a fluid, structural universe in which the emphasis is on interdependence...to a universe of impenetrable blocks, self-sufficient, essentially identical and in competition with one another, a universe in which caste appears...as a substance' (1970: 222). Ethnicity thus became, in Joan Vincent's (1974) oft-quoted phrase, 'the ascriptive mask of confrontation'.

Ethnicity, as stated above, is an identity game played for high stakes. The players cannot afford to be rigid. If the mask that proclaims identity cracks, one must have another ready to continue the play. This is best illustrated by the stratagems that the Muslims of Bengal have employed from time to time, so that while they are Bengali *Muslims* at certain times, they are Muslim *Bengalis* at others. The masks have fitted the face so well that it seems futile to ask which is the real thing, the face or the mask. Let me provide very briefly the main details of what happened in that part of the world between the 1940s and 1970s.

BENGALI MUSLIM ETHNICITY:
THE CASE OF WINNERS

Islam was brought to Bengal by invading Muslim armies from north India in the early thirteenth century. Force alone could not have, however, achieved the mass conversions that eventually took place in the late medieval period in the eastern parts of the province, which are more or less coterminous with the territories of Bangladesh as established in December 1971. Although the rigidities of the caste-based Hindu social organization had been softened by the impact of Buddhism before the arrival of Islam, the deprived and exploited lower castes, which are an inalienable component of the caste system, must have welcomed the egalitarian message of the religious leaders who went wherever the Muslim armies led, but who were themselves peace-loving seekers. Recent research on the subject has revealed other highly significant factors contributing to the unusual phenomenon of mass conversion, notably, ecological and economic changes (see Eaton 1994). When the first modern census was taken in 1872, the province of Bengal (as it was then, including not only the areas that constitute Bangladesh today but also the Indian states of West Bengal and Assam) was found, to everybody's surprise, preponderantly Muslim.

In short, the twin processes of incursion and conversion were responsible for the emergence of a loosely structured Muslim Bengali community. It comprised a non-Bengali-speaking, immigrant, social and cultural elite, who considered themselves the guardians of Islamic orthodoxy, and Bengali-speaking, generally illiterate, native masses, drawn through conversion mostly from lower Hindu castes. The latter were, in the eyes of the elite, only imperfectly Islamized, retaining a great deal of their pre-Islamic cultural baggage. Efforts were afoot in the sixteenth century, which continued into the seventeenth, by concerned persons who have been called 'cultural mediators', to gradually improve the quality of Islamic awareness and practice among the ignorant masses through carefully designed communication strategies that paradoxically depended upon the use of Hindu cultural tradition as a resource for Islamization. The result was the shaping of an Islamic syncretistic tradition in Bengal (see Roy 1983).

These Muslims did not, of course, live by religion alone. By the nineteenth century patterns of economic exploitation had emerged: these opposed the backward, predominantly Muslim parts of the province to the relatively advanced and predominantly Hindu west, and within the eastern parts, Muslim peasantry to Hindu and Muslim landlords. Religiosity may well be, as suggested by Karl Marx, the sigh of the oppressed, but the religious fundamentalism that made its appearance among Bengali Muslims in the late nineteenth century had other causes also than only the economic: it was partly a reaction to the syncretistic tradition mentioned above (see Ahmed 1981), which was an anathema to orthodox Muslims.

The Indian Muslim League, which later successfully campaigned for the establishment of Pakistan, was founded in Dacca (Dhaka), the largest city of east Bengal, in 1906 under the shadow of communal violence directed against Hindu landlords and merchants. The previous year the British government of India had partitioned the undoubtedly unwieldy province (Presidency) of Bengal, ostensibly for reasons of administrative convenience, but also motivated by the desire to contain a late nineteenth century nationalist upsurge under upper middle class Hindu leadership of high caste background that had come to stay. The division was welcomed by the Muslim leadership—they were openly assured of more job opportunities and other economic gains—and opposed by the Hindu, which regarded it as yet another instance of the colonial policy of 'divide and rule' and an attempt to weaken the nationalist challenge. The opposition to the partition was stronger than the support: it appealed to Bengali cultural pride and memories of regional independence and inter-communal unity. Consequently, the partition was annulled in 1911, much to the dismay of the Muslim leadership. With the passage of time, the Hindu–Muslim divide became wider.

Bengali Muslims were the single largest ethnic group among Indian Muslims and accounted for over half of all Bengalis. From the early years of the century they had constituted the vanguard of Muslim separatism, and they themselves were led by a burgeoning middle class. The latter felt trapped between the persistent threat of Hindu domination and the indifference of the Muslims of the north and north-west to both their political predicament and numerical weight. When the Muslim League met for its annual session in 1940 in Lahore, it was a prominent Bengali Muslim leader, namely A.K. Fazlul Huq, who moved the resolution demanding independent Muslims states in north-western and eastern India. In the event, a single Muslim state, Pakistan, was established in 1947 with an eastern and a western wing, separated by well over a thousand miles of Indian territory.

By aligning themselves with the Muslims of the north and the north-west, the Muslims of Bengal had chosen to ignore their ethnic distinctiveness, comprising racial, cultural, and linguistic attributes. They identified themselves with non-Bengali Muslims in furtherance of their 'dream' of a South Asian Muslim homeland and of their economic and political interests. It is clear that religion was being employed as an integrative device—as a mask—to cover significant cultural differences that clearly distinguished them from other South Asian Muslim communities. Herein lay the possibility of future deconstruction of Pakistan. It would be misleading to suggest, however, that the Muslims of Bengal were deliberately indulging in a masquerade, but what they did amounted to doing so.

Before long, resentment about being treated as the culturally inferior wing of the country began to emerge in East Pakistan. There were other problems too. The political and administrative centres were in the western wing, which was also economically dominant. But the raw materials that helped earn foreign exchange and pay for West Pakistan's industrialization came from the eastern wing. It would be a mistake to consider its economic structure, in which the eastern wing became an internal colony, as the primary determinant of Pakistan's eventual breakup. Cultural differences were equally important. The first attack on Bengali cultural distinctiveness, so perceived, was the decision of the federal government in 1948 to make Urdu the sole official language of the country. Agitating for the status of the second official language for Bengali, on par with Urdu (which was in any case the mother tongue of only the migrants from north India to West Pakistan), Bengali Pakistanis achieved their objective in 1954.

The relationship between the two wings was never cordial again, and found expression in many mutually culturally derogatory statements by prominent politicians, including a particularly crude one by President Ayub Khan, who was a Pathan, in his autobiography. He wrote about East Pakistani Muslims as people who had 'not known any real freedom or sovereignty' in the past, who were still 'under considerable Hindu cultural and linguistic influence', and exhibited 'all the inhibitions of down-trodden races', such as 'exclusiveness, suspicion and a sort of defensive aggressiveness' (1967: 187). What made the characterization particularly odious, was that he wrote about West Pakistanis in glowing terms.

When Pakistan held its first nationwide elections in 1970, 23 years after independence, East Pakistani Muslims had come a long hard way: they had redefined their identity and in the process their significant 'others'—their political friends and foes and their cultural familiars and strangers. In other words, they decided to discard the old mask, wear a new one, and continue to play the identity game. In the 1940s, they had projected themselves as Muslims living in Bengal out of which East Pakistan was carved out. In 1970 they went to the polls as Muslim *Bengalis* rather than as Bengali *Muslims*, and emerged triumphant. By the end of the next year, after enormous sacrifices including a war, the new state of Bangladesh was born. Indian training of Bengali youth for armed combat, and eventually direct participation by India in the war, helped expedite the process of the breakup of Pakistan.

The main credit (or blame) for the birth of Bangladesh (or the disintegration of Pakistan) lies elsewhere. It was the victory of Bengali ethnicity, that is, of the ability of an ethnic group to pursue its economic and political interests and preserve its over-all cultural identity by playing down the importance of religion—which had earlier yielded the desired results—stressing the significance of language, and valorizing the culturally homogeneous nation-state. Pakistan was an Islamic state by proclamation; Bangladesh under the leadership of Mujibur Rahman was formally secular to begin with (according to the Constitution adopted in 1973), but there have been changes made subsequently, as part of *realpolitik*, beginning with the assassination of President Rahman.

I should emphasize that analysing the events leading up to the birth of Bangladesh in the framework of ethnicity leads to the conclusion that the choice that was made by the Muslims of Bengal in the 1940s was not erroneous or invalid. It seemed the rational thing to do then. The threatening 'other' at that time were the Hindus—economically exploitative, politically dominant, and culturally arrogant.

After independence, all these negative roles vis-à-vis the East Pakistani Muslims came to be performed by the Pathans and the Punjabis of West Pakistan. The bond of Islam was no longer useful from the Bengali point of view. Responding pragmatically to the negative feedback, the Muslims of Bengal redefined their identity in territorial (*sonar Bangla*, the golden Bengal), linguistic and broad cultural terms. Religion was not thrown out, but its significance was redefined. It had to share the political space with other symbols that too partook of the sacred but were not religious in the narrow sense: the example that comes readily to mind is that of the powerful metaphor of 'soil' (*māti*), or 'the country's soil' (*desher māti*), that occurred prominently in the rhetoric favouring independence during 1970–1. The lesson was that there are no fixed or objective attributes of ethnic identity; there are predictable economic, political, and cultural objectives, however, which may be combined in different ways, varying the emphasis on the individual elements, and thereby setting up a hierarchy of values.

A final comment. In a paper on Bengali ethnicity that I wrote in 1971 around the time Bangladesh was born, I cautioned: 'It is not at all unlikely that in the years to come, the salience of religion will re-emerge among the Muslims of Bengal—though in a changed context—for Bangladesh exists independently of the Indian state of West Bengal because it is predominantly Muslim' (Madan 1994a: 219).

Today we know that this is precisely what has happened. General Zia-ur-Rahman, the third President of Bangladesh amended the 1972 constitution to delete secularism as a principle of state policy and substituted it by 'Absolute Trust and Faith in the Almighty Allah as the basis of all actions'. He introduced Islamic teachings into general education, lifted the ban on the fundamentalist organization called the Jamat-i-Islami, and brought his country into the Islamic Conference; but he did not tamper with Bangladeshi identity defined in cultural-linguistic terms and acknowledging common ancestry. In 1988, General Ershad, the sixth President, declared Islam as the state religion of Bangladesh. Islam has indeed become salient again in the country, but not at the cost of the racial, cultural, and linguistic markers of national identity. The boundary between Hindus (about 15 per cent of the population) and the Muslims defined in terms of religion, however, remains in place.

Ethnicity is a game of chance; it follows that it may not always succeed. It does not seem to have succeeded in the case of the Sikhs of Punjab, although I am not sure whether the present situation warrants the conclusion that they have been finally 'de-ethnicized' (see Gupta 1996: 85–9). There seem to be no final outcomes in this game: they are usually deferred. What looks like a final conclusion may turn out to be only a long interval. Let me then turn to a brief examination of the vicissitudes of Sikh identity.

PUNJABI SIKH ETHNICITY: THE CASE OF LOSERS

It is instructive to consider Punjabi Sikh ethnicity alongside Bengali Muslim ethnicity because the two cases are similar in terms of ethnic identity being made the basis for state formation, but are otherwise significantly different in many ways, including historical origins and the subsequent course of events, symbol selection and strategy, and political goals and outcome.

In striking contrast to the manner in which the Bengali Muslim community came into existence, the Punjabi Sikhs first made their appearance early in the sixteenth century by distancing themselves from some of the crucial features of the parental Hindu community, such as social institutions (for example, caste and priesthood), religious beliefs (for example, polytheism and miracles), and practices (for example, idol worship, elaborate life-cycle rituals, and renunciation of domesticity). Later, the numbers of Sikhs increased considerably through the entry of low-caste Jats (originally non-Hindu pastoralists of areas in Rajasthan to the south of Punjab) into their fold. Armed invasion or aggressive proselytization did not play any role in either of the two processes just described—namely, fission and fusion—by which the Sikh community took shape in the sixteenth century. These processes were wholly peaceful, non-political, and voluntary. This may have been expected, for the founder of Sikhism, Guru Nanak (1469–1539), known for his piety, pacifism, and trust in the goodness of common people, had little use for formal political institutions such as kingship. Moreover, the Sikhs strove for internal harmony, playing down caste differences.

The distinction between Hindu and Sikh identities remained vague, however (see McLeod 1989). The Hindus revered Guru Nanak as a man of God, respected his teachings, and regarded his disciples (the Sikhs) as brothers—as a sect, perhaps, but not a distinct religious community. Indeed, many Hindu families comprised members who were by choice brought up as Sikhs. Inter-marriage also was commonly practised. This contrasted with the situation in Bengal, where, as was stated above, once community-based or communal politics emerged in reaction to nationalist mobilization, Muslims always saw themselves in opposition to an oppressive other, whether the Bengali Hindu—in which case religion was valorized—or, later, the West Pakistani Muslim—here secular components of culture, particularly language, acquired salience.

While the Bengali Muslim self-perception of victimhood may not have been recognized by the designated others, the latter acknowledged the fact of religious or cultural difference. In Punjab, the perception of difference was largely one-sided—on the part of the Sikhs—but this did not entail the allegation of oppression until after independence from British rule in 1947. Indeed, the Sikhs were seen as, and gloried in being, the 'sword arm' of the Hindus, for they, unlike many Rajputs (warrior caste Hindus), had consistently questioned the legitimacy of Muslim rule in India, and taken up arms against it at the beginning of the eighteenth century under the leadership of the tenth and last personal guru of the Sikhs, Gobind Rai (1666–1708).

It was interestingly Guru Gobind who defined the fundamentals of the Sikh faith in terms of personal identity rather than religious belief or doctrine alone. The Sikhs, he declared, would be unlike the Hindus, unshorn and, unlike the Muslims, uncircumcized (see Uberoi 1991). The Sikh's body, sanctified by the ritual of initiation, which he prescribed, became the supreme symbol of identity. The guru and his wife were cast in the role of parents of all baptized Sikhs for all time to come. This was a highly imaginative step of far-reaching significance, for it introduced the idea of common ancestry, overriding diverse tribal and caste origins. The guru also initiated the practice of codifying the norms of correct behaviour (*rahitnāma*), which translated into Sikh culture. Ironically, in respect of religion, Guru Gobind apparently came very close to certain forms of Hinduism (for example, worship of an all-powerful goddess). The Hindus were not Sikhs but they were not enemies either; the enemy was the Mughal (Muslim) state.

The state plays a crucial role throughout the eighteenth century. The self-image of the Sikh as the warrior fighting against unjust rulers gains strength, but the idea of a Sikh territory or sacred homeland is absent. It is noteworthy that Guru Gobind was neither born in Punjab nor did he die there, and he never visited the Golden Temple in Amritsar, which is today considered the holiest of Sikh holy places, for he never visited the city. It was considered unsafe for a self-proclaimed rebel to be in these parts of the country. The state that Ranjit Singh, a baptized Sikh, established in 1799, extended beyond Punjab in the west, and it was not a Sikh state in concept or practice: it was so by association, however. The ruler himself acknowledged, despite many critical transgressions, his Sikh identity, which entailed submission to the codes of conduct as interpreted by the guardians of the faith. But Ranjit Singh's state collapsed within half a dozen years of his death in 1839. The British claimed his territories and the Christian church, his successor.

Just as the Muslims had in the eighteenth century attributed loss of political power to the corruption of religious faith, many Sikhs too blamed their relapse into Hinduism at the level of practice—which was a fact—for their own political misfortunes. The enemy came to be redefined: it was now the turn of the lax or fallen Sikhs to be cast in this role. They were considered to have reverted to Hindu beliefs and rituals. Religious revitalization was, therefore, combined with deliberate efforts to create a cultural distance between the Hindus and the Sikhs. Popular beliefs, customs, life-cycle rituals, etc., which the Sikhs traditionally shared with the Hindus on a local basis, came to be gradually replaced to add cultural weight to the political slogan of the 1890s, 'we are not Hindus (*ham Hindu nahin hain*)!' (see Oberoi 1994). These efforts culminated in a successful agitation in the early 1920s for driving out Hindu ritual functionaries from the gurdwaras (Sikh temples of worship) with the help of the government.

The Gurdwara Reform Act of 1925 put the seal on the demarcation of the cultural boundary between the Hindus and the Sikhs—at least in the eyes of those Sikhs who followed, in cultural life, the reformist as against the traditional, and, in politics, the communal as against the secular approach. The demand for Pakistan put forward in the 1940s made the reformist–communal Sikhs realize that, although they were concentrated in Punjab, about as many Sikhs lived outside it. This problem would have to be overcome if they were to be a strong regional political force. No Sikh leader has ever advocated movement of populations, but a most interesting redefinition of Punjab as the symbolic land has indeed been attempted, pointing to its importance in both the religious and the political history of the Sikhs, irrespective of a particular family's or individual's domicile. This redefinition eventually became the basis for the demand for Khalistan, comprising Punjab and some adjacent areas, and the transformation of a communal into an ethnic movement. I say 'eventually' because one would have to also take note of certain events in the 1950s and 1960s, leading to the differentiation of Punjabi as a secular language (that is of the Punjabi Hindus and Muslims) and as the religious language of the Sikhs written in a script that, they maintained, had been specially evolved by the second Sikh guru in the middle of the sixteenth century. This differentiation became the basis for the second division of the province/state of Punjab in 1966.

A new confrontation was set up between the Sikh majority Punjab state, the Hindu dominated Haryana state, and the Union of India over territorial and river water-sharing issues. It is out of this confrontation, which was primarily economic and political in character, that the militant secessionism of the 1980s, apparently a religio-ethnic movement, was born. I say 'apparently' because it was flawed as an expression of ethnicity. Common ancestry was present, but it was derived from ritual rather than race. The Sikhs were united by a common religion that was seen by at least the reformists among them as a rejection of Hinduism. But the Hindus of Punjab have always revered the Sikh gurus and continue to do so. They sing hymns from the Sikh holy book, the

Guru Granth Sahab, visit gurdwaras for religious devotions, and sometimes raise a son of the family as a Sikh as an act of piety.

In short, the Hindus of Punjab have never acknowledged that they could be the threatening 'others', although they were economic competitors and political opponents of the Sikhs. Politically opportunist Punjabi-speaking Hindus did disown their mother tongue in the 1960s in an effort to prevent a second partition of the state, but this had more to do with politics per se than cultural boundaries. In fact, they continued to speak the language. Moreover the distribution of population—a two-thirds Sikh majority in the new state but nearly half of all Sikhs living outside Punjab—militated against the idea of Khalistan as an independent Sikh homeland. Hostility towards the Indian state, which was characterized as both godless and anti-Sikh, was, however, mitigated by the participation of millions of Sikhs in the Indian economy, polity, and government.

How then did Sikh ethnicity emerge rather suddenly in the 1980s? A careful examination of the evidence reveals that, as in East Pakistan, in Punjab also a dominant state (that is, the Union of India) succeeded in transforming a combined sense of ethnic distinctiveness and discriminatory treatment at the hands of the federal government into not exactly an armed rebellion (as happened in Pakistan) but a violent (terrorist) secessionist movement. In both cases, a foreign neighbouring state provided significant help: India in the movement for an independent Bangladesh and Pakistan in the movement for an independent Khalistan. Why did the Bengali Muslims succeed but not the Punjabi Sikhs—at least not so far? What does the retreat of Sikh separatism in Punjab signify?

Obviously answers to the two questions involve a combination of many significant factors—including, for example, the 'distance' of Islamabad from Dacca and the 'proximity' of Delhi to Amritsar—into all of which I cannot go here: selection is necessary. The Punjabi Sikhs, like the Bengali Muslims, felt that they were being subjected to political and economic discrimination (by a Hindu-dominated state) because of their ethnic identity, but they did not initially moot the idea of secession. This is clear from a perusal of the text of the set of twelve resolutions adopted in 1977 at a conference attended by Sikh delegates from all over India and owing allegiance to the Akali party. Known collectively as the Anandpur Sahab Resolution, it opens with an affirmation of India as 'a federal and republican geographical entity of different languages, religions and cultures', and proceeds to list grievances which concern territorial, economic, cultural, and related matters (see Gupta 1996: 212–18).

While it was the army generals who contributed significantly to the insularity of the federal government in Pakistan in 1970–1, it was the Congress party, which ruled at the Centre as well as in Punjab from time to time (not in 1977), that did so in India in 1977–8. Its leaders were quick to characterize the Akali demands as communal or ethnic, which they partly were, and anti-national, which they apparently were not. More grievously, they tried to cut at the support base of the Akalis by introducing a Sikh religious preacher, Jarnail Singh Bhindranwale, into the political arena, but this move backfired.

Bhindranwale had his own agenda of rejuvenating the Sikhs as an orthodox religious community, strictly following the precepts of Guru Gobind; he was virulently hostile to sectarian groups among the Sikhs. Bhindranwale refused to be a tool of the Congress party (see Kapur 1986; Madan 1997). While he himself remained non-committal on the issue of Khalistan, he drew support for his fundamentalist programme from active supporters of secession, who included a large number of unemployed youth. He openly accused the central government and the Hindus of being opposed to the legitimate politico-economic demands of the Sikhs.

This combination of perspectives of what the political unrest in Punjab was all about was, as it were, sealed by the decision of the central government (headed by Prime Minister Indira Gandhi) to use military force in June 1984, in an operation code-named Bluestar, to capture Bhindranwale and his armed supporters, who had taken sanctuary in Akal Takht, the second of the two temples in the Golden Temple complex at Amritsar. The force required to achieve the objective proved to be much more than was anticipated with disastrous consequences. The Akal Takht was destroyed, the Golden Temple itself damaged, and Bhindranwale alongside most of his supporters killed. Also killed were several hundred Sikh pilgrims who happened to be at the temple purely for devotions.

The attack on the Golden Temple complex caused immense resentment among Sikhs everywhere (and among many Hindus too), but particularly among the Sikhs in Punjab. In October Prime Minister Indira Gandhi was assassinated by her two Sikh body-guards in an act of retaliation. This dastardly act was immedi-ately followed by anti-Sikh mob violence in Delhi and many other cities, and this claimed several thousand lives. The cumulative impact of the assault on the Golden Temple complex and the massacre of the Sikhs generated widespread sympathy for Sikh grievances among members of the community generally and, in some circles, active support for the militants. It must be emphasized, however, that the support for militancy, even when at its peak, did not embroil all the Sikhs living in Punjab.

There is a two-fold contrast with the East Pakistani situation of 1970–1: not only were virtually all Bengali Muslims of Pakistan resident in East Pakistan, they generally, and all but a very small minority of senior civil and military officers, actively supported the movement for secession from Pakistan. Military intervention by India finally clinched the issue in favour of the East Pakistanis. As stated above, Sikh militants never succeeded in their efforts to garner total support in the community despite appeals in the name of common Sikh identity and interests. Assistance by Pakistan to Sikh militants in the form of money, arms, and training remained covert, and did not escalate into open intervention.

In the event, Sikh militancy in Punjab was ruthlessly managed by the Indian government through combined police and military operations. As soon as these operations were seen to have reached a satisfactory conclusion, democratic government, which had remained suspended for over half a dozen years, was restored in 1992, with only the Congress party supporters among the Sikhs, and of course the Hindus, participating in the elections. Within a year, the Sikhs generally expressed a clear preference for electoral politics, and normalcy began to be restored after a decade of unrest.

Looking at the Punjab situation today (in 1997), Sikh ethnicity apparently has run out of steam and there are no immediate signs of its being recharged. The right-wing Sikh political party, the Akali Dal, is in power in the state of Punjab, paradoxically in coalition with the right-wing Hindu Bharatiya Janata Party.[1] Akalis sit in the Parliament at Delhi and participate in national politics. How has this change come about? Absence of general, active, support among the Sikhs, astute political management by some relatively unknown and therefore non-controversial Congress Sikhs, police determination often indistinguishable from ruthlessness under the overall direction of a tough chief who is himself a Sikh, the militants' excesses which victimized Sikhs as well as Hindus, and fatigue among the supporters—all these have been put forward as the causes of the return of normalcy in Punjab in the 1990s. What has not received adequate attention, I think, is the failure of ethnicity to take hold there the way it did in east Bengal.

What is the critical difference between the two cases? Obviously, the elements out of which an ethnic movement may be successfully constructed—namely common ancestry, common culture, threatening others who have a different ancestry and a different culture, and a state that is seen as oppressive—were present in both situations but not all of them carried comparable weights. Consciousness of participating in a common culture and speaking the same tongue enjoys facticity in both the Bengali and the Punjabi cases and is, therefore, of similar significance. The remaining factors are not, however, strictly comparable. The differences in respect of the character of common ancestry and emotional identification with the soil have been discussed above. The attitudes of the two federal governments were also not strictly comparable. Although both were seen as dominated by the opponents of the victims and, therefore, oppressive, Pakistan was headed in 1970–1 by a military dictatorship, but India was a functioning federal democracy throughout the period under consideration (1978–92).

The most critical differences between the east Bengali and Punjabi situations were, I think, two. First, while the threatening others in Pakistan, namely, the West Pakistanis were geographically distant, culturally and linguistically different, and economically dominant, the Punjabi Hindus shared the same habitat, culture, and language with the Sikhs and did not enjoy as a community decisive advantage vis-à-vis the latter in economic terms. Secondly, the kind of mass mobilization in support of independence that occurred in East Pakistan did not materialize in Punjab. I will not invoke psychological predispositions (Bengali emotionalism versus Punjabi pragmatism), but only point out that it has been suggested that, in its earlier phase (in the late 1970s and early 1980s), an emerging Sikh movement was characterized as secessionist by its political opponents: the participants spoke in terms of economic, political, and cultural demands within the existing political framework (see Gupta 1996). In other words, the marriage of ethnic self-consciousness and the demand for an independent state based on it, occurred first in the minds of people other than those who were to be its bearers and soldiers, both as fear and as allegation, and only afterwards in the minds of the Sikhs. It was derivative rather than original. In east Bengal it all came from within.

The experiments with ethnicity of Bengali Muslims and Punjabi Sikhs have lessons for others—for example, the Muslims of the Kashmir Valley (in the Indian state of Jammu and Kashmir), most of whom claim freedom or autonomy in the name of ethnic identity. I now turn to this third and last case in this discussion of the strategies of coping with ethnicity in South Asia.

KASHMIRI MUSLIM ETHNICITY: THE CASE OF NON-STARTERS[2]

For over fifty years now—since the partition of the Indian subcontinent on the basis of differences of religious identity and the birth of the independent states of India and Pakistan in 1947—the state of Jammu and Kashmir has been a major trouble spot of the world where two inconclusive wars have been fought. The issue at stake is whether this state should be a part of India or Pakistan. In recent years certain political groups have argued in favour of a third option, namely independence (*āzādī*). Various arguments have been put forward of which one is based on the assertion of a distinctive Kashmiri ethnic identity (Kashmiriyat). The situation is complex and some background information should be of help in coming to grips with it (see Ganguly 1997).

When the British decided to transfer power to two successor states, they also announced that the rulers of the quasi-independent native states of the subcontinent, who acknowledge Great Britain as the 'paramount power', would each be free to choose to accede to one or the other of the new states, or to stay independent. While most of the five hundred odd states speedily opted for accession, keeping in mind the compulsions of geographical contiguity and the religious composition of the population, the two largest states, namely Hyderabad and Jammu and Kashmir, deferred a decision.

Hyderabad was surrounded on all sides by Indian territory, its population was predominantly Hindu, but its ruler was a Muslim. Limited military action by the Indian government settled the issue in a matter of a few days.

Jammu and Kashmir presented unique features that made for a very complex situation. It had common borders with both India and Pakistan and also with Afghanistan, the USSR, China, and Tibet. Its ruler was a Hindu. In the state as a whole the Muslims enjoyed a two-thirds majority but they accounted for 95 per cent of the population of the Kashmir Valley, a constituent part. In other parts, Hindus or Buddhists were in the majority. The Kashmir Valley occupied a special place not only because it attracted tourists from all over the world, but also because it had been for the previous decade and a half the political centre of the state. A secular political party, headed by the best known mass leader of the state, Sheikh Abdullah (a Kashmiri Muslim), had spearheaded a movement for democratic rights and economic reforms. This party was opposed to the communal politics that had been the basis for partition.

In October 1947, Muslim tribal invaders from Pakistan, backed by the Pakistan army, entered the state and headed for the capital city of Srinagar in the Valley, obviously to force accession of the state to Pakistan. Caught unprepared in this critical situation, the ruler acceded to India. The military operations that followed drove the invaders back towards their bases, but before they were completely overcome, the matter was referred by India to the United Nations Security Council, which still has the problem on its agenda. India had originally offered to decide the issue of accession (although it was legally complete) through a plebiscite provided that Pakistan withdrew all its troops (the demand was endorsed by the UN), which it never did. Instead it launched a second war in 1965 which was of short duration and produced no tangible result. The state of Jammu and Kashmir as it was in October 1947, before the tribal raiders came in, stands divided by a 'cease-fire line' which has since 1972 (after the third Indo-Pakistan war over Bangladesh) been referred to by both sides as the 'line of actual control'.

Now, the natives of the Kashmir Valley (henceforth referred to as Kashmir or the Valley) are of one physical stock—anthropologists attest this—and share at the broadest level a common culture—ethnography describes and self-ascription confirms it. When they speak of themselves as Kashmiris (or, to use the native term, Kashir), they usually have two things above all others in mind. These are, first and concretely, their being speakers of two mutually intelligible varieties of the same tongue and, secondly and somewhat vaguely, their being natives of the Valley, which is not a vast place, being only 85 miles long and 25 miles broad. Folklore and poetry have helped the Kashmiris, who rarely travel around in Kashmir for sight seeing, to imagine their homeland as a paradise on the earth (*gulshan vatan*, 'the native land that is a flower garden').

Within the commonalities of culture there are differences. I just mentioned two varieties of speech. The grammar is the same; the variety is of lexical elements. Significant words and phrases, as for instance mutual greetings, identify a speaker or listener, or both, as Muslim or Hindu. The difference of religion is, of course, most critical: for the Muslims the Hindus are 'misbelievers' (kafir); for the Hindus the Muslims are ritually impure (*mleccha*). All native Hindus belong to the Brahman (highest) caste, and are known as the Pandits. There are no other Hindu castes in Kashmir, a situation without parallel anywhere in India. Muslim occupational groups, themselves descendants of converts from Hindu castes, provide the services needed by the Hindus. Mass conversion to Islam during the early years of Muslim rule, beginning in the late fourteenth century—comparable to the conversion in Bengal mentioned earlier—is responsible for this socio-demographic peculiarity.

Despite the conspicuous or subtle differences of religion, language, custom, clothing and diet, there was much goodwill and harmony among the people. In a paper based on fieldwork done in the 1950s and 1960s, I wrote about the success of the Kashmiri Muslims and Hindus in building agreement on difference (see Madan 1994b: 167–201). The politically correct statement would have been that the Kashmiris have a composite culture, but this would not have been equally true of all aspects of life. For instance, it would not be quite accurate to say that all specificities of Islamic belief and practice in Kashmir, which deviate from Sunni orthodoxy, reflect Hindu influence.

In the wake of the accession of Jammu and Kashmir to the Indian Union (in 1947), an existing political division among the

Muslims of Kashmir between secular and religious nationalists respectively hardened into support for either the state remaining in India or joining Pakistan. A new significant element was introduced into this situation in the 1980s, following the emergence of Islamic fundamentalism in the Valley, which was different from earlier reformist movements insofar as it had explicit political objectives. The fundamentalists are generally politically pro-Pakistan. The new development was that many of the supporters of accession to Pakistan, along with some pro-India elements, now called for a third option, namely an independent state based on the secular ideology of Kashmiriyat, or Kashmiri ethnic identity. The three political options correspond to three kinds of nationalism: religious nationalism divides Muslims and Hindus into Pakistan and India supporters respectively. Secular nationalism makes both Muslims and Hindus India supporters. Ethnic nationalism is the basis for independence (see Varshney 1992).

The problem with this neat tripartite division is that the Hindu minority almost completely migrated out of the Valley in 1990–1, when fundamentalists gave the call for an Islamic regime in Kashmir, denying Kashmir's syncretic cultural tradition, and pro-Pakistan and pro-independence elements joined hands to mount an insurgency directed against the Indian state. Many Pandits lost their lives; many more, their properties. They were branded as Indian agents (*mukhbir*) in view of their explicit preference for the full integration of Jammu and Kashmir in the Indian Union. It is estimated that not more than fifteen thousand out of about 200,000 Pandits still live in the Valley. Among the stories of ethnic cleansing in our times, the Pandit story has not received much attention, perhaps because their numbers are relatively small and their political influence is negligible.

The dilemma that the leadership of the pro-independence, professedly secular, party, namely the Jammu Kashmir Liberation Front, face is that they need the Pandits as an emblem or sign of their secular credentials. At the same time they need to affirm the crucial importance of Islam in the making of Kashmiri culture and identity if they have to keep their following among the Muslims generally. For these Muslims, Kashmiriyat under fundamentalist pressure can be, and indeed has been, described as Islamization. But Islamization is context-sensitive. M. Ishaq Khan puts it thus: 'The syncretism of Islamic beliefs and local practices is actually the beginning of a movement for the realization of the ultimate, if not immediate, objectives of Islam at both the individual and social levels' (1994: 222).

The Pandit point of view, on the contrary, traces the roots of Kashmiri identity to its pre-Islamic days, recalling achievements in the fields of religion, philosophy, literature, architecture, etc. The Pandits consider themselves an inalienable people of India and their culture as part and parcel of Hindu culture. They take pride in what emigré Pandits have contributed to the making of modern India. Jawaharlal Nehru, the first Prime Minister, was one such Pandit. If absent from the Valley, the Pandits are a problem for the pro-independence elements, because they are needed to maintain a secular Kashmiri identity. If present, they are again a problem, because they harken to a past that the Muslims have rejected, and they value the cultural and political bonds with India that the ethnic nationalists want to sever.

Another major problem, it seems to me, is the non-availability of a key symbol of collective identity other than religion to mobilize support across the religious boundary. Kashmiri is not comparable to Bengali as it is not a written language and its literary heritage is oral. The use of the Persian script in modern times is unacceptable to the Pandits, some of whom prefer the ancient Sharada, which is, however, known only to the priests. Most of them prefer the phonetic Nagri script in which Hindi, the first official language of India, is written. Although this too cannot capture all Kashmiri phonemes, it certainly does so much better than the Persian script which has had to be altered. The use of Urdu written in the Persian script as the official language of the state, going back to pre-independence days, has not exactly helped the cause of Kashmiri. Moreover, the older composite nature of Kashmiri (comprising Sanskrit, Persian, Arabic, and other lexical elements) is being altered by the Muslim elite in an effort to standardize it through the elimination of readily recognizable Sanskrit words. The Pandits look upon this too as part of the process of Islamization, and a none too subtle way of changing the common cultural heritage in a manner that eliminates its Hindu elements. On an overall view, Kashmiri has not and is unlikely to play the kind of role that Bengali, despite its association with the Hindus exemplified by its vocabulary and script, played in the evolution of Bangladeshi ethnicity.

The Muslims as the principal players of the game of ethnicity in Kashmir have not yet worked out a solution to the foregoing problems. Until they do so, their management of Kashmiriyat remains flawed. The mask of ethnicity does not quite fit the Muslim face in Kashmir today. The Pandits too have not yet got their act together. The only sensible course for them would be to support secular nationalism, but they seem to be leaning towards Hindu religious nationalism. In short, those who would carve out an independent state in the Valley on the basis of ethnic identity in the manner of Bengali Muslims can only be called non-starters at present.

CONCLUDING REMARKS

To conclude: I have presented above three cases of coping with ethnicity, from the people's point of view rather than that of the state. These two points of view are, as stated at the very outset, mutually opposed: where people seek to establish a new state on the basis of putative ethnic identity, the success of the people is the failure of the state, and vice versa. From the people's perspective Bangladesh has been a unique success story; there is no chance that what has come to stay will be reversed. The demand for Khalistan has apparently been unsuccessful, although one feels less confident of the finality of its failure than one does of the stability of Bangladesh's success; Sikh fundamentalism survives in enclaves, but militancy on a large scale is unlikely to stage a come back. The nascent movement for a Kashmiri state has really not taken off, although it has been accompanied by as much violence and violation of human rights from both sides as was witnessed in Punjab.

Punjab and Kashmir are not the only militant movements that the Indian state has faced. The north-eastern states of India, where militant ethnicity first surfaced among the Nagas and the Mizos, is still in the grip of ethnic movements, notably in the state of Assam; Mizoram and Nagaland, particularly the former state, are relatively peaceful. There are restive ethnic groups elsewhere in the country. What is distinctive about Punjab and Kashmir, and of course Bangladesh, is the role of foreign intervention. In its absence in the north-east, the Indian state has so far coped reasonably well with the challenges of ethnicity through a mixture of political accommodation, economic aid, and suppression through the employment of armed police forces and the military. It has also depended upon the factor of fatigue setting in among not only the people in general, but also the militants themselves. Indeed, the same combination of factors has played a crucial role in Punjab also, and it now seems to be doing the same in Kashmir. Unlike Punjab, however, Kashmir has been on the top of Pakistan's agenda—it has been officially referred to as 'the unfinished business of partition'—since its birth in 1947 and, by its efforts, Kashmir has remained a concern of international bodies such as the Organization of Islamic Countries and, of course, the United Nations. No easy or early solution to the larger problem of the status of the state of Jammu and Kashmir is yet in sight. But the problem of the Kashmiri Muslims' demand for an independent ethnic state, which would really be an Islamic state, is, as I have tried to show, another matter.

At the beginning of this chapter I had posed a methodological question, namely, what is it that the notion of ethnicity, as defined here, enables us to do that other concepts, notably caste, which have long done service in the sociology of India, do not? Let me end with a set of answers that are inescapably provisional (by virtue of the very nature of the scholarly enterprise).

First, it helps in describing situations in which power is a visible key variable that it was not in the caste system before independence, and for which the contest is ultimately not between ethnic groups alone, but between an ethnic group and a central authority (the state).

Secondly, it enables one to take a multidimensional view of ethnic identity in a way communalism did not.

Thirdly, it makes it possible to overcome an old but mistaken opposition between the objective and subjective aspects of social identity, between other-ascription and self-ascription.

Fourthly, it brings out the interplay of moral worth and material interests in the construction of identity and dispenses with the mistaken notion that culture is merely an epiphenomenon.

And, fifthly, it enables us to take a processual or generative view of what people do, through as well as at the behest of their leaders, to pursue collective goals, which include protection of cultural pride no less than the pursuit of economic advantage and political power.

Conceptual refinement is not, however, an end in itself. It is worthwhile only if it leads us to a deeper understanding of concrete social situations. It has been my effort in this chapter to understand the dynamics of three recent South Asian ethnic movements by introducing some analytical ideas into the description and comparing the three cases. The results obtained are, I think, interesting and amenable to further generalization through an encounter with more data from diverse settings.

NOTE

1. The political scenario has changed since 1997, and the Congress party is now (in 2005) again in power. This does not, however, affect my argument.
2. The discussion of the situation in Kashmir in this section of the chapter is presented again in historically situated and much greater detail in the next chapter. There is an overlap between the two chapters, but I have refrained from removing the same in order to preserve the completeness of the argument presented here. Chapter 7 also updates the discussion as it was written in 2004–5, seven years after this essay.

REFERENCES

Ahmed, Rafiuddin. 1981. *The Bengal Muslims 1871–1906: A Quest for Identity*. New Delhi: Oxford University Press.

Bailey, F.G. 1996. *The Civility of Indifference: On Domesticating Ethnicity*. New Delhi: Oxford University Press.

Dumont, Louis. 1970. *Homo Hierarchicus: The Caste System and its Implications*. London: Weidenfeld and Nicholson.

Eaton, Richard. 1994. *The Rise of Islam and the Bengal Frontier, 1204–1760*. New Delhi: Oxford University Press.

Ganguly, Sumit. 1997. *The Crisis in Kashmir: Portents of War, Hopes of Peace*. Cambridge: Cambridge University Press.

Geertz, Clifford. 1973. 'The integrative revolution: primordial sentiments and civil politics in the new states'. In *The Interpretation of Cultures*. New York: Basic Books, pp. 225–310.

Gupta, Dipankar. 1996. *The Context of Ethnicity: Sikh Identity in Comparative Perspective*. New Delhi: Oxford University Press.

Khan, Mohammad Ayub. 1967. *Friends not Masters: A Political Biography*. London: Oxford University Press.

Khan, M. Ishaq. 1994. *Kashmir's Transition to Islam: The Role of Muslim Rishis*. New Delhi: Manohar.

Kapur, Rajiv. 1986. *Sikh Separatism: The Politics of Faith*. London: Allen and Unwin.

Kroeber, A.L. 1930. 'Caste', *Encyclopedia of Social Sciences*, vol. III, pp. 254b–7a.

Leach, E.R. 1960. 'What should we mean by caste?' In E.R. Leach (ed.). *Aspects of Caste*. Cambridge: Cambridge University Press.

Madan, T.N. 1994a. 'Two faces of Bengali ethnicity: Bengali Muslim or Muslim Bengali'. In *Pathways: Approaches to the Study of Society in India*. New Delhi: Oxford University Press, pp. 202–25.

———. 1994b. 'The social construction of cultural identities in rural Kashmir'. In *Pathways: Approaches to the Study of Society in India*. New Delhi: Oxford University Press, pp. 167–201.

———. 1997. *Modern Myths, Locked Minds: Secularism and Fundamentalism in India*. New Delhi: Oxford University Press.

McLeod, W.H. 1989. *Who is a Sikh? The Problem of Sikh Identity*. Oxford: Clarendon Press.

Oberoi, H.S. 1994. *The Construction of Religious Boundaries. Culture, Identity and Diversity in the Sikh Tradition*. New Delhi: Oxford University Press.

Roy, Asim. 1983. *The Islamic Syncretistic Tradition in Bengal*. Princeton, N.J.: Princeton University Press.

Shils, Edward. 1975. 'Primordial, personal, sacred, and civil ties'. In *Centre and Periphery*. Chicago: University of Chicago Press, pp. 111–26.

Uberoi, J.P.S. 1991. 'Five symbols of Sikh identity'. In T.N. Madan (ed.). *Religion in India*. New Delhi: Oxford University Press, pp. 320–32.

Varshney, Ashutosh. 1992. 'Three compromised nationalisms: Why Kashmir has been a problem'. In Raju G.C. Thomas (ed.), *Perspectives on Kashmir*, Boulder: Westview Press, pp. 191–234.

Vincent, Joan. 1974 'The structuring of ethnicity', *Human Organization*, 33: 375–9.

Weber, Max. 1968. *Economy and Society*, 3 vols, New York: Bedminster.

7

*Kashmir, Kashmiris, Kashmiriyat**

Kashmīramandalam chaiva pradhānam jagati sthitam
Kashmir verily occupies a premier place in the world.

Nīlamata Purāṇa (AD c. 7th cent.)

In the lake the arms of temples and mosques
are locked in each other's reflections.
But the mutual need of the Pandit and
Muslim is so deep it can turn bitter...
Your memory gets in the way
of my memory.

Agha Shahid Ali (1949–2001)

mashīdan mandran girjan daramsālan ta astānan
yiman sārnai garan atsanuk kunai darvāza thāvun chhum

Mosques, temples, churches, hospices, and holy places:
To enter these many homes I will build but one doorway.

Ghulam Ahmad Mahjoor (1885–1952)

Myths, Legends, and History

The Kashmir Valley has now been for over four centuries a much
favoured destination of travellers from near and far in search of
unparalleled scenic beauty and, perhaps, escape from the hot
summers of the sub-tropical plains of north India. The Mughal

* This essay has been specially written as the introductory chapter in
The Valley of Kashmir: The Making and Unmaking of a Composite Culture
edited by Aparna Rao (forthcoming from Manohar Publishers, New
Delhi). I am grateful to Aparna Rao, Sudhir Chandra, and Edie and
Satish Sabarwal, and to Uma and Vini for their advice on an earlier draft.
It is dedicated to the memory of Aparna Rao.

emperor Jahangir (ruled 1605–27) journeyed summer after summer across the Pir Panjal mountains for rest and recreation in Kashmir. (This road is now under reconstruction for general use in the near future.) There he laid a beautiful fountain and flower garden, called the Shalimar, on the bank of the Dal lake in the outskirts of the ancient city of Srinagar. The tribute to Kashmir attributed to him is famous: 'If indeed there be paradise on the earth, it is this, it is this, it is this' (*agar firdaus bar ruye zamin ast, hamin asto hamin asto hamin ast*)! Two hundred years later, the poet Thomas Moore in faraway England, who had never been to India, asked 'Who has not heard of the Vale of Cashmere...?'

Many people today know about Kashmir for another less fortunate reason. Since the late 1980s, it has been one of the contemporary world's most troubled and dangerous places, even a 'nuclear flashpoint', in the grip of what India calls 'terrorist insurgency' and Pakistan, 'a freedom movement'. Over fifty thousand people, mostly Muslims but including Hindus, Sikhs, and security personnel, are said to have lost their lives in militancy related operations,[1] and nearly two hundred thousand Kashmiri Hindus have fled their homes. The disturbances in Kashmir originate in disaffection among the people generally owing to corruption in public life, bad governance, and the disputed constitutional status of the Indian state of Jammu and Kashmir, often briefly referred to as Kashmir. Earlier it had been an independent princely state, which formally became a part of India in 1947, under the shadow of a violent incursion of tribal groups (Afridis and others) engineered by Pakistan. How the Kashmir Valley became part of the Kashmir state in the middle of the nineteenth century will be described below.

The Valley is an oval-shaped basin, approximately 134 kilometres in length and 40 kilometres in breadth (total area 15, 120 sq. kms.), at an average altitude of 1800 metres above sea level. Its largest city and summer capital, Srinagar (Shrīnagara, said to have been founded by Ashoka, ruled 268–231 BC, but perhaps rebuilt in the sixth century) lies at 34°N, 75°E. Surrounded by mountains, dotted with lakes (including Wular, the largest fresh water lake in Asia), and drained by rivers of which the Jhelum (*Vitastā*) is the longest, the Valley was, Kashmiri Hindus believe, once in the ancient past a large mountain lake. The legend of the lake has found support in the researches of geologists and paleobotanists, and it is likely that a volcanic eruption followed by millennia of erosion may have led to the emptying of the waters. According to legend, it was literally an act of god.

The earliest extant text about Kashmir is the *Nilamata Purāna* (in Sanskrit, AD 6th–7th century). Kashmir (Kashmīra of which the native Kashīr is a direct phonetic derivative) is mentioned as a kingdom at the very beginning of this work. Kashmīra is linked to Kashmīrā, one of the names of the goddess Uma, Shiva's consort. Further it is stated that, what was formerly an 'enjoyable, heart-capturing lake', for very long, later became a 'beautiful land' after the water had been drained off by Ananta, the snake deity, on the command of Vishnu, the supreme god in the Vaishnava tradition. The lake had been the abode of a demon Jalodbhava who was invincible under water (Ved Kumari 1968: 16; 1973: 4). The problem with this story is that Uma and Vishnu belong to different pantheons but Kashmir probably evolved a syncretic religious tradition quite early. Kashmiri Brahmans today are Smartas, that is worshippers of Shiva, Shakti, and Vishnu, and upholders of the householder tradition. Domestic puja comprises the adoration of the panchayat (so named) of Ganapati, Surya, Vishnu, Shiva, and Devi.

There are other versions of the myth of genesis. One that is commonly told is that when all gods, including Shiva and Vishnu, had failed to vanquish Jalodbhava, they prayed to the supreme goddess for help. She transformed herself into a *shārika* (mynah) bird, picked up a pebble in her beak, and dropped it on the demon. The pebble instantaneously became a hillock and the demon was crushed to death under it. A hillock in the north of the city of Srinagar is known as Sharika Parbat and identified as the very 'pebble' that killed the demon. Sharika, a Shakta deity ('eighteen armed, dark complexioned, beautiful'), is worshipped as the Mother Goddess by Kashmiri Brahmans and circumambulation of the hillock is an act of religious devotion. The Valley, after it had surfaced, received different names including Kashmir and Satidesha, Sati being yet another name of Uma.

The new land was peopled by the serpent (dragon?)-worshipping Nagas (*nāg* in Kashmiri means a serpent as well as a spring). They were later joined by the Pishachas, who do not seem to have been welcome, and other migrants called Manavas and including Brahmans. One of these Brahmans, Chandradeva, became a mentor of the Naga chief Nila, and instructed him to compose Nilamata, the Naga code of conduct. The Brahmans seem to have tried to help produce a socially harmonious though internally diversified society by maintaining that they were all the descendants of the sage (rishi) Kashyapa. The word Kashmir has also been said to be derived from Kashyapa-*mar*, the abode of Kashyapa. Archaeological evidence that bears witness to neolithic settlements of 5000 years ago (notably at Burzahom and Gufkral) does not fire the popular imagination in the same manner as the imagined pasts.

The beginnings of the land, the significance of its name, and the origins of its inhabitants are by and large shrouded in myth and legend. Even a Jewish connection has been suggested (comments on the Semitic features of Kashmiris are numerous in travellers' accounts) by those who believe that Jesus survived the crucifixion, escaped to Kashmir with his mother and intimate followers, and lies buried in Srinagar (Kersten 2001). What is of real significance is that the social, religious, and economic organization of the Valley had come to be of a common pan-Indian type by the time the *Nīlamata Purāna* was composed. Besides tribal communities, the four principal varnas (Brahmans, Kshatriyas, Vaishyas, Shudras) and many castes including those resulting from inter-varna marriages are mentioned. The Naga cult, Shaivism, Vaishnavism, and Buddhism had their adherents among the people, but, as the Chinese traveller Hiuen Tsang noted in the mid-seventh century, Brahmanical religions had become ascendent at the cost of the other faiths. Agriculture, artisanate work, and trade seem to have been the principal types of economic activity. Politically, Kashmir was a kingdom with frontiers that often spilled over its geographical boundaries.

Nīlamata Purāna was one of the works consulted by Kalhana, author of the remarkable *Rājataranginī* ('river of kings'), a regional history in Sanskrit, composed between AD 1148 and 1150. He begins his chronicle in the hoary past, but soon comes to Ashoka, whom he identifies as a follower of the teachings of the Buddha, in the third century before the commencement of the Christian era. Kanishka of the central Asian Kushana dynasty also is named, but no mention is made of the famous fourth Buddhist ecumenical council that was convened under his royal patronage near Srinagar in the second half of the first century AD. The chronology remains a mixture of fact and fiction; it becomes surer only after the ninth century. It is clear that politically Kashmir was not isolated, and at the level of the people also movement and exchange were common. While Harsha of Kanauj (ruled AD 606–47) is believed to have subjugated Kashmir, Lalitaditya (ruled AD 724–61) of Kashmir presumably extended his dominions by conquering Kanauj, Punjab, and Tibet. Lalitaditya also had a passion for religious architecture, which is best exemplified by the massive Martand (sun) temple in south-east Kashmir. Severely damaged under the rule of the iconoclastic Sikandar, it survives today as a magnificent though forlorn ruin, a specimen of the Kashmir school of architecture (Wink 1990: 249–52).

Within Kashmir, increasing complexity marked all areas of life. Kings and queens often were powerful and cruel, court intrigues and debauchery were common, the bureaucracy (Kayasthas) became unscrupulous, Brahmans were characterized by greed as much (if not more) as by learning, and an uncultured but dominant landowning class (called the Damaras) emerged as a rival centre of power as did mercenary groups like the Tantrins (see Pandit 1968). The religious scene remained rather fluid, with Buddhists, Vaishnavas, Shaivas, Shaktas, and others comprising the population, without any group being preponderant.

The darker side of society and polity should not, however, be allowed to obliterate from view impressive developments characterizing cultural and religious life. Thus, Kashmiri Brahmans evolved a non-dualistic system of esoteric thought and practice (including yoga) between the fifth and eleventh centuries, generally known as Kashmir Shaivism, which is different from the Shaiva schools of south India. The earliest of the Kashmiri schools is that of the Kaulas; with strong Tantric affiliations, it is said to have been elaborated into a system in the early ninth century. The central quest is for the true knowledge of reality. The Kaula and the later Krama schools were integrated into the Trika ('threefold') system, which included new elements also. Its basic concept is the possibility of liberation of the individual seeker through the recognition (*pratyabhijna*) of Shiva as the source of all reality (Chatterji 1914; Singh 1979).

The most famous exponent of Trika philosophy was Abhinavagupta (ca.960–1025). In his exposition, the Absolute (or reality) is conceived as pure consciousness, different from appearances, which permeates the external objective world. 'The whole universe is created by God', he taught, 'in his own nature, just as one finds the reflection of the world in a mirror' (Hughes 1994: 22). Abhinavagupta was also a luminary in the fields of aesthetics and poetics (see Pandey 1963). The continuity of Brahmanical tradition over the longue durée finds daily expression in the recitation at home and in temple of a Sanskrit hymn composed by Abhinavagupta in praise of Shiva, who is hailed as the 'embodiment of Knowledge, unique, without beginning or end (*chinamayam ekam anantam anādim*)'. The best known and authentic exponent of Kashmir Shaivism in the twentieth century was Swami Lakhimanjoo (1907–84). Reviving the oral tradition, he focused in his discourses on both the cognitive and the experiential aspects of the *kundalinī* (creative energy) yoga (see Hughes 1994).

Another reminder of the longevity of the Brahmanical tradition is the annual pilgrimage to the cave of Amarnath, which was already an ancient ritual when Kalhana wrote the *Rājataringinī* (Pandit ibid.: 38) 850 years ago, and attracts today hundreds of thousands of pilgrims from all over India despite the disturbed conditions. It would seem though that during the medieval period the pilgrimage had been discontinued, and the route to the cave lost. It was a Muslim Gujjar shepherd who rediscovered it in the late nineteenth century, a fact gratefully acknowledged by the Pandits: the Gujjar family is given a share of the cash offerings made at the cave by the pilgrims.

ISLAM, CONVERSIONS, AND COMPOSITE CULTURE

A steady political decline from the death of the great king Avantivarman (in AD 883) onward brought the situation to such a pass that the takeover by Muslims, who had been around as mercenaries since the late eleventh century (Kalhana mentions Turushkas or Turks) became easy and virtually inevitable. In AD 1320, a Tartar warlord Dulucha invaded Kashmir; the Hindu king Suhadeva fled the Valley, but Dulucha did not stay long. Soon afterwards power was seized by a Tibetan fugitive, Rinchana. He became a Muslim but died before long (in 1323). It was one of his courtiers, Shah Mir (originally from Swat), who can be said to have firmly established Muslim rule in Kashmir in 1339. It lasted almost 500 years during which time local dynastic rule gave way to the Mughal imperium (in 1586), of which event the major surviving symbol is the fort atop Sharika Parbat built by the emperor Akbar. The pleasure gardens and retreats for meditation by Sufi masters came later. In the memory of Kashmiris, Mughal rule ended their independence. The last but one of their pre-Mughal rulers, Yusuf Shah, is fondly remembered as the husband of Habba Khatun, a commoner reputed to have been a legendary beauty and a gifted romantic poet. She is regarded as a maker of modern Kashmiri. Mughal control too disintegrated making it easy for Afghans under Ahmad Shah Abdali to take over Kashmir in 1753, initiating a period of extreme persecution of the people that lasted three quarters of a century.

Rapid and large-scale conversions to Islam in the Valley (comparable to similar but later developments in Bengal) call for some explanation. Marshall Hodgson's discussion of the subject in the context of the thirteenth to sixteenth centuries can serve as a useful backdrop. He mentions social and economic advantages, psychological pressures, discriminatory treatment of non-Muslims under sharia law, and even large scale persecution as contributory factors. He notes the 'steady tendency' of non-Muslim lands to become 'solidly Muslim' under Muslim rule (Hodgson 1961: chapter IV). In Kashmir, conversion had behind it a number of causes most notably: (i) mutual antagonism and internal corruption of the Brahmanical and Buddhist traditions; (ii) acute socio-economic and political degeneration of Kashmir in the last years of Hindu rule; (iii) sustained exertions of immigrant Sufi masters to propagate their faith; (iv) emergence of an eclectic and accessible folk version of Islam; and (v) acute intolerance of some of the early Muslim kings (Hangloo 2000: 59–60).

Among the Sufi masters, the contributions of Mir Sayyid Ali Hamadani of the Kubrawi order, who arrived in Kashmir in around 1379–84 as an upholder of pure Islamic faith and practice, are noteworthy. He was a zealous missionary but stayed only a couple of years during which he became the mentor of the king, Qutub-ud-Din (1372–89), advising him about the virtue and importance of being the true exemplar in a society in which Muslims were still a minority and Hindu practices rampant among the converts. This required a mixture of firmness and persuasiveness. The Mir's work was carried forward a decade later by his son, Mir Muhammad. The senior Mir's memory is enshrined in one of Srinagar's most beautiful sacred spots, the mosque of Shah-i Hamdan, also known as Khanaqah-i Mualla, on the riverbank, believed to have been built over a shrine dedicated to the Shakta goddess Kali. Even into the late 1980s, the site was available to Muslims (inside the mosque) and Hindus (outside on the ghat) for their respective modes of prayer and worship.

The first three hundred years of Muslim rule witnessed three different kingly styles in Kashmir. The first king, Shah Mir, had followed the path of gradual assimilation. A later king, Sikandar (ruled 1389–1413), resorted to coercion and persecution, reportedly under the influence of his prime vizier, Suhabhatta, a Brahman who had converted to Islam. He patronized immigrant Turkish and Persian Muslims, and displayed enormous enthusiasm for the destruction of Hindu temples, which won him the sobriquet of *butshikan*, idol breaker. He imposed punitive taxes on the Hindus and banned many religious practices and ceremonies. Inevitably large-scale conversions occurred and some Hindus (mainly Brahmans) migrated out of the Valley. The curious fact that all the native Hindus of Kashmir toward the end of the nineteenth century, when the German indologist Georg Bühler visited the Valley (in 1875), happened to be a single community of Brahmans numbering about 40,000 (Bühler 1877), was soon afterwards confirmed by the British civil servant Walter Lawrence (1895, 1909). The absence of non-Brahman castes was telling evidence, perhaps, of large-scale conversions to Islam, for the Brahmans must have been here as elsewhere a superior category within an internally heterogeneous social order. Inter-caste relations did not disappear, however; converted Muslims continued to provide hereditary caste services to their Brahman patrons well into the middle of the twentieth century (Madan 1994).

The third kingly style was that of Zain-ul-Abidin, Sikandar's younger son, who succeeded his elder brother as king in 1420. He revoked most of the anti-Hindu laws and strove to restore confidence among his non-Muslim subjects. He encouraged those who had fled to come back, stopped the burning of Brahmanical scriptures and the destruction of temples, allowed cremations, pilgrimages and sacrifices, and encouraged the ethos of cultural pluralism and religious tolerance. He is said to have even proclaimed that those forcibly converted could return to their ancestral faith. This was, however, impossible because the Brahmans considered ritual pollution caused by conversion irreversible.

Zain-ul-Abidin himself showed considerable interest in Brahmanical philosophies and sciences, anticipating in this and many other respects the Mughal emperor Akbar, a century and a half later, as the embodiment of the Sufi ideal of *sulh-i-kul* (total peace, peace towards all). Zain-ul-Abidin also took enormous interest in the secular affairs of his subjects, encouraging them to widen their economic activities to include stone cutting, wood carving, papier maché work, shawl and carpet weaving, embroidery, etc., which skills had arrived with the Turkish and Persian immigrants. The king's grateful subjects, of all faiths and occupations, revered him as the *bad shah*, the great king. Indeed, it is said that the Kashmiri Brahmans hailed him as *batta shah* (the king of the Bhattas, that is Brahmans) (see Kilam 1955).

By the time of Zain-ul-Abidin's death in AD 1470, Kashmiri society had begun to acquire the socio-religious composition that, barring changes in numbers, survived into the twentieth century. The majority of the people were and today are Muslims, mainly Sunnis but include a sizeable proportion of Shias. Ethnically, the overwhelming majority of the Muslims are descended from native converts of all castes; the rest, descendants of immigrants, include Afghans, Mongols, Persians, and Turks. The most recent of the immigrants are the nomadic pastoralists known as the Gujjars and the Bakkarwals. Their culture is based on continuous crossings of geographical and cultural boundaries (Rao 1998). The Hindus were and are exclusively Brahmans and use the community name Bhatta (Batta), 'learned persons' (teachers, priests, etc.). Actually many Muslims, descendants of Brahmans, also continue to use the family name Bhatta as also several others indicative of pre-conversion Hindu caste identities, high and low.

There are distinctions also within the Brahman community, who consider themselves Saraswats (one of the original divisions of this varna), reflecting sectarian divisions (Shaivas, Shaktas, Vamapanthis, Vaishnavas), occupational classes (Karkun, followers of secular occupations, and Gor or Guru, the priests), and calendrical preferences (Banamasi, Malamasi), etc. (Bühler 1877; Madan 2002: 19–23). It should be noted here that the community name of Pandit, which is most widely used and better known

today, came into use much later. Jai Narain Bhan, a Bhatta court-
ier of the Mughal emperor Muhammad Shah (1719–49), requested
that Kashmiri Brahmans at the court be addressed as Pandits,
rather than by such honorifics as Khwajah; the request was
granted through a royal proclamation (Sender 1988: 43).

The corrupt state of the upper echelons of Hindu society in the
fourteenth century has already been mentioned above as one of
the reasons for the rapid passage of Islam into Kashmir. Mention
must now be made of a development within the Hindu fold itself
that gave expression, on the part of at least some thoughtful
minds and sensitive souls, to strong disapproval of the ritualistic
ruts into which Brahmanical orthodoxy had fallen. The most
distinguished of them all was the mystic Lalla (b. circa 1320, see
Kaul 1973: 7), a gifted woman within the Shaiva (Trika) tradition.
Her thoughts or teachings have come down to us in the form of
her oral poetic utterances (*vākh, vākya*). Inevitably, they have
suffered distortions, and often sayings have been attributed to her
which are at variance with the rest, lexically, syntactically, and
substantively. What after critical scrutiny may be considered her
authentic reflections embody the core message of *advaita* (non-
dualism) and yoga (mystical union of the internal and the external)
leading to self-realization. For the attainment of such a higher
consciousness, self-control, purity of body and mind, and constant
meditation on the indivisible Absolute were, in accordance with
the Shaiva tradition, deemed essential by her. She called for the
abandonment of external forms of religious behaviour, including
priestly rituals, idol worship, pilgrimages, and the rest. She was
also against social conventions that, she believed, hindered higher
pursuits. The following two verses are illustrative of her thought
in which the cosmic and the social form one seamless whole:

gvaran vonnam kunuy vatsun	The Guru said but one thing to me:
nebra dopunam andar atsun	'The outside abandon, inward turn';
suy gav Lalli mey vākh to vatsun	That was for Lalla the Holy Word
tavay hyotum nangay natsun	Hence I roam 'naked', freed of
	illusions!
Shiva chhuy thali thali rozān	Shiva resides everywhere,
mo zān Hyond ta Mussalmān	Do not distinguish the Hindu from
	the Muslim;
trukay chhukh ta pān praznāv	If you are wise, know thy true self,
soy chhai Sāhibas zāni zān	Which indeed is to know the Lord!

It has been suggested by some historians that the Islamic notion of unity (*wahdat, tauhīd*), and some Buddhist and Nath Yogi ideas and practices too, must have influenced Lalla, given the times in which she lived (Khan 1994: 70, 73 et passim). This may be so, but it is hard to deny that her basic inspiration was that of her own family's Trika tradition (Kaul 1973: 70, 82f.). The language of her sayings provides ample evidence of the same: not only is it grounded in Sanskritized Kashmiri but it also includes many keywords and technical terms from the Brahmanical and Shaiva traditions and hardly any from the Islamic and Sufi traditions (see, for example, verses 89 to 96 in Kaul ibid.: 118–20). Indeed, it has been argued that she was one of the makers of the Kashmiri language as a suitable vehicle for philosophical thought (ibid.: 65). Although she was not alienated from Brahmanical thought, she was severely critical of prevalent Brahmanical religious and social practices. No wonder that the Brahmans were hostile to her and her recognition in her own community came relatively late (in the mid-nineteenth century). Further, it is not unlikely that her monist philosophy may have facilitated the conversion of many Hindus to Islam, with its own emphasis upon the oneness of God.

There is only one more seer of whom Kashmiris generally speak in the same breath as Lalla, namely Nur-ud-Din or (to use his popular name) Nunda Rishi (1379–1442). Son of a village watchman who had embraced Islam, Nur-ud-Din, however, traced his spiritual lineage from the Prophet Muhammad himself. He is the best known luminary of the unique Kashmiri mystic order of Muslim Rishis, distinguished by its native roots and eclecticism from the orthodox Sufi orders (Khan 1994). As is obvious from its name, the Rishi movement originated in the encounter between a proselytizing Islam, represented by the zealous ulama and the gentler Sufis who came to Kashmir from Central Asia and Persia, and a socially and politically decadent Hindu society that, however, still harboured true seekers like Lalla. It seems that many Brahman ascetics found refuge in and helped to shape the emergent, mainly rural Rishi order, which was enlivened by the impact of an orthodox God-centred, socially egalitarian Islam. Thus, the practice of *pās-e-anfās* ('watching the breath'), characteristic of the Muslim mystics, was probably derived from the yogic control of breath (*prānāyāma*). The Mughal emperor Jahangir was sufficiently struck by the vegetarianism and the practice of celibacy of the Rishis to take note of it in his memoirs (Rafiqi n.d.).

For Nur-ud-Din, the *Qur'ān*, the example of the Prophet Muhammad (*Sunna*), and the Law (sharia) were the true foundations of the religious life of Muslims; at the same time he paid homage to great Sufi masters (such as Sayyid Husain Simnani who had come to Kashmir), and went further on the path of religious syncretism in acclaiming Lalla as an avatār in the eyes of all Kashmiris (Khan 1994: 77, 83). Time and again his sayings echoed Lalla's. Her affirmation that, having long searched in vain for 'the Pandit' (knower of true knowledge, Shiva) in the outer world, she ultimately found Him in her 'own home' (in herself) (Kaul 1973: 120), is the very same as Nur-ud-Din's confession (Khan ibid.: 102):

su mae nishay ba tas nishay	He is with me and I with Him,
mae tas nishay qarār āv	In his presence I find peace;
nahaqai chhondum su pardishay	Foolishly I looked for Him elsewhere,
pananay deshay mae yār āv	My Beloved is no further from me than my sight.

The life of the Rishis was originally characterized by austerities combined with a radical, all-embracing, pantheistic altruism that was directed towards not only human beings but also animals, birds, trees, and plants (ibid.: 38). The Rishis emphatically were not renunciants: their asceticism was inner worldly and they showed a deep consciousness of social purposefulness and the importance of productive work. Nur-ud-Din despaired of the ways of the Ulama, and asked his followers to put their trust in the *Qur'ān* itself and in the Sufi practice of repeating God's name (*dhikr*) as a form of discipline and devotion. He was, like Lalla, a great communicator, using versified speech and homilies with great effect. Like her, he too contributed significantly to the making of the Kashmiri language enriching it with Arabic and Persian words. He was a mediator between the Great Tradition of Islam and Kashmiri beliefs and practices that had grown over the centuries under the umbrellas of Brahmanical and Buddhist traditions. The veneration of places of worship (*asthāpan, ziārat*) and the abodes of Sufi masters (*khānaqah*), common among Kashmiri Muslims, recalls to one's mind Hindu temples and Buddhist monasteries. The observance of anniversaries (*urs*), veneration of relics, and singing of songs of praise and thanksgiving addressed to God, the Prophet, and local saints following formal prayers (*nimāz*), while standing with folded hands, also are reminiscent of Hindu and Buddhist devotional styles.

And yet, basically, Kashmiri Islam as it was shaped over five hundred years or so always maintained a somewhat uneasy relationship between the Arabic (classical) and local traditions, never deaf to the call of the former but never also in denial of the latter. The ulama, the Sufis, and the Rishis have been in their respective and often contrary ways the exemplars of Islam in Kashmir from the fourteenth century to the present day, and people have made their choices. Syncretism involving bilateral compromises, historians tell us, has not been characteristic of Islam in Kashmir in the context of inter-religious (Muslim–Buddhist/Hindu) or intra-religious (within Islam) relations. But there has been convergence in both contexts. The Kashmiri practice of Islam in some of its aspects may seem opposed to the Great Tradition of Islam but, in fact, it is encompassed by the latter, such that the universal prevails over the local: neither is denied by the other. Thus understood, some scholars argue, Islamization efforts are uncalled for: Kashmiri Islam has been and is Islam, true to the twin calls of the Ka'ba and the local shrine (see Khan 1997: 86–96).

The relationship between the two varieties of Islam in Kashmir is perhaps best understood as a historical process rather than as a state of being. What the future will unfold is, of course, hard to predict. I presume that the split between the universalists and the upholders of the local tradition will not be easily bridged, and the latter will outnumber the former in the foreseeable future. Then there is the related question of how effectively Kashmiri Muslims generally will withstand the pressures of Islamic fundamentalism as a global phenomenon. The answer is contingent upon, first, how soon the political future of Kashmir is determined, and secondly, how comprehensive the processes of secularization in the Muslim world generally will be. These are currently marked by significant diversities.

JAMMU AND KASHMIR: AUTOCRACY AND DEMOCRACY

Muslim rule in Kashmir fell on bad days, as Hindu rule had earlier. The province (*subah*) became virtually independent of

Delhi in the mid-eighteenth century, but it soon came under Afghan rule, which was cruel and rapacious. The Brahmans and the Shias were subjected to severe persecution. It was the Kashmiri Pandits (some of whom had actually selfishly done quite well by themselves in Kashmir as well as Kabul) who decided to approach Maharaja Ranjit Singh of Lahore to end their misery. Kashmir was annexed by Lahore in 1819, but not for very long. The brief duration of the Sikh rule was no mercy for it too turned out to be oppressive.

The kingdom of Lahore capitulated to the East India Company's government in 1846, and two treaties were signed for subsequent governance of the areas concerned. By the second of these treaties, the British handed over to Raja Gulab Singh, the Dogra ruler of Jammu, all the hilly and mountainous country situated east of the Indus and west of the Ravi in exchange for seventy-five lakh rupees and some other tokens of gratitude and loyalty. This should have included the Kashmir Valley too, but that came into his possession with British military help only a little later, ending the suzerainty of Lahore there. Ladakh, the western part of Tibet, was conquered by Gulab Singh earlier in the century (in 1834). His son Ranbir Singh further expanded his territories, conquering Gilgit in 1860. Baltistan too had come into the possession of the Dogras. Thus, a process that had started early in the nineteenth century to expand the domain of the small principality of Jammu (absorbing Basoli, Chenani, Kishtwar, Poonch, Rajaori, etc.) became, by the end of the century, the large enterprise of constituting the state of, as it was called, Kashmir and Jammu or, for short, Kashmir (Lawrence 1909; Bamzai 1962; Rai 2004).

Territorially the largest princely state in the subcontinent in the twentieth century, it comprised two provinces (Kashmir, Jammu) and the frontier districts (Ladakh, Gilgit), with a total area of 80,900 square miles and a population of 2, 905, 578 (1901 census), of whom only 158,478 (about 5 per cent) lived in urban areas. Religion-wise, Muslims accounted for 74 per cent and Hindus 23 per cent; Sikhs and Buddhists made up the remaining 3 per cent. In these figures we have an anticipation of later problems: an overwhelmingly rural and poor people, predominantly consisting of Muslims, ruled by a Hindu Maharaja, who being ethnically a Dogra, belonged to the province of Jammu, which was smaller than the Valley both area-wise and population-wise (Rai 2004).

Between 1846 and 1925, the first three Dogra rulers of the state (father, son, and grandson) were devout Vaishnava Rajput Hindus, who claimed to belong to the very same 'sun' lineage as the god and ideal king Rama, and considered their rulership a religious obligation. This perspective generated two interrelated moral judgements, namely, first, Hindus were religiously the better guided people than the others, and secondly, among Hindus, the Vaishnavas were superior to the Shaivas and the Shaktas. Pursuantly, the new rulers promoted Vaishnavism in various ways, including notably the construction of a magnificent temple complex for the worship of Raghunath, the tutelary deity of the Dogras, in Jammu. Ranbir Singh, the second Maharaja, let it be known that Vishnu appeared to him in a dream, and asked him to have a marble image of him as the mace holding Gadadhar sculpted (by a Rajasthani sculptor, who too received divine instruction in a dream in this regard), and establish it in Srinagar. The image was placed in a boat and allowed to float downstream on the Jhelum. A temple-cum-palace complex (Shergarhi) was constructed on the left bank of the river above the spot where the boat had stopped. The point of this miracle story is obvious to need elaboration.

When the opportunity arose, Ranbir Singh also promoted the worship of a new Vaishnava goddess, Ragnya or Khir Bhavani ('Milk Goddess') at a spring about a dozen miles downstream from Srinagar, and had a suitable liturgical text (*mahātmya*) composed in her honour. Miracles and dreams occur in this story also. She thus emerged as a rival to the ancient Sharika Bhagvati (mentioned earlier), whose worship had traditionally included offerings of raw and cooked sheep's meat. The killing of cattle for beef was banned and the buying of milk products by Hindus from Muslims was prohibited.

Altogether the Dogra rulers thought poorly of the quality of the religious life of the Pandits. The celebration of Rama Navami (Rama's birthday) and Janma Ashtami (Krishna's birthday) in temples and homes was encouraged, and the Dussehra, commemorating Rama's triumph over the demon king Ravana, was publicly celebrated by the Maharaja himself at the Parade Grounds in Srinagar. This became an annual celebration. Besides, financial support was provided for the repair and reconstruction of old temples. No comparable steps were taken for the promotion of

Islam and the repair of old mosques. Actually financial support to the famous Rishi shrine at the village of Aish-Muqam was withdrawn (Rai ibid.: 102). As for the ethnic divide, preference was given to the Hindus of Jammu over the Pandits in making appointments to administrative posts; Kashmiri Muslims, generally illiterate, were almost wholly outside the pale of government patronage.

On the secular side, it must be conceded that, after the long and dark night of Afghan and Sikh rule, the Dogras took some minimal positive steps, or promoted private initiatives, to improve the quality of life of the Kashmiris generally. Modern education and physical culture and modern medicine-based health care were introduced in the Valley late in the nineteenth century by Christian missionaries (Biscoe 1971). Facilities for affluent Western and Indian tourists (hotels, houseboats, merchandize stores, etc.) also came up around the same time.

Public works (roads, drainage, sanitary water supply, electricity generation) were added to the state's responsibilities. Some first steps were taken towards the setting up of small-scale industrial units (a government-owned silk factory, privately owned carpet weaving, and safety-match making units, etc.), promoting tourism, which in turn helped boost handicrafts, and preventing land alienation through legislation. Superior quality shawls (*pāshminā, jāmawār*), papier maché products and carved walnut furniture— all the work of hereditary Muslim craftsmen—attracted worldwide attention. Poverty, illiteracy, and ill-health were, however, such colossal problems in the Valley that whatever was done was too little. The total number of schools maintained by the state was still as low as 87 in 1901 and the overall literacy was a mere 2 per cent (Lawrence 1909: 79). One of the striking symbols of the downtrodden condition of the people was the legal fiction that since Kashmir had been 'purchased' by Gulab Singh from the British, *all* land was the personal property of the ruling family, and those who deemed themselves owners of agricultural land were in fact only tenants: this atrocious position was corrected only in the 1930s.

The Muslim majority of the Valley, exploited or at best uncared for, was not totally dormant. If anywhere, religion was among them the sigh of an oppressed people. The practice of Islam, such as it was, however, came under unprecedented pressure. The creation of the state of Kashmir and Jammu (later redesignated Jammu and Kashmir, J&K) and the establishment of reasonably stable conditions therein, opened the Valley to subcontinental influences. One of the significant intrusions early in the twentieth century was that of the reformist Islamic movement Ahl-i-Hadis, which promoted a purist Islam, based exclusively on the *Qu'rān* and the example and sayings (Sunna, Hadis) of the Prophet Muhammad. From its perspective, the veneration of saints and shrines and the adoration of relics were indisputably unacceptable as valid Islamic practices. The votaries of reforms in Kashmir were some ulama and lay persons who came into contact with the leaders of the movement in places like Delhi. An Ahl-i-Hadis mosque came up in Srinagar to serve as a nerve centre, and the widely respected Mirwaiz (principal preacher) of the Jama Masjid in Srinagar was believed to be supportive; he had also been dubbed a sympathizer of fundamentalist (Wahhabi) Islam. Traditional Kashmiri Islam found its supporters among other Mirwaizs, and the government invoked the policy of state neutrality in matters pertaining to religion (which was only an excuse for lack of interest) to stay out of the controversy (Zutshi 2003: 150–1 et passim). The divide between the followers of an Arab and a Kashmiri Islam survives to this day, and has had some tragic consequences. By and large, however, Kashmiri Muslims not only remain steadfast within their own tradition, they also have scholars among them today who are learned and persuasive enunciators of the distinctiveness and validity of Kashmiri Islam.

But religion alone does not constitute the life of Kashmiri Muslims: increasingly through the greater part of the twentieth century economics and politics have gained salience. The roots of the awakening lay in the emergence of a tiny but purposeful Muslim educated class in the late 1920s. The big turning point was a violent confrontation on 13 July 1931 between the state police and a Muslim crowd in the vicinity of the main jail in Srinagar, where a non-Kashmiri Muslim was on trial on the charge of sedition. The police opened fire on the protesters, killing some of them. The dispersed demonstrators proceeded towards the city centre and made sporadic attacks on the Pandits and their properties. Remembered to this day by Muslims generally as the 'Martyrs' Day' and by most Pandits as 'The Loot', the events marked the beginning of a political movement against autocratic

Dogra rule. What began as a communal disturbance, in which the Pandits identified themselves and were identified by Muslims with the Hindu-dominated state, was before long consciously sought to be restructured by some Muslim leaders on economic (landowner versus tenant), political (ruler versus subjects), and ethnic (Kashmiri versus Dogra) lines.

Organizationally, these efforts led to the division of Kashmiri politics into the National and Muslim Conferences in 1939, with the former commanding much greater influence under the leadership of a charismatic leader, Sheikh Mohammad Abdullah (1905–82), who belonged to the first generation of university educated Muslim youth (he studied at Aligarh Muslim University) in Kashmir. He was able to attract the following of some Pandits and Sikhs also, and tried to present his political objectives as secular and state-based (and not confined to the Muslims and the Valley). These developments in Jammu and Kashmir were welcomed by the Indian National Congress; in fact, Jawaharlal Nehru, who was the President of All India States Peoples' Conference, declared the demand for 'responsible government' as the objective of progressive political elements in all Indian states. Nationalist Kashmiris were thus cast in the role of the torch bearers of this freedom movement.

During the 1940s, Kashmir, the state as well as the Valley, was in a state of political turmoil. In 1946 Sheikh Abdullah gave the call for the abrogation of the 1846 treaty (under which Kashmir had come into the possession of the Dogra rulers) and the vacation of the Valley by the Maharaja. He dramatically offered to raise 75 lakhs of rupees from the public to pay off the ruler. Abdullah and other top leaders of the National Conference were tried for sedition and imprisoned.

It was not politics alone that was aflame in the Valley in the 1930s and 1940s. There was an enormous release of energy and creativity in many other fields, most notably education, journalism, and literary activity. Public enterprise more than matched governmental initiatives in opening schools, colleges, and hospitals. By the mid-1940s, Srinagar had two government and three private (two Hindu, one Muslim) colleges. A small group of progressive Pandit doctors, instead of entering government service, chose to set up the Kashmir National Hospital in Srinagar, run on a shoestring budget, which became a symbol of Pandit participation in people's causes on secular lines. Daily and weekly newspapers in Urdu (*Hamdard, Rahbar, Martand, Desh, et al.*) were started not only by political and cultural organizations but also by public spirited individuals. The poetry of Ghulam Ahmad Mahjoor (1885–1952) was the supreme symbol of both political awakening and cultural creativity. Kashmiri as a spoken language without a script had a long tradition of song and folktale; the dominant themes of lyrical poetry were romantic love and religious devotion. It was the talented and socially conscious Mahjoor who introduced the themes of love of one's land, communal harmony, and the assertion of human dignity and political rights. (His choice of the pen-name of 'Mahjoor', a slave without any rights, was itself a bold challenge to autocracy.) His 'call to the gardener' (1938) to create a 'new spring' acquired the status of a revolutionary anthem:

agar vuzanāvahan bastī gulan hanz,	Should you want to arouse this
trāv zero bam	land of flowers,
bunyul kar vāw kar gagrāy kar	Abandon your song and dance;
toophān paidā kar	Shake the earth, unleash
	raging winds and thunderclaps!
	Give birth to a great storm!

RELIGION, NATIONALISM, AND ETHNICITY

When the British Government announced in 1947 its decision to transfer power to a successor (India) and a new (Pakistan) state in August that year, it also notified the lapse of its status as the paramount power in relation to the 'native' states, which would thus become wholly sovereign. It was, however, obvious to everyone concerned that these states would have to 'accede to' (merge with) one or the other new state of the subcontinent, mainly on the basis of territorial contiguity. While other princes proceeded accordingly, the biggest two, Kashmir and Hyderabad, vacillated between possible options. The Kashmir Maharaja's problem was partly like Hyderabad's (the prince and the majority of the people belonged to different religions) but, while Hyderabad was embedded in India, Kashmir's borders were contiguous with both India and Pakistan. In October 1947, Pakistan-backed tribal mercenaries intruded into Kashmir and headed for the capital city of Srinagar, indulging in rape, pillage, and killings along the way, ostensibly to put an end to the repression of Muslims in the state. Lamb (1992) has written of the 'horrors of tribal invasion'. This sudden development convinced the Maharaja that his only option in the circumstances was to accede to India, which he did forthwith, so that the Indian army and air force could come in to push back the raiders. This proved a much harder undertaking than anticipated as regular Pakistan army units were sent into Kashmir in 1948.

The fast developing scenario led to the installation of a National Conference government headed by Sheikh Abdullah in the state late in 1947, and the abdication by the Maharaja in favour of his son the next year (Singh 1994). To completely overcome the aggression, India had to choose between permitting its troops to cross into Pakistan, a course that Abdullah's government favoured, or to seek intervention by the United Nations, which India did. The India–Pakistan dispute over Kashmir has remained on the agenda of the Security Council ever since. Its recommended solution, after asking for a UN-supervised ceasefire, was a plebiscite to ascertain the wishes of the people of the state, but a precondition for this was the complete withdrawal of its troops and mercenaries by Pakistan, which has never happened. The ceasefire has held, leaving areas in western and north-western parts of the state in Pakistani hands, where Pakistani military remains in control. No plebiscite has been held over half a century after the proposal was made in a Security Council resolution in 1949, and is now generally considered unworkable (Dasgupta 2002; Jha 1996; Lamb 1992).

When East Pakistan broke away in 1971 to emerge as Bangladesh, Pakistan, anxious to regain lost territories in the west, and obtain release of nearly 100,000 soldiers who were being held as prisoners of war by India, was in no position to dictate the terms of peace. The tacit understanding between Indira Gandhi and Zulfikar Ali Bhutto at Shimla in 1972 was to gradually convert the ceasefire line in J&K into an international frontier. P.N. Dhar, one of the architects of this agreement, has written that this still is the only feasible solution of the Kashmir problem in its international aspect (Dhar 2000: 189–97). The recent conversion in 2005 of the 'line of control' (the old ceasefire line) into a 'soft border', permitting easy travel across it to separated Kashmiri families, seems to be a crucial step in this direction.

Going back to the assumption of power by Abdullah, he proceeded quickly to enact land and tenancy reforms that were more radical than those of any other state, and went a long way towards empowering Kashmiri peasantry, which was predominantly Muslim. He also tried to limit the powers of the Indian Union and enhance those of the J&K state by emphasizing the terms of the accession, limited as these were to matters such as defence, external affairs, currency, and communication. Unlike any other state comprising the Union, J&K acquired a constitution and a flag. The central government was supportive: the Indian Constitution, which became effective in 1950, confers a special though temporary status on the state through Article 370. This temporary status has by now acquired quasi-permanent status (Behera 2000).

Abdullah's ambitions soared. He envisaged an autonomous and perhaps independent status for his state and for himself the crown, as it were. He soon began to loose the common touch and the loyalty of some of his closest colleagues. The vigilant Mahjoor had seen very early the coming of a new aristocracy. In a 1948 poem on the theme of freedom, he had lamented:

Yi āzādī chha svarguch hoor	Freedom is a houri of Paradise,
pheryā khāna path khānai	Will it wander house to house?
fakat kentsan garan andar	In a few homes alone,
marān grāyi āzādī	She showers her favours!

Abdullah was dismissed in 1953 when proof came to hand that he was seeking international backing for his plans. He was put under detention (Abdullah 1993), and succeeded by his close associate, Bakshi Ghulam Mohammad. During the eleven years that Bakshi headed the state government, J&K witnessed considerable progress on the educational and economic fronts, and stronger ties were forged with the Union. Abdullah now repudiated the accession and this ensured that he stayed in prison. But the Bakshi's regime came to be characterized by deep corruption and erosion of the rule of law. The alienation between the three cultural regions (Jammu, Kashmir, Ladakh), which began in Abdullah's time, continued unabated.

The 1960s were a time of drift in J&K, but the process of closer integration with India was continued by the governments that held power. Perhaps the most notable thing to happen was that, when in 1965 Pakistan sent in infiltrators into the state, triggering the second Indo-Pakistan war, Kashmiri Muslims, who were expected by Pakistan to play a supportive role, generally did not do so. Fortunately, the hostilities ceased within weeks. Their outcome was more favourable to India than Pakistan, and the peace was ratified through the Tashkent Agreement (1966). On the negative side, the alienation of the National Conference and the state government from the people deepened, creating a vacuum that was sought to be filled by new political elements, notably the anti-secular Jamat-i-Islami. The Jamat spread its influence through madrasas and also tried to penetrate the political arena, but without much success. Its significance lay, however, in the promotion of fundamentalist exclusivity (Schofeld 1997).

Abdullah, characteristically blowing hot and cold, alternately in and out of prison, finally arrived at an understanding with the Union government, and once again headed the J&K administration in 1975 (Qasim 1992). He tried to arrest the influence of the Jamat-i-Islami by banning its schools. Old age, the years out of power, the deepening of economic ties with the rest of the country, and the emergence of a Muslim educated middle class, had together produced a politically self-aware Kashmir Valley which was a stranger to the once charismatic and autocratic Abdullah. Acknowledging candidly that the clock could not be turned back, he reconciled himself to the role of an elder statesman: the days of the revolutionary rebel, and subsequently of the ambitious ruler, were clearly over.

Political developments of another kind were on the horizon by the time Abdullah died in 1982. A year later elections were held in the state. The electorate included an increasingly literate and economically better off Muslim middle class that was well informed about international developments, including the Iranian Revolution of 1979. The election results brought to the surface the dangerous trends of communalization and regionalization in the politics of the state, to which all political parties made their contribution. The pattern of the distribution of population provided the basis for such a turn of events. According to the 1981 census, while Muslims were 64 per cent of the total population of the J&K state, their percentages for the Kashmir Valley, Ladakh-Kargil, and Jammu provinces were 95, 46, and 30 respectively. The Buddhists accounted for 51 per cent of the population of

Ladakh-Kargil, but the Hindus in the Valley, mostly Pandits, were a mere 4 per cent (Joshi 1999: 451). While the call of Islamic fundamentalists was heard in the Valley, Hindu communalists raised their own divisive slogans in Jammu. Abdullah's son Farooq, the new chief minister, was unequal to the task of handling the developing scenario. His work was not made any easier by the opportunistic and manipulative policies of the Union governments under Indira Gandhi and her son, Rajiv.

While the politicians engaged in their battles of self-aggrandizement, the people's resentment against the state and the Union governments, and against the infamous practice of rigged elections in J&K deepened. They looked for new political goals, new leaders, new methods, and new international allies. In the changing situation, the allies for some of the severely disgruntled elements were those who provided money and guns. The training of Kashmiri youth in armed insurgency is believed to have begun in Pakistan in 1987–8 (Behera ibid.: 164). The Jammu Kashmir Liberation Front (JKLF) emerged as the leading organization demanding freedom (*āzādī*). It projected itself as a secular democratic body and stressed the relevance of armed struggle, a far cry from the pacifist traditions of the people of Kashmir. Before long the movement developed fundamentalist and communal orientations, and targeted Kashmiri Pandits as 'informers' (*mukhbir*) and 'enemy agents', the enemy being the Indian government. Street bombings and selective killings of the Pandits began in mid-1989, and within months the militant cadres of JKLF clarified their concept of *āzādī* as Nizam-i-Mustafa, Islamic rule.

Very rapidly the Valley was in the throes of a mass movement in 1990. The abduction in December 1989 of a daughter of Mufti Mohammad Sayeed, a Kashmiri politician who had just assumed charge as the Union Home Minister in Delhi, and her release in exchange for several militants who were under detention, gave much confidence to the secessionist elements, particularly in Srinagar and other towns. The Pandits felt deeply threatened, following warnings in some newspapers and on neighbourhood public address systems asking them to support Islamic rule or leave the Valley. What began as isolated incidents of migration rapidly ended up as a near total exodus. Of the estimated 200,000 Pandits, all but about 10,000 persons, or even less (living in about

270 locations), have left their homes, jobs, businesses, and properties to seek shelter in refugee camps in Jammu, Delhi, and elsewhere, or with relatives (Madan 2002: xvii–xxii). They have not yet been able to return fifteen years later. The traditional pluralist and tolerant character of the Kashmir Valley (Madan 1994: chapter 9) has been irreparably damaged. To maintain, as is sometimes done by some Kashmiris and non-Kashmiris, that the Pandits left without sufficient reason, or because a crafty governor engineered their departure so that he could deal with the Muslims without any hindrance, reveals a woeful lack of both empathy and commonsense, for a beleagured microsopic minority can ill afford to take risks with life and honour, and no one in his or her senses would abandon home, work, and property because of a bus at the doorstep.

It is not only intercommunity relations that have been damaged, the characteristic eclectic ethos of Kashmiri Islam itself has been brought under severe strain by non-Kashmiri fundamentalist elements who have penetrated the Valley as *mujāhideen* or the soldiers of holy war. Some of them, earlier active in Afghanistan, headed for Kashmir once the curtain came down on the Taliban government. Such elements are believed to have played a crucial role in the arson that consumed the resting place of Nur-ud-Din, the great Muslim Rishi (mentioned above), in Chrar-i-Sharif in 1994 (Joshi 1999: 352–66). Two episodes of the brutal killing of the remnants of the Pandit community, in the villages of Wandahama and Nadimarg in April 1998 and March 2003 respectively, in which about fifty innocent and trustful men, women, and children were killed, put paid to hopes of an early return of the refugees to their homes.

By the mid-1990s, the JKLF found itself marginalized by a large number of more aggressively militant Muslim outfits. Among these, the Hizbul Mujahideen displaced JKLF as the principal recipient of Pakistani patronage. The overall situation in the Valley and some border districts in Jammu amounted to a 'proxy' war between militants and the state and central security forces. The government's early strategy of coping with the situation with 'the mailed fist' left much to be desired (Ganguly 1997). A change in the Kashmir policy of the Government of India emerged during the years (1999–2004) that the National Democratic Alliance was in power in New Delhi. On the initiative of Prime Minister

Atal Bihari Vajpayee, the central government took the first steps towards a dialogue with Pakistan and the representatives of a group of about two dozen political parties, collectively known as the All Party Hurriyat Conference (APHC), founded in 1993, whose stated political objective is the establishment of an independent state. But a rift between the extremist (pro-Pakistan) and moderate (pro-independence) groups in 2003 has weakened the APHC. The promising meeting between President Pervez Musharraf of Pakistan and Prime Minister Manmohan Singh of India in New Delhi in April 2005 has raised cautious hopes of a 'final solution' of the Kashmir problem based on radical rethinking of the notion of 'border', but it is too early to celebrate.

It must also be noted that numerous Muslims in the Valley are now deeply conscious of the fact that, from their perspective, the violent struggle for freedom, whether conceived as jihad or in secular terms, has brought with it frightful disruption of normal life for them too. Caught between the gun-wielding militants and armed security forces, they have suffered heavy losses of life and property. The Valley has become a prison for them. The worst sufferers have been young children robbed of their innocence; those older have been deprived of proper education; and those still older find themselves ill equipped for the privileges and responsibilities of adult life. A whole generation of Kashmiri Muslim youth have grown up in the Valley since the early 1990s without knowing any Pandits intimately. Likewise, Kashmiri Muslims are the unseen but not unheard of 'terrorists' for Pandit children in the refugee camps of Jammu.

Looking at the events in the Valley over the last half century, it is clear that political opinion among Kashmiri Muslims runs along three conceptions of nationalism, namely religious, secular, and ethnic (pp. 167ff. above). Adherents of the first variety want Kashmir to be a part of Pakistan on the basis of religious identity, the principle that underlay the partition of the subcontinent. The secular nationalists believe that their traditional Kashmiri ethos of religious pluralism is wholly compatible with the secular state of the Indian constitution and Kashmir's destiny binds it with India's. As against these two views, the currently dominant view appears to be that the composite Kashmiri culture is unique and strong enough to serve as the ideological basis of an independent state, which would, however, need economic support and defence and diplomatic guarantees by both India and Pakistan. On closer examination, and in the prevailing circumstances, with the Pandits excluded from the Valley physically as well as politically, Kashmiri religious and ethnic nationalisms are different only in terms of the future political status that they envisage for the Muslim majority areas of the state including the Valley. Religion is the key element in both these nationalisms, but it could be argued, that the conceptions of Islam (universal or local) in the two cases are not the same.

The ideological foundation of ethnic nationalism is nowadays referred to as *Kashmīriyat*, 'the state of being a Kashmiri'. It is not a Kashmiri word and has become current usage only in the last twenty years or so. Kashmiriyat was not a part of the vocabulary of Kashmiri politics of the 1930s and 1940s (Zutshi 2003: 233 et passim) as were socio-economic categories such as landlord and cultivator/tenant. The Kashmiri word that comes closest to it is the collective name 'Kashir' for the Kashmiri speaking natives of the Valley.

What Kashmiriyat connotes today depends upon whom you ask, a votary of the idea or a sceptic. Generally, it refers to Kashmiri identity cutting across the religious divide and defined by, above all, the key elements of the love of the homeland (Kasheer) and of common speech (Koshur). Besides, similar customs and practices (for example, distribution of cooked or uncooked food as a token of goodwill, visits to shrines, and reverence for the relics of holy men), similar culinary and sartorial styles, shared folklore and folk music, etc., had in past contributed to an ineffable sense of mutual recognition and togetherness that was both physical and cultural.

In more concrete details, inter-community differences in respect of all the foregoing and other criteria have also been present. To give but a few examples: Keywords for religious and moral concepts differ between the two communities as do their conceptions of the Valley (Sharada Peeth or the land of learning, gods and goddesses for Pandits and the land of Islam for Muslims); similarly not all items of food, kitchenware, and traditional dress are identical, and they do not interdine; Muslims and Pandits do not intermarry, and they follow very different rules of marriage and inheritance; Muslims are not allowed inside Hindu kitchens, worship rooms, and temples, and Pandits would neither wish to nor be allowed to join community-prayers in a Muslim mosque. The conceptions of the socio-economic order in which they participated overlapped but were not identical: the society was one but its perceptions were various (Madan 1994; Wani 2005: 273–97).

Most significantly, the memories of the past that the two communities have are not always the same. It is arguable that the distinctiveness of traditional Kashmiri society lay in the Muslims and Pandits having built agreement (a kind of social contract) on the basis of the legitimacy of religious and cultural differences. In psychological terms, one could speak of the existence of genial amity, or more perceptively, of a subtle sense of 'mutual need' that was not wholly free of tension. If anything could be called Kashmiriyat, I think, it would be this pluralistic culture of tolerance that yet was not syncretism. The political awakening of the 1930s and its further course into the 1980s, combined with the restructuring of the feudal economy, gradually undermined the structure of harmonious inter-community relations as well as the sentiment of amity. In short, the secular concept of Kashmiriyat is in today's circumstances rather vague, it has an uncertain future, particularly because the events of the last quarter century have sharpened communal identities in all regions of the state (Jammu, Kashmir, and Ladakh).

An alternative perspective is that Kashmiriyat was the gradual outcome of the mutual adaptation of the various pre-Islamic religious traditions and the Great Tradition of Islam. The most profound exemplars of this dialectic were the Rishis. The spirit of the dialectic was mystical religious experience and universal love. The maturation of Kashmiriyat was, however, impeded and even distorted, it is argued, by the fabrication in the mid-nineteenth century of the state of Jammu and Kashmir, a Hindu polity, and its intrusion into the cultural life of the peoples of the Valley. Their identities were redefined in exclusive in place of inclusive terms. The heightened communal consciousness came to a head in the 1930s. This alienation provided the basis for the events of the last two decades. So understood, Kashmiriyat refers to a historical promise that was not fully realized (Khan 2004), indeed it was reversed. Kashmiri Muslims may still talk about Kashmiriyat, and so may the Pandits, but the prospect of a merger of cultural horizons, while it produces nostalgia, seems unrealizable, particularly following the Pandit exodus.

One still hears about the government's resolve to bring the Pandits back to the Valley. Kashmiri Muslims generally, echoing Sheikh Abdullah's sentiment that Kashmiri culture without Pandit contributions would lose its 'flavour' (1986: 883), say that they miss their Pandit 'brethren'. No Muslim organization has, however, so far come forward with a formal plan for the return of the Pandits. In 2002, a governmental committee estimated that the cost of bringing back and rehabilitating the migrants would be 2300 crores of rupees. In the summer of 2004, the media reported a 240 crore rupee project of the J&K Government to build 200 two bedroom flats in a village in Badgam district of the Valley for Pandits wishing to come back. Similar schemes elsewhere would add another 400 flats. How many Pandits would thus come home (if they do)? Perhaps 5000 or may be 10,000, if more accommodation is made available, security guaranteed, and economic opportunities provided. How many swallows make a summer? And one should recall that no Pandit family, howsoever poor, ever lived except in a three floor house, which was more than house, it was home (see Madan 2002: 39–48). The 2005 Report of the Parliamentary Committee on the Home Ministry has castigated the Union Government for its 'lack of clear vision' on the future of Kashmiri Pandits. More need not be said.

On their part, some Pandit migrant organizations have asked for resettlement in their 'own Kashmir (Panun Kashmir)', if necessary in a specially carved out area in the Valley. Appeals are issued from time to time by Pandits of the senior generation for the preservation of cultural roots and of physical ties (for example, through pilgrimages) with the Valley. The unbearable miseries of those thousands who still live in cramped refugee camps, the 'migrants' of officialese, under appalling conditions of poverty in Jammu (where their number was officially put at 34,000 in 2001) and elsewhere (the total number registered migrants is 56,487), arouse both anguish and anger among the Pandits generally, although nobody else seems to bother, perhaps because they are too few to qualify as a vote-bank. Those qualified to make the judgement have spoken of the 'psychological traumas' and 'moral degradation' of the camp dwellers, recovery from which will not be easy.

But this is not the whole picture. There are also thousands of Pandit young men and women, who have grown into adulthood in the last fifteen years, acquired educational and professional skills, and spread far and wide in search of work opportunities and a new life—and in many cases succeeded remarkably in doing so. The backdrop of these individual success stories, namely the sudden and traumatic loss of homes and homeland under threat to life and honour, should not be, however, forgotten. The migrants also know that their cultural identity will gradually lose its depth and vigour, but then time flies only forward like an arrow. The first cultural trait to be lost will be, significantly and sadly, the mother tongue, the key marker of identity. Without a script, enshrined in speech and song, it already seems alien with a load of neologisms. I have been told that not all Pandit children in the refugee camps are proficient in the language. Other cultural traits too will flounder. Like the Nehrus and Saprus of yore, today's Pandit refugees will enter into their own double-edged exchanges with the languages and lifestyles of the areas they settle down in. The tunes of Kashmiriyat, for all their melody and nostalgia, will begin to sound mute to them. Well may they recall a poem by one of their best modern poets, Dina Nath Nadim (1916–88), but give it new meanings:

mea chham āsh pagahuch	My hopes rest in the morrow:
pagah sholi duniyah	Tomorrow the world will be gorgeous![2]

Indeed, this is the fond hope of all Kashmiris today, each and everyone having his or her own vision of the future, but for now uncertainty is the dominant mood. The old world, such as it was, has been lost; a new one has yet to be won.[3]

NOTES

1. According to Lt. Gen. (retd) S.K. Sinha, Governor of the state, speaking in New Delhi on 29 April 2005, the figures for deaths are: 20,000 militants, 15,000 civilians ('almost all killed by terrorists'), and 5000 security personnel (*Daily Excelsior*, Jammu, 30 April 2005). He characterized the manner of killings by terrorists as generally brutal.
2. The translations throughout this essay are mine. The transcription of Kashmiri in Roman is far from satisfactory. Agha Shahid Ali wrote in English.
3. This has not been an easy essay to write. The reader should know that I was born and brought up in a Kashmiri Pandit home in Srinagar, but have since 1949 lived mostly outside Kashmir, except

for a year in 1957–8 when I was engaged in a field study of family and kinship among the Pandits of rural Kashmir (Madan 2002). The eruption of violence in 1989–90 compelled my parental family and all kith and kin to leave their homes, two of which were burnt by terrorists. Our own home in Srinagar (one of the finest specimens of Pandit domestic architecture, with its carved walnut wood panellings, showing Iranian influence in design and construction) was vandalized, ripped, and robbed. My deepest regret is about the loss of books and manuscripts, some of them rare, collected over two generations.

REFERENCES

Abdullah, Sheikh Mohammad. 1986. *Atish-i Chinar* (in Urdu). Srinagar: Ali Mohammad & Sons.

————. 1993. *Flames of the Chinar: An Autobiography*. Abridged and translated by Khushwant Singh. New Delhi: Viking.

Bamzai, P.N.K. 1962. *A History of Kashmir*. Delhi: Metropolitan.

Behera, Navnita Chadha. 2000. *State, Identity and Violence: Jammu, Kashmir and Ladakh*. New Delhi: Manohar.

Biscoe, C.E. Tyndale. 1971. *Kashmir in Sunlight and Shade*. New Delhi: Sagar.

Bühler, Georg. 1877. *Report on Search for Sanskrit Manuscripts, in Kashmir, etc.* Bombay: Royal Asiatic Society.

Chatterji, J.C. 1914. *Kashmir Shaivism*. Srinagar: Research Department, Kashmir State.

Dasgupta, C. 2002. *War and Diplomacy in Kashmir*. New Delhi: Sage.

Dhar, P.N. 2000. *Indira Gandhi, the Emergency, and Indian Democracy*. New Delhi: Oxford University Press.

Ganguly, Sumit. 1997. *The Crisis in Kashmir*. Cambridge: Cambridge University Press.

Hangloo, R.L. 2000. *The State in Medieval Kashmir*. New Delhi: Manohar.

Hodgson, Marshall G.S. 1961. *The Venture of Islam*. Vol. 3. *The Expansion of Islam in the Middle Periods*. Chicago: University of Chicago Press.

Hughes, John. 1994. *Self Realization in Kashmir Shaivism*. Albany: State University of New York Press.

Jha, Prem Shankar. 1996. *Kashmir 1947: Rival Versions of History*. New Delhi: Oxford University Press.

Joshi, Manoj. 1999. *The Lost Rebellion*. New Delhi: Penguin.

Kaul, Jaylal. 1973. *Lal Ded*. New Delhi: Sahitya Akademi.

Kersten, Holger. 2001. *Jesus Lived in India*. New Delhi: Penguin.

Khan, Mohammad Ishaq. 1994. *Kashmir's Transition to Islam*. New Delhi: Manohar.

Khan, Mohammad Ishaq. 1997. *Experiencing Islam*. New Delhi: Sterling.
———. 2004. 'The Rishi tradition and the construction of Kashmiriyat.' In Imtiaz Ahmad and Helmut Reifeld (eds). *Lived Islam in South Asia*. New Delhi: Social Science Press.
Kilam, J.L. 1955. *A History of Kashmiri Pandits*. Srinagar: G.M. College.
Lamb, Alastair. 1992. *Kashmir: A Disputed Legacy, 1846–1990*. Karachi: Oxford University Press.
Lawrence, Walter R. 1895. *The Valley of Kashmir*. London: Oxford University Press.
———. 1909. *Imperial Gazetteer of India*. Calcutta: Government Press.
Madan, T.N. 1994 [1973]. The social construction of cultural identities in rural Kashmir. In T.N. Madan, *Pathways: Approaches to the Study of Society in India*. New Delhi: Oxford University Press. Reproduced in T.N. Madan (ed.). *Muslim Communities of South Asia: Culture, Society and Power*. New Delhi: Manohar, 2001, pp. 229–68.
———. 1998. 'Coping with ethnicity in South Asia: Bangladesh, Punjab and Kashmir compared'. *Ethnic and Racial Studies* 21, 5: 969–89.
———. 2002 [1965]. *Family and Kinship: A Study of the Pandits of Rural Kashmir*. New Delhi: Oxford University Press.
Nilamata Purana. See Ved Kumari (q.v.).
Pandey, K.C. 1963. *Abhinavagupta: An Historical and Philosophical Study*. Varanasi: Chowkhambha.
Pandit, R.S. (trs.). 1968. *Kalhana's Rajatarangini*. New Delhi: Sahitya Akademi.
Parimu, R.K. 1969. *History of Muslim Rule in Kashmir*. New Delhi: People's Publishing House.
Qasim, Syed Mir. 1992. *My Life and Times*. New Delhi: Allied.
Rafiqi, Abdul Qaiyum (n.d.). *Sufism in Kashmir*. Varanasi: Bharatiya Publishing House.
Rai, Mridu. 2004. *Hindu Rulers, Muslim Subjects: Islam, Rights, and the History of Kashmir*. New Delhi: Permanent Black.
Rājataraṅgiṇī. See Pandit (q.v.)
Rao, Aparna. 1998. *Autonomy: Life Cycle, Gender and Status among Himalayan Pastoralists*. New York: Berghahn.
Schofield, Victoria. 1997. *Kashmir in the Crossfire*. New Delhi: Viva Books.
Sender, Henny. 1988. *The Kashmiri Pandits: A Study of Cultural Choice in North India*. New Delhi: Oxford University Press.
Singh, Jaideva. 1979. *Siva Sutras: The Yoga of Supreme Identity*. Delhi: Motilal Banarsidass.
Singh, Karan. 1994. *Autobiography*. Rev. edn. New Delhi: Oxford University Press.
Varshney, Ashutosh. 1992. 'Three compromised nationalisms: Why Kashmir has been a problem'. In Raju G.C. Thomas (ed.). *Perspectives on Kashmir*. Boulder: Westview Press.

Ved Kumari. 1968. *The Nilamata Purana. Vol.I. A Cultural and Literal Study of a Kashmiri Purana.*1973. Vol. II. Text with English Translation. Srinagar: J&K Academy of Art, Culture and Languages.

Wani, Muhammad Ashraf. 2005. *Islam in Kashmir.* Srinagar: Oriental Publishing House.

Wink, André. 1990. *Al-Hind: The Making of the Indo-Islamic World.* Leiden: E.J. Brill.

Zutshi, Chitralekha. 2003. *Languages of Belonging: Islam, Regional Identity, and the Making of Kashmir.* New Delhi: Permanent Black.

Part Three

Religious Traditions and Values

It has been convincingly argued that religions are best understood as multifaceted traditions, evolving social phenomena rather than frozen stocks. Religions have their cosmologies, theologies and eschatologies, their metaphysics and ethics, but they also have their histories, sociologies, and politics. They are significant—in some cases defining—components of the cultural heritage within which social institutions operate. India is the native land of or the host to most of the major religions of the world. Whether one is a Jain, Buddhist or Hindu, Christian, Muslim or Zoroastrian, or Sikh, India is home. The different religious traditions have grown here in a state of mutual interaction, borrowing from each other in the areas of belief and practice, and yet retaining their individual characteristics. The Indian religious space is not merely plural; India's religious traditions, one and all, have strong pluralist tendencies.

In Chapter 8, selected conceptual categories of the Indic religions are presented and medieval syncretistic developments discussed. The impact of the West in both politico-economic and religio-cultural arenas in the seventeenth and eighteenth centuries resulted in a radical social transformation of the country, generating both reform movements and revivalist tendencies. The challenge of secularism in more recent times that all the religious traditions face is again mentioned, having been earlier discussed at length in the first part of the book. The future, it is suggested, lies with cultural pluralism, and with (to borrow a phrase of Martin Marty's) a religio-secular world view. When this essay was written (in 1988), religious fundamentalism had already emerged as a worldwide phenomenon and India had not escaped its impact, but I did not discuss it because mainly of the limitations of space.

There is also the argument that while fundamentalist tendencies within the Sikh and Islamic traditions are undeniable, what often passes for Hindu fundamentalism, while reactionary and intolerant, lacks the essential association with scripturalism. I have already touched on this point in Chapter 5.

The next chapter looks upon the householder tradition in Hindu society, the beginnings of which perhaps go further back in time than the organization of society on the basis of caste. Textual and ethnographic data are discussed and regional diversities noted. The continuity of this tradition is a remarkable feature of the stability of Hindu society. If the householder within the domestic domain is the base of the social order, the king at the head of the kingdom is its ultimate upholder. The notion of dharma is of central importance; what may seem to be an autonomous secular domain is, in fact, part of the sacred order. And kingdoms in turn, since they do not exist in isolation, constitute what could be called the political 'world order' in Hindu classical thought. Needless to emphasize, this world order was only subcontinental. This idea is briefly examined in the annex to Chapter 9. The contemporariness of some of the formulations in the ancient texts is indeed striking.

To talk of the life of the householder, and the values by which he or she lives, leads one to the critical issue of the conceptualization of death in both traditional (religious) and contemporary (secular) perspectives. This has been presented in Chapter 10 from the point of view of Christian, Hindu, and Jain traditions and also within the framework of modern medical discourse. Their apparent mutual unintelligibility may be an obstacle that ought to be overcome in the interest of a deeper understanding of the phenomena of aging, death, and bereavement in our times.

A religious tradition is a living heritage providing purposes and procedures for the everyday life of the people. It is, of course, also available for study to anyone, insider or outsider. In Chapter 11 I have tried to bring out the complementarity between the 'field view' and the 'book view' in the study of Hinduism, best exemplified by the works of M.N. Srinivas and Max Weber respectively. Around the middle of the twentieth century the study of Hindu society by Indian sociologists was dominated by Indology. This resulted in a wide gap between the lived social reality and sociological accounts of it. The publication of Srinivas's

Religion and Society among the Coorgs of South India in 1952 was a landmark in the empirical study of Hinduism: it brought to life what otherwise remained cold in the pages of the books devoted to it. Srinivas's book set a trend for fieldwork-based studies of all aspects of Hindu society including religion, caste, and kinship. The gains in the understanding of the social reality were enormous.

Within a few years, however, Louis Dumont reminded us (in 1957) that in the study of Hindu society, with its rich literary heritage of self-representation and reflection, the ethnographic and Indological approaches would have to be combined. Soon afterwards the English translation of Max Weber's *The Religion of India* (1958) became available. Weber had drawn upon the resources of both the sacred literature and the colonial archive with, notwithstanding several shortcomings, excellent results. I also have argued (in the concluding essay of this part of the book) for bridging of the textual and empirical perspectives and for the continuing relevance of the sociology of religion.

Blank (p. 210)

8

India's Religious Traditions
Some Conceptual Categories*

Ekam sad viprā bahudhā vadanti.
(The Truth is but one, though the learned state it in many ways.)

Rig Veda, c. 1200 BC

Personally, I think the world as a whole will never have, and need not have, a single religion.

Mahatma Gandhi, 30 May 1913

To write about religion in India without querying the notion of religion as a discrete element of everyday life is to yield to the temptation of words. The point is not that the religious domain is not distinguished from the secular, but rather that the secular is regarded as encompassed by the religious—even when considered opposed to it—and not independent of it. The relationship is hierarchical. That is, religion in indigenous cultures is believed to be the foundation of society, and the traditional vision of life

* Reproduced with minor verbal changes and bibliographical additions from *Daedalus*, Fall 1989, pp. 115–46. Original title, 'Religion in India'. The text of this essay was finalized in 1988. If it were to be rewritten now, I certainly would conclude it more cautiously, emphasizing that humanism is but one variety of religion in our times. More visible than it and no less widespread, but perhaps no more significant, is religious fundamentalism and extremism. Religion as personal faith is virtually everywhere, including India, opposed by religion as ideology or collective power, religiousness by (as Clifford Geertz has put it) religious-mindedness.

Acknowledgements. In the preparation of this essay I was greatly helped by the constructive criticisms and encouragement of Arjun Appadurai, Stephen Graubard, the late Ravinder Kumar, Ashis Nandy, and Nur Yalman. My thanks to all of them.

is holistic. This is the first principle for any discussion of religion in India.

It is an irony of history that modern intellectuals, Indians as well as Westerners, have generally considered religion (or religiosity) the bane of the good enlightened life in South Asia and indeed everywhere. Considering the abuse of religion in our times, this opinion is not surprising. Thus, Jawaharlal Nehru wrote: 'We have to get rid of that narrowing religious outlook, that obsession with the supernatural and metaphysical speculations, that loosening of the mind's discipline in ceremonial and mystical emotionalism, which come in the way of our understanding ourselves and the world' (1961: 552–3). Needless to emphasize, *understanding* here means comprehension in terms of Western rational thought.

There are other modern Indians who have wondered if the religious label that has stuck to Indian culture is genuine or only spurious. Dhurjati Prasad Mukerji (one of the founding fathers of sociology in India) wrote about fifty years ago: 'Our material conditions, our political subjection, our nationalism conspire in the currency of the story started by the West for its own purposes that Indians, by and large, are... addicts to religion, that both the body and the soul of Indian culture are annexed and possessed by the Divinity' (1948: 6). He felt constrained to add, however, that those 'progressives' in India who dismiss religion as the opium of the people not only ignore social facts but also 'the historical process by which these have assumed the attached social values' (ibid.: 7).

Contrast these expressions of the negative or apologetic attitude toward religion with the characteristically simple but emphatic expression of faith by Mahatma Gandhi: 'For me every, the tiniest, activity is governed by what I consider to be my religion' (1986: 391). For Gandhi and the millions of Indians he represented, religion was indeed constitutive of society. This is as true of Indian Muslims, for whom the ultimate reality is spiritual and for whom consequently there is no such thing as a profane world, as it is of the Sikhs, who deny the separation of spiritual goals from the pursuit of political power, and of the Hindus, who see the cosmos as a single whole, a unity, comprising all creation animated by one spirit.

Let me state here that I am inclined to believe that the religious, or traditional, view of life has not really been the source of conflict between peoples, that it is its perversion which has been so. The scope of inter-religious understanding is, in my opinion, immense, and it is in no way contradicted by the holism of the religious traditions of mankind. And yet, one surely may not turn a blind eye to the conflicts between religious communities which have for so long caused untold suffering to innocent people everywhere. The historicity of such conflicts does not, however, constitute an argument against religion or signify its irrelevance; it only points to the unrealized promise of cultural pluralism. The history of India is the history of syncretism among religious traditions as well as conflict between religious communities, and should have a great deal to tell us about both processes. It is therefore important that we read history carefully, for while the clash between obscurantist-revivalist ideologies has turned out to be not only barren but also bloody, secularism (in the Enlightenment sense of the term) has nowhere—not even in Europe—succeeded in providing a comprehensive alternative to the religious world view. In fact, secularization has entailed the loss of meaning in human life about which Max Weber wrote so eloquently.

Now, all world views, whether religious or secular, have their metaphysical foundations, which are the basis and an integral component of social activity everywhere. In India, the root paradigm of all the major indigenous religious traditions is that of the cosmic, moral social order, of dharma. It is to an interpretation of this that I now turn.

METAPHYSICS: DHARMA

Dharma, a Sanskrit word, is generally employed in contemporary writing in most Indian languages to stand for religion, but this usage is not satisfactory. According to Hinduism, Jainism, Buddhism, and Sikhism, the universe is sustained by dharma. The great Indian epic *Mahābhārata* (c. 400 BC–AD 400) says: '*Dharma* is so called because it protects *dhārnāt* (everything); *Dharma* maintains everything that has been created; *Dharma* is thus that very principle which can maintain the universe' (Lingat 1973: 3). Today, we do not need old texts or modern philosophers to tell us that 'next to the category of reality, that of *dharma* is the most important concept in Indian thought' (Radhakrishnan 1923: 52). Almost every Hindu, Jain, Buddhist, or Sikh, even if he is illiterate and of humble origin, knows that dharma is the foundation of the good life. Whether this is seen naively as an instance of equal social distribution of knowledge, or critically as the hegemonic imposition of the thought of the Brahmins on others, the fact remains that dharma is a rich word of everyday speech in India. This does not, however, mean that its meaning is easily conveyed in non-Indian languages. It is broader and more complex than the Christian notion of religion and less jural than our current conceptions of duty. It emphasizes awareness and freedom rather than the notion of *religio*, or obligation.

A concept of multiple connotations, dharma includes cosmological, ethical, social, and legal principles that provide the basis for the notion of an ordered universe. In the social context, it stands for the imperative of righteousness in the definition of the good life. More specifically, dharma refers to the rules of social intercourse laid down traditionally for every category of actor (or moral agent) in terms of social status (varna), the stage of life (āshrama), and the qualities of inborn nature (*guna*). Put simply, for every person there is a mode of conduct that is most appropriate: it is his or her *svadharma*, which may be translated as 'vocation'. The emphasis here is upon legitimacy in terms of authenticity; and authenticity flows from one's social position and physical nature; external coercion is of no real value. So much so indeed that the *Bhagavad Gītā* (c. 200 BC–AD 200), which is in our times the most widely known text of the Hindu religious tradition, repeatedly exhorts the actor to prefer failure in the pursuit of his vocation to success in someone else's role. Action to which one is born arises spontaneously and is easily performed: it is not a burden. When one achieves such a state of dharmic existence or moral perfection—the mystic Jiddu Krishnamurti called it 'choiceless awareness'—contexts are dissolved, specificities disappear, dualities are transcended, and what survives is a seamless moral sensibility.

Many scholars—Indians as well as foreigners—have commented on the absence of 'natural law' from Hindu thought and its alleged ethical relativism. What I have just said about the dissolution of contexts may be seen to underscore this problem rather than to resolve it. It is therefore relevant to mention here that the Hindu tradition does in fact entertain the notion of universally applicable law, *sādhāran* or *sāmānya* dharma, which is the foundation for all specific dharmas. Thus, untruthfulness, wanton killing, stealing, sexual assault, or self-seeking endeavour at the cost of others may never be justified under any circumstances, though the punishment for transgression is not the same in all cases. Similarly, forgiveness, application to work, sincerity, personal cleanliness, and moral watchfulness are virtues that Hinduism calls for everybody to cultivate. The charge of absolute ethical relativism does not really hold. Moreover, the unease of modern scholars when faced with complex Indian traditions is a result of their distrust of pluralism; but pluralism is not a self-evident moral flaw; it is in fact the strength of many non-Western ethical traditions.

Dharma as the foundation of the good life consists of the rational pursuit of economic and political goals (*artha*) as well as pleasure (*kāma*). Taken together, these three constitute the goals of life (*purushārtha*), and are hierarchically related: the pursuit of pleasure ought to be subordinated to economic and political goals, and the pursuit of economic and political goals must likewise conform to dharma. In other words, one must avoid the acquisition of wealth and the gratification of desires if they involve the violation of dharma.

Although only three principal goals of life are mentioned in the earlier texts, a significant fourth goal is discussed at much length in the *Mahābhārata* and has since remained prominent. This is the goal of moksha, or freedom through transcendence from the cycle of birth, death, and rebirth, and therefore from the pursuit of the other three goals. Dharma, inclusive of *artha* and *kāma*, is a grand design of life, and moksha is the alternative. There is no contradiction here. Dharma is the basis of the householder's life, which is highly prized (see Chapter 9). Its repudiation is renunciation, or *sannyāsa*. Ideally, however, one may become a renouncer only after fulfilling the obligations of householdership. As for the renouncer himself, he too is bound but by his own dharma.

Non-Indian students of the Hindu way of life have been deeply impressed with renunciation as an ideal for personal life just as they have been by the caste system as a framework for social life. Hindus themselves acknowledge the fascination with renunciation, and yet postpone it to the very end of a person's life as its fourth stage, after the stages of study, householdership, and retirement. In fact, only a microscopic minority actually renounce the world. Not only is the renouncer a striking figure, dressed in ochre robe, carrying his staff and begging bowl, a living embodiment of self-control and asceticism; he is also an exemplar of values. As the French social anthropologist Louis Dumont has reminded us, renouncers have often been founders of sects in the caste-based Hindu society (1980: 275, 284–6).

Perhaps because this ideal is so noble and lofty, reverence for it as an ideal is combined with a healthy scepticism about real-life renouncers. Hindu tradition stresses the importance of overcoming dualistic choices and the possibility of doing so without renouncing, by means of detachment and the overcoming of all passions. Sociologically, the householder who follows dharma is the true hero. Everyday the renouncer knocks at his front door, asking for alms: by his very presence, he invites the householder to renounce the world. And the householder hears equally often, if not oftener, the muffled yet powerful knock of the sensualist at his back door, as it were, tempting him to a life of pleasure. The householder's heroism lies in the good sense of the middle path, which the *Katha Upanishad* tells us is sharp like the razor's edge (see Madan 1987a).

The middle path (*mādhyamika*) is also what is extolled above all in the Buddhist tradition. It comprises 'the noble eightfold path' based on 'the four noble truths'. Gotama the Buddha (563–483 BC), in his first sermon at Sarnath to the five disciples who had stood by him set in motion, as the Buddhists say, 'the wheel of the cosmic law of righteousness' (*dhammachakka*). The enlightened Gotama stressed the folly of the pursuit of pleasure, for it produces pain and suffering. The first truth of life, he said, is sorrow; the second, that the source of sorrow is desire; the third, that sorrow can be ended if craving is eliminated; and the fourth, that the eightfold path leads to *nibanna*, the 'blowing out' of both desire and suffering. We see that no sooner had the seer stated the truth than he pointed to action in a striking unity of the theory and the art of life.

The noble eightfold path is, then, dharma (dhamma in Pali). It consists of right views, right resolve, right speech, right conduct, right livelihood, right effort, right mindfulness, and right concentration. This exhortation in all its nobility and severity is addressed to the monk who seeks refuge in the community of monks (sangha). Monks and lay Buddhists seek the protection of the Buddha and dhamma. Dhamma is equally acknowledged as the foundation of the universe by all schools of Buddhism—Hinayana, Mahayana, Theravada, and others.

It would be an oversimplification to treat the Buddhist dhamma and the Hindu dharma as essentially the same, though they are similar. For one thing, the Buddhist notion of cosmic and moral law is in no way whatsoever linked with any notion of the supernatural, while such an association acquires increasing importance in the history of Hinduism. Moreover, the hierarchical triad of dharma, *artha*, and *kāma* is significantly restated so as to stress that dharma as the cosmic law, or the Truth, absolutely encompasses the righteousness of the ruler. Dhamma is indeed called the 'king of the righteous king'. It is this absolutist conception of dhamma that resulted in the elevation of non-violence (ahimsā) and compassion as supreme values.

In Jainism ahimsā forms the very core of dharma; indeed, ahimsā is dharma. There is also a special use of the term, according to which it denotes a spatial category in Jain physics—the space in which movement takes place. Movement is central to Jain practice in many ways; as moral exertion, it is the essence of life. In its more basic sense, dharma in the Jain tradition is the eternal law of respect for life; and for the Jains life is an attribute of practically everything that exists, including earth, water, and wind, so even the wind must not be harmed. As far as possible, nothing must be destroyed.

The notion of destroying or killing to protect dharma was, however, developed within the Hindu tradition. The war described in the *Mahābhārata* is called the dharmic war. In fact the *Bhagavad Gītā* puts forward the notion of avatār, or divine incarnation, as a means of destroying the wicked and restoring dharma. This idea has been incorporated into the Sikh tradition also.

Sikhs employ the word *dharam* (dharma) to describe their way of life, which is the same for all Sikhs irrespective of differences of social origin or personal conditions. It is a universally applicable code of conduct taught by the Divine Preceptor (guru) and expressing the Divine Commandment (*hukam*). Nanak, the founder of the Sikh faith, spoke of the five 'domains' (*khanda*) that constitute what I would call 'life space'. Of these, the first is dharma, or moral duty. The others are the domains of spiritual knowledge, human effort, divine benevolence, and truth. Sikh men consider it a moral duty to carry a small sword (*kirpān*) on their person to symbolize both the divinity and the individual's determination to kill or be killed in the defence of dharma. The congregational prayer of the Sikhs includes a reference to those who 'offered their heads at the altar of *dharma*'.

An examination of the notion of dharma in India's cultural traditions reveals that in the earliest formulations it had less to do with supernatural powers or rituals than with human activity and the moral integrity of the actor. The notion of a supreme being or divinity has remained alien to Jainism and Buddhism, but it gradually gained ground in the Hindu tradition. By the time the *Bhagavad Gītā* came to be composed, the idea of dharma being divinely instituted and protected had become established.

According to the *Manusmriti* (AD c. 200), there are four sources of dharma—namely, the original teaching, remembered traditions, the conduct of good people, and personal judgement. Whether what was originally taught and heard is revelation and, if so, whether revealed knowledge is to be traced to a divine origin, are questions that have been long debated within the tradition but need not detain us here. More important, surely, is the mutual relationship between the four sources. A narrow exegesis of the texts might suggest a descending order of preference, but a more insightful interpretation would look upon the sources as a matrix of interacting factors. Dharma is not law or custom or conscience but all these in different combinations. Some of the truly significant interpretations of dharma have been provided by those who defied tradition and sought to discover it in their own conscience or, to put it differently, in moral reason. This is what Yudhishthira, the hero of the *Mahābhārata*, did; in our own time this is what Mahatma Gandhi did. And surely it is this acknowledgement of the superiority of moral reason to customary usage that underlies the power of the notion of dharma: it not only sustains but also transforms society.

PRAXIS: KARMA

Dharma as the abstract principle of the social order is a metaphysical concept. As a disposition of the mind, it is a subjective quality. As metaphysics and as psychology, it has practical consequences—namely, the obligation and the tendency to act in a particular way in specified situations. The synthesis of thought and action—of theory and practice—is even more clearly expressed in the notion of karma, another key concept of India's indigenous cultural traditions. Dharma and karma are inseparable and in certain contexts indistinguishable. If dharma is the social consensus about the good life, karma is the individual actor's effort to live according to it.

Karma literally means action. The *Bhagavad Gītā* (3: 24) makes creativity obligatory for the Supreme Being himself, for if he did not act, the world would fall into ruins and there would be chaos. Divine creation is thus the paradigmatic karmic act. For human beings, the emphasis is on tasks to be accomplished, on desires to be fulfilled. The tasks may be traditionally commanded; the desires or goals are often empirically motivated. Traditionally, karma is said to be of three kinds—of the body, of speech, and of the mind—but it is best when it is all three together. The karmic act is value neutral. While *adharma* would mean evil, the opposite of dharma, the opposite of karma is absence of karma (*akarma*). It follows that while dharma *produces* dharma, the consequences of particular karmic acts may be meritorious or evil. This is the notion of the fruits of action, of compensation or retribution, which was regarded by Max Weber (1958: 118) as 'the unique Hindu theodicy' of the existing social order. He saw in karma the nearest that one could get to doctrinal belief in Hinduism, revealing more about his own Christian anxieties, perhaps, than about Indic cultures. Be that as it may, karma does stand for what may loosely be called a theory (see Chapter 11 below).

In all Indian cultural traditions, human actions have consequences that are inescapable. The fruits of action bring joy or sorrow depending on whether certain actions have been good or evil. Whatever cannot be enjoyed or suffered in the present life must be experienced hereafter in another birth, which may not be a human birth. To be born a human being is a rare privilege because it is only through such a birth that a soul may be freed from reincarnation.

An emphasis on the metaphysics of karma characterizes Western scholarship on India in our own time no less than in the late nineteenth century. Within the indigenous Hindu discourse, however, the emphasis is on pragmatics, on karma *in* action or *as* action. This is particularly true of the original Buddhist teaching.

According to it, everybody is the architect, here and now, of his own destiny, for better or worse, depending on the moral choices he makes. The notion of karmic legacy is rejected. The Jains do, however, entertain the notion of karmic burden, which they seek to 'burn up' through the practice of severe austerities (something that the Buddha clearly disapproved of). They conceive of karma as a substance that accumulates in the process of transmigration and envelops the soul as a form of matter.

The Hindu concept of karma is, however, essentially pragmatic. Ask an orthodox Hindu about karma and he is more likely to talk of it as ritual than as abstract belief. In his life millennia of experience are summed up. Thus, karma will stand for prayer and worship addressed to favourite gods and goddesses; this is the popular ritual called puja. Its origins go back three thousand years, when the early Vedic seers, overwhelmed by the power of nature and by its beauty, anthropomorphized it—saw aspects of it as gods—and prayed to these gods for boons and protection. (Incidentally, the Vedic chant is said to be the beginning of the northern and southern Indian classical music traditions.)

Later, in the evolution of Hinduism, karma became identified with sacrificial rituals that were believed to produce results simply because the rituals were performed, and not because they were offerings to deities or mediating links between human beings and supernatural powers. It was against such intense and exacting ritualism, and the attendant power of ritual specialists, that the Buddha revolted two and a half thousand years ago. During the post-Buddhist revival, the great eighth-century Hindu Vedantist philosopher from South India, Shankara, uncompromisingly downgraded ritualism and placed the way of knowledge and wisdom high above it as a means to spiritual good. Seven hundred years later, a devout Hindu householder of North India, Nanak, taught his disciples, the Sikhs, the superiority of moral righteousness over mechanical ritualism. And yet rituals have not wholly disappeared from the life of the Hindus or the Buddhists or the Sikhs. In fact, rituals define these and other religion-suffused ways of life all over South Asia, but they do so in rather flexible ways.

Rituals thus survive as rites of passage. Every Hindu, no matter what caste or community he belongs to, is the subject of rituals at birth, marriage, and death. Such rituals are intended for the moral refinement of the individual. Life-cycle rituals constitute *samskāra*, that is, the process whereby one is 'made complete or perfect' and, ultimately after death, transformed into an ancestor. As an ancestor, one is in contact with ones's descendants through the rituals of feeding that the latter perform. If the ancestors are not at peace, there will be no births. Rituals protect the seed and the foetus. They give the newborn child her individual and social identity. They bestow on the so-called 'twice-born' Hindus their upper-caste status. In marriage, as a vedic hymn puts it, parental love gives way to conjugal love: love gives, love receives, and with love is the ocean of life filled. The so-called rites of passage are in fact rituals of transformation and continuity in one great chain of being. They are supplemented by rituals that protect the body against disease and physical dangers. There are also the expiatory rituals of atonement and moral purification.

Important as karma (in the foregoing sense of ritual) is, it is not self-sufficient. Man is ever in need of divine favour and one seeks this through pūjā and pilgrimage. Pūjā, the Hindu ritual of adoration, may be performed at home or in a temple. Its recipient is one's favourite deity—Shiva, Vishnu, or Devi—iconically represented and treated as an honoured guest. It is bathed, anointed, fed, entertained with song and dance, praised and prayed to, and put to bed. While sacrificial rituals also were performed to win divine favour, pūjā emerged as a distinctive mode of worship characterized by intensity of emotion. Although the home was regarded as good as the temple for this purpose, the latter enjoyed a special status.

Temple art and architecture of ancient and medieval India survive to bear witness to the primacy of the religious over the secular in Hindu society. According to an old Tamil saying, one should not build a house in a town without a temple. Even kings obviously paid greater attention to the temple than to the palace: as a rule the palace had to be lower than a temple and the Brahmins' houses lower than the palace. The temple was the centre of the town. Its spire, visible from a long distance, indicated its very existence. The temples in turn took interest in mundane affairs, using their landed and other forms of wealth to promote the economic well-being of the priestly class and occasionally and derivatively of the larger community as well. As is well known, temples provided loans and promoted irrigation works in South Asia.

Prayers are also offered at sacred spots such as the source of a river or the meeting place of rivers. Every day in India Hindu pilgrims walk to some such sacred place (*tīrtha*), an *axis mundi*, far away from home, to wash off their moral impurities and attain merit. To go on a pilgrimage one becomes a 'wanderer', *yātrika*, for the specific purposes of accumulating merit. In a well-known ancient text, we hear the god Indra, presiding deity of pilgrims, pronounce the following exhortation: 'The fortune of him who is sitting, sits; it rises when he rises; it sleeps when he sleeps; it moves when he moves. Therefore, wander!' (Eck 1982: 21). Indeed, going on pilgrimages, particularly to highly esteemed places, and on particularly auspicious occasions, is scripturally recommended karma. Thus, every twelve years, on the astrologically auspicious occasion called Kumbha, millions of Hindus visit the holy city of Prayag in North India at the confluence of the rivers Ganga and Jamuna. All of India gathers there, as it were. Walking together, bathing together, or having *darshan* (seeing an image or icon) together, each pilgrim is yet alone in the crowd: being a pilgrim is an intensely personal experience (see Karve 1988: 142–71).

The practice of pilgrimage knows no community barriers. The Jains are the pilgrims par excellence, always on the move visiting temples and holy places. The most notable among the latter is Shravana Belgola in South India, where the world's largest monolith, the sixty-foot image of Gomateshvara, a Jain spiritual teacher, sculpted late in the tenth century, is venerated daily and especially at periodic festivals. The Buddhists from India and abroad go on pilgrimage to Bodh Gaya, where Gotama received enlightenment, or to Sarnath, where he preached his first sermon, or to Kandy in Sri Lanka, where the holy relic of his tooth is venerated. Similarly, Sikh pilgrims from India and elsewhere go on pilgrimage to Nankana Sahib, the birthplace of Nanak, in Pakistan. For Muslims anywhere, one of the five key religious obligations is, of course, to visit Mecca if they have the means to make it; but practically every Muslim in India goes on pilgrimage to the shrine of one Sufi saint or another within a reasonable distance of where he lives. As modern means of communication and transportation become available more generally, holy places attract larger numbers of pilgrims (and also secularly minded tourists, since many of these shrines are scenic or architecturally interesting).

For the Hindu in search of liberation from the cycle of birth, death, and rebirth, the karmic store of accumulated merit is a trap—hence the appeal of renouncing all worldly karma. But this ideal—itself probably a reversal of an earlier notion that one needs more than a lifetime to fully partake of worldly joys—is difficult to achieve. It is in this context that the teaching of the *Bhagavad Gītā* acquires critical importance. Emphasizing the performance rather than the abandonment of karma, it teaches the ethics of altruism. If one performs one's duty in a spirit of sacrifice, eliminating one's ego and self-interest, one is liberated from the fruits of action even before death. One of the most crucial statements in the *Bhagavad Gītā* (2: 47) bears on this point: 'Your entitlement is to *karma* alone, never to its fruits. The hope of such fruit should not therefore be the motive for action, nor should one therefore become inactive.' In the twentieth century, Mahatma Gandhi has been the most distinguished teacher of this view of karma. He added a note of caution, however, for those who would endeavour to convert this precept into practice: without surrender to divine will as an act of devotion, the Mahatma taught, the practice of karma yoga will not succeed.

AGAPE: BHAKTI

Vedic polytheism and ritualism gave way to Upanishadic philosophizing about the metaphysics of the act. There was a transformation then rather than a sharp break, an attempted synthesis rather than a flat repudiation. Still later, the *Bhagavad Gītā* acknowledged both ritual and knowledge as legitimate ways to attain self-realization, which, according to Hindu tradition, is the highest goal of human life. To the ways of action (karma) and intelligence (*jñāna*), the *Gītā* added the way for devotion (bhakti), thus reviving the theistic element that post-vedic Hinduism had played down. After describing the ways of action, knowledge, and devotion, the *Bhagavad Gītā* in one of the concluding verses (chapter 18, verse 66) enjoins the seeker to abandon all three ways and to seek refuge in God so as to be free of the burden of all moral imperfections. This call to total surrender is as much intellectual as it is devotional. It was an idea fashioned by the

Brahmins, the guardians of the sacred tradition and the ideologues of Hindu society.

Many centuries later (toward the close of the ninth century) a devotional movement flowered in South India among non-Brahmin groups, who gave it utterance in Tamil rather than Sanskrit, which the Brahmins called the language of the gods. These groups represented a longing for theism after a millennium of Jain and Buddhist influence had swept over India, pushing the existence of God into the sidelines of religious thought and practice. They also expressed a moral weariness about the dharmas of caste and gender and sought to transcend such relativism by concentrating on personal devotion to their favourite deities. Shiva devotees took the lead, but Vishnu devotees followed soon later. The latter came to be known as Alvars—that is, those with an intuitive knowledge of God who were engaged in contemplative 'immersion' in him. These devotional movements became widespread, embracing high castes as well as low by the end of the eleventh century.

The best known among the Alvars is Nammalvar. In his 'hymns for the drowning' (to use A.K. Ramanujan's [1981] felicitous phrase), Nammalvar puts forward a novel notion of devotion as the assumption of femininity by the devotee in relation to the one supremely noble man, Vishnu. While the Upanishads taught man to realize his own divinity and the *Bhagavad Gītā* advised surrender, the Alvars stressed either the constant companionship of God or separation from him and the consequent longing, amorous in character, for union with him. But the preoccupation is with separation (*viraha*). While other Alvars covered a wide range of emotions, including those experienced by parents, sons, companions, servants, and women in love, Nammalvar sang particularly of the last of these (Ramanujan ibid.: 52).

Is that you, little bird?
When I asked you to go
as my messenger to the great lord
and tell him of my pain, you
dawdled, didn't go.
I have lost my looks,
my dark limbs are pale.
Go look for someone else
to put sweet things in your beak,
go now.

The intoxication of love also found expression among the devotees of Shiva in South India. The pangs of separation are typically described thus by Mahadevi, a woman from Karnataka who was a devotee in the twelfth century (Ramanujan 1973: 124, 125):

Four parts of the day
I grieve for you.
Four parts of the night
I'm mad for you.
I lie lost,
sick for you, night and day.
O Lord white as jasmine.

Describing the imagined ecstasy of union, she sang:

He bartered my heart,
looted my flesh,
claimed as tribute
my pleasure,
took over
all of me.
I'm the woman of love
for my lord, white as jasmine.

The most celebrated Sanskrit text of *viraha* bhakti is the *Bhāgvata Purāna* (ninth century), which was most probably composed in South India. It contains much metaphysics and, laying particular stress on his childhood and youth, tells the tale of Krishna, the most illustrious avatar of Vishnu. Stories of his dalliance with young cowherdesses occupy a central place in the bhakti tradition, for the love of these women for Krishna is seen to symbolize the love of all devotees for God or, more abstractly, the longing of the individual soul for merger with the supreme soul, of which it is an emanation. This love, while all-consuming and incessant, is totally selfless and therefore pure. The *Bhāgavata Purāna* describes nine modes of bhakti: 'Listening to the Lord's glory, singing of Him, thinking of Him, serving His feet, performing His worship, saluting Him, serving Him, friendship with Him, surrendering oneself to Him' (de Bary 1958: 333).

The story of the unmarried love of Krishna and the cowherdess Radha has had wide influence all over India. Many Vaishnava sects owe their origin to it. In the late twelfth century in eastern India, the poet Jayadeva composed a religious-erotic poem of great beauty (the celebrated and much translated *Gītā Govinda*), describing the love of Radha and Krishna, their separation, and eventual reunion. Soon this poem became a part of temple worship and was set to music. It became an expression of spiritual quest. Gradually it spread to southern and western India and was incorporated in temple dance and music.

Later, in the sixteenth century, a Bengali devotee called Chaitanya became possessed with the love of Krishna and identified himself with Radha agonizing over the pangs of separation from the Lord. Dancing and singing along with his followers, he travelled all the way to Vrindavan in North India, where, according to legend, Krishna had been born and had spent his youth. This dance-song form of worship with the agony of love as its theme came to be called *kīrtan*. Chaitanya looked upon union with fear and even hatred, for it is in separation that the devotee, with all his or her senses, experiences God. In Gujarat, a contemporary of Chaitanya called Vallabha composed a treatise on aesthetic theory as a commentary on the love-play of Krishna as narrated in the *Bhāgavata Purāna*. Vallabha spoke of the complementarity of 'total love' and 'constraint'. For him, bhakti was the contemplative endeavour of achieving union but the search for it was superior to finding it, so one must hold oneself back and experience in separation the love of God in full measure.

Bhakti imagined as conjugal love found its most poignant expression in the deeply moving lyrics of Mira, a Rajasthan princess of the late sixteenth century. While for Mahadevi, Shiva had been the lover, for Mira, Krishna was the longed-for husband. The pain of separation was no more bearable for that reason: 'I will build myself a pyre of fragrant wood and beseech you to set it aflame with your own hand. The fire will consume me and I will be a heap of ashes. Won't you rub your body with these ashes, in the manner of the mendicant?'

Intense religious emotion found other kinds of expression also. In the sixteenth century, Sur sang joyously in Brijbhasha (a dialect of Hindi) of Krishna, child and young man, and Tulsi composed in Avadhi (another dialect of Hindi) the epic story of Rama, avatar of Vishnu, originally written in Sanskrit (c. 200 BC). Tulsi's bhakti was that of the servant (*dāsa*) devoted to the service of his divine master. The love of God for the devotee, who dwells on his own imperfections and therefore on divine grace, is a central theme of Tulsi's sublime poetry. His *Rāmacharitamānas* is a widely read, recited, and enacted vernacular religious text of India.

Sur, Tulsi, and Kabir, another devotee from a century earlier, are not only luminaries of the medieval bhakti movement but also the three great pillars of Hindi literature, a fact that draws our attention once again to the all-encompassing nature of religion in India. Kabir's devotionalism was centred not on a personalized god in human form, however, but on an abstract and formless conception of the divine (*nirguna*). He considered the religious experience more important than its ground in some conception of a divinity. Alongside bhakti Kabir echoed the metaphysics of the Upanishads and reflected in some measure the influence of Sufi ideas on his upbringing as a Muslim.

SYNCRETISM: SUFIS, SANTS, AND SIKHS

Hinduism, Buddhism, and Jainism are indigenous religious traditions: it is from India that they—particularly Buddhism—have spread to other parts of Asia and the world. Buddhism was practically wiped out of India by the eighth century, but only after many of its ideas and ideals had been absorbed into Hindu thought. In fact, the Buddha was deified by the Hindus, not by the Buddhists. Jainism has remained very close to Hinduism, especially in the realm of practice. In terms of the number of adherents, however, it is Islam that has become the second most important religion of India. In fact, there are more Muslims in India now (over 120 million) than in any other country except Indonesia.

Islam was brought to India by Arab traders toward the close of the seventh century, within living memory of the prophet Muhammad. Subsequently, the conquerors came and with them, the 'doctors' of Muslim law called the ulama. They stressed the realization of the true spirit of Islam through submission to 'the way' (sharia) God had ordained for his true followers and faith in the example and sayings of Muhammad. Simultaneously, the Sufi seekers of God also came to India. They tended to keep aloof from the kings, but the kings often sought them out. The Sufis evolved their own way (*tarīqa*) of realizing God—through love and the intermediary role of saints. The chasm between sharia and *tariqa*, between the ulama and the Sufis, has been a factor of immense importance in the history of Islam in India. While the original tradition emphasized living in faith through the material world, the Sufi quest was essentially spiritual. 'If knowledge strikes the heart,' the Sufis taught, 'it is welcome: if it strikes the body it is a burden.' The idea of realizing the true nature of God, and even attempting to become one with him, was anathema to the ulama, who denounced many Sufi orders as heretical. The Sufis' quest was, however, very similar to that of the Upanishadic seers: the latter's *soham* ('I am He') was echoed by the former's *anal-haqq* ('I am Truth').

The scope for religious syncretism was not perceived immediately. In fact, anti-Hindu polemics were characteristic of Indian Sufism in the pre-Mughal period. Leaders of various Sufi orders were active in converting Hindus to Islam. Kashmir and Bengal, where mass conversions took place, were won over more by Sufis than by kings. The promise of syncretism was realized better in areas such as Bengal, where Hindu mythology and cosmology became the vehicles for Islamic dogmas and practices. As Bengal was Islamized, Islam itself became Hinduized. Muhammad's biography became a variant of Krishna's early life (see Roy 1983); Hindu gods rubbed shoulders with Muslim saints. In the heartland of India, two royal brothers, Dara Shukoh and Aurangzeb, the former a follower of the Sufis, and the latter of the ulama and the more orthodox Sufis, fought the battle to the finish. The ulama won. This was perhaps one of the most critical events in the history of Islam in India, and I will describe it in some detail.

Dara Shukoh (1605–59), son of Shah Jahan, was great grandson of the Mughal emperor Akbar, who had valiantly tried to bring the various religions of his realm together. But the special hall for discussions among scholars professing different faiths that Akbar had had built in his capital city of Fatehpur-Sikri ended up being a hall of disharmony, a Tower of Babel. Not to be defeated, Akbar assumed the role of religious leader and formally promulgated a new religion combining elements of Islam, Christianity, and Upanishadic Hinduism. But this too failed, and Akbar's *dīn-i-Ilāhī* (religion of God), which never made much headway beyond the court except to antagonize the ulama, died with him in 1605.

In his zeal for religious syncretism, Dara Shukoh was Akbar's true heir and also a scholar of the religious classics of Islam and

Hinduism. Taking his stand on the revelation in the *Qur'ān* that God had sent his messengers to all peoples and given them their scriptures, Dara maintained that it was the moral duty of a Muslim to learn from these other religious traditions. He believed that the Upanishads must be the 'concealed scripture' spoken of in the *Qur'ān*. He considered them, a such, the original source of monotheism. Not surprisingly, he translated the *Bhagavad Gītā* and a number of Upanishads into Persian. He maintained that the translation was intended to clarify the Quranic revelation, not to devalue it. He also wrote a treatise on comparative religion, in which he compared the technical terms of Upanishadic pantheism with what he believed, perhaps mistakenly, to be their equivalents in Sufi thought. Apart from his Sufi preceptors, Dara consulted Brahmins as well as Hindu mystics and saints on aspects of the spiritual quest (see Mujeeb 1967).

Dara's younger brother, Aurangzeb, disapproved of Akbar and Dara's quest for religious syncretism. Getting the ulama to pronounce Dara an apostate, for maintaining, among other things, that Islam and Hinduism were 'twin brothers,' Aurangzeb had Dara executed in 1659. For Aurangzeb, Islam and Hinduism were as irreconcilable as truth and error. The Akbar–Dara quest for inter-religious understanding was not, however, a total failure. It gradually led to a change in the attitudes of some Sufi orders (notably, the Qadiri with whom Dara was associated and later the Naqshbandi with whom Aurangzeb had his ties). They moved from hostility to tolerance and even understanding of Hinduism. In fact, the exclusive and syncretic tendencies ran parallel to each other, often in the thought and action of the same person. After reading the *Bhagavad Gītā*, Shah Abdul Aziz (d. 1824), for example, who was at the forefront of the 'purifiers' of Indian Islam and worked for the return of Sufi orders to orthodoxy, also regarded Krishna as a saint.

If the Akbar–Dara experiment had succeeded, perhaps Hinduism would have evolved in a manner consistent with its monotheistic potential and Islam perhaps would have been absorbed into it just as the Buddhist and Jain heterodoxies had been. But these changes did not occur. The role of Sufism in bringing Islam and Hinduism close together must not be overestimated. Even the outstanding contributions of the gifted Sufi Amir Khusrau in the late thirteenth century to a composite literary and musical culture, and his obvious pride in being an Indian, did nothing to soften his ambivalence about, if not hostility toward, Hinduism.

Some contemporary Indian thinkers, confronting history with metaphysics, maintain that a synthesis between Hinduism and Islam was never truly possible because their basic value orientations are irreconcilable (Ahmad 1964). The lure of synthesis, according to these scholars, turned out to be elusive. In terms of the fundamentals of belief and practice, their opinion may well be true, but the unthinkable (namely synthesis) did take place in medieval India, and not only in art and architecture, painting and music, language and literature, but also in religion and philosophy—though in a much more limited way in the latter than in the former three domains.

And yet the coming of Islam was indeed a revolutionary event: it broke the ancient bond between India and her indigenous religious traditions. Although Christianity had arrived here with the apostle Thomas, who established the Syrian church in southwestern India, it had not sued for the state, and no Christian kingdoms were established. It is in this sense that the coming of Muslims to India was undeniably a political act, an invasion.

Cultural synthesis at the high philosophical level had its counterpart at the popular level. The latter in fact anticipated the former and was also more successful. Kabir, whom I have already mentioned in connection with bhakti, had preceded Dara Shukoh by almost a hundred years. Looking back, social historians consider him the originator of a new religious tradition, namely the Sant tradition. The word *sant* is derived from the Sanskrit *sat* for 'truth' or 'reality', and means one who knows the Truth or who has experienced Reality.

Rejecting the external authority of the Vedas and the *Qur'ān*, Kabir, who was brought up in a Muslim family, preached the goal of inner realization based on the love of transcendent and formless divinity. He was influenced by Vaishnava bhakti primarily but also by yogic and Sufi ideas and practices, such as the ideals of self-perfection and the oneness of God respectively, and the meditative recitation of God's name as an expression of one's love for him, common to both Hindu devotees and Muslim Sufis. His followers were drawn mostly from lower, often untouchable, Hindu castes, and included Muslims. The latter saw him as an exponent of the Sufi notion of the 'unity of being' (*wahdat-al-wujūd*).

The Sants stressed the fulfilment of essential social obligations such as the need to support one's family through personal effort. Kabir himself is said to have practised the craft of weaving. Although socially involved, the Sants advocated an inner detachment from worldly ties. Seeking a true guru, keeping the company of like-minded seekers, and dedicating themselves to the incessant remembrance of God, they abandoned traditional rituals and rejected caste and religious barriers. Their creed of love embraced humanity as well as the abstract supreme being. Rabindranath Tagore called this the religion of man. Sociologically, the Sant reformation is important because it gave birth to a large number of sects in northern, central, and western India. Many of these sects, including the Kabir Panth, survive until today.

One sect that was to grow into a world religion was that of the followers of Nanak (1469–1539) in the Punjab. Born an upper-caste Hindu, deeply influenced by the Sant tradition as well as by Upanishadic metaphysics, and clearly aware of the teachings of Islam and the practice of the Nath Yogis (members of a Hindu sect who focus on self-perception and inner awareness), Nanak revolted against ritualism and caste rigidities, particularly the former. He also sought to combine elements from the various religious traditions of India and to transcend them. Worship of and submission to the will of God, honest labour, and collective sharing of the fruits of labour are believed to be the principles of his teaching. His companions and followers came to be called Nanak Panthis as well as Sikhs (disciples, or learners), and their religious tradition, the Sikh *dharam*.

Nanak was the first guru of the Sikhs. He was followed by nine others. The Mughal emperor Akbar was tolerant of the new sect and is believed even to have visited the third guru. The political environment after Akbar's death became increasingly hostile under the Naqshbandi Sufi reaction to Akbar's alleged apostasy. Sikh tradition holds Jahangir (Akbar's son) responsible for the death of the fifth guru. Around the same time the social composition of the Sikh community, which had been confined largely to a small number of clean Hindu castes, also changed. The large-scale entry of Jat agriculturalists into the Sikh fold contributed to the shaping of its militant character. The original pietist and pacifist message of Nanak was gradually transformed without being abandoned completely. On the one hand, Hindu ritualistic practices were gradually revived; on the other, the Sikhs came into armed conflict with the Mughals, who considered them rebellious and tried to suppress, if not exterminate, them. The sixth guru, Hargobind, proclaimed himself the spiritual and temporal leader of the Sikhs. Distinguishing between the two functions, subordinating the temporal to the religious, he yet insisted on combining them both in his own person.

Finally, the tenth guru, Gobind (1666–1708), took up arms against Aurangzeb and presented the two-edged sword as the symbol of the deity to his followers. More than any of his nine predecessors, Gobind brought the Sikh faith closer to completion philosophically; he also highlighted the distance between the Sikhs and the followers of the two main faiths through an emphasis on behavioural differences. Obviously influenced by the *Bhagavad Gītā*, he presented himself as the protector of dharma; also he composed a hymn in praise of the Hindu goddess Chandi, whom he worshipped. He translated the *Bhāgavata Purāna* and some other Sanskrit texts into the vernacular. At the same time he instituted a ritual of initiation and a code of conduct for his followers. The latter included the injunction to remain unshorn (unlike the Hindus) and uncircumcized (unlike the Muslims). Besides their head and facial hair, the Sikhs were to wear other visible markers of their distinctive identity. He put an end to the institution of personal gurus and declared the Sikh holy book, the *Granth Sahab*, originally compiled by the fifth guru and containing the hymns of Nanak and many Sants and Sufis, as the eternal spiritual guru. Temporal power would vest in the Sikh congregation itself.

Theologically, the Sikh faith is syncretistic. Sociologically, the Sikh community is a reproduction of Hindu society, being characterized by caste distinctions to this day. Politically, it had remained opposed to the Muslims since the seventeenth century, and began to distance itself from the Hindus towards the end of the nineteenth century. Those Sikh 'Sants' of today who are politicians, or who patronize terrorists in the name of the unity of religion and politics, have hardly any claims to membership in the Sant tradition of which Nanak was a flower or of the Sikh faith to which he gave birth.

Religious syncretism bore witness to the vitality of the religious life in medieval India. But religion was to become perverted in the modern age. The coming together of religious traditions was to give way to the falling apart of politicized religious communities. The encounter of Hinduism and Christianity in the sixteenth and following centuries was to generate one last syncretic movement before the parting of ways—or what seems so just now—between the adherents of different faiths in India.

Bengal, which had seen the coming together of Buddhism, Hinduism, and tribal religions, and later of Hinduism and Islam, and which had also witnessed an upsurge of Vaishnava bhakti, was to be the home of an experiment in syncretism in the nine-teenth century. Its moving force was Rammohun Roy (1772–1833), a Hindu of wide sympathies and vast scholarship. He operated on two fronts. Convinced of the need for the elevation of the religious life of the Hindus in the direction of a monistic theism, he launched a multipronged drive to synthesize whatever he considered most valuable in vedantic Hinduism, Islam, and Prot-estant Christianity. He also initiated and supported campaigns to eradicate social abuses of various kinds in Hindu society. The most remarkable feature of his syncretic quest was, perhaps, its rootedness in Hinduism, Roy's great admiration for the moral precepts of Jesus (on which the wrote a book) notwithstanding. His religious philosophy was perhaps too austere and intellectual for the Hindus to accept. Not surprisingly, therefore, the universal religion he dreamed of died with him. His successors split up and the majority returned to the Hindu fold before long.

COMMUNALISM AND SECULARISM

Rammohun Roy had hoped for a sociocultural and a religious renaissance under British rule (which he considered a civilizing force) and as a result of India's encounter with Christianity. The search for syncretism on the part of some was, however, more than matched by the fear of an imperial proselytizing religion on the part of others. The encounter of religious traditions was in-evitably linked to the clash of imperialism with nationalism. Given the holist perspectives characteristic of India's cultural traditions, nationalism was presented as a religious quest. Thus, Aurobindo Ghose proclaimed: 'nationalism is not a mere political programme; nationalism is a religion that has come from God' (de Bary 1959: 727).

The dawn of the twentieth century saw political organizations draw upon religious symbolism to mobilize people in the struggle for independence. What is most significant is that the use of such symbolism was resorted to not only by exclusively Hindu or Muslim organizations but also by the multi-religious Indian National Congress. This was no less true of the Congress under Mahatma Gandhi (1869–1948), the Mahatma, than it had been earlier when the reins of leadership were in the hands of militant leaders who projected a more emphatic Hindu personality. Bal Gangadhar Tilak (1856–1920) and Gandhi presented new and divergent interpretations of the *Bhagavad Gītā* that were reminiscent of old controversies, but unlike some of the commentaries which had been renunciatory, argued a this-worldly philosophy of action.

Gandhi's approach to religious pluralism was transcendental rather than simply syncretic. Throughout his long political career he stressed the inseparability of religion and politics. But, he maintained, religion should not entail sectarianism: 'This religion transcends Hinduism, Christianity, and Islam'. Convinced of the truth of all religions and of the limitations of human under-standing, he considered conversion an expression of lack of genuine religious faith. He was horrified by the so-called religious conflicts: 'Religion is outraged when an outrage is perpetrated in its name' (1961: 47).

Gandhi set himself three major goals: freedom from British rule, inter-religious harmony, and the improvement of the socio-religious life of the Hindus. He sincerely believed that the goals entailed one another and were pragmatically related. Much to the dismay of secular-minded nationalists, he tied up the national movement after the First World War with Khilafat (the movement against termination of the caliphate) and later with the eradication of untouchability among the Hindus. He never waivered in his commitment to a holist world view: each religion was all-comprehensive though there were many religions.

The Mahatma's efforts to unite Hindus and Muslims in the pursuit of the national goal of independence from foreign rule failed in the end. His conception of religion as faith wedded to moral reason was not shared by his followers, whether Hindus or non-Hindus. The religiosity which won against him was of the miracle-haunted rustic and the rootless urbanite on the one hand,

and of the profit-seeking politician on the other. Extremist elements among Hindus and Muslims alike repudiated his leadership: to the former he was a foe of Hinduism, to the latter of their aspiration for a separate homeland. Nationalism in India became polarized, with Hindus and Muslims generally pitted against each other. Although most Hindus stayed with the Congress, the two turbulent streams of communalism flowed along their separate courses, as the subcontinent lurched forward toward independence. Communalism in the sense of struggle for independence and power on the basis of religious identity rather than on the principle of territory—which is the usual basis of nationalism—thus came to dominate the internal politics of India.

Gandhi and like-minded people, especially the Muslim theologian and politician Maulana Abul Kalam Azad and the secularist Jawaharlal Nehru, could not stem the tide of communalism. India was partitioned in 1947 and the Islamic state of Pakistan was born in the midst of communal riots on an unprecedented scale, resulting in the killing of thousands of Hindus, Muslims, and Sikhs in many parts of the subcontinent but most of all in the provinces of Bengal and the Punjab. Millions became refugees and fled across the newly created international frontiers. Gandhi's dream of a united independent India went up in smoke, but he did not have to suffer long: he was assassinated early in 1948 by a group of Hindu militants.

Instead of cleansing politics of its unsavoury aspects, as men of faith such as Mahatma Gandhi had believed it would, religion was reduced to being a mere 'sign of distinction' between politically mobilized human groups. It became a 'shadow' of itself (Dumont ibid.: 315–16). Millions of people felt revulsion towards the political abuse of religion, particularly by leaders who had no use for religion in their own lives. In such a situation, there were many who still believed in the idea of inter-religious understanding, but there were numerous others who looked forward to the elimination of religion from public life. Jawaharlal Nehru (1889–1964) was one such rationalist and he committed independent India to the custody of a modern state. Secularism in India has, however, had far from an easy passage. Asked by André Malraux what his greatest difficulty had been since independence, Nehru had replied, 'Creating a just state by just means', and, after a pause, 'Perhaps, too, creating a secular state in a religious country' (1968: 145). This was in 1958, eleven years after India had gained freedom.

Nehru was a modernizer who was deeply conscious of the harm that religiosity had done to India. He had written just three years before he became the prime minister of India in 1947 that it was 'with the temper and approach of science allied to philosophy, and with reverence for all that lies beyond' that Indians must face life. He had further observed that 'the day-to-day religion of the orthodox Hindu is more concerned with what to eat, who to eat with and from whom to keep away, than with spiritual values.... The Moslem...has his own narrow codes and ceremonials, a routine which he vigorously follows, forgetting the lesson of brotherhood which his religion taught him' (1961: 553).

Nehru's views are important because they are the best possible statement of the liberal secular outlook, which is widely regarded as a precondition of modernization. In fact, what is remarkable is the need Nehru felt to defend religion as philosophy or as a concern with 'all that lies beyond'; otherwise, he was an agnostic and favoured a rationalist, and even a historicist, world view.

An examination of Nehru's published work brings out clearly his conviction that religion is a hindrance to 'the tendency to change and progress inherent in human society' and that 'the belief in a supernatural agency which ordains everything has led to a certain irresponsibility on the social plane, and emotion and sentimentality have taken the place of reasoned thought and inquiry' (ibid.: 543). But, then, he did not worry too much about religion and its political expression as communalism because 'the real thing' was 'the economic factor' (1973: 203). He expected communalism to recede in the face of a reordered economic structure. But this proved a false hope, perhaps because no real economic restructuring was possible in the short run. Secularism as the basis of the state had therefore to be a policy of strict neutrality on the part of the state in its dealings with citizens irrespective of their various religious faiths. This policy is more a defensive strategy to help tide over the intervening period until the anticipated transition to a truly secularized society than a positive philosophy of life (see Madan 1997).

It is pertinent to recall here that the emergence of secularism in Europe, in the sense of 'disenchantment with the world' (as Schiller and Weber put it), was not only an expression of repugnance toward the corruption of institutionalized religion but was also aided by developments in the teachings of Christianity. The basis for the separation of state and Church is to be found in the New Testament itself. The privatization of religion, through the assumption by the individual of the responsibility for his own salvation without the intervention of the Church, was a later development. All this is well known. A similar ideology is, however, absent from the cultural traditions of India. The idiom in which to express the ideal of secularism has, therefore, yet to be constructed. This is not an easy task, because the great majority of the people of India are adherents of one religious faith or another and also because in such matters borrowed ideas do not carry us very far (see Chapter 3 above).

As for the vitality of the religious life of the people, it is unfortunate that what attracts attention most is the so-called fundamentalism among Muslims and Sikhs and revivalism among Hindus. There is no doubt that communal politics, which had been weakened considerably in the wake of Gandhi's martyrdrom, has become strident again. Non-political expressions of this vitality are also available, testifying to the capacity of the Hindu tradition to continuously spawn not only new cults and sects but also new gods and goddesses. The secularists consider this wholly regrettable because they see such developments as evidence of the persistence of anti-rational attitudes and social backwardness.

Arguably, their conceptions of rationalism and social advancement are unreasonably restrictive. They fail to realize that religiously minded people are not necessarily bad or stupid— certainly not more than the secularists themselves. It should be realized that secularism may not be restricted to rationalism as understood in the West, that it is compatible with faith, and that it need not be the sole motive force of a modern state. For the secularist minority to stigmatize the majority as superstitious and to preach secularism to them as the law of their being is both moral arrogance and political folly.

What, then, is the way out of the present predicament in the history of religions in India? The question is more easily posed than answered; but it is quite clear that the solution will have to be broadly humanist rather than narrowly sectarian or naively secularist. Maybe Gandhi's approach still has its uses. For Gandhi, religion was a matter of faith but not blind faith. He placed moral reason above scriptural authority. Religion, he maintained, is the source of absolute value and hence constitutive of social life; politics is the arena of public interest; without the former the latter becomes debased. But the multiplicity of religious faiths would generate conflict in the value domain itself. He considered the quest for a single religion neither feasible nor indeed desirable. There was thus no escape from a transcendentalist approach and the quest for inter-religious understanding; a simple pluralism advocating respect for all religions would not do.

Gandhi's secularism was a restraint on the state, not because this was expedient but because society would ultimately be reformed by good people and not by governments. In saying so, he reiterated such old and enduring ideas as dharma, karma, and bhakti. He also sought to carry forward the syncretic tendencies that have always been present and that had become particularly salient in the medieval period. In doing all this, he also showed a keen awareness of the spirit of the age in which he lived, as, for instance, when he maintained that morality in our time finds expression through politics.

* * *

As an interpretive essay on religion in India, this has been an exercise in selection. The terrain to be covered is vast and bristles with many complex problems of fact and interpretation. To cut a way through it, I have focused on some points on high ground, as it were, in the hope that, seen together, they would provide a coherent picture. Doubtless there are other perspectives and other profiles. The issue is not that but rather that the interpretation offered here should be based on a fair reading of the history of religions in India. Naturally, I believe it to be so. I certainly have my preferences in relation to the available interpretations, but they are not peculiarly mine. And, as the German philosopher Hans-Georg Gadamer (1983: 105) has emphasized, 'The very idea of a definitive interpretation seems to be intrinsically contradictory. Interpretation is always on the way.'

At this point it seems pertinent to state very briefly that I was born a Hindu and had a Hindu upbringing combined with a 'modern' education—a common enough experience in contemporary India. I became an anthropologist, which means, I guess, that I have tried to look upon my cultural heritage with an attitude that stands in the twilight zone between sympathy and scepticism, admiration and distaste. But, then, there is really no minimum definition of what it requires and means to be a Hindu other than in terms of birth, and that gives me release. Although I do not believe in or do a hundred things that my grandfathers believed in or did, yet I do not feel I am not a Hindu; nor has anybody suggested otherwise. There are no practising Hindus in the sense in which there are practising Christians; there are no 'five pillars' of Hinduism as there are of Islam. But my personal beliefs and behaviour are beyond a certain point irrelevant to my concerns as a scholar. If I find that religion is a significant element in the constitution of society in India, that does not mean that I wish it to be so. One does not wish that the Himalayas were or were not there; they *are* there.

What, then, distinguishes the perspective offered in this essay? It is above all the effort to look upon religion not as a reflection or a subsystem of society but as society, viewed primarily in terms of axiologically grounded social action, and as something on the move. Whether in its cosmological, moral, theological, or social aspects, the religious landscape in India has been characterized by pluralism for more than two thousand years. Holism and pluralism are not necessarily in conflict. Syncretic movements as well as inter-religious antagonisms have been present throughout the history of India. If anybody should think that my emphasis on syncretism is misplaced, I would ask such a critic to ponder the Sant tradition. If India has ever had a religion that cut across traditional religious, social, and gender boundaries, that combined the intellectual and the emotional, that unified rather than divided people, it is the Sant tradition. It is up to us to realize the potential for good that is inherent in religion.

In the modern age, while conflict between politically mobilized religious communities has become a salient phenomenon in India, conscious efforts have been made to replace syncretism with secularism. Secularism is generally understood as both the limitation of the role of religion in public affairs and the policy of neutrality on the part of the state in relation to the citizens who are followers of various religious traditions. Secularism would have had wider acceptance if it had not been so utterly uncritical in its rejection of religion and its acceptance of a technological view of the world.

Meanwhile, the present is marked by the return of religion to the secular city, as Harvey Cox (1984) has said, and also by a resurgence of violence, even terrorism, in the name of religion (see Casanova 1994 and Juergensmeyer 2000). The secularists, whether liberals or Marxists, seem unable to appreciate that the ideologies of secularism themselves have partly contributed to the present impasse. The prospect is uncertain. The history of humankind, however, teaches us that, as Émile Durkheim (1965) observed, there is something eternal about the role of religion as the moral foundation of social life, and that religion is more likely to be transformed rather than eliminated from society. It is possible that in India, and indeed everywhere else in the postmodern age, religion may yet be rediscovered as humanism, and find expression in a variety of ways, *excluding* theocracy, fundamentalism, and intolerance. In the words of T.S. Eliot,

The only hope, or else despair
Lies in the choice of pyre or pyre—
To be redeemed from fire by fire.

REFERENCES

Ahmad, Aziz. 1964. *Studies in Islamic Culture in the Indian Environment.* Oxford: Clarendon Press.

Casanova, José. 1994. *The Public Religions in the Modern World.* Chicago: University of Chicago Press.

Cox, Harvey. 1984. *Religion in the Secular City: Toward a Postmodern Theology.* New York: Simon & Schuster.

de, Bary, Wm. Th. (ed.). 1958, 1959. *Sources of Indian Tradition.* Vol. 1 (1958), Vol. 2 (1959). New York: Columbia University Press.

Dumont, Louis. 1980. *Homo Hierarchicus: The Caste System and its Implications;* Chicago: University of Chicago Press.

Durkheim, Émile. 1965. *The Elementary Forms of the Religious Life.* J.W. Swain (trs.). New York: The Free Press.

Eck, Diana. 1982. *Banaras: The City of Light.* New York: Alfred Knopf.

Gadamer, Hans-Georg. 1983. *Reason in the Age of Science.* F. Lawrence (trs.). Cambridge: MIT Press.

Gandhi, M.K. [Mahatma]. 1961. *The Way to Communal Harmony.* U.R. Rao (ed.). Ahmedabad: Navjivan.

Gandhi, M.K. [Mahatma]. 1984. *All Men are Brothers*. K. Kripalani (ed.). New York: Continuum.

————. 1986. *The Moral and Political Writings of Mahatma Gandhi*. Raghavan Iyer (ed.). Oxford: Clarendon Press.

Juergensmeyer, Mark. 2000. *Terror in the Mind of God: Global Rise of Religious Violence*. Berkeley: University of California Press.

Karve, Irawati. 1988. 'On the road: A Maharashtrian pilgrimage'. In Eleanor Zelliot and Maxine Bernsten (eds). *The Experience of Hinduism*. Albany: State University of New York Press.

Lingat, Robert. 1973. *The Classical Law of India*. Berkeley: University of California Press.

Malraux, André. 1968. *Antimemoirs*. London: Hamish Hamilton.

Madan. T.N. 1987a. *Non-renunciation: Themes and Interpretations of Hindu Culture*. New Delhi: Oxford University Press.

————. 1987b. 'Secularism in its place'. *The Journal of Asian Studies* 46, 4: 747–59.

————. 1997. *Modern Myths, Locked Minds: Secularism and Fundamentalism in India*. New Delhi: Oxford University Press.

Mujeeb, M. 1967. *The Indian Muslims*. London: Allen & Unwin.

Mukerji, D.P. 1948. *Modern Indian Culture*. Bombay: Hind Kitab.

Nehru, Jawaharlal. 1961 (1946). *The Discovery of India*. Bombay: Asia Publishing House.

————. 1973. *Selected Works of Jawaharlal Nehru*, Vol. 5. New Delhi: Orient Longman.

Radhakrishnan, S. 1923. *Indian Philosophy*. Vol. 1. London: Allen & Unwin.

Ramanujan, A.K. 1973. *Speaking of Siva*. Harmondsworth: Penguin Books.

————. 1981. *Hymns for the Drowning*. Princeton: Princeton University Press.

Roy, Asim. 1983. *The Islamic Syncretic Tradition in Bengal*. Princeton, N.J.: Princeton University Press.

Weber, Max. 1958. *The Religion of India: The Sociology of Hinduism and Buddhism*. H.H. Gerth and D. Martindale (trs.). Glencoe, Ill.: The Free Press.

9

*The Householder Tradition in Hindu Society**

Student, householder, forest hermit, and ascetic: these four distinct orders have their origin in the householder.... Among all of them, however, according to the dictates of Vedic scripture, the householder is said to be the best, for he supports the other three. As all rivers and rivulets ultimately end up in the ocean, so people of all the orders ultimately end up in the householder.

Mānava Dharmashāstra

DEFINING THE TERMS

To write about the householder tradition in Hindu society, it seems desirable that we begin with a brief clarification of the key terms 'householder', 'tradition', and 'Hindu society' as employed in this essay.

A household is a group of persons who own or 'hold' a house: they are the householders. They may as well be seen as a group that is held together, as it were, in or by a house. The idea of ownership is mutual and dynamic: it is a durable relationship made of many strands. A house is of course a building of some kind intended for human habitation, but in many cultural settings, including the Hindu, it is more than that. Besides a material (architectural, allodial) aspect, it has ritual, symbolic, and emotional significance, establishing richer bonds between the house and the householders, and among the householders, than those of mere co-residence in a dwelling.

* Reproduced from Gavin Flood (ed.), *The Blackwell Companion to Hinduism.* Oxford: Blackwell, 2003, Ch. 13, pp. 288–305.

Co-residence is, however, a crucial aspect of the life of the householders. It arises from the ties of kinship, which may be biological or fictive but modelled on the biological, and of marriage. To elaborate, the household comprises at least a married couple and their naturally born or adoptive children. In pre-industrial societies the household is usually more ramified structurally and may even include distantly related or unrelated helpers and dependents. In such societies, the family and the household usually are, unlike in contemporary Western society, differentiated. A family usually comprises many households which live in separate sections of a house or in separate houses. The houses may be built around a compound or may be scattered. The failure to recognize the embedded character of the household within the family has given rise to the somewhat misleading notion of the Hindu 'joint' family (Madan 1962). Some perceptive scholars have rightly observed that from the Hindu perspective the Western household, which is also the immediate family, may well be characterized as being 'restricted'.

Apart from having a structural or formal aspect, the household also has functional and cultural aspects. Householders do many things together. Most notably they produce and socialize children. They act as an economic group engaged in productive and distributive activities, and marked by a division of labour on the basis of (among other considerations) age and sex. They participate in domestic rituals focused on particular household members (for example, birth, marriage, and death rites) or on other religious concerns (for example, propitiation of supernatural 'beings'). They work, gossip, tell tales, sing, and dance together. All these and other related activities comprise a significant part of the way of life of the householders—their culture. What they do not only fulfils certain practical needs, but also bestows meaning and significance on their lives. The practical and the symbolic aspects of the householders' lives, their interests and values, are closely intertwined. They are a legacy that is ever being reaffirmed and reformulated.

This brings us to the second term, 'tradition', which is used here to denote the established ways of living in a society, and their underlying principles and values, accumulated over time. Traditions may be written or they may be oral. All that is remembered may not, however, be currently alive, nor may it be dead, for it may be revived and in the process reinvented. The householder tradition in Hindu society today had its beginnings in the so-called Vedic age about 3000 years ago, and has inevitably undergone many significant changes. Given such a length of time, what is remarkable is perhaps not the extent of change, but the measure of continuity.

This continuity, however, is often questioned because the very idea of Hindu society is said to be relatively recent. What, then, do I mean when I write of Hindu society in this essay? Existentially, Hindu society comprises all those Indians who consider themselves Hindus and make public acknowledgement of this identity, for example when the decennial census is taken. It accounts for four-fifths of the population of India of over one billion. If the so-called Scheduled Castes of officialese, or Dalits (the oppressed) of popular discourse, formerly known as the 'untouchables', are excluded—as some vocal Dalit intellectuals demand (see Ilaiah 1996)—Hindus still account for over two-thirds of the population.

The word 'Hindu' is of course not new: even as term of self-ascription it has been employed at least since the fifteenth century (Thapar 1989: 224). The idea of a large, multimillion-strong, community of subcontinental distribution, however, emerged strongly only in the nineteenth century in response to the Western colonial and Christian missionary challenges, and as a result of improved means of transport and communication. Such an encompassing idea brought together, but did not merge into one, a multitude of communities, each identified by regional culture and language, religious belief and practice, hereditary occupation and caste, and other criteria (see pp. 298–9 below).

Thus, Bengali Brahmans, Tamil Shaivas or Vaishnavas, Gujarati Patidars, north Indian Kayasthas, and numerous other communities acquired an additional shared identity as Hindus. The immediate significance of this development was primarily political. It also highlighted a sense of cultural togetherness in terms of the recognition of a common textual tradition of long duration, beginning with the Vedic corpus and including the later Puranas and epics. The extent and nature of the knowledge of this tradition was (and is) variable, being derived from the texts themselves or their exegeses among the literate elite, or received through verbal exposition by professional story tellers and family elders among the non-literate, largely rural populace.

It has been suggested that acknowledgement of the ultimate authority of the Veda may well be the minimum definition of Hinduism and Hindu identity today (Smith 1989: 13–14), irrespective of how much or how little is known about it. But Hinduism is not identical with Vedism or Brahmanism (Flood 1996). In its growth other sources too, notably the folk traditions—some of them predating the Vedic period—have contributed significantly. In fact, a two-way flow has been at work. Elements of the textual ('Great') tradition have been restated and re-enacted in the idiom of the folk ('Little') traditions (the process has been called, somewhat infelicitously, 'parochialization'). Likewise local beliefs and practices have been built into the textual tradition through 'universalization' (Marriott 1955). Other process of communication or combination have also been at work, such as the identification of critical resemblance between different traditions (Hiltebeitel 1999).

In short, both existentially and historically one can speak and write of Hindu society meaningfully. Its boundaries are flexible, however, and even at its centre 'an inner conflict of tradition' (Heesterman 1985) has been manifest. One of the most significant such antagonisms is between householdership (*gārhasthya*), firmly embedded in society, and renunciatory withdrawal from social obligations (*sannyāsa*). And this dichotomy is as old as the Vedic tradition itself.

GĀRHASTHYA: WAY OF LIFE OR STAGE OF LIFE?

Domestic groups of one kind or another are a cultural universal. Even food-gathering and nomadic tribes periodically settle down to rest and residence in open camps or covered huts before they set out again in search of food for themselves and their domesticated animals. Relatively permanent households are generally but not always associated with cultivation of the soil. They are characterized by rites and symbols that, among other things, valorize domesticity.

Among the Vedic Aryans the domestic fire was more than a hearth for cooking food: it was also the locus of rites of various kinds and thereby acquired a symbolic character. The Aryan householder (*shālīna* from *shālā*, hall) did not, however, immediately qualify for the performance of the prescribed *shrauta* sacrifices that occupied a central place in his and his household's life. For this purpose he had to establish several fire altars. The first of these (*agnyādheya*) was lit with fire taken from the domestic hearth but, after some ceremonial cooking of grain, it was extinguished. One then set out from home to relight it elsewhere with a fire drill after a lapse of time, say a year. More altars (two or four) were set up subsequently. The process completed, the *shālīna* became the *āhitāgni*, that is one who has made the transition from the world in which he was born to one that is transcendent. Two options were apparently available.

The householder could choose to settle down in the second abode, after leaving the first, and establish the sacrificial fires there, and acquire the various accoutrements of a householder, namely a fixed residence, grain, cattle, and other kinds of wealth including servants. Alternatively, the householder could opt for the life of a wanderer (*yāyāavara*). Although he might not have settled down long anywhere, his wandering had a clear purpose, namely the performance of the very same *shrauta* sacrifices to which the householder devoted himself. Indeed, the wanderer travelled to acquire the means, by force if necessary, to do so. Those from whom he took included the settled householders, whose antagonist he would have seemed to be. But his ultimate aim, after the years of wandering and violence, apparently was to settle down to the life of a peaceful householder. Although less glamorous it was regarded a welcome way of life.

In the event, the *shālīna* and the *yāyvara* were really not opposed to each other in their aims but only in their methods. The householder does leave home once to become the *āhitāgni* householder, and the wanderer eventually settles down to domesticity. Both are united in the role of the *shrauta* sacrificer, who is a householder although, paradoxically, he also performs rituals that are extra-social. Making their appearance in the Vedic texts, the householder and the wanderer are present in the Dharma literature also as two types of householders.

Jan Heesterman, on whose discussion of the original Sanskrit sources the foregoing account is based (see Heesterman 1982 and 1985), points out that while all Dharma texts prescribe the departure of the *shālīna* from home before he may establish the sacrificial fires, the *yāyāvara* emerges as the renouncer (sannyāsī) in some of them. Like the *shrauta* sacrifice, renunciation is an act that transcends society. But while the sacrificer periodically reverts to the life of the householder (after each sacrificial performance), or even does so for good, the renouncer turns his back on both the domestic and the sacrificial fires. According to Heesterman, the renouncer better fulfils 'the inner logic' of the Vedic tradition, wherein the desire for breaking away from society is first articulated. The wish for transcendence, however, never wholly repudiates the human world but rather encompasses it. 'The householder adds an extra-social dimension to his quality by becoming a *shrauta* sacrificer and finally withdraws from society into a renunciatory mode of life. But even then he retains the quality of *grihastha* and [of] an *āhitāgni*' (Heesterman 1982: 268).

Patrick Olivelle, another authority on the subject, is even more emphatic in presenting the early primacy of the householder's way of life. He writes: 'The ideal and typical religious life within the Vedic ideology is that of a married householder. The normative character of that life is related to the two theologically central religious activities: offering sacrifices and procreating children' (Olivelle 1993: 36). The scope of sacrifice was vast with cosmo-moral significance and included the three (or five) daily obligations of the householder in redemption of the 'debts' mentioned in Vedic literature. These number three in some texts and five in others: the debts to gods, seers, and fathers, and additionally to all men and non-human creatures. To discharge the debt to the ancestors, adult men of the 'twice-born' (*dvija*) varnas were expected to marry and beget sons. Implicit in the notion of the discharge of debts was an enlarged conception of the moral agent, comprising not only the male sacrificer but also his wife ('one half of the husband') and their offspring. From the *Rigveda* down (in time) to the *Manusmriti* this idea of the man–wife–son triad holds ground and idealizes the life of the householder. Through the performance of sacrifices and by begetting a son, a householder achieves the prized goal of immortality.

The foregoing view of life underwent a radical transformation as a result of both an inner dynamism and significant socio-economic changes between the sixth and fourth centuries BCE. The latter included the introduction of wetland rice cultivation in the lower regions of the Ganges valley resulting in the generation of an agricultural surplus that facilitated an increase in population and the emergence of urban settlements. With the latter came the merchant class, the notion of kingship, and an individualistic spirit. 'The freedom to choose' that one would associate with individualism was, according to Olivelle (ibid.: 58), 'at the heart' of the challenge to 'the vedic religious ideal', which led to the formulation of 'the original *āshrama* system that permitted a choice among several modes of religious life'.

The alternatives to the life of the married man and the householder that now became available comprised the life of the celibate and the ascetic respectively. For the ascetic and the renouncer the ultimate aim of moral striving was liberation from the cycle of birth, death, and rebirth in place of the Vedic householder's quest for immortality. Comparing the ideology of the early āshrama system to that of the varna and caste systems, Olivelle observes: 'The creators of *āshrama* system intended to do to the diversity of religious life styles what the creators of the *varna* system did to the diversity of social and ethnic groups': instead of 'eliminating' it, they accommodated 'the diversities within an overarching system' (ibid.: 101).

The āshrama system as originally conceived was, however, transformed by the beginning of the common era into what Olivelle calls the classical āshrama system. Whatever the reasons for this transformation, which can only be speculative and do not directly concern us here, it comprised two significant elements. The alternative modes of life of the worldly householder and the ascetic renouncer now became stages in the life of the moral agent. Of the four stages of studentship (*brahmacharya*), householdership (*grihastha*), retreat (*vānaprastha*), and renunciation (*sannyāsa*), the first three were by the very nature of the scheme temporary (each stage leading to the next), and the last one permanent as long as one lived. Moreover, a sense of obligation in the pursuit of ideals, which had been overtaken by the notion of choice, was revived.

To quote Olivelle again, 'the four āshramas came to be regarded as constituting four ideals of the Brahmanical ethic' that were, 'as far as possible', to be 'realized by each individual' (ibid.: 129–30). And each stage was inaugurated by the rites of passage appropriate to it. The Brahmans were less tolerant of choice than their ancestors and provided an ideological back-up to the scheme of stages through the notion of *svadharma*, that is dharma appropriate to each stage of life and, concomitantly, each varna.

It was thus that the compound notion of *varnāshrama* dharma came to be the definition of the religio-moral life of the Brahmans and derivatively of the other twice-born varnas.

While the notion of the householder as a choice for life is present in the Dharmasūtras, the later notion of āshramas as stages of life is elaborated in the Dharmashāstras, belonging to the first five centuries of the common era. Of these the most frequently cited, perhaps, is the *Mānava Dharmashāstra*, also known as the *Manusmriti* and believed to have been in existence already in the second century (see Buhler 1964: xiv). The householder's stage in the life of the individual is prescriptively introduced early in the text: 'When, unswerving in his chastity, [the student] has learned the Vedas, or two Vedas, or even one Veda, in the proper order, he should enter the householder stage of life' (3.2 in Doniger and Smith 1991: 43; all further quotations from the *Mānava Dharmashāstra* are from the foregoing translation).

One notices a certain urgency in the text, a desire not to postpone too long the inauguration of the householder's life. Appropriately, the making of a proper marriage is taken up first (3.4–66). The qualities of a woman that make her a good wife are listed. Eight forms of marriage and their varna-wise appropriateness are described. Exhortations on the duties of spouses and the respect due to women follows. The men of the household are advised to 'revere' and 'adorn' women if they wish for 'good fortune': 'The deities delight in places where women are revered...and [the family] thrives where women are not miserable' (3.55–58).

The law book then proceeds to prescribe the establishment of the domestic fires for cooking food and performing 'five great sacrifies' as well as other domestic rituals. These sacrifices, it is explained, enable the householder to expiate the sins that are daily committed as a matter of necessity at the five slaughter-houses of the home, namely the fireplace, the grindstone, the broom, the mortar and pestle, and the water jar (3.68). The expiatory rites are: 'The study (of the Veda) is sacrifice to ultimate reality, and the refreshing libation is the sacrifice to the ancestors; the offering into the fire is for the gods, the propitiatory offering of portions of food is for the disembodied spirits, and the revering of guests is the sacrifice to men' (3.7). The continuity of the tradition from the Vedic sacrifices (mentioned earlier in this essay) down (in time) to shāstric rituals is noteworthy.

The argument is enlarged to bring in the other three orders (corresponding to the other stages of life): 'since people in the other three stages of life are supported every day by the knowledge and food of the householder, therefore the householder stage of life is the best' (3.78).[1] In the giving of offerings and alms nobody is left out, not even dogs, those who have fallen, 'Dog-cookers', those whose evil deeds have made them ill, birds and worms (3.92).

Guests come in for detailed mention, and even a deserving Vaishya or Shudra, approaching a Brahman's house in the proper manner must be given food, although only alongside the servants (3.112). Not everyone qualifies to be a guest, however, certainly not Brahman householders in their own village, who can only be called foolish, for they run the risk of being reborn as 'the live-stock of those who have given them food' (3.104). It is only after one and all have been fed that the pious householder shall him-self eat. 'The householder should eat the leftovers only after he has revered the gods, the sages, humans, ancestors, and the household deities. The person who cooks only for himself eats nothing but error [sin], for the food left over from the sacrifice is the food intended for good men' (3.117–18).

A large part of the third book of *Mānava Dharmashāstra* (122–286) has *shrāddha*, the sacrifice to the ancestors, for its theme. The central rites consist of offering rice balls (*pinda*) to specified deceased ancestors and feeding invited Brahmans who represent them.

The fourth book attends to the issue of the means of subsistence of the householders. An interesting classification is presented. Subsistence by gleaning corn and gathering grains is 'lawful'; unsolicited gifts are 'immortal' and acceptable; farming, although the 'deadly' mode of life, is legitimate; trade is 'simultaneously good and unlawful' and yet permissible. But servility must be avoided for it is 'the dog's way of life' (4.5–6). Detailed rules of behaviour not only in respect of diet but the whole range of natural and legitimate activities are listed.

Altogether, a view of the householder's life is presented in which a great deal is permitted including profit and pleasure, so long as it is lawful, prudent, generally acceptable to good people, and in conformity with tradition (see for example, 175–80). What is more, the conception of the householder's life presented in the *Manusmriti* is inclusive and incorporates through subtle devices 'the values of other *āshramas* without abandoning home and family' (Olivelle 1993: 140).

The conflict between the two views of *gārhasthya*—as a permanent alternative to other ways of life, notably that of the renouncer, or as a temporary stage in the life of a twice-born man—was apparently never completely resolved in the textual tradition of the Dharmashāstras and subsequently. What is clear, however, is that, even when the idea of āshramas as stages of life prevailed, the virtues of the householder's way of life were uniformly eulogized. Thus the *Mahābhārata*, which is a truly oceanic source of the precepts and practice of dharma, endorses 'the superiority of the householder' and promotes the idea that renunciation of the householder's life is appropriate only in old age (ibid.: 148–51).

Although Olivelle argues persuasively that the notion of choice in the original āshrama did not completely disappear from subsequent formulations, contemporary Indological literature has generally favoured the idea of an ordered sequence of stages. This is true of both earlier works and the more recent ones, but Olivelle's seminal work is bound to generate rethinking on the subject. The prevailing consensus regarding āshramas as stages of life may be illustrated by referring to two widely read studies of Hinduism by Zaehner (1962: 146–50) and Flood (1996: 61–5, 87–90). In considering the householder's state the very foundation on which the other states rest, contemporary scholarly opinion follows the standard reading of *Mānava Dharmashāstra*.

The influence of Indology on social anthropological studies of the family and household in Hindu society has been negligible. Indeed many anthropologists and sociologists writing in the 1950s and 1960s emphasized the desirability of freeing ethnographic inquiry from Indological assumptions about the character of the Hindu family and the household (see, for example, Shah 1973). The one major dissenter was Louis Dumont who maintained that the sociology of India should lie at the confluence of the findings of Indology and the sociological vantage point (1957: 7). Following this methodological perspective, he produced a seminal essay on world renunciation in Indian religions in which he suggested that 'the secret' (or core principle) of Hinduism (and the structure of Hindu society) may be found in 'the dialogue between the renouncer and the man-in-the-world' (Dumont 1960: 37–8).

As Heesterman has pointed out, 'In the classical Brahmanic view the pivotal actor on whom the *dharma* turns is the typical man-in-the-world, the substantial "twice-born" householder, the *grihastha'* (1982: 251). He disagrees with Dumont regarding the notion of the dialogue because, according to him, the renouncer and the householder lack a common ground, and stand for genuinely dichotomous, mutually antagonistic—rather than complementary—lifestyle choices. What interests us here is that both recognize the traditionally central position of the householder in Hindu society.

Taking that agreement as the point of departure, we now turn to an examination of the ethnographic evidence accumulated in the recent past.[2]

THE HOUSEHOLDER IN ETHNOGRAPHY

In the clarification of the definitional conventions (in the first section of this essay), the attention paid to the house may have seemed somewhat excessive. In the classical textual tradition, the building of temples, royal palaces, and cities expectedly received much more attention than ordinary houses (see Rowland 1953), but some of the basic principles (concerning, for example, the choice of the site and the size and orientation of the building) were the same. The applicability of these principles to house building varied according to the varna of the household, more choices being open to the Brahmans and Kshatriyas than to the others. The abundance or meagreness of the material resources of the household also was a significant factor influencing, if not determining, the choices that were made. Some of the traditional considerations have survived until today; indeed there is today a resurgence of interest in urban India in Vedic architectural principles of house-making.

The folk traditions are not lacking in this respect. Indeed, there are not only explicit guidelines about house-making, which combine ritual and practical considerations, but a vast lore about the character of the houses, and its significance for the well-being of the household also exists.

Thus, among the Brahmans of the Kashmir Valley, widely known as the Pandits (see Madan 1989),[3] the house is the abode of gods as well as human beings. It has a guardian deity (*grihadevatā*) who is identified (through the rituals associated with him) with Vāstupati, the Vedic lord of the earth. The bonds between the house, the deity, and the household are intimate. It is noteworthy that, traditionally, a Kashmiri Pandit household never sold or bought a house. On building a new house, the protective deities would be ritually reinstalled there before entering it, and the old house would then be demolished or, rarely, abandoned.

The sentiments of love, sharing, and solidarity that characterize interpersonal relations in a well integrated household are, in the Pandit's estimation, the highest ideals of human conduct, the acme of morality. The house is loved and valued because of the sanctity and the sentiments associated with it and not merely because of its material value. It is regarded as a moral space par excellence. The home is said to be neither the place for the indulgence of one's physical appetites (*bhogashālā*), nor for the performance of austerities (*yogashālā*) (ibid.: 256–7). In other words, it is the narrow middle ground, the 'razor's edge' of the Upanishads.

An even richer conception of the house in relation to the householders than among the Pandits is found in Tamil Nadu. Here houses are material structures like they are everywhere, but they also partake of the properties of personhood. Valentine Daniel writes:

> Not only are houses, as are [villages] and persons, [made of] substance that can be contaminated and changed by mixing with other substances (hence the concern with what kind of substance crosses the vulnerable thresholds—windows and doors—of the house and affects its own substance and that of its inhabitants) but houses are also 'aware' of their vulnerability. They have personlike needs for companionship, and experience loneliness and fear when isolated (1984: 114).

Houses here are believed to have a life cycle: they are conceived and born, they grow, and may eventually die. Houses, like human offspring, have astrological significance and may bring good or bad fortune to the household. They have feelings and attitudes. It is not therefore without trepidation that the decision to build a house is taken. To minimize the risks and uncertainty strict rules are followed in the selection of the site. It must be judged to be auspicious, and appropriate rituals (for example, Vāstu Purusha puja, although everybody is not sure who Vāstu is) may be performed.

Conception is said to occur when a corner post or cornerstone is installed by a member of the artisan caste who is traditionally entrusted this work. While at work, he must observe rules pertaining to himself. For example: he must eat only vegetarian food or else ghosts and evil spirits will take possession of the house under construction; he must avoid bodily contact with members of lower jātis or goods in the house will disappear; he must abstain from sexual intercourse or else the house will be eroded by white ants. Another set of rules concerns the construction. Scarecrows must be planted in the four cardinal directions to ward off the evil eye. When the roof is laid, only an odd number of beams must be used, as a result of which it is deemed to be incomplete. Incompleteness is a blemish and helps in warding off the evil eye. Moreover, incomplete houses may be expected to grow further.

When a house is ready for occupation, it is said to have been born. A horoscope is cast for it to figure out what the future holds for it. In addition to the nine planets of horoscopes for human beings, the influence of the qualities of the first occupants also are crucial for a house. Houses acquire the same jāti status as the householders and must observe the same rules of inter-caste conduct as is applicable to them. In short, there is a structural homology between the human body and the house, which is culturally constructed.

That the house–householder relationship is an intrinsic one is well illustrated by the distinction that Bengali Hindus make between the *bāsā* ('nest' abode) of a man, his wife and children, and the *bārī* (also called *griha*, house) in which his parents (and other family members) live. Until his father's death he and his immediate family are deemed to be part of the larger family and he may not claim to have his own separate *bārī*. Needless to add, not all sons may live away from the parental home (Inden and Nicholas 1977: 7).

The Bengalis think of a house as shared space, and this makes room for unrelated dependents (for example, servants) to live in it along with those who constitute the family and who share bodily substance. The Kashmiri Pandits make a similar distinction between one's *gara* (house, home) and *dera* (place of temporary residence), but the latter may be *gara* to someone else. Moreover, a son may establish his own household even during the life time of his mother, but this normally does not happen while the father is alive.

The issue here is the manner in which a household is constituted. Among the Pandits, the family (*kutumba*) usually comprises a number of households, each living in a house or a part of a house, and known as *chulahs* (hearth, hearth group). They make a clear distinction between those members who are born into the family / hearth group (*zāmati*), and those who are married into it (*āmati*, 'incomers'). Consanguinity and affinity are mutually exclusive principles. Besides birth and marriage, fictive kinship in the form of adoption also is a recognized mode of recruitment to the family. At the household level unrelated persons may also be present, in some cases on a permanent or quasi-permanent basis (see Madan 1989: chapters 5 and 6). Moreover, families are not thought and spoken of in terms of a beginning and an end, but the household is subject to a developmental cycle. Births and marriages are the incremental events; deaths and partitions result in the loss of members. A household may even die as when the surviving spouse of a childless couple, or of a couple that have only daughters who have moved out on marriage, dies (ibid.: chapter 4).

Although parental love, filial piety, and fraternal solidarity are said to be the foundation of the householder's life, abandonment of joint living as one chulah, and complete or partial partition of the jointly owned estate, are commonly expected to occur among the Pandits (ibid.: chapter 8). In terms of the ideology of the householder, fraternal strife is considered morally reprehensible, but practical considerations are allowed to override morality. Moreover, the blame for intra-household bickering is cleverly placed on the shoulders of the wives who are, of course, the *zāmati* and not the *āmati*. And the decline of morality in the dark age of *kaliyuga* is always cited as a cause of things that should not happen.

In this context, it is noteworthy that the domestic scene two thousand years ago was essentially the same as it is today in most Hindu homes. Thus, we read in the *Mānava Dharmashāstra* (9.104 and 111): 'After the father and mother (are dead), the brothers [may] assemble and divide the paternal estate equally, for they have no power over two of them while they are alive.' More significantly, apropos the contention of the decline of morality: 'They [the brothers] may live together in [mutual respectfulness], or they may live separately if they wish for religious merit; for religious merit increases in separation, and so separate rituals are conducive to religious merit' (Doniger and Smith 1991: 209, 210). It is, of course, questionable how much considerations of religious merit count in contemporary times, but division of jointly owned estates does often occur with a view to reducing income tax burden.[4]

The question of religious merit apart, performance of rituals is indeed a major concern of Brahman and other upper caste households even if only as a matter of convention. There are two main types of domestic rituals. Firstly, those associated with life-cycle events (notably birth, initiation, marriage, and death), known as *sanskāra*, and those that affirm the bonds between ancestors and descendents, called the *shrāddha*. Secondly, there are the rituals that seek to establish purposive and meaningful communication between householders and supernatural 'beings'. These may be supplicatory in character, as is the daily worship one's chosen deities, or contractual, or even coercive. The rituals performed by lower caste Hindu households may not be an exact replica of upper caste rituals, and may not involve the specialist services of a Brahman priest, but they too fall into the two categories mentioned above. Work related rituals also take place in artisan and peasant households.

Sustained by economic activity, reinforced by religious observances, the life of the Hindu householder is nourished and legitimized by the values of love, sharing, and solidarity. It has been explicated that, while 'authority, rights and duties, land, inheritance, the distribution of resources within the joint family, prestations, reproduction, and so forth' are critical factors in the construction of interpersonal relations in Bengali households, often providing the basis for conflict, love (*prīti, prema*) holds them together. 'If kinsmen have the proper kind of love for one another, then they will enjoy well-being and they will not be divided by greed, selfishness, or envy' (Inden and Nicholas 1977: 87–8).

A variety of loves is said to be discernible, namely conjugal, filial, fraternal, parental, and the love between brothers and sisters. Love may be egalitarian or hierarchical. In all cases, it is expressed through spontaneous and selfless feelings of caring (*pālana*), nourishing (*poshana*), and supporting (*bharana*) for one another. Delight (*ānanda*), gratification (*tripti*), and contentment (*santosha*) are the fruit of such feelings (ibid.: 21).

An elaborate ideology of love in Tamil Nadu comprises the ideas of *anpu* (love), *pacam* (attachment), *ācai* (desire), *kāppu* (bonding), *pattu* (devotion), etc. These are articulable, and sometimes articulated, in explication of how the members of a household relate to one another (see Trawick 1966: chapter 3). *Anpu* is a complex notion that connotes a multitude of emotions and moral judgements. Thus, love must be contained (*adakkam*, containment), for excess is harmful; moreover 'love grows in hiding'. Even a mother's love for the child must be 'kept within limits', for 'letting love overflow its bounds could be harmful not only to the recipient, but to the giver as well' (ibid.: 94). While the legitimacy and power of sexual love and pleasure (*inpam*, 'sweetness') may not be denied, the love of spouses is also best contained to the point of concealment. Such concealment takes diverse forms including, particularly among the lower castes, the derogation of the husband by the wife.

Love is a force, but its essence is tenderness. It grows slowly by habituation; indeed it becomes a habit (*parakkam*) that even death does not destroy. The loved person becomes a part of oneself. *Parakkam* implies friendliness, easiness, and grace (ibid.: 100). But it has its emotional costs. Love and attachment have a cruel aspect, for they produce restlessness. Moreover, being parted from the loved person is painful; it is like having a part of oneself severed. Love makes one do strange and even improper things, such as defiance of the rules of purity: picking up the leaf from which someone has eaten, and which is therefore impure, is an act of love and meritorious. It conveys a message of union and equality. Love teaches humility (*pani*). 'In acts of love, the humble became proud, the servant became master, the renouncer became possessed' (ibid.: 106). Love normally produces servitude (*adima*), a sense of being controlled by another person, but then this feeling itself is 'a powerful expression of love' (ibid.: 111). Ultimately, love means that the members of the household 'are all one' within the 'four walls' of the house. As a Tamil householder (a woman) has put it, 'In order for you to understand my heart, you must see through my eyes. In order for me to understand your heart, I must see through yours' (ibid.: 115, 116).

There is a gentle and authentic simplicity about the manner in which the Tamil villager articulates the place of love in the ideology of the householder. There are other values too that are generally affirmed elsewhere by other Hindu communities, but raised above them all is the ideal of domesticity itself. The Kashmiri Pandits are the self-aware ideologues of *gārhasthya* within the value framework of Hinduism, expressed, for example, in the notion of *purushārtha* comprising the goals and orientations of dharma, *artha*, and *kāma*. The Pandit ideology of the householder is lukewarm about the fourth *purushārtha* of moksha, and explicitly negative about renunciation (*sannyāsa*) as a way of life or as the last stage of life. As a householder, a Pandit may legitimately seek joy and plentitude, but ideally this endeavour should be subordinated to dharma and combined with detachment (*virakti*) and the love of one's chosen personal deity (*ishtadeva, istadevī*). As a well-known Pandit poet, Krishna Razdan (1850–1925), who was a devout Vaishnava, put it: 'Why should we renounce the lovely world? Our love of Him is our austerity...' (see Cook 1958).

The Pandit's ideology of the householder is, in fact, more than just that: it is their ideology of humanity. While all sentient beings are born (and die), human beings are made and matured through the *sanskāras* and achieve different degrees of moral perfection by their conduct. A boy attains the ritual status of an adult when he receives the girdle (*mekhalā*) and the holy neck threads (*yajnopavīta*). In the case of girls, it is marriage that bestows similar status on them. Marriage is crucial for men as well as women, for it is only through it that they become householders. Bachelors, childless widowers, and widows are normally members of households but not themselves *grihastha*, and are therefore considered unfortunate. The greatest desire of a Pandit, whether man or woman, is to be a full-fledged householder.

The Pandit ideology of the householder is constructed around men. Women and children are spoken of in relation to them. But the men themselves recognize that in the reality of everyday life women are significant role players. They are referred to as *grihasthadhārinī*, the upholders and the bearers of the burden of *gārhasthya*. A man works out his destiny as a Pandit and a human being in the company of women: without them his ritual, personal, and social life is incomplete. Among the most coveted meritorious acts that a Pandit may perform, the giving away of his daughter in marriage (*kanyādāna*) ranks very high. Men are hierarchically superior to women, but it is together with them that they constitute the core of the life of the householder.

Being a Pandit is as much a concern of women as it is of men. In the domain of domestic activity, however, women's roles are different, and their work in the kitchen as well as their participation in religious rites is severely but discretely restricted during the periods of menstruation. Moreover, women do not offer water and food to ancestors; they do not have the ritual status and authority to initiate their sons into adulthood or give their daughters in marriage. And yet the wife is always present by the husband's side on all major ceremonial occasions. She is one-half of his self (*ardhāngini*).

The ideology of the householder clearly establishes the Pandit as the man-in-the-world. Such a person's prime concern in the midst of worldly activities is with the maturation of his self. This is ensured if he organizes his domestic life in strict conformity with traditional purposes (*purushārtha*), employing appropriate procedures for their achievement. Release from the chain of transmigration (*samsāra*) is a high but frankly distant goal—so distant indeed as to be virtually beyond reach. A prudent person concentrates on the slow but steady accumulation of merit by the conscious effort to lead a disciplined life.

Renouncers are conspicuous by their absence in Pandit society. Self-styled renouncers are distrusted as men who, with a failed domestic life behind them, make a virtue of necessity. At a deeper level, however, one might detect a fear of the renouncer, for he poses a threat to the ideology of the *gārhasthya*. The sannyāsī is too powerful an adversary to be contemplated with equanimity. Individual renouncers, if judged to be genuine, will be accorded respect. But renouncers as a category are caricatured: that the caricature is only too often an accurate enough portrait of the 'holy men' one actually meets is another matter though not totally irrelevant. The real point seems to be that only when the renouncer is thus portrayed may he be convincingly employed as a foil to highlight the virtues of the life of the householder. These are said to flow from 'detachment in enjoyment', which is the essence of renunciation. *Gārhasthya* is not to end in renunciation, but it should be guided by the values of *sannyāsa*. For the rest, everything is dependent upon divine grace (*anugraha*).[5]

The foregoing summary of the Pandit ideology of the householder is based on my fieldwork in the village of Utrassu-Umanagri (south-east Kashmir) carried out mainly in 1957–8 (Madan 1989). It is noteworthy that, despite over five hundred years of life lived as a small minority (about 4 per cent of the population in the 1950s) amongst Muslims—who are mainly descendants of Hindus converted to Islam *en masse* in the fourteenth century— and under Muslim rule between the early fourteenth and mid-nineteenth centuries, the Pandits have managed to preserve many core ideas and values of the Brahmanical tradition *via* oral transmission. In an essay based on Sanskrit texts of the medieval period (9th–13th centuries) unknown to the rural Pandits among whom I engaged in fieldwork, Alexis Sanderson observes (1985: 197–8).

> The Brahmanism of the middle ground…offered the Brahman householder a monism for the ritual agent which admitted renunciation but tended to confine it to the last quarter of a man's life (after the payment of the three debts), and at the same time made it unnecessary by propagating a doctrine of Gnostic liberation within the pursuit of conformity to the householder's dharma…. [Moreover, the householder] was to protect himself through disinterested conformity to God's will manifest as his dharma.

Needless to emphasize, it is the continuities between the ideas of the two periods (pre-Muslim and composite) that are remarkable rather than the differences, which are essentially those of emphasis. It follows that in the study of the householder tradition in Hindu society, the bringing together of the perspective of Indology and sociology, is not only justifiable but indeed imperative.

CONCLUDING OBSERVATIONS

The two most characteristic institutions of Hindu society are caste and the family/household. Kane in his monumental survey of the *Dharmashāstra* concludes that the overall tendency 'is to glorify the status of an householder and push into the background the two āhsramas of *vanāprastha* and *sannyāsa*, so much so that certain works say that these are forbidden in the Kali age' (1941: 424). Ethnographic evidence also underscores the importance of the life of the householder in contemporary Hindu society.

Looking back over time, it is noteworthy that various developments in the history of Hinduism have reinforced the householder tradition. Thus, many of the major protestant sectarian movements of medieval times, which today have millions of followers, emphasized the virtues of disciplined domesticity as against renunciation. Basava (c. 1106–67), the founder of the Virashaiva (or Lingayat) sect in Karnataka (in the south), himself moved to and fro between withdrawal from and participation in worldly activities, but his followers have remained wedded to the householder's life. In Punjab (in the north) all but one of the ten Sikh Gurus were married men with families, and explicitly opposed the renunciation of the householder's life. (The eighth guru died during his boyhood.) Similarly, Vallabha (c. 1479–1531), promulgator of *pushti mārga* ('the way of abundance'), whose followers are found mainly in western India, was a householder, and so are his followers. Although Chaitanya (c. 1485–1533), founder of the Gaudiya movement in the east devoted to Radha–Krishna worship, did himself abandon family life in his exultation of divine, conjugal love, his followers include householders as well as ascetics. All these sects extol domesticity as the preferred state so long as it is an affirmation of the bliss of the union of the devotee and the deity.

In popular imagination, however, particularly outside India, the renouncer looms large. This may be so because he is a magnificent, even theatrical figure, who gives away all his possessions, performs his own mortuary rites to proclaim the severance of all social bonds, and lives a highly disciplined life of austerities (see Madan 1987: 1–16 et passim). Although he may be impressive, the renouncer is not the only actor on the Hindu stage of life; in fact, he is not on the stage at all, but looks at it from the outside. That his gaze is powerful may not be, however, denied. The figure in the centre of the stage is the homely householder. If not exactly cast in a heroic mould, he is not a shadowy figure either. And, in his own manner, he is a fighter.

The everyday life of the householder is marked by temptations that he must resist. On the one hand, he hears on his front door the knock of the sannyāsī, who stands there in the guise of the mendicant asking for alms, but also suggests the possibility of an alternative way of life. On the one hand, the *bhogi* ('enjoyer') knocks on his back door, as it were, inviting him to a life of pleasures. The values of *gārhasthya* are challenged and threatened by both the visitors. The householder's success lies in his ability to resist the extremist alternatives and to tread the middle ground, combining the values of domesticity and detachment. For the Hindu, of whatever caste or sect, domesticity is marked by the feeling of well-being and happiness.[6] It embodies the value of righteousness and action, purity and auspiciousness, and purposefulness and contentment. It is the good life.[7]

NOTES

1. In the original: *yasmāt trayo 'pvāśramiṇo jñānenānnena mānhavam/ gṛhsthenaiva dhāryante tasmājjyeṣṭāśramo gṛhi.*
2. We may briefly note here the reading of the tradition by the scholars of what is known as 'Hindu law' (a product of British colonial administration). Thus, it is stated that, 'the joint and undivided family is the normal condition of Hindu society. An undivided Hindu family is ordinarily joint not only in estate, but also in food and worship' (Desai 1998: 314). From the sociological point of view this statement suffers from the conflation of two analytically and often empirically distinct groups, namely the family and the household. The law qualifies the foregoing characterization by maintaining that, 'the existence of joint estate is not an essential requisite to constitute a joint family and a family, which does not own any property, may nevertheless be joint' (ibid.). It is obvious that it is a larger grouping than the household to which the law refers; it is equally clear that without constituent households, there would be no joint families. The foundational nature of the household in relation to Hindu society is thus implicitly recognized in Hindu law.
3. Virtually all but 5000 to 10,000 persons of this community of about 300,000 persons have been driven out of Kashmir following the eruption of a Muslim militant, secessionist movement in 1989. The refugees live in temporary camps in Jammu and Delhi, or have taken up residence in various towns and cities of India, mainly in the north. The hope that they will be able to return to their homes are not bright. In describing aspects of their domestic life, the present tense has been retained here. See Chapter 7 above.
4. The Hindu undivided family has tax saving privileges that maybe availed by individual members. These are not available to non-Hindu households (see Gulati and Gulati 1962).
5. A negative attitude towards renouncers is widespread, and may go so far as to ascribe a malignant influence to them, responsible for misfortune among householders, as do the residents of the village Ghatiyali in Rajasthan. For them the sannyāsī is the threatening outsider (see Gold 1988: 53). But there are exceptions. In Rajasthan itself, the pastoral Raikas consider renouncers auspicious, even like

gods, and their blessings are valued by householders. The house-holder–renouncer relationship is not antagonistic here but 'interwined' (Srivastava 1997: 266).

6. For vignettes of domestic life among four castes of north India (Brahman, farmer, carpenter, and oil-presser), which show interesting similarities and differences, see Wiser 1978.

7. That would be a neat way to conclude this essay, but we must note (at least in a footnote) that the values by which many secularized, Hindu urban households live today come from sources other than traditional culture. The process of change had already become manifest in the late nineteenth century in cities such as Calcutta and Bombay. Individualism was on the rise and large households were being viewed negatively by social reformers. The process of social transformation has deepened and become more widespread, particularly since independence. More and more people of means in urban India today live in rented apartments, have small 'households', affirm the values of individual choice and achievement, and gender equality, and generally participate in a global culture of Western origin. But, as the ethnographic content of this essay shows, the old household tradition is by no means dead, particularly in the rural areas where three quarters of the people of India live.

REFERENCES

Bühler, G. 1964. *The Laws of Manu*. Delhi: Motilal Banarasidass.

Cook, Nilla Cram. 1958. *The Way of the Swan: Poems of Kashmir*. Bombay: Asia.

Daniel, Valentine. 1984. *Fluid Signs: Being a Person the Tamil Way*. Berkeley: University of California Press.

Desai, S.T. 1998. *Mulla: Principles of Hindu Law*. 2 vols. New Delhi: Butterworths.

Doniger, Wendy and Brian K. Smith. 1991. *The Laws of Manu*. New Delhi: Penguin Books.

Dumont, Louis. 1957. 'For a sociology of India'. *Contributions to Indian Sociology*, 1:7–22. Reprinted in Dumont 1970: 2–18.

————. 1960. 'World renunciation in Indian religions'. *Contributions to Indian Sociology*, IV: 33–62. Reprinted in Dumont 1970: 33–60.

————. 1970. *Religion, Politics and History in India*. Paris: Mouton.

Flood, Gavin. 1966. *An Introduction to Hinduism*. Cambridge: Cambridge University Press.

Gold, Ann Grodzins. 1988. *Fruitful Journeys: The Ways of Rajasthani Pilgrims*. Berkeley: University of California Press.

Gulati, I.S. and J.S. Gulati. 1962. *Undivided Hindu Family and to Tax Privilege*. Bombay: Asia.

Heesterman, J.C. 1982. 'Householder and wanderer'. In T.N. Madan (ed.). *Way of Life: King, Householder, Renouncer*. pp. 251–72. New Delhi: Vikas.

————. 1985. *The Inner Conflict of Tradition*. Chicago: University of Chicago Press.

Hiltebeitel, Alf. 1999. *Rethinking India's Oral and Classical Epics: Draupadi among Rajputs, Muslims and Dalits*. Chicago: University of Chicago Press.

Ilaiah, Kancha. 1996. *Why I am not a Hindu: A Sudra Critique of Hindutva Philosophy, Culture and Political Economy*. Calcutta: Samya.

Inden, Ronald B. and Ralph W. Nicholas. 1977. *Kinship in Bengali Culture*. Chicago: University of Chicago Press.

Kane, Pandurang Vaman. 1941. *History of Dharmashāstra*. Vol. II, Pt. I. Poona: Bhandarkar Oriental Research Institute.

Madan, T.N. 1962. 'The joint family: A terminological clarification'. *International Journal of Comparative Sociology* 3: 7–16.

————. 1987. *Non-renunciation: Themes and Interpretations of Hindu Culture*. New Delhi: Oxford University Press.

————. 1989. *Family and Kinship: A Study of the Pandits of Rural Kashmir*. 2nd edn. New Delhi: Oxford University Press.

Manu. *Mānav Dharmashāstra*. See Olivelle 2005.

Marriott, McKim. 1955. 'Little communities in an indigenous civilization'. In M. Marriott (ed.). *Village India*, pp. 171–222. Chicago: University of Chicago Press.

Olivelle, Patrick. 1993. *The Asrama System: The History and Hermeneutics of a Religious Institution*. New York: Oxford University Press.

Rowland, Benjamin. 1953. *The Art and Architecture of India: Buddhist, Hindu, Jain*. London: Penguin Books.

Sanderson, Alexis. 1985. 'Purity and power among the Brahmans of Kashmir'. In Michael Carrithers et al. (eds). *The Category of the Person*, pp. 190–216. Cambridge: Cambridge University Press.

Shah, A.M. 1973. *The Household Dimension of the Family in India*. New Delhi: Orient Longman.

Smith, Brian K. 1989. *Reflections on Resemblance, Ritual and Religion*. New York: Oxford University Press.

Srivastava, Vinay Kumar. 1977. *Religious Renunciation of a Pastoral People*. New Delhi: Oxford University Press.

Thapar, Romila. 1989. 'Imagined religious communities? Ancient history and the modern search for identity'. *Modern Asian Studies* 23, 2: 209–31.

Trawick, Margaret. 1996. *Notes on Love in a Tamil Family*. New Delhi: Oxford University Press.

Wiser, Charlotte V. 1978. *Four Families of Karimpur*. Syracuse: Syracuse University.

Zaehner, R.C. 1962. *Hinduism*. London: Oxford University Press.

Annex to Chapter 9

The Concept of 'World Order' in Classical Hindu Thought*

INTRODUCTORY REMARKS

The Hindu conception of the social order is holistic and hierarchical. The domestic domain is not a self-sufficient enclave, but is encompassed by wider and ascending (higher level) orders to create a single moral universe. The family, caste, and the local community, comprising the micro level, are embedded in the kingdom at the meso level. The head of the household, the village headman, and the king is each the upholder of dharma in his domain, that is, at his level. In a brief extension of the discussion of the householder tradition in Hindu society, I present below an outline of the political or 'world' order.

At the very outset, let me clarify that what is generally referred to as the Hindu (religious) tradition is primarily the textual tradition associated with the Brahmans. They have been for more than three thousand years the specialists responsible for the construction, evolution, and transmission of this tradition. Needless to emphasize, evolution includes transformation. Not that the three other major social categories (varnas, castes) comprising Hindu society (namely, Kshatriyas, Vaishyas, and Shudras) have not made any contributions—they indeed have—but in the division of responsibilities and hereditary occupations evolved over time from early on (say circa 1200 BCE onward), it was the Brahmans

---

* If the householder's life provides the foundation on which the Hindu social order is built, one could well argue that its capstone must be an elaborate and overarching conception of the world order. In this note (originally prepared for the Religion in World Order Project directed by Samuel P. Huntington at the Weatherhead Center for International Affairs at Harvard), a brief outline of the dimensions of the world order in the Hindu classical (textual) tradition is presented. Fuller discussion must await another occasion. Meanwhile, I would like to thank Mark Juergensmeyer for persuading me to undertake this short exercise and for his support.

who emerged as the authors and teachers of scriptural 'texts' (even before these came to be committed to writing) and as priests. Moreover, they also were the principal contributors to secular knowledge including, among other subjects, the science of governance.

An outstanding characteristic of Brahmanical thought throughout the ages is its preoccupation with 'ordering' within the framework of holism. That is, various human activities and their foundational principles (the parts) acquire their significance from placement and inter-relatedness within a conceptual whole. This does not mean, however, that Brahmanical thought is internally undifferentiated. In fact, ontological, epistemological, and material distinctions (classifications) are a defining characteristic of this thought. Differentiation is not, however, allowed to produce distinct social strata or cultural enclaves. The urge to integrate is as strong (if not stronger) as that to differentiate. A major principle/ procedure of integration is what Louis Dumont (1980: 19 et passim) calls hierarchy/hierarchization. Vertical orders are constructed in such a manner that a domain of action or knowledge encompasses (or is encompassed by) its opposite below (or above) it. An outstanding example of this mode of ordering is the inclusion of the social order (sociology, economics, politics) within an all-inclusive cosmic order (cosmology) (Smith 1994).

The foundational principle of the cosmos in Vedic thought is *rita*, which is a Sanskrit word connoting 'fixed order'. This principle is manifest, for instance, in the fixed cycle of seasons (*ritu chakra*). The cycle is autonomous and beyond the control of human agency or supernatural powers. It is an expression of natural law and an unalterable causality. The breakdown of *rita* would be a cosmic collapse of the kind that the failure of the law of gravitation would be so. At the encompassed social level, *rita* appears as dharma (from the Sanskrit root *dhar*, 'hold' or 'uphold'), an idea that gained prominence in course of time at the cost of *rita*. Dharma in its broadest connotation stands for moral righteousness; narrowly it means law and more loosely, custom. The emphasis is on the moral agent's conscious decision to conform, to act according to group (varna, jāti) dharma and in harmony with one's inborn nature (*svabhāva*). The opposite of dharma, *adharma* (moral turpitude) also is conceivable (see Selwyn 1982): it would have immense consequences. Large scale decline of dharma could eventually culminate in the catastrophic end of an age through total dissolution (*pralaya*). Before that, however, the dharmic order could be restored by divine retribution. This possibility defines the notion of avatāra, the descent of the deity in incarnate form to protect the good and destroy the evil doers (*The Bhagavad Gītā* 4, 7–8). Vedic cosmology is thus tempered with Vaishnava theology.

The foundation of the social order still is dharma. Without a grammar of values and traditions of law and custom the maintenance of the social, economic, and political orders is impossible. Dharma is the highest (overarching) value; it encompasses all rational secular behaviour including economic and political activities (*artha*). Dharma inclusive of artha encompasses the pursuit of physical and aesthetic pleasures (*kāma*). In other words, the pursuit of *kāma* must not violate the imperatives of *artha* and dharma; and the pursuit of *artha* must be in conformity with the dictates of dharma.

It is clear that this hierarchy of goals (*purushārtha*) is also a hierarchy of values. The domain of *artha* (more specifically of *kshatra* or concrete ruling power, sovereignty) does not generate its own principle of legitimization. The same is provided by dharma conceived of as both a set of universal principles and a set of context-sensitive guiding principles specific to the caste of rulers and warriors, the Kshatriyas, which is the second from above in the four-fold ordering of social categories. And since the social order is part and parcel of the cosmic order, the Kshatriyas, notably the king, are the protectors of the latter. The domain of the king is also the domain of god: the secular world order is in principle an aspect of the cosmic order.

It is the moral duty of the king (and the corresponding role players at lower/narrower levels, all the way down to the village headman) to ensure that every social group conforms to, and is enabled to do so, its specific set of responsibilities. Thus alone may the ordered universe be upheld. The wielder of ruling power obviously must have the power to punish the transgressors of dharma, and to do this he must himself be morally superior to the people in general (a consideration that Aristotle [*Politics* VII, 14] regarded as unusual but to be the case among Indians). *Dandanīti* is the morality of punishment. It is dealt with in both general and specific treatises, the *dharma shāstra* and the *artha shāstra*.

Before turning to a brief, illustrative discussion of a core text from each category, focused on the problem of the political order, I may mention that ancient materialist philosophies, notably Lokāyāta (circa 6th century BCE?) critiqued dharma as a human construction that was far from a universal law but only a device to serve the interests of the powerful.

THE LAW CODE OF MANU

Mānava Dharmashāstra ('The Law Code of Manu') is believed to have been composed by a single author, presumably a north Indian Brahman, sometime between the first century BCE and the second century CE. It is an ambitious and comprehensive (indeed hegemonic) text for the guidance and governance of the various sections/strata of society, although most of it is concerned with the rules of conduct for the two top social categories (varna). The general rules of proper (righteous) conduct that apply to the Brahmans also hold good for the rulers. Besides, a specific set of detailed instructions is laid down for the king.

The king, according to Manu, was divinely created to maintain order, protect the entire creation, and prevent chaos through the instruments of reward and punishment, with the emphasis clearly on punishment (*danda*), which is not, however, brute force but a form of morality (*nīti*). To quote from a recent literal translation:

> The king should administer appropriate Punishment on men who behave improperly...Punishment is the king...the leader...the ruler...Punishment is the Law...when...wielded properly...he gives delight to all the subjects; but when he is administered without careful examination, he wreaks total havoc.... The whole world is subdued [*kept in order*] through Punishment.... All the social classes would...revolt, as result of blunders committed with respect to Punishment.... The administrator of Punishment...is a king who speaks the truth, acts after careful examination, is wise, and has masterly grasp of [the goals/values of] Laws, Wealth, and Pleasure (Olivelle 2004: 106–7).

The above, drawn from the first two of the 17 pages devoted to the laws of kingship (Chapter 7), is merely illustrative of the manner Manu constructs the notion of the politico-moral order within the kingdom. (Chapters 8 and 9 deal with the justice system.) It is necessary to stress that punishment was not the first or sole concern of the king: the welfare of the people came first, and this was achieved by a variety of means, with the back-up of force. Nor was punishment absolute, unbridled power, but (to repeat what has already been noted above) the coercive arm of moral law (dharma) which is the foundation of the internal order of the polity/kingdom. For the external order—relations between king-doms—that could be deemed to be the equivalent of 'world order' in Indian classical thought, Manu places the principal emphasis on the army (warfare) and the envoys (diplomacy) (7.65). It is the envoy's duty to forge alliances and to split allies, all in order to serve the interests of his master. For more elaborate treatment of these ideas, I will now turn to another body of texts, those concerned specifically with the science of governance.

THE SCIENCE OF GOVERNANCE

Arthashāstra is a corpus of texts pertaining to the rational pursuit of economic and political objectives. The best known of these texts is the *Arthashāstra* believed to have been authored by Kautilya, also known as or identified with Chānakya, the chief adviser of the emperor Chandragupta (c. 321 BCE). The extant text of the work dates from the third century CE, and is described by the author as the 'compendium' on the 'acquisition and maintenance of the earth'. It is important to note here that the *Arthashāstra* is a theoretical (normative) text, not the description of any particular state. Moreover, the Kautilyan world order is expectedly confined to India.

Kautilya's *Arthashāstra* (henceforth *KA*) acknowledges four fields of knowledge: metaphysics, revealed scripture, economics (dealing with agriculture, cattle-breeding, and trade), and the science of governance (*dandanīti*, the ethics of punishment or the legitimate exercise of coercive power). *KA* has been compared to Machiavelli's *The Prince* for its valorization of power/punishment, but this is misleading. Some textual ambiguity notwithstanding, the subordination of political and economic ends (*artha*) to moral law (dharma) is clearly affirmed. The affirmation having been made at the very outset, the work focuses on various aspects of governance or, to put it in other words, on the securing of ordered and orderly secular life. It deals with a large number of topics, one of which is 'sovereignty' (Book 6).

Eight elements of sovereignty are identified: The king, the minister, the country, the fort, the treasury, the army, the friend, and the enemy. Sovereignty is thus a holistic concept. Not to speak of absence, even the weakness or flawed nature of any element disrupts the political order. Thus:

> A king of unrighteous character and of vicious habits will, though he is an emperor, fall a prey either to the fury of his own subjects or to that of his enemies. But a wise king, trained in politics, will, though he possesses a small territory, conquer the whole earth with the help of the best fitted elements of his sovereignty, and will never be defeated (Sastry 1967: 291).

The expansion of territory ('the conquest of the whole earth' is surely a hyperbole) is a legitimate objective with obvious economic (land is the principal source of wealth) and political (respect of power and the securing of peace through war) justifications.

> The possession of power and happiness in a greater degree makes a king superior to another; in a less degree, inferior; and in equal degree, equal. Hence a king shall always endeavour to augment his power and elevate his happiness (ibid.: 293).

KA expounds the notion of 'circle of states' as the basis of what may be called the world order. A circle comprises three primary kings, namely a conqueror, his friend (ally), and his friend's friend. The conqueror's enemy has his own similar circle. Besides, a circle each, with a mediatory king, and a neutral king at its centre, is also visualized. Thus there is a constellation of four interacting circles (neutrality is not the absence of relations) comprising 12 (3×4) kings (ibid.: 292–3).

Interstate relations are of six types, namely peace, war, neutrality, alliance (coalition), making preparations for marching, making peace with one state, and simultaneously waging war with another. As *KA* puts it, a king must make the appropriate choice.

> Whoever is inferior to another shall make peace with him; whoever is superior in power shall wage war; whoever thinks, 'No enemy can hurt me, nor am I strong enough to destroy my enemy', shall observe neutrality; whoever is possessed of necessary means shall march against his enemy; whoever is devoid of necessary strength to defend himself shall seek the protection of another, whoever thinks that help is necessary to work out an end shall make peace with one and wage war with another. Such is the aspect of the six forms of policy (ibid.: 295).

The seventh book of *KA*, comprising 18 short chapters (ibid.: 295–352), contains a detailed discussion of the various policy options. A notable aspect of the discussion is that, if making peace or waging war appears to be of equal advantage, a king (state) should make the former choice, for going to war carries with it the risk of the loss of both power and wealth. A war may be 'open', 'secret', or 'undeclared'. One must always be prudent, calculating possible losses and gains, and striking the right balance. While going to war against a less powerful (inferior) king is a defensible choice, even in that case peace should be made, once the opponent admits defeat and is duly submissive.

Wars end in treaties (*sandhi*) of one kind or another: for example treaties with or without specific obligations. Treaties with obligations are further classified into seven types according to different combinations of the variables of place, time, and objective. Treaties may of course be entered into to gain time or to facilitate gathering of intelligence. It follows that treaties may be broken or renegotiated. A conquered or vassal king would have different reasons for renegotiating a treaty (only if he can manage doing so) than a conqueror (see Rangarajan 1992: 580ff.). In short the Kautilyan world is a flux.

Depending upon whether one is a conqueror, a defeated king, a mediator, or a neutral king, different policy options (including combinations) should be considered. Pragmatism is the key to the right package of choices; an overall acknowledgement of the moral law notwithstanding, in the conduct of states, in internal as well as external matters, ends justify the means. Thus *KA* gives equal attention to spies (espionage, gathering of intelligence) and to envoys (diplomacy) in interstate relations; in fact the two categories seem to overlap—as indeed they do in our times.

KA goes into many other aspects of domestic and interstate orders, including finances, fortifications, bureaucracy, army, and the actual conduct of war. Wars are a key theme of certain kinds of classical literature within the Hindu tradition, notably the two great epics, the *Rāmāyana* of Valmiki (c. 500 BCE) and the *Mahābhārata* of Vyāsa (c. 500 BCE 500 CE).

Rāmāyana and *Mahābhārata*

At the centre of each epic is a great war—the causes, preparation, course of events, and the aftermath are discussed. This is not the place to raise the question of whether the wars actually took place: we are concerned with the substance of the texts and not their historicity. Neither war is about conquest or the acquisition of territory, although the author of the *Mahābhārata* has a more positive attitude to territorial conquest. Both have been traditionally described as 'righteous' wars (*dharma yuddha*), that is wars fought to reestablish the disrupted politico-moral order.

The root cause of the threatened order in the *Rāmāyana* is the existence of barbaric, even demonic, non-Aryan societies/polities. The latter must be eradicated so that cultured ('noble', *ārya*) people can live in peace according to the dictates of dharma, each community or caste following its own customs (*lokāchāra*) within the framework of a common morality. The king is the guardian of the pluralist social order in the Hindu tradition. His duty, *rājadharma*, is to protect the many dharmas that together institute the social order. Any transgression of norms, even within the four walls of a community's life, upsets the entire social order, and the king must act to repair and restore it. He is, in a manner of speaking, a democrat rather than a despot. The king does not legislate, and even when it comes to making choices (deciding a course of action where several are possible), he is guided by those who are adept in dharma, like the Brahman Vasishta in the *Rāmāyana*, or in just policy (*nīti*) like the Kshatriya Vidura in the *Mahābhārata*.

The war in the *Mahābhārata* involving coalitions of states on both sides, is a fratricidal war of patrilineally related clans and their respective circles of support comprising kin, affines, and friends. The root cause is greed and deceit in the quest for an illegitimate share of royal power and privilege. The victory in the end rests with the upholders of dharma among the principals. A detailed discourse on statecraft (*rājadharma*, royal duties) is to be found in book 12 of this very long epic. It is not an original discourse and derives many of its ideas from the older tradition of the *Mānava Dharmashāstra* and *KA* considered above. An outstanding characteristic of the *Mahābhārata* is that it allows more room for expediency than does the earlier *Rāmāyana*.

Among other themes, interstate relations are discussed. Expediency is the watchword: 'the king should make peace with those with whom it should be made and wage war with those with whom it should be waged' (Ghoshal 1959: 221). In dealing with an enemy, the king 'should break up the enemy's ranks by straightforward as well as deceitful means' (ibid.). One should not go to war against a king perceived as hostile without adequate preparation, but once one is in it, one should 'wage a war of complete extermination', employing not only military power ('fire and sword') but also 'the methods of unscrupulous diplomacy and calculated treachery based upon unquenchable distrust of the enemy', and even use 'poison and stupefying drugs' (ibid.: 225). Self-interest and self-preservation are the ultimate consideration. Interstate relations are, according to the *Mahābhārata*, essentially fluid in character: there are no permanent friends or foes.

Both epics speak not only of kings and kingdoms, but also of the ultimate possibility, emperors and empires, or, in other words, of a unipolar world order. Lest all this royal rhetoric should be considered lacking in any historical value, it may briefly be mentioned here that in what are called the early and medieval periods of Indian history, empires were constructed, and they rested on a clear configuration of interstate relations. Thus, during the early medieval periods, normative texts as well as historical records 'represented kings as organized into a single hierarchy. This hierarchy had a paramount "king of kings", overlord of the "entire earth" at the top, and countless little kings, lords of ten (or fewer) villages, at the bottom' (Inden 1982: 99). It was not merely a question of scale ('sizes or quantities'), but also of quality (an enhancement of the complexity of features) such that the king of kings was called the *chakravartin*, sovereign of the world, and indeed deemed an incarnation of the 'cosmic overlord'.[1] This notion was elaborated within the Buddhist tradition to which I now turn. If I do so at all, it is because this tradition arose out of, although only partly in opposition to the Hindu (Brahmanical) tradition.

THE BUDDHIST CONCEPTION OF POLITICAL AND WORLD ORDERS

The Buddhist conceptions of society and polity deviate from the Hindu in denying the divine origin of both, repudiating the caste (varna) basis of society, and rejecting punishment (*dandanīti*) as the key principle of statecraft. This tradition did not, however, give up the notion of cosmic law (dharma, dhamma in Pali) as the basis of order in all its manifestations including that of the political order. The Buddhist conception of the king is that of the righteous ruler (*dharma rāja*) who yet seeks to be the world conqueror (*chakkavatti*, one who rolls the wheels, *chakka*, of the moral law, dhamma), rather than wielder of the 'rod' of punishment, with a view to promote universal righteousness. His alter ego is the renunciant monk (*bhikhu*) who is a seeker of universal truth. Dharma has both connotations, moral law and truth, and as such is the foundation of all that exists.

As the 'world' conqueror, the Buddhist king must follow the path of peace once the conquest has been made: he does not seek territory but righteousness. The Indian emperor Ashoka (ruled 268–31 BCE), who renounced violence at the end of the only war he fought (the Kalinga war), and became a Buddhist, is the paradigmatic king, a promoter of dharma. The example he set was influential. Writes Stanley Tambiah:

> We cannot emphasize strongly enough how important in the actual history of Southeast Asian polities has been this pattern of over-rule and conversion to the dharma of the conquered rulers or subjected peoples. This conversion is co-extensive with the process of political expansion by monarchs or of political unification, which is more an embracing of diversity around a centre than a centralization of power itself (1967: 46–7).

Tambiah maintains that in practice interstate political order in Southeast Asia was modelled upon the geometrical/visual notion of *mandala*, which has four images or symbols located at the four cardinal points on the four sides of a central image or symbol. The idea is familiar: Kautilya's *Arthashāstra*, as noted above, speaks about circles of states. Calling such a geopolitical order 'the galactic policy', Tambiah (ibid.: 102–31 et passim) documents in rich detail the widespread distribution of this configuration (a 'centre-oriented concentric-circle view'), and how the centre holds together the totality, in Southeast Asia.

CONCLUDING REMARKS

In the Hindu tradition, prior to righteous (rooted in dharma) kingly rule, there was the dispensation or logic of the fishes (*matsya nyāya*)—the big fish eating the smaller one: in other words, there was anarchy. Divine intelligence conceived of the royal function, namely the protection of the people, and the king incarnated the divinity. The society and the polity both are of divine origin and, therefore, grounded in the moral law. The king's dharma comprises all other dharmas, according to the *Mahābhārata* and he is their guarantor. As Lingat puts it, '*Dharma* is essentially a rule of *interdependence*, founded on a hierarchy corresponding to the nature of things and necessary for the maintenance of the social order' (1973: 211).

The Hindu tradition combines the rhetoric of moral rectitude with the acknowledgement of the compulsions of the lived-in world. Hence, 'Dharma is the sovereignty of sovereignty', according to the scripture, and the rod of punishment (*danda*) is acknowledged as the king's emblem and instrument. But the king does not act alone: the Brahman priest (*purohita*) stands ahead of him, even as he is the king's servant. Temporal *power* is here (as in the Buddhist and also Christian and Islamic traditions) legitimized and constrained by spiritual *authority*.

Righteousness (moral law), wealth (economic strength), and coercive power (physical force) in judicious combination are the foundation of the kingdom's political order. And derivatively such too is the basis of the world (interstate) order. The kingdom will not survive without the king; similarly the circle of states will not survive without centre. Like the king must punish but not unjustly, the central state must wage war but not arbitrarily or unilaterally, for it may not act alone without bringing about the collapse of the alliance (coalition). Order of whatever kind (social, economic, political), both internal and external, and at whatever level, is ultimately a combination of authority and responsibility, a matter of checks and balances. The classical Hindu tradition will have it no other way.[2]

NOTES

1. Even in the twentieth century, Hindu princes usually sought legitimacy for their various conceptions of royal duty and royal power in the classical tradition. This is illustrated felicitously in an excellent essay on perceptions of princely rule by Adrian Mayer (1982).

2. Going by the texts, in conceiving of an interstate order, the emphasis is exclusively on the kingly function narrowly defined, that is on wars and alliances. Little is said of trade and cultural exchanges. This is rather puzzling because, not to mention local and regional flows of goods and services, even maritime trade is known to have flourished in western India as long as 5000 years ago. As for the movements of peoples and the fusion of lifestyles, the Vedic corpus bears witness to these phenomena. And then there was the famous expansion of Buddhism and Hinduism, particularly the former, into South and Southeast Asia, and north-ward, but this was almost entirely non-political, 'dumb and deedless' in Hegel's ironic phrase. A Hindu adventurer voyaged east in the first century CE and founded a kingdom comprising Cambodia and the adjacent lands. These happenings must have not been heard of back home. In short, the texts on which this note is based do not look beyond the Indian shores; only the north-western frontier lay somewhere in today's Afghanistan.

REFERENCES

Dumont, Louis. 1980. *Homo Hierarchicus: The Caste System and its Implications.* Chicago: University of Chicago Press.

Ghoshal, U.N. 1959. *A History of Indian Political Ideas. The Ancient Period and the Period of Transition to the Middle Ages.* Bombay: Oxford University Press.

Inden, Ron. 1982. 'Hierarchies of Kings'. In: T.N. Madan (q.v.), pp. 99–125.

Lingat, Robert. 1973. *The Classical Law of India.* Berkeley: University of California Press.

Madan, T.N. (ed.) 1982. *Way of Life: King Householder, Renouncer.* New Delhi: Vikas; Paris: Maison des Sciences de l'Homme.

Mayer, A.C. 1982. 'Perceptions of princely rule: Perspectives from a biography'. In T.N. Madan (q.v.), pp. 127–54.

Olivelle, Patrick. 2004. *The Law Code of Manu.* New York: Oxford University Press.

Rangarajan, L.N. (ed. and trs.). 1992. *Kautilya: The Arthashastra.* New Delhi: Penguin India.

Sastry, R. Shama. 1967. *Kautilya's Arthasāstra.* Mysore: Mysore Printing and Publishing House.

Selwyn, Tom. 1982. 'Adharma'. In T.N. Madan (q.v.), pp. 381–401.

Smith, Brian K. 1994. *Classifying the Universe: The Ancient Indian Varna System and the Origins of Caste.* New York: Oxford University Press.

Tambiah, Stanley J. 1976. *World Conqueror and World Renouncer. A Study of Buddhism and Polity in Thailand.* Cambridge: Cambridge University Press.

10

Dying with Dignity*

Great is death...Sure as life holds all
            parts together, death holds

all parts together;
Sure as the stars return again after they
            merge in the light, death is
great as life.

Walt Whitman
Leaves of Grass

INTRODUCTION

In what turned out to be the last of his numerous talks to Western
audiences, delivered at Sanen in Switzerland in the summer of
1985, some months before his death early in the following year,
the well-known Indian mystic, Jiddu Krishnamurti, said:

> Death, talking about it, is not morbid. It is part of our life. From
> childhood maybe till we actually die, there is always this dreadful
> fear of dying.... We have put it as far away as possible. So let us
> enquire together what is that extraordinary thing that we call death
> (1986: 103).

* Reproduced from *Social Science and Medicine* vol. 35, no. 4 (1992),
pp. 425–32. Originally presented as a background paper at the Social
Science and Medicine Conference held in Peebles (Scotland) in September
1992. I would like to record here my deep appreciation of the interest
and support over many years of Peter McEwan, founder-editor of the
journal. Similar gratitude is due to Charles Leslie and (belatedly) the
late V. Ramalingaswami.

I have chosen to begin this essay with the foregoing quotation because it juxtaposes in clear and simple language the modern and traditional attitudes to dying, represented respectively by silence and speech. The former is rooted in deep hopeless fear and the latter in equally deep, if not deeper, confidence. The hopelessness flows from seeing death as the end of a good thing, namely life, while the hopefulness or confidence arises from the faith or conviction that life encompasses death and is not overwhelmed by it. The speechlessness of incomprehension is confronted with the articulation of the affirmation of death as an aspect of life. Hence Krishnamurti's invitation to his audience to talk about it.

Folklore, ethnography, literature, religious philosophy, psychoanalysis, systems of medicine, etc., all bear witness to the universal concern about death as a threat to life. All cultures see the threat emanate sometimes from outside the individual and sometimes from within him or her. (Henceforth, for the sake of convenience, male pronouns will be used to refer to both genders.) Malevolent spirits, vengeful human beings, poisoned foods, polluted environment, and other such phenomena may be seen to invade and break through the spiritual and physical protective boundaries of the individual. Or, he may be threatened by some internal flaw, whether ignorance', 'karma', or the 'death wish'. What is a threat to life is not yet its cessation. It is only when these external and internal threats are regarded as more real than life, at least more powerful, that the loss of confidence and despair, and indeed the loss of dignity, set in.

WESTERN PERSPECTIVES

In his erudite inquiry into changing Western attitudes to death over a thousand years, Philippe Ariès (1981) maintains that the early Christians inherited from the Greco-Roman world an attitude towards death which was not marked by fear. Death was a collective destiny and therefore not fearful. Moreover, there were other comforting ideas, notably those of the 'second coming' of the Saviour and the promise of a blissful afterlife. Ariés calls this the 'tame death'.

According to him, a major shift in consciousness occurred, mainly during the eleventh century, coinciding with the emergence of the individual and the retreat of the group or community. An intense concern with one's sense of the self, and also with the death of the self, were the key characteristics of the new attitude. This 'turning of the tide' led in modern times (that is, in the nineteenth century) to the notion of death as separation, as a catastrophe, and as sorrow. Finally, in the present century, a further radical alteration in the Western man's consciousness of death occurred through the 'medicalization' of death, as a result of which it came to be denied. Death became a shameful thing, an embarrassment, even dirty and indecent. 'Death has ceased to be accepted as a natural, necessary phenomenon. Death is a failure, a "business lost"' (ibid.: 586). In short, death loses contact with human dignity.

Ariès concludes his study pointing out that by transforming the phenomenon of death from a religious and social to a technical and individual problem, modernity offers two choices.

> The first is a massive admission of defeat. We ignore the existence of a scandal that we have been unable to prevent; we act as if it did not exist, and thus mercilessly force the bereaved to say nothing. A heavy silence has fallen over the subject of death. When this silence is broken...it is to reduce death to the insignificance of an ordinary event that is mentioned with feigned indifference (ibid.: 613–14).

Either way, dying is robbed of dignity: neither the individual nor the community has the moral strength to recognize the ever-present possibility of death as a *normal* phenomenon.

The seeds of the attitude that sees death as defeat lie in the secularized world view of the Age of Reason. By inviting man to dare to know and to take charge of his fate, that is, to make his own history, the Enlightenment rendered the idea of the limitation of human capabilities unintelligible, if not illegitimate. The birth of the clinic and the 'power' of the physician over other human beings—through a supposed ability to prolong life (Francis Bacon, among others, propagated this idea)—and over human life follow from this development (Foucault 1976).

The 'disenchantment of the world' and the processes of rationalization of which Max Weber wrote, also meant the displacement of ultimate values by instrumental values. The latter, when elevated to the level of the former, contradict themselves and life becomes meaningless, and so indeed does death. Weber maintained that nobody in the modern West had confronted this question more directly than Leo Tolstoy, according to whom death had no meaning for civilized man. Weber commented:

> it has no meaning because the individual life of civilized man, placed into an infinite 'progress', according to its own immanent meaning should never come to an end; for there is always a further step ahead of one who stands in the march of progress.... And because death is meaningless, civilized life as such is meaningless; by its very 'progressiveness' civilized life gives death the imprint of meaninglessness (1948: 139, 140).

Other scholars, too, have linked the meaninglessness and lack of dignity in the modern concepts of death and dying to the invasion of human life by technology. Thus, Ivan Illich points out that, in Western society, the medicalization of death redefines death, which as a 'natural' phenomenon might have some meaning and even dignity attached to it, and reduces it to something very mechanical, 'the ultimate form of consumer resistance': 'natural death is now that point at which the human organism refuses any further input of treatment' (Illich 1975: 149). This might well be seen as the ultimate indignity in which the modern world envelops dying. And, as Illich points out, 'The white man's image of death has spread with medical civilization and has been a major force in cultural colonization' (ibid.: 123).

Modern notions of institutionalized care of the ageing and the dying, and the institutions of the old-age home and the hospital, on which modern society prides itself, initiate a process of isolation of those who are still alive and even healthy at their age (Elias 1985; Myerhoff 1979), or dying but not unaware of their condition and of the reaction of normal people around them. As N. Elias puts it, 'if a person must feel while dying that, though alive, he or she has scarcely any significance for other people, that person is truly alone' (ibid.: 64).

The loneliness of the ageing or dying person is multi-dimensional and includes removal from amidst one's family members and friends to be placed among strangers and specialists. One loses significance as an active decision-making member of society and is reduced to being a dependent of those whose professional duty (which is very different from kinship obligation or friendly concern) it is to take care of such 'cases'. If ageing or dying is accompanied by excitement, depression or pain, as it often is, one is put on tranquilizers, anti-depressants, or pain killers, which are undoubtedly welcome to the subject in his helplessness as they relieve him of immediate distress, but which also gradually erode his self-esteem. One is no more oneself. As Illich puts it, perhaps with brutal frankness, 'increasingly pain-killing turns people into unfeeling spectators of their own decaying selves' (1975: 108).

The dying sometimes graduate into the special category of terminally ill patients. In technologically advanced countries, they are handed over to machines and monitors to which they are chained by the wires and tubes of dependency. The patient is now dehumanized and the decision as to when to stop is that of the specialists, sometimes doctors, and sometimes lawyers. There is an emphasis on so-called scientific objectivity, and emotions— the doctor's, the patient's, and the relatives'—are banished. The irony of it all is that the patient, being a terminal case, is offered no assurance of anything beyond that the offerings of modern medicine will be pressed into service to prolong life and, perhaps, deaden the capacity for feeling.

David Moller (1990), a sociologist, in his study of dying cancer patients in America, calls this a 'double failure': the dying patient is denied humane care and understanding and is at the same time stigmatized, without being offered any hope of recovery. The only question that then remains, as one of the doctors quoted in Moller's book asked his superior, is, 'what do we do with the body?' Such a patient crosses before his death the threshold, beyond which dignity or its lack, the comfort of company or loneliness, lose all meaning. And yet modern medicine deems it a challenge to keep him alive, and the same is clothed in high-sounding, but empty, rhetoric about medical ethics. Any consideration of the quality of life is pushed aside.

It is not at all surprising that the modern medical culture has come to generate extremely critical reactions on both philosophical and practical grounds. There is not only passionate criticism (Illich 1975; Nandy 1988), but also heightened interest in euthanasia (Thomasma and Graber 1990). Widely publicized cases of people like Nancy Cruzan (d. 1991) and Janet Adkins (d. 1991) further highlight the fact that extremist situations generate extremist solutions.

To recall briefly, Nancy Cruzan suffered brain damage (due to oxygen deprivation for a quarter of an hour) following a car accident in 1983 when she was 24 years old. Her parents and husband sought the best medical help, but it was clear within a few months that it would be impossible to bring her out of her vegetative state. They then sought disconnection of the support systems to let her die. The hospital refused to do this without legal authorization, but this was not forthcoming because the law in the state of Missouri required the patient's consent. It took seven years to overcome this hurdle and Nancy was allowed to die only towards the end of December 1991. Meanwhile her husband had ceased to be her husband, but her parents had fought with great perseverance to restore some dignity to their daughter's 'life' and end their own deep suffering.[1]

While Nancy Cruzan was still in an unconscious state, Janet Adkins, a 53-year-old, physically fit woman, recently diagnosed to be suffering from some early symptoms (such as forgetfulness, etc.) of Alzheimer's disease, and unwilling to see herself gradually losing self-control and dignity, ended her life. She was able to do this painlessly by injecting a lethal substance into her body with the help of Dr Jack Kevorkian and his 'suicide machine', the use of which he had explained over television earlier in the year. The Michigan court, which was asked to determine if Dr Kevorkian was guilty of abetting the murder, ruled that Janet Adkin's decision was freely and entirely her own. Doubts, however, remain as to whether her decision was not a hasty, premature action arising out of depression and whether the doctor had not violated professional ethics. He has since published a book defending his position.

The involvement of the legal process in both these cases brought up a fundamental issue which the courts were asked to decide, namely, who is the ultimate repository of the right to decide if and when to end a human life—the state, the doctor, the individual's next of kin, or the individual himself? The rights of the state in this regard are not well defined in respect of situations of the kind that were under consideration, for Nancy Cruzan was guilty neither of murder nor of high treason. Moreover, did the state have a constitutional right to keep people alive? Given the central importance that individualism has acquired, over the last several hundred years, as a dominant ideology in Western culture (deriving strength from classical Greek thought and from the later teachings of the Christian Church), it was only to be expected that the right to die would be regarded as one among the fundamental rights of the individual. The state through its judicial arm would be the guarantor of this right.

Naturally, the US Supreme Court decided (though only by a majority of 1, 5 against 4), on 25 June 1990, that Nancy Cruzan's parents could not exercise on her behalf the constitutional right of *competent* people to refuse medical aid (Dworkin 1991). And the unconscious Cruzan was not competent. It is obvious that under exaggerated emphasis, a value becomes a *dis*-value: the subject of this case was a victim of one of her own inviolable rights as an individual. The failure to raise and answer the question of whether such assertion of an individual's rights truly enhances his dignity, or prevents unnecessary human suffering, was the proverbial default. Public pressure finally persuaded a lower court to accept the testimony of Nancy Cruzan's friends that, before her accident, she had said that she would not want to live in the vegetative state which was later to become her own condition, and she was allowed to die.

Dramatizing the conflict of strongly-held opinions, we have the runaway success of Derek Humphrey's book, *The Final Exit* (1991). Here a whole range of options are explained in the typical American 'do-it-yourself' style for the benefit of those who want to end their life. The numerous buyers who purchased the book must have included thousands who were simply curious (that is non-serious) rather than contemplating suicide. The phenomenon thus underscores the fact that dying is trivialized as much by making it easy as it is robbed of dignity by its being made difficult.

We are here faced with a total collapse of values. To quote Weber again:

> Whether life is worth living and when—this question is not asked by medicine. Natural science gives us an answer to the question of what we must do if we wish to master life technically. It leaves quite aside or assumes for its purposes, whether we should and do wish to master life technically and whether it ultimately makes sense to do so (Weber 1948: 144).

Weber's inspiration was Tolstoy's message, conveyed through his later novels and stories, including *The Death of Ivan Illich*, that only those who know how to answer the question 'How shall we live?' can cope with dying gracefully.

Dignity does not come to the dying from immortality fantasies, or compensatory ideas, such as reincarnation and paradise, nor does it come from empowerment through modern medicine. It comes from the affirmation of values, not only up to the boundary of death as some scholars seem to suggest (Bowker 1991), but in a manner that encompasses dying under living and does not oppose the two in a stern dualistic logic. To illustrate what I mean by this, I will turn briefly to thinking about death in Hindu and Jain cultural traditions. Needless to say, this thinking has been evolved in pre-technological environments, but survives, even if weakly, in modern times.

INDIAN PERSPECTIVES

The quotation from Jiddu Krishnamurti with which this essay opens refers to death as an *extraordinary* thing. The extraordinari-ness of death implies a positive value. In the Hindu tradition, Death is defined as the personification of time (*Mahakala*) as also of the very foundation of the cosmo-moral order (Dharma). Without death, in other words, there will be neither meaningful life nor ordered society. This is, of course, a metaphysical idea, and that should be permissible, for I have tried to show in the second section of this essay that a technological or legalistic view of death leads to its trivialization. There are many ways in which Hinduism copes with the problem of death, but, owing to limitations of space, I can present only two statements here, one very briefly and derived from the Sanskritic literary tradition, and the other in some detail and based on ethnography.

Hindu Textual Tradition

It used to be customary among high caste Hindu families—and the practice is continued until today in many tradition-oriented homes—to read aloud certain parts of the religio-philosophical text, the *Bhagavad Gītā*, in the presence of a dying person. The passages usually chosen introduce an inner-self and outer-self, or subtle-body and physical-body, dichotomy. This dichotomy is not employed to dismiss the physical body as dross or evil, but to characterize it as perishable, and therefore impermanent, by its very nature. One's sense of personal identity is sought to be constructed from the totality so that death is not seen as threatening to one's sense of 'selfhood', and the idea of prolonging the life of the physical body is seen as unnecessary, although its maintenance in a state of health (for example, through yoga) is emphasized. Actually, ancient Hindu medicine is called ayurveda, the science of longevity; moreover by including it in the vedic corpus it is given the status of the highest knowledge.

The problem of the finiteness of the physical body is tackled by refusing to give it the status of a problem and by accepting death as a normal happening. What is expected to happen should not be a cause for sorrow and grief. The *Bhagavad Gītā* says that the worn-out body is like an old set of clothes, and that 'all things born in truth must die; and out of death in truth comes life' (Mascaro 1962: 50). If dying is such an ordinary, routine, though in a sense important, occurrence, how then does one refer to it as 'extraordinary'? And Krishnamurti was only echoing the Hindu metaphysical texts, the Upanishads, when he used the term.

The Hindu answer to this question would seem to be that it is in the presence of death that life's deepest significance becomes manifest, and the moment of death certifies the encompassing character of life or, in other words, the supremacy of life over death. In the *Katha Upanishad*, the questioner learns from Yama, the god of Death, the secret of life in answer to his question about the significance of 'the great passing on' (Radhakrishnan 1953: 607), namely that the knowing self is never born, nor does it ever die (ibid.: 616). If texts that are more than a thousand years old seem remote, let me add that many contemporary Hindu religious philosophers base their thinking on ideas derived from them. Thus, J.L. Mehta, a philosopher who was equally at home in Western and Indian philosophies, told a Harvard audience of theologians and students of comparative religion in June 1988, just a month before his own death: 'Not until living itself is transformed into a pilgrimage, which is nothing if not living in the face of death, one's own, does Scripture disclose its sovereign majesty, become truly Scripture' (1988–9: 12).

And not only philosophers, but also common people, who are the subjects of ethnography, do so. But before I present the evidence of ethnography, I would like to emphasize that the upanishadic idea of the illumination of life by death is the very opposite of the notion of modern medicine, couched in Bichat's prescription, 'Open a few corpses: you will dissipate at once the darkness that observation alone could not dissipate', which was paraphrased by Foucault thus: 'The living night is dissipated in the brightness of death' (1976: 146).

Ethnographic Evidence

I have conducted fieldwork among Hindu villagers in the Kashmir Valley in north India. These Hindus, known in ethnographic literature as Kashmiri Pandits, belong to the Brahman caste and have a well-developed lore about death and dying (Madan 1987). They maintain that the most irrefutable evidence of how good a life, in moral rather than material terms, has been, becomes truly known only at the time of death: *a good death certifies a good life*. In the Pandits' judgement, death is not the ending of an individual life, but its completion for the time being, for they entertain the idea of reincarnation. The hour of death finally portrays the goodness or otherwise of a person's life and also uniquely anticipates the future. In other words, the manner of one's passing outweighs all previous claims and intimations of one's moral worth. Death is, therefore, indeed an extraordinary event.

The Pandits have evolved an elaborate typology of deaths. Thus, they speak of the good death, 'the great passing on' (*parmagati*) that does not just happen, but has to be achieved or attained. If one is able to let go or renounce the 'life-breath', in full consciousness, at a time and place of one's choosing, one dies in a state of dignity. This folk idea, of course, echoes the upanishadic last wish of the dying person that, at the moment his body turns to ashes (the reference is to the Hindu practice of cremation) and his life-breath merges with the undying wind, he should be in full command of his faculties and remember all past deeds (Radhakrishnan 1953: 577): *aum krato smara kritam smara krato smara kritam smara!*

The main elements of the notion of the good death are the place (*desh*), the time (*kāla*), and the moral-physical state of the person (*pātra*) at the time of his death. The best place to die, according to the Pandits, is in one's home, the house in which one has lived. For many men, this would be the house where one was born, but in the case of women it would be the house where one has lived after marriage and where one has borne and raised children. The house is not regarded merely as a dwelling, but as the microcosm of the universe. It stands on sanctified ground and has a presiding deity. Inside it, the Pandit householder pursues his legitimate worldly goals of self-fulfilment and seeks to improve the moral quality of his self or person (see pp. 252–3 above and Madan 1989). It is, therefore, right and proper that he should die here.

The only preferred alternative is to die in a holy place of pilgrimage (such as Haridwar or Kashi in north India), but this is perhaps considered more appropriate for unattached persons who do not have any immediate kin, or who are believed to have overcome worldly attachments in the manner of, for example, renunciants. Jonathan Parry, a British anthropologist, has written that the significance of dying in Kashi (Parry 1981) lies not only in the high sanctity of the place but also in the deliberate choice that is made to die there. It should be added that there are interesting variations on this theme, and tradition-minded men of the second highest caste, the Kshatriyas or Rajputs, consider dying on the battlefield as the most glorious death, 'the brave man's way of passing on' (*vīrgati*). The emphasis, it should be clear, in both cases, is on choosing: one must be in command and should not be overtaken by death. To be so overtaken is the loss of dignity.

To die at home is not enough to constitute a good death. The second crucial element is the hour of death, that is, one must die at an astrologically appropriate time so that a smooth passage from the world of human activity to the worlds beyond is assured. Again, the Pandits emphasize that those who have attained moral excellence through knowledge, good deeds, yoga, etc., can indeed choose the moment of death just as they can choose the place of death. Stories of particular deaths are told to illustrate and validate this contention. Needless to say, a great deal of myth-making and fabrication goes into the making of these tales of edification. Their significance does not lie in their veracity but in the values and ideals they uphold.

Then there is the third and last element of the good death, namely, the personal condition of the subject. Has he lived a long life marked by the fulfilment of the legitimate worldly goals of righteous actions, religious devotions, and the attainment of wealth, progeny (particularly sons), and 'good name' (even fame) in society?

Has he discharged all family and social obligations and not been predeceased by those younger than himself? In the case of women, the husband, though older, should be one of the survivors. Finally, were the last moments of death conscious, easy and peaceful, without being preceded by a long painful illness? If the answer to all these questions is in the affirmative, then one has indeed died in not only peace but also dignity. Such a death is dignified and extraordinary because it symbolizes so many positive values of Pandit culture—in fact of Hindu culture in general.

A community which entertains a notion of the good death may be expected to complement it with a notion of the bad, undignified death. It is marked, the Pandits maintain, by the loss of control over one's worldly position, family affairs, and, above all, over one's body and mind. Further, these Hindus also entertain the notion of what may be called 'anomic' death, that is death which raises misgivings, even if only temporarily, regarding the fragility of the moral foundations of human life. The death of an old couple's youthful son, married and having young dependent children, is the prime example of what the Pandits call 'untimely' death, but this literal translation of the Sanskrit words *akāla mrityu* hardly captures the intensity of personal sorrow and moral horror which are sought to be conveyed when they use it. They also refer to such a death as *anartha*, unfortunate and meaningless,[2] and even as *pralaya*, or the dissolution of the cosmo-moral order, for it upsets the normal moral ordering of events.

The foregoing brief characterization of the good death in relation to the bad brings out clearly that in Hindu morality what cannot be cured has to be endured. If the end of one's life is to be enveloped in the indignity of total loss of control, one can only submit to this fate, one's karma, in the hope that whatever follows death may be better. Weber has pointed out that, looked at from the Western perspective, the 'karma doctrine transformed the world into a strictly rational ethically-determined cosmos; it represents the most consistent theodicy ever produced in history' (1958: 121). That such a world view, perhaps, had its cost— 'other-worldliness' in Weber's judgement—is an issue that does not concern us here.

The Hindu attitude is shared in some measure by the other indigenous religio-cultural traditions of India. The Jains, although a small minority (less than 1 per cent of the population), are an important presence in the mosaic of Indian culture, and share the Hindu concept of the good or dignified death as one that is marked, above all, by the dying person being in full control of the happening. Their view of how this may be achieved, and their interpretation of it are, however, radically different from the general Hindu standpoint.

Jain Tradition

Jainism predates post-vedic Hinduism by many centuries and the latter derives some of its key motifs from Jainism and Buddhism including, notably, the ideas of ahimsā (non-killing or, more generally, non-violence) and nirvāna (liberation). The inner/outer-self dichotomy of Hinduism mentioned above appears as a much sharper opposition, but the physical body is still not wholly rejected at the outset, as it were, so that suicide is considered an act lacking in merit. It contradicts the value of ahimsā. Like the Pandits, Jains of the Digambara sect, too, have an elaborate typology of deaths consisting of forty-eight named types broadly grouped into, first, 'childish or foolish death', second, 'wise death', and third, 'the wisest of the wise deaths' (*pandita-pandita-marana*) (Shettar 1986, 1990). Suicide falls in the first category and the fact that it may be a consciously chosen death is of little avail. It is marred by attachment (the desire to die) as well as violence.

There is ample evidence, however, that the Jains have practised self-initiated ritual death for a very long time and considered it to belong to the category of the 'the wisest of the wise deaths'. There are many recognized ways of achieving it, such as renunciation, worship, prayer, meditation, knowledge, and above all, fasting (*sallekhanā*). Before a monk or nun embarks upon such austerities, he or she has to be fully convinced that the outer-body (*kāyā*) is the enemy of the inner-self (*ātmā*) and, therefore, slow withering of the body is the best way to burn out the burden of karma that remains at the end of a lifetime of virtue, cleanse the inner self, and thus obtain release from reincarnation. Fasting may last many years, consisting of gradual reduction in the intake of nutrition, and 'the aspirant is taken through a series of fifteen intermediate observances leading to the *pratyākhyāna* or complete abstinence from every kind of intake, save air' (Shettar 1986).

Jain ethics teaches that when a householder believes that death is near because of incurable disease or old age, or fears death at the hands of an enemy, an appropriate method of abandoning one's body should be chosen. Death is not desired because it is at hand, nor feared, for one can still be one's own master. *One must not lose control.* When an aspirant *finally* sits down to die, he must choose the time, place, body posture, etc., with great care, for these must remain unchanged until the moment of death. The second main Jain sect of Shvetambaras also subscribe to a similar notion of living and dying with dignity.[3]

Needless to say, the numbers of those who choose to die thus, considering it the most dignified death, is small, though it may have been proportionately larger in earlier times: epigraphical and archaeological evidence lends support to such a belief. But death through fasting is not unknown among Jains and Hindus even in contemporary times.

The best known fairly recent example is that of Vinoba Bhave, Mahatma Gandhi's most distinguished non-political disciple. In 1983, when he was in his late eighties, he suffered a heart attack. He refused medication, despite the best efforts of everybody concerned, including the Prime Minister of India, and within a few days he abstained from nourishment as well. Soon afterwards, he died in his hermitage, on the eve of the Hindu festival of lights (Deepavali), a very auspicious occasion in the Hindu calendar. His passing was, in terms of the tradition, a paradigmatic death, surcharged with dignity—indeed an extraordinary thing. As may have been expected, some English language newspapers commented editorially that the doctors who let this death happen were guilty of unprofessional conduct, and that such deaths should not be countenanced in modern times.

CONCLUDING REMARKS

Dying and death are part and parcel of human life. In modern society, which is the actual or desired social condition of our times, one does not anticipate one's death any more than one can anticipate one's birth, but one does live under the shadow of death due to disease, old age, accidents, and even violence. This shadow covers more and more adult lives as work situations and residential locations multiply and life expectancy increases among all peoples.

The expanding diagnostic abilities of modern medicine make death a constant presence, particularly in the lives of the elderly, and generate a dependence on specialists and technological intervention. Increasingly, one is infantalized and finds oneself incapable of describing, and to a great extent understanding, one's condition. One becomes metaphorically, and even literally, speechless. Isolated, taken over by specialists, bound to machines, one feels not only lonely but even remorseful and guilty ('if only I had taken these symptoms seriously', 'if only I had not done those things…'). One loses both one's freedom and one's dignity.

Freedom and dignity are, of course, cultural constructs. While the ideas are universal, their precise content admits of cultural variability. Indeed, this can go very far as is evidenced by B.F. Skinner's (1972) attack on them as antiquated, futile, and even harmful ideas in the context of modern society where everything, or almost everything, can be fixed, by designing cultural practices in an appropriate manner. However, those who still see some virtue in these ideas, will find it remarkable how across many cultures (and not only in Christian, Hindu, and Jain cultural traditions) the loss of autonomy, and loss of control over oneself in the context of death, are seen to result in undignified death, that is death which lacks nobility, distinction, and illustriousness. Drawing upon half a dozen cultures from distant parts of the world, Jonathan Parry and Maurice Bloch observe that the 'good' (we might say the 'dignified') death is 'one which suggests some degree of mastery over the arbitrariness of the biological occurrence' (Parry and Bloch 1982: 15). I have tried to show in this essay that modern medical and legal procedures increase, perhaps paradoxically, the range of this arbitrariness. What is arbitrariness from the victim's perspective is power from the perspective of those who control others with the help of specialized knowledge. As Foucault (1976, 1977) has pointed out, various mechanisms of power have in the last two hundred years established their control over the body in both its living and dead states (see also Armstrong 1983).

In drawing attention to traditional Hindu and Jain views of death and dying, which have some points in common with the Christian view, I am not suggesting that all one has to do to restore dignity to death is to make a turn-about and proceed from modernity towards tradition. The point of the comparison very briefly undertaken here is that the so-called modern attitudes, instead of being held in stark opposition to the traditional, can have their excesses corrected by a recognition of alternative perspectives, whether traditional or themselves modern.

One of the central ideas from the traditional perspectives, with which I will conclude, is that which does not oppose life and death in stern opposition, reserving dignity, if at all for anything, for the former, and consigning the latter to utter meaninglessness. The following words of the fourteenth-century Kashmiri Pandit mystic poetess, Lalla (Kaul 1973: 123),

Alike for me is life and death:
Happy to live and happy to die
I mourn for none, none mourns for me!

were echoed five hundred years later by Walt Whitman (*Leaves of Grass*):

Have you supposed it beautiful to be born?
I tell you I know it is just as beautiful to die!

These affirmations call our attention to the value of holism in the midst of fragmentation that characterizes modern life everywhere, valorizing life in instrumental terms, and designating death an indignity.

NOTES

1. Since the above was written, another case has been followed worldwide with much interest. An American young woman, Terri Schiavo, suffered a heart attack in 1990 that left her severely brain damaged, unable to move, talk, or feed herself. Eight years later, her husband moved court seeking permission to disconnect her feeding tube, but her parents opposed this move. They invoked the support of the Church on the ground that the right to give and take life is not in human hands. Finally, the tube was removed in March 2005 following court permission. Frantic efforts by Terri's parents and siblings with the support of the 'pro-life' groups to get the Supreme Court overturn the lower court's decision failed and she died on 31 March.
2. The notion of meaningless death in the sense implied here may be found in many cultures. Thus, Elias, writing from the perspective of Western culture, observes: 'It is terrible when people die young

before they have been able to give their lives a meaning and taste the joys of life' (1985: 66).

3. Like the Jains, the Buddhists too have a highly developed tradition of 'meditations' on death, but they are an even smaller component of the Indian population than the Jains. However, an excellent account of this subject is available in respect of Tibetan Buddhists drawing upon, among other sources, the famous *Tibetan Book of the Dead* (Mullin 1986). Needless to add, the Buddhists generally, like the Jains and Hindus, do not look upon death as the enemy or destruction of life. At the same time, they do not approve of self-mortification or other procedures of 'inviting' death.

REFERENCES

Ariès, Philippe. 1981. *The Hour of Our Death*. New York: Alfred Knopf.

Armstrong, D. 1983. *Political Anatomy of the Body: Medical Knowledge in Britain in the Twentieth Century*. Cambridge: Cambridge University Press.

Bowker, John. 1991. *The Meanings of Death*. Cambridge: Cambridge University Press.

Dworkin, R. 1991. 'The right to death'. *The New York Review of Books*: 14–17.

Elias, Norbert. 1985. *The Loneliness of Dying*. Oxford: Blackwell.

Foucault, Michel. 1976. *The Birth of the Clinic: An Archaeology of Medical Perception*. London: Tavistock.

————. 1977. *Discipline and Punish: The Birth of the Prison*. London: Allen Lane.

Humphrey, D. 1991. *The Final Exit*. London: The Hemlock Society.

Illich, Ivan. 1975. *Medical Nemesis: The Exploration of Health*. New Delhi: Rupa.

Kaul, Jailal. 1973. *Lal Ded*. New Delhi: Sahitya Akademi.

Krishnamurti, J. 1986. *Last Talks at Sanen 1985*. San Francisco: Harper and Row.

Madan, T.N. 1987. 'Living and dying'. In *Non-Renunciation: Themes and Interpretations of Hindu Culture*. New Delhi: Oxford University Press.

————. 1989. *Family and Kinship: A Study of the Pandits of Rural Kashmir*. Second enlarged edition. New Delhi: Oxford University Press.

Mascaro, Juan (trs.). 1962. *The Bhagavad Gita*. Harmondsworth: Penguin Books.

Mehta, J.L. 1988–89. 'Problems of understanding'. Cambridge, MA: *Bulletin of the Centre of the Study of World Religions* 15: 2–12.

Moller, D.W. 1990. *On Dying without Dignity: The Human Impact of Technological Dying*. New York: Baywood.

Mullin, G.H. 1986. *Death and Dying: The Tibetan Tradition*. Boston: Arkana.

Myerhoff, Barbara. 1979. *Number Our Days*. New York: D.P. Dutton.

Nandy, Ashis (ed.). 1988. *Science, Hegemony and Violence: A Requiem for Modernity*. New Delhi: Oxford University Press.

Parry, J.P. 1981. 'Death and cosmogony in Kashi'. *Contributions to Indian Sociology* 15: 337–65.

Parry, J.P. and Maurice Bloch. 1982. 'Introduction: Death and Regeneration of Life'. In *Death and Regeneration of Life*. Cambridge: Cambridge University Press.

Radhakrishnan, S. 1953. *The Principal Upanishads*. London: Allen and Unwin.

Shettar, S. 1986. *Inviting Death: Historical Experiments on Sepulchral Hill*. Dharwad: Karnatak University.

————. 1990. *Pursuing Death: Philosophy and Practice of Voluntary Termination of Life*. Dharwad: Karnatak University.

Skinner, B.F. 1972. *Beyond Freedom and Dignity*. New York: Alfred Knopf.

Thomasma, D.C. and G.C. Graber. 1990. *Euthanasia: Toward an Ethical Social Policy*. New York: Continuum.

Weber, Max. 1948. *From Max Weber: Essays in Sociology*. H.H. Gerth and C.W. Mills (trs.). London: Routledge and Kegan Paul.

————. 1958. *The Religion of India: The Sociology of Hinduism and Buddhism*. H.H. Gerth and D. Martindale (trs.). Glencoe, Ill.: The Free Press.

11

The Sociology of Hinduism
Reading Backwards from
Srinivas to Weber*

Do not stay in the field!
Nor climb out of sight.
The best view of the world
Is from a medium height.

Nietzsche
The Gay Science

M.N. SRINIVAS: SOME REMINISCENCES

May I begin with a few reminiscences by way of a personal tribute to Professor M.N. Srinivas (1916–99)? I first saw and heard him half a century ago, late in 1954. He was then Professor of Sociology at the M.S. University of Baroda, and had come to Lucknow, where his reputation as the acclaimed author of *Religion and Society among the Coorgs of South India* (1952) had preceded him. He had come, it was said, to consider the possibility of becoming the Director of UP government's newly established institute of rural analysis. Professor D.N. Majumdar invited him to speak in the Department of Anthropology at the university. An interdepartmental group of teachers and students had gathered to hear him, as had been announced, talk on fieldwork.

* This is the text of the Fifth M.N. Srinivas Memorial Lecture delivered under the auspices of the Indian Sociological Society on 25 October 2005 at the 31st All-India Sociological Conference held at the University of Jammu. The footnotes and some references have been added. Forthcoming in *Sociological Bulletin* 55, 2 (2006). I am grateful to the Indian Sociological Society for permission to include the essay in this book.

Srinivas made a measured plea for empiricism in the social sciences and for the method of 'participant observation' in anthropological research. Successful fieldwork, he maintained, required total commitment, even the holding in abeyance of family and personal obligations. Incidentally, Srinivas, who was 38, was still a bachelor. All this was of course received well by Majumdar, who was himself an indefatigable and exemplary fieldworker.

The discussion that followed produced some excitement when A.K. Saran, a sociology lecturer respected for his scholarship, accused Srinivas of being a positivist and 'cavalier' to deductive reasoning as a mode of knowing in social research. While the evidence of the senses may not be ignored, he argued, it necessarily is limited. Observation could at best reveal patterns of behaviour; it would not unveil their significance.[1] It was clear from Srinivas's terse response that he considered Saran's objections an exercise in obfuscation. If empiricists might have been compared to polytheists and deductivists to monotheists, we were the audience at an inconclusive theological debate: neither Srinivas nor Saran yielded any ground! The incident was remembered on the campus for quite some time. And Srinivas, with his pipe and beret and formal style, left behind him the image of a soft-spoken and rather reserved professor.

A few months later Srinivas was again in Lucknow as an examiner at the university. Also there at the same time were the avuncular A. Aiyappan from the Government Museum of Madras and the debonair S.C. Dube of Osmania University. Dube's *Indian Village* (1955) had just arrived in the bookstores. Although the Aiyappan–Majumdar generation was still in command, Srinivas and Dube were in our eyes the new exemplars pointing to new ways of doing anthropology and sociology.

Now, Srinivas wanted to buy a pillow for his return train journey to Baroda (his servant had forgotten to pack one in his bedroll), and Majumdar asked me to be his shopping escort. This then was my opportunity. Hopeful that he may have seen my enthusiastic review of his Coorg book in *The Eastern Anthropologist*, but apprehensive that he may have found it insignificant, I waited for him to say something about it; he didn't! But he listened to me attentively when I talked to him about my plans for doctoral research involving fieldwork among my own people, the Kashmiri Pandits, and was quite supportive.

Later that year, 1955, I wrote him asking if he would write a letter of recommendation supporting my application for the award of a research scholarship at the Australian National University. I enclosed a copy of the review of McKim Marriott's *Village India* (1955) that I had written and solicited his advice. To my very pleasant surprise, he responded soon, agreeing to write the letter of recommendation, and also commented on my review at considerable length.

From then on, I remained in continuous contact with Srinivas until the very end. In 1959 he was one of the examiners of my Ph.D. dissertation. I visited him in his office at the Delhi School of Economics, where he had moved recently, for my viva voce examination, which he conducted with solicitude and meticulous care, writing down my answers to the queries of the other two examiners, who could not be present. His own questions were more in the nature of advice on revision for publication. And he asked me to come home for dinner. I knew I had made it!

Six years later he strongly supported my move from Karnatak University to the Institute of Economic Growth in Delhi. As the years passed by, I came to deeply respect Srinivas for his seriousness as a scholar and for his unfailing courtesy, charm, and wit as a human being. He was an engaging raconteur. His stories about such diverse topics as the zest for life of Punjabi immigrants in England and the eccentricities of Professor G.S. Ghurye are still fresh in my memory!

In 1999, the last year of his life, I met Srinivas twice. He invited me to speak on religious fundamentalism at the National Institute of Advanced Studies (NIAS) in Bangalore, where he held the JRD Tata Visiting Chair. Soon afterwards he came to Delhi to give the inaugural silver jubilee lecture of the Delhi School of Economics. He told me of his plans to organize an international conference on religion and society at NIAS the following year with the focus on the imperative need to avoid confusion between religion as such and the political abuse of religion. There was a dangerous slippage, he said, from the legitimate disapproval of religious fanaticism to an uncritically negative attitude towards religious faith. He wanted me to participate in the conference. Alas, he died before the year was out. The quiet manner of his going was characteristic of Srinivas's style of life.

When Director Roddam Narasimha invited me to deliver the

first M.N. Srinivas Memorial Lecture at NIAS in January 2001, I spoke on the persistence of religion in the modern world in fulfilment of the promise, as it were, I had given Srinivas to participate in his conference (see Madan 2001 and Chapter 1 above). And now, when the Indian Sociological Society has honoured me by naming me as this year's M.N. Srinivas Memorial Lecturer, I have decided, once again, to engage with the theme of the relationship of religion and society, this time in the specific context of the sociology of Hinduism. I will highlight some of Srinivas's own seminal contributions and then move backwards, as it were, to revisit the classic study of Hinduism by Max Weber (1864–1920). A comparison of the two approaches is, I am convinced, worthwhile both for its methodological interest and substantive results. I can only touch upon a few points; a fuller discussion is precluded by lack of time.

IS A SOCIOLOGY OF HINDUISM POSSIBLE?

To begin, I would like to briefly address two objections to the project of a sociology of Hinduism. Hinduism, it is said, is not a religion, for it does not have a founder, or a single foundational scripture, or a set of fundamentals of belief and practice. A notion of the supernatural is not central to it, and the idea of moral law that may be considered a substitute is highly relativistic. These and other similar doubts have been around a long time. Srinivas (1952, 1958, 1968) himself acknowledged them, and wrote about the 'amorphousness' and 'complexity' of Hinduism and the difficulty of defining it. All this did not, however, deter him from writing about it.

Weber (1958: 27) considered reverence for the Vedas and belief in the sacredness of the cow defining features of Hinduism, but he too noted the virtual lack of dogma in Hinduism (ibid.: 21) and the fact that the term itself was a recent Western coinage (ibid.: 4). He observed: 'Hinduism simply is not a "religion" in our [Christian?] sense of the word. What the Occidental conceives as "religion" is closer to the Hindu concept of *sampradāya*' (ibid.: 23). He paid no further attention to the issue. Whether Hinduism is a religion or not, and whether religion itself is a meaningful cross cultural category, it would be pointless to deny that Hinduism is a cultural tradition and thus a legitimate subject for study.

But some historians have objected that Hinduism is not an old tradition, that it is only a nineteenth century fabrication by Christian missionaries, Orientalists, builders of the colonial archive, and would-be makers of an Indian nationalism. 'What has survived over the centuries', Romila Thapar writes, 'is not a single monolithic religion but a diversity of sects which we today have put under a uniform name' (1997: 56). This is, I am afraid, questionable.

There are other historians who have documented the continuities as well as the discontinuities between the early religion of the Vedas and the later religion of the Smritis, Shastras, Puranas, and the epics. They have also drawn attention to the 'family resemblance' among the regional traditions of myth and ritual to come to the conclusion that, whatever may have been the earlier connotations of the Persian-Arabic term 'Hindu', by the medieval times it certainly identified most of the known peoples of India by their religious beliefs and practices (see, for example, Lorenzen 1999 and Michaels 2005).

For this we have the testimony of the great traveller–scholar al-Biruni, who came to India with Mahmud Ghaznavi, and composed his famous work, *Tārikh-ul Hind*, around AD 1030 after living in India as a participant observer for a dozen years. Beginning with the Hindu conception of God, his wide ranging ethnography covers, among other topics, sacred texts, mythology, metaphysics, ritual, custom, law, and the sciences to distinguish and even contrast the Hindus as a socio cultural and religious category from the Muslims. He sarcastically notes the Hindus' willingness to argue with words in defence of their religion but not die for it as apparently every good Muslim would.[2]

I will mention only a few other witnesses. In the middle of the fourteenth century, the chronicler Abd al-Malik Isami categorized the people of the Deccan as Hindus and Muslims in his account of the victories of the sultans. In the north, the Shaiva mystic Lalla of the Kashmir Valley (see p. 184 above), however, called upon the thoughtful and the wise to abandon the distinction between Hindus and Muslims as followers of different faiths, and recognize the in-dwelling Divinity in all human beings. By the sixteenth century the religious connotation of the terms Hindu and Muslim was well established, for instance, in the vernacular literature of eastern, northern, central, and western India. In the seventeenth century, Shivaji spoke of his sacrifices for the Hindu dharma. And so on, until we read about 'Hinduism' early in the nineteenth century. Rammohun Roy was perhaps the first Indian to use it, in 1816 (see King 1999: 100). The roots of the authentic (as against the degenerate) 'Hindooism' lay, he argued, in the Vedanta. He regretted that the 'ancient religion had been disregarded by the moderns' (Kopf 1979: 13).

Srinivas on the 'Spread' of Hinduism and 'Sanskritization'

In short, the recognition of the diversities of belief and custom among self-knowledged Hindus on a regional or local basis—the proverbial trees of ethnographic description—does not require us to deny the existence of a more than a millennium-old evolving subcontinental religious heritage—the sociological wood. An insightful way of doing this was provided by Srinivas in the Coorg book. In a summing up towards its end, he recalls his use of the concept of 'spread' throughout the book, categorizing Hinduism for heuristic purposes as 'All-India', 'Peninsular', 'Regional', and 'Local'. All-India Hinduism, he writes, 'is Hinduism with an all-India spread, and this is chiefly Sanskritic in character'. After drawing attention to the step-by-step change of scale, Srinivas continues: 'In a very broad sense it is true that as the area of spread decreases, the number of ritual and cultural forms shared in common increases. Conversely, as the area increases, the common forms decrease' (1952: 213–14). That is, they do not disappear completely.

The sceptical historians will perhaps fault Srinivas for making the methodological error of category assumption, illicitly smuggling in a fictional Hinduism into his analytical framework. The charge will not stick, for he provides ethnographic ballast for his framework by pointing out that the different levels of Hinduism are not hermetically sealed, but the stages of a two-way social process characteristic of the caste-based social structure of South Asia. While the Sanskritic (or Brahmanical) Hinduism, the one with the all-India spread, had shown a remarkable capacity for absorbing local cultural elements, 'local' Hinduisms too have borrowed from the Sanskritic reservoir of belief and practice. This latter process has had its roots deep in history with significant consequences; Srinivas famously called it 'Sanskritization'. He wrote:

> The caste system is far from a rigid system in which the position of each caste is fixed for all time. Movement has always been possible, and especially so in the middle regions of the hierarchy. A low caste was able, in a generation or two, to rise to a higher position in the hierarchy by adopting vegetarianism and teetotalism, and by Sanskritizing its ritual and pantheon. In short, it took over, as far as possible, the customs, rites, and beliefs of the Brahmins, and the adoption of the Brahmanic way of life by a low caste seems to have been frequent, though theoretically forbidden (ibid.: 30).

The extreme caution that marks this initial formulation of the notion of Sankritization is noteworthy. It generated an enormous body of ethnographic work—more perhaps than any other theoretical construct in the history of the sociology of India—and was in the process refined by Srinivas himself and by others in the mid 1950s. Notable among these were McKim Marriott (1955), who used the terms 'universalization' and 'parochialization' for the two-way process; Fred Bailey (1958), who introduced the important notion of limits, showing how those below the barrier of pollution do not have this route of upward mobility open to them, and Surajit Sinha (1962), who wrote about Rajputization or state formation among the tribal peoples. Srininvas (1966a) himself presented more nuanced formulations, linking Sanskritization to Westernization and secularization, almost in linear progression, as strategies of status enhancement. His virtually unqualified positive assessment of Sanskritization as productive of socio-cultural cohesion (Srinivas 1967) provoked some criticism of his failure to unmask the hegemonic character of the process. My concern here is not to make an overall assessment of his paradigm of social change, but only to look at it for the light it throws on the processual nature of Hinduism.

All this is of course well known; let me just add that some of the most significant long-term evidence of the two-way process of cultural borrowing has been provided by historians themselves (Clio be praised!). One of the richest such works that I have read is Kunal Chakrabarti's (2001) insightful account of the cultural and religious history of medieval Bengal, in which the wily Brahmans are shown to have played a most significant role in the creation of what in Srinivas's terms is an example of regional Hinduism.

SRINIVAS ON RITUALS AND SOCIAL SOLIDARITY: A FIELD VIEW

Let me now turn to another crucial aspect of Srinivas's study of Hinduism. A casual look at his bibliography reveals not more than about ten titles that would suggest that Hinduism, or more generally religion, was one of his principal concerns as a sociologist; but titles can be deceptive. If one were to think of him as primarily a sociologist of caste, one would have to note that, in his judgement, caste as a social institution derived its legitimacy from religious values. His first major publication, based on his M.A. dissertation at the University of Bombay, was entitled *Marriage and Family in Mysore* (1942), but the focus, as he himself states at the very beginning, is very much on the family as a site for the performance of rituals: puberty rites, marriage rites, delivery and naming rites, and celebratory periodical rites (fasts and festivals) are described. The practices of the Brahmans are distinguished from those of the 'non-Brahmans' among the Kannada castes. Little is said about the economic side of family life, although there is a short chapter on bride price, or of interpersonal relations, beyond a brief discussion of the conflict-ridden relations between mothers-in-law and daughters-in-law. What is equally noteworthy is that the beliefs that go with the rites receive little attention. Thus, 'the purpose of death ceremonies' is described in a short quotation from Monier-Williams (ibid.: 150–1).

In continuation of this emphasis, religion in the Coorg book also is structured around what Srinivas calls the 'ritual idiom'. 'Every society', he writes, 'has a body of ritual, and certain ritual acts forming part of the body of ritual repeat themselves constantly. Not only ritual acts but also ritual complexes, which are wholes made up of several individual ritual acts, frequently repeat themselves' (1952: 70). It is thus that ritual contributes to social solidarity. What we have here is near reification of ritual, as if the act moves under its own steam. The connected beliefs, notably ritual purity and pollution, with which the book is significantly concerned, and notions like dharma and karma, *pāpa* and *punya*, provide only an underpinning. The same cluster of values finds mention again in *The Remembered Village* (1976: 312–19) and, in likewise manner, as a backdrop of behaviour. There are no detailed descriptions of rituals here, presumably because processed fieldnotes of the observations made may have been lost in arson in his office at Palo Alto (ibid.: xi).

I find the emphasis on observable behaviour an intriguing aspect of Srinivas's methodology and would like to dwell on it briefly. We are told by A.M. Shah that Srinivas's impressionable childhood was spent in the setting of a long house in the city of Mysore in which five Sri Vaishnava Brahman families had their abode (Shah 1996: 198). Writing himself about the life of the Brahman families of the village of Rampura, Srinivas observes that it was 'permeated by ritual' (ibid.: 293); so must have been, one imagines, the daily life of his own natal household. The preoccupation of the Brahman householders everywhere with *karmakānda*, that is with the performance of life-cycle rituals, is well known. Moreover, the *karmakānda* is behaviouristic insofar as the efficacy of the mantra is believed to lie in the utterance and of the associated bodily movements and gestures (*mudrā*) in correct procedure. Any search for the meaning of the ritual act as a whole is considered redundant if not injurious to the purpose of the ritual.

The writing of Srinivas's doctoral dissertation under the supervision of Radcliffe-Brown at Oxford must have been a felicitous meeting of minds. In his Foreword to the Coorg book, Radcliffe-Brown wrote:

> For the social anthropologist the religion of a people presents itself in the first instance not as a body of doctrine, but as what we may call 'religious' behaviour as a part of social life. Social anthropology is behaviouristic in the sense that we seek to observe how people act as a necessary preliminary to trying to understand how they think and feel (Srinivas 1952: vi).

There would be little to complain about this procedure if all it meant was that it is in social activity that the meaning of concepts and beliefs is located, not in themselves. But in practice it has usually resulted in religious beliefs being pushed into the background, rendered secondary in ethnography.

At the very commencement of the post-Enlightenment study of religion, some of the pioneers were sceptical about the existence of religious belief outside the fold of what they considered the fully evolved religions. William Robertson Smith in his classic *Religion of the Semites* (1894), stated that 'antique religions had for the most part no creed; they consisted entirely of institutions and practices' (2002: 16–17). Earlier, Fustel de Coulanges in another classic, *The Ancient City* (1864), opened the discussion with an affirmation of 'the necessity of studying the earliest beliefs of the ancients in order to understand their institutions' (nd: 11ff.), only to conclude that in those cultural settings beliefs (for example, about the inseparability of body and soul) were forgotten in course of time and the connected rites alone (for example, burial and the building of tombs) survived as evidence of their existence. 'Thus a complete religion of the dead was established', he wrote, 'whose dogmas might soon be effaced, but whose rites endured until the triumph of Christianity' (ibid.: 21).

Fustel de Coulanges was one of the teachers of Émile Durkheim, who defined religion as 'a unified system of beliefs and practices' (1995: 44), but devoted more attention to the latter. Edward Tylor's speculation about the origin of primitive religion in the notion of the individual soul (Tylor 1913), and the earlier characterization of belief as an 'act of the mind' by David Hume in his *Natural History of Religion* (1757), would have stood precisely for the kind of psychologism, and in effect reductionism, to which Durkheim was firmly opposed. For him the social fact, comprising both collective representations and group activities, could be legitimately explained only in sociological, not psychological, terms. Durkheim in turn influenced Radcliffe-Brown (in Evans-Pritchard's [1965: 74] judgement 'the weakest link of the chain'!), who wrote in his ethnography of the Andaman Islanders (1922) about their beliefs (for example, in 'a class of supernatural beings'), but by his own declaration he foregrounded ritual.

The point of the digression is to suggest that, intellectually, Srinivas belongs to a celebrated but not uncriticized tradition in the sociological study of religion, which valorizes behaviour at the cost of belief. To be fair, I must mention that in his studies of Hinduism there are references to beliefs, but these are brief and remain confined to a mention of sectarian differences in the conception of deities (theology) and to a more general set of metaphysical ideas, notably *samsāra*, karma, dharma, and moksha. The practical notions of ritual purity and pollution, however, receive rich treatment in the Coorg book.

It is likely that Srinivas's distrust of 'bibliocentrism' in the study of Hindu society held him back, but the 'field view' itself would have revealed a great deal more about beliefs than is to be found in his book had he been theoretically differently oriented than he was, beliefs of the kind that we find in the doctoral dissertation of Jayanthi Beliappa, a Coorgi scholar. I should add here parenthetically that Srinivas (1973) himself later on expressed dissatisfaction with the limitations of the functionalist framework.

Like Srinivas, Beliappa too set out 'to comprehend the nature of the relationship between religion and social reality'. Bypassing Radcliffe-Brown, she turns to Durkheim to emphasize that for him 'the concreteness of social reality was embedded in a cognitive system' just as 'systems of knowledge were grounded in a social framework' (1979: 1.9). This is elaborated to lead to the study of how the Coorgis 'comprehend and construct their cosmology in order to derive from it a system of meanings that help their social life as a small community to endure'. She explores 'areas of religious experience in which there is a clear delineation of religious discourse for the routines of everyday life' (ibid.: 2.1). Beliappa acknowledges the great value of Srinivas's pioneering study, but suggests that an alternative approach, grounded in structuralism rather than functionalism, may reveal to us more about how the Coorgis themselves *conceptualize* their social life. For instance, birth and death are for them 'meaningful' events, besides being occasions for the performance of appropriate rituals. 'Function' and 'meaning' are of course intertwined aspects of these rituals. And the question of 'meaning'—the question of making sense of the world—engaged Max Weber deeply.[3]

WEBER ON THE PLACE OF BELIEFS IN HINDUISM:
A BOOK VIEW

I would like to begin my discussion of some aspects of Max Weber's 'view from afar' of Hinduism with the thought that he nailed to the masthead of his celebrated (although in some respects flawed) study of the rise of the spirit of capitalism in the West. In the opening paragraph of the book, he maintained that the offspring of 'modern European civilization, studying any problem of universal history', were bound to reflect on the circumstantial uniqueness of certain 'cultural phenomena' that have 'appeared' there, and which they would 'like to think...lie in a line of development having *universal* significance and value' (1930: 13, emphasis original). Paradoxically, uniqueness is here considered generalizable, and the history of the West is privileged. As Marx put it, it was the mirror in which the pre-industrial world could see the face of its future.

Given such a point of departure for his massive project of the study of the economic ethics of world religions, Weber's study of Hinduism was inevitably cast in the mould of otherness. While Srinivas was born into Hindu society and studied it from within although as an anthropologist—he wrote eloquently about 'the study of one's society' (1966b)—Weber was distant from it in every conceivable respect, the absolute outsider. Srinivas wrote about Hinduism from personal experience and fieldwork study. He used secondary sources also in both the Mysore and Coorg books but sparingly, and these were contemporary English language rather than traditional texts.

Weber drew heavily upon the colonial archive (including descriptive and census reports) but he also delved into the traditional texts (in German or English translation). The Brahmanical ideas that he examined for their secular sociological significance came from his obviously selective reading of the Vedic corpus, the *smriti, shāstra*, and *nīti* literatures, the *Mahābhārata* and the *Rāmāyana*, the Upanishads, even the *tantra* texts. He also consulted contemporary exegeses and commen-taries by Western and Indian scholars. In short, Weber's view of Hindu society and religion was the 'book view' par excellence. Now, as I have already said, Srinivas was deeply suspicious of 'bibliocentrism'; he was equally wary of 'paleocentrism'; they were for him two sides of the same counterfeit coin. The aridity of the book view, its lack of contact with lived reality, were known to him from the work of some of his Bombay University colleagues. That Weber's approach was different was not known to Srinivas when he formulated his early views, because, although the original work was published in 1920, he did not read German, and the English translation, *The Religion of India*, was published only in 1958.[4]

Differences of method notwithstanding, what I find striking in the first place is the similarity of substantive conclusions arrived at by Srinivas and Weber, but there are significant differences too.

For both, the caste system was the fundamental institution of Hinduism, and the Brahmans were the crucial mediators in the relationship of religion and society. Both recognized them as ritual specialists and repositories of sacred knowledge, but Weber especially stressed their role as the 'cultural literati', weaving out their webs of metaphysics that had for very long ensnared the 'masses'. What the creative minority thought up, the mimetic majority acquiesced in one way or the other.

All Hindus, Weber wrote, 'accept two basic principles: the *samsara* belief in the transmigration of souls and the related *karman* doctrine of compensation. These alone are the truly "dogmatic" doctrines of Hinduism' (1958: 118). Such acceptance had become manifest in the ordering of social relations, in the caste system. The bond between 'idea' and 'action' is summed up in one of the most memorable passages of *Religion of India* (pp. 121–2):

> *Karma* doctrine transformed the world into a strictly rational, ethically determined cosmos; it represents the most consistent theodicy ever produced by history. The devout Hindu was accursed to remain in a structure which made sense only in this intellectual context; its consequences burdened his conduct. The *Communist Manifesto* concludes with the phrases 'they (the proletariat) have nothing to lose but their chains, they have a world to win'. The same holds for the pious Hindu of low castes. He too can 'win the world', even the heavenly world; he can become a Kshatriya, a Brahman, he can gain heaven and become a god—only not in this life, but in the life of the future after rebirth into the same world pattern.[5]

I would like to draw attention to two aspects of Weber's statement. First, he highlights a view of society that emphasizes its embeddedness in a morally determined universe in which good fortune or bad fortune is a deserved condition, and society is not a matter of customs and transactions but of moral imperatives and social obligations. One does what one ought to do and not what is personally pleasing or profitable: one must be true to one's group dharma.

But—this is the second aspect—dharma is absent in the passage, although it is almost invariably bracketed with karma by most authorities including Srinivas. Dharma is, in fact, introduced at the very beginning of the work, given the broad connotation of all social action as ritual, a kind of social liturgy, and contrasted to dogma (ibid.: 21). 'Hinduism is primarily ritualism', Weber observed, 'a fact implied when modern authors state that *mata* (doctrine) and *marga* (holy end) are transitory and...freely elected, while *dharma* is "eternal"—that is, unconditionally valid'. But *'dharma* differs according to social position...*dharma* depends upon the caste into which the individual is born...*dharma* can be developed...by finding thus far unknown but eternally valid consequences and truths' (ibid.: 24–5). Weber's conception of Hinduism as ritualistic is not the same, it should be emphasized, as Srinivas's conception of it as a configuration of domestic and extra-domestic rituals associated with the human life-cycle and religious devotion.

Srinivas regards the 'ideas of *karma, dharma* and *moksha*' as 'intimately related to the caste system', and acknowledges that, their Sanskritic origin notwithstanding, they have reached 'the common people' through various channels of communication (1968: 359). In the Rampura book, he describes how in the judgement of the villagers generally, dharma refers to good liberating conduct and karma to evil actions which have consequences that hold one in karmic bondage (1976: 312–19). But he does not engage with these ideas in any great detail.

Srinivas rather focuses, as I said earlier, on another set of ideas in his writings, particularly in the Coorg book: these are the ideas of good-sacred and bad-sacred, of ritual purity and pollution (*madi* and *polé* in Coorgi speech). It is these that he sees as the principal determinants of interpersonal and inter-group relations in the contexts of the family and caste. Needless to emphasize, these ideas are more readily discernible in everyday behaviour— relating to, for example, food taboos, bodily contact, and occupational choice—*but not more important* than the more abstract ideas of dharma and karma that Weber focused on. In this Srinivas anticipated Louis Dumont's later valorization of ritual purity as the cardinal value that defines hierarchy (Dumont 1970). It is not therefore surprising that Dumont (1959: 9) should have hailed the Coorg book as a modern classic half a dozen years after its publication. Notwithstanding his programmatic declaration that the sociology of India lies at the confluence of Indology and sociology (1957: 7), Dumont the fieldworker is closer to Srinivas than Dumont the textualist is to Weber (see Chapter 12 below). I cannot, however, pursue this trail here. I must return to Weber.

Weber was not, of course, a fieldworker, but he was sensitive to such ethnography as was available to him and his perspective was processual. The best way to illustrate this is to recall what he wrote about the diffusion of Hinduism over time, and here he anticipated Srinivas most remarkably. He called this process Hinduization, and believed that Hindu 'propaganda in the grand manner', or simply 'missionary propagation' (1958: 9), had been going on for close to a millennium: Hinduism had thus spread from the heart of northern India (Aryavrata) to the rest of the country. This extensive Hinduization (as he called it) sucked local tribal communities into a subcontinental religio-social milieu. Indeed, the propagators are 'met halfway' by the 'outsiders' (ibid.: 14).

The process, Weber noted, was multi-stranded, involving the selective but expanding use of the expert services of the Brahmans, adopting new kinds of work and occupations, altering dietary habits and social customs, and accepting new modes of religious behaviour. Gradually, the outsiders would usually find themselves transformed into impure Hindu castes. Within the broader framework of extensive Hinduization, Weber noted, there was a tendency to engage in intensive (or internal) Hinduization in pursuit of status enhancement (ibid.: 11). If material gain motivated the Brahman to be accommodative (a player of the game), the quest for social legitimation drove the climbers forward and upward, hoping to bridge 'the abysmal distance Hinduism establishes between social strata': Weber called it the peculiar 'religious promise' of Hinduism (ibid.: 17).

What all this means we know very well indeed, thanks to the vast body of ethnographic studies generated by N.K. Bose's seminal essay on 'the Hindu method of tribal absorption' (Bose 1941) and, of course, Srinivas's discussions of Sanskritization. Weber appreciated as well as Bose and Srinivas that the processes were collective and not individual, that it could not be 'otherwise' since individuals can never rise except as a 'caste' (ibid.: 11ff). The similarity between Weber's and Srinivas's views is so striking that it is puzzling that not much attention has been paid to it. (Kulke 1986 is a notable exception.) Srinivas himself never mentions it in his published work.

The only reference to Weber in Srinivas's writings that I know of is to the argument about the lack of appropriate ideological resources in Hinduism for the endogenous development of capitalism. It is a very short comment (in a co-authored article), criticizing Weber for 'a partial view of Hinduism', but noting that 'Weber himself [had] identified a few elements of "rational ethic" in Hinduism', and concluding with a reference to the managerial and administrative abilities often displayed by 'Hindu ascetics' who head 'large and wealthy monasteries and temples' (1968: 364).

Weber's views about Hinduism and capitalism have been subjected to much criticism, some of it based on misreading what he actually wrote. This is how he describes the scope of his study: 'Here we shall inquire as to the manner in which Indian religion, *as one factor among many, may have prevented capitalistic development* (in the occidental sense)' (ibid.: 4, emphasis added) Could any formulation be more cautious even if it is not wholly open minded? Nor can Weber's thesis be disproved by describing what Indian entrepreneurs achieved in the nineteenth century, often in competition with British entrepreneurs. Weber's concern was with *initial* development (or the first appearance), and he held the hereditary and non-innovative character of caste-based division of work as much responsible for the non-emergence of capitalism as any religious ideas as such. It is not my contention that Weber's thesis, whether about Europe or about its generalizability, is above criticism (see, for example, Munshi 2003 for an excellent recent critique), but lack of time does not permit fuller discussion here.

In any case, the question about capitalism with which Weber begins *The Religion of India* is not all that interested him in Hinduism. In the first part of the book, after introducing the ideological backdrop, he discusses the Hindu social system comprising tribe, caste, sect, etc. It is in this discussion that the convergences between him and Srinivas are pronounced. Part two, which is about as long as the first, focuses on 'orthodox and heterodox holy teachings'; in the concluding part he moves into east Asia with the Buddhist missions to return to nineteenth century India's restoration movements.

For a final comment on Weber's work, to illustrate his interest in the role of ideas, I would like to recall his insightful discussion of the *Bhagavad Gītā* (ibid.: 180–91), which, he says, 'in a certain sense represents the crown of the classical ethics of Indian intellectuals' (ibid.: 185). Here he lays bare 'the inner conflict' of the Hindu tradition, notably that between the Brahmanical and

Kshatriya ways of life, and between two modes of salvation represented by, first, the moral agent's assumption of responsibility for breaking out of the karmic chain and, secondly, his seeking refuge in divine grace (*prasāda*) (ibid.: 187), a radical departure from the classical Brahmanical tradition.

A key question is posed by Draupadi in the *Mahābhārata*, writes Weber, when, apropos Yudhishthira's 'blameless misfortune', she tells him that 'the great God only plays with men according to his whims'. Yudhishthira's response is: 'one should not say such things, for by the grace of God the good receive immortality and, above all, without this belief people would not practice virtue' (ibid.: 182). And without virtue there is no social life: social norms ultimately arise when individuals learn to care and give, trust and conform.

But, then, how does one practice virtue? The *Bhagavad Gītā* teaches the ethic of conformity to one's varna dharma or obligations established by nature, Weber notes: right knowledge (*jñānyoga*) for the Brahman and right action (*karmayoga*) for the rest. The Kshatriya must wage war and rule—'without any concern for consequences', especially not for personal success (ibid.: 184). 'The inner-worldly ethic of the *Bhagavadgītā*', Weber observes, 'is "organismic" in a sense hardly to be surpassed. Indian "tolerance" rests upon this absolute relativising of all ethical soteriological commandments' (ibid.: 189–90). In his apprehension of absolute relativism in Hindu ethics, and the resultant tolerance, Weber is of course mistaken: maybe fieldwork in an Indian village would have brought to his notice the widely known fact, recorded by ethnographers (see, for example, Mathur 1965), that there are shared values also, the *sādhāran* dharma that defines one's humanity and cuts across varna boundaries. And there is exploitation, oppression, and violence. Weber obviously did not know certain things and got others wrong. (I wonder if he ever knew a Hindu or met one.) That is not remarkable: what is so is how much he knew right, and how comprehensive his outline of a sociology of Hinduism—and indeed of the comparative sociology of religion—was.

CONCLUDING REMARKS:
THE RELEVANCE OF A SOCIOLOGY OF RELIGION

It is time to wind up. I trust I have been able to bring out in some small measure that, while the 'field' or ethnographic view of

Hinduism brings into sharp focus the lived social reality, the 'book' or bibliographic view provides the background that illumines the foreground. Reading 'backwards' from Srinivas to Weber is not a retreat from fieldwork and the personally observed microcosm into the textually described macrocosm, from the concreteness of rituals into the abstraction of beliefs. It is rather the establishment of balance between the two perspectives, a fusion of horizons. Needless to emphasize, the double perspective generates questions and yields answers that neither of its two constituents do. If *Religion and Society among the Coorgs of South India* is the one bookend of the sparse sociological corpus on Hinduism (sparse compared to what sociologists have written about other world religions), then *The Religion of India* is the other. We need both bookends to hold the shelf together and indeed expand it. It is work in progress, and I invite our younger colleagues to participate in it.

There are hesitations, I know, that keep them away. For instance the mistaken belief that the study of religion does not have the same social relevance or academic value as some other subjects, such as economics and politics, or class and gender, because religion is illusory, reactionary, and in retreat.[6] Referring to the lack of scholarly interest in folk religions, Srinivas observed in the Rampura book that 'leading Indian anthropologists and sociologists profess to be rationalists' (1976: 290). Weber noticed this failing early. Acknowledging the unresolvable conflict between religion and modern rationality, he wrote in the concluding paragraph of his Protestant Ethic book: 'The modern man is in general unable to give religious ideas a significance for culture and national character that they deserve' (1930: 183). Developments worldwide in the last quarter of the twentieth century in the relationship of religion, politics, and society have added a new significance to Weber's acute observation. There is urgent need today, more than ever before, to *understand* religion as a social force for good or evil in the modern world. I do not really need to remind you about what happened in Poland and Nicaragua, in Iran and Afghanistan, in Sri Lanka and India, and elsewhere including, most notably, the USA, where Christian fundamentalism re-emerged with explicit political goals in the 1980s, and the USSR, which disintegrated in the early 1990s, not only constitutionally but also and more importantly, ideologically.

Another but not unrelated hesitation arises from a method-ological doubt: Does an agnostic make a good student of the sociology of religion? During a conversation we had in Delhi in 1998, Srinivas asked me rhetorically why Raymond Firth's writings on religion compared so poorly with Evans-Pritchard's, and proceeded to give me his answer: 'Firth is a rationalist', which of course he was (Firth 1996). And Srinivas himself was, as he publicly acknowledged (1974, 1993), a believer.

Srinivas's greatly admired mentor and friend, Evans-Pritchard, a late life convert to Catholicism, shared his doubts about ratio-nalists as credible students of religion. He quotes Wilhelm Schmidt with approval: 'There is too much danger that the [non-believer] will talk of religion as a blind man might of colours, or one totally devoid of ear, of a beautiful piece of music' (1965: 121).[7] But then we have Weber's affirmation that he was personally 'unmusical religiously' although not 'anti-religious' or 'irreligious' (see Weber 1975: 324); indeed at times he wondered, to the utter bewilderment of his wife Marianne, that he might after all be a mystic (Mitzman 1985: 218). His uncertainties did not, however, stand in the way of his wide ranging and deeply insightful studies of several world religions. His formulation of the consequences of the historic process of rationalization in the West, of which 'disenchantment' was an aspect—the retreat from 'public life' of 'the ultimate and most sublime values...into the transcendental realm of mystic life or into the brotherliness of direct and personal human relations' (1948: 155)—brought out his pessimism about the fate of moderniz-ing societies. He may well have partly imbibed this pessimism from Nietzsche for whom the notion of the death of God opened several possibilities including that of nihilism, the loss of all values (see Nietzsche 1974: 181 and pp. 8–9 above).

Weber saw the possibility of 'refuge' in religion (Evans-Pritchard 1965: 118), but as a rationalist that was not the road he took. His agonizing finds echoes in the life and work of his great contem-porary, Émile Durkheim (1858–1917), co-founder with him of the sociology of religion.[8] I do not have the time to elaborate, but let me remind you that Durkheim had his own religious anxieties, converting from Judaism to Catholicism, and then, yielding to the prevailing anti-clericalism in Paris, he ended up as a rationalist. For the rest of his life, he searched for a civic morality to fill the vacuum created by France's rejection of her Catholic past (see Lukes 1973). He asserted that, for himself, he was 'quite indifferent' to the 'choice' between 'God and Society' since he saw 'in the Divinity only society transfigured and symbolically expressed' (1953: 52). Durkheim had concluded his 1915 classic study of 'the religious life' with the observation that, in the face of the unstoppable advance of science, religion seemed 'destined to transform itself than to disappear' (1995: 432). Later, he explained that 'the fusion of consciences' that constitutes 'a source of religious life as old as humanity...can never dry'. More emphatically, he declared, 'The only thing that matters is to sense above the moral coldness which prevails on the surface of collective life, the sources of warmth which our societies carry in themselves (Pickering 1975: 185, 187).[9]

One's being a believer or an agnostic does not, I am convinced, by itself make or mar one's chances of being a good sociologist of religion. One has only to ensure that one's faith or ideology does not prejudice the outcome of one's inquiries. Let me turn one last time to Weber, and remind you that his methodological stance on objectivity in social research, abjuring 'value judgements', which has of course been much criticized, did not exclude the study of values ('value references') (Weber 1949). And what is religion all about if it is not about values? What we need in the study of religion, as of any other social phenomenon, is genuine interest, theoretical self-consciousness, methodological rigour, sociological imagination, and above all intellectual honesty. None of these requirements is a gift of the gods; they are all eminently cultivable research skills or, if you prefer, scholarly virtues. Let me, then, hope that our younger colleagues will not stay away from the study of religion, as Srinivas thought they were doing, that they will come forward. This is indeed the tribute he would have most appreciated.[10]

NOTES

1. Saran developed his critique of positivism in a number of papers and review articles. Notable among these are his discussion of positivist sociology (Saran 1962) and a suggestive (unpublished?) paper characterizing Max Weber's work as 'the end of Comtean Sociology' (Saran 1987). He also wrote a searching critique of Marxian sociology with special reference to its theory of social change

(Saran 1963). While agreeing with Peter Winch's scepticism about 'the idea of a social science' (Winch 1958), he rejected the alternative of a Wittgensteinian sociology (Saran 1964). Saran's writings on methodology have not had any significant impact on the work of sociologists and social anthropologists in India: these have been regrettably considered too heavily metaphysical to be of interest.

2. Al-Biruni wrote: '...they [the Hindus] totally differ from us in religion, as we believe in nothing in which they believe, and *vice versa* [an echo of the Quran 109]. On the whole, there is very little disputing about theological topics among themselves; at the most they fight with words, but they will never stake their soul or body or property on religious controversy' (Sachau 2002: 3).

3. I should mention here that Srinivas was an examiner of Beliappa's Ph.D. dissertation and commended it highly. Her supervisor, Veena Das, had in her own doctoral work, conducted under Srinivas's supervision, opened discussion of the dialectic of 'structure' and 'cognition' in the study of ritual (Das 1976). This indeed is how intellectual traditions grow, through critical engagement, and we owe a deep debt to Srinivas for his encouragement.

4. I regret never having asked Srinivas when he first learnt, and what exactly, about Weber's study of Hinduism. Parsons (1937: 55 ff.) contains a short summary; the Gerth and Mills edition of Weber's selected essays (Weber 1948) also includes some discussions. I am not sure Srinivas knew about these books when he first formulated his own ideas about Hinduism at Oxford, where Durkheim rather than Weber provided the stimulus to thinking about religion (see Evans-Pritchard 1965).

5. It may be helpful here to quote Weber's gloss of the notion of theodicy (1948: 122):

> The age-old problem of theodicy consists of the very question of how it is that a power which is said to be at once omnipotent and kind could have created such an irrational world of undeserved suffering, unpunished injustice, and hopeless stupidity. Either this power is not omnipotent or not kind, or, entirely different principles of compensation and reward govern our life—principles we may interpret metaphysically, or even principles that forever escape our comprehension.

He acknowledges the inspiration of the Upanishads in arriving at the above formulation. The word 'theodicy' we, of course, owe to the late seventeenth century German philosopher Gottfried Liebniz, who derived it from Greek roots (*theos, dikē*) to connote the 'justice of gods'. Such justice was for him proof that the world we live in is the 'best of all possible worlds'.

6. Cp. Béteille (2005: 53): 'I believe that the sociological study of religion brings sharply into focus certain interesting questions of approach and method, and a discussion of these may be of wider interest in the study of society as a whole, including the study of such subjects as class, gender, nation, and, more generally, politics.' I agree. There are some other arguments and emphases in Béteille's essay which I find problematic, but this is not the place to go into them. I may note, however, that he recognizes the differences between the Durkheimian and Weberian approaches to the study of religion, and implicitly favours the former. I have already indicated above the reasons for my preference for the Weberian approach.

7. This is problematic. Evans-Pritchard's 1937 work on the religious life of the Azande, marked by a rationalist attitude to the understanding of witchcraft, magic, and the work of oracles, is in no way a less masterly study than the 1956 work on Nuer religion completed after his conversion. In fact the latter has been said to be marked by a personal (Christian?) bias (see Douglas 1980: 87).

   The image of the blind man and colours is interestingly invoked by Durkheim also: 'what I ask of the free thinker is that he should confront religion in the same mental state as the believer... he who does not bring to the study of religion a sort of religious sentiment cannot speak about it! He is like a blind man trying to talk of colour' (Pickering 1975: 184). This is, of course, a plea for empathy not for religiousness.

8. A word about the exclusion of Marx. The core idea of 'projection' as the essence of religion is not his; he took it over from Ludwig Feuerbach (1957). The Marxian approach, with its emphasis on the illusory, although socially functional, character of religious belief, and the consequent certainty that it can be and should be abolished (alter the social conditions that produce it and the religion will disappear), I think, forecloses fuller understanding of religion even in the class-based Western society. Marx did not really construct a general theory of religion. Moreover, it is arguable that the roots of Marxian humanism lie in Christianity and that its own version of dogmatism or creedal fundamentalism makes it akin to religion. These are large questions and outside the scope of the present discussion.

9. Georg Simmel (1858–1918), another contemporary and friend of Weber (he too converted, from Judaism to Protestantism), was convinced that the methods and tempers of religion and science were in conflict, and the proving of the verities of religious faith was 'completely outside the sphere of scientific interest' (1997: 4). But he maintained that religion as a quality of social relationships was a fit subject for sociological study; he indeed found 'strong similari-

ties between the religious and the sociological forms of existence'
(ibid.: 157).
10. Written at 'Zabarwan', Berwyn, PA (USA) in August–September
2005.

REFERENCES

Bailey, F.G. 1958. *Caste and the Economic Frontier: A Village in Highland Orissa*. Bombay: Oxford University Press.

Beliappa, Jayanthi. 1979. *A Study of the Religious Concepts of the Coorgs*. Ph.D. dissertation, University of Delhi.

Béteille, André. 2005. Religion as a subject for sociology. In Dipankar Gupta (ed.). *Anti-Utopia: Essential Writings of André Béteille*. New Delhi: Oxford University Press.

Bose, N.K. 1941. The Hindu method of tribal absorption. *Science and Culture:* 7: 188–94. Reproduced in N.K. Bose, *Culture and Society in India*, 1967, Bombay: Asia.

Chakrabarti, Kunal. 2001. *Religious Process: The Puranas and the Making of a Regional Tradition*. New Delhi: Oxford University Press.

Coulanges, Fustel de. (1864) n.d. *The Ancient City: A Study on the Religion, Laws and Institutions of Greece and Rome*. New York: Doubleday Anchor.

Das, Veena. 1977. *Structure and Cognition: Aspects of Hindu Caste and Ritual*. Delhi: Oxford University Press.

Douglas, Mary. 1980. *Evans-Pritchard*. London: Fontana.

Dube, S.C. 1955. *Indian Village*. London: Routledge and Kegan Paul.

Dumont, Louis. 1957. 'For a sociology of India'. *Contributions to Indian Sociology* 1: 7–22.

———. 1959. 'Pure and Impure'. *Contributions to Indian Sociology* 3: 9–39.

———. 1970. *Homo Hierarchicus: The Caste System and its Implications*. London: Widenfeld and Nicholson.

Durkheim, Émile. [1915] 1995. *The Elementary Forms of Religious Life*. Karen E. Fields (trs.). New York: The Free Press.

———. 1953. *Sociology and Philosophy*. D.F. Pocock (trs.). London: Cohen & West.

Evans-Pritchard, E.E. 1937. *Witchcraft, Oracles and Magic among the Azande*. Oxford: Clarendon Press.

———. 1956. *Nuer Religion*. Oxford: Clarendon Press.

———. 1965. *Theories of Primitive Religion*. Oxford: Clarendon Press.

Firth, Raymond. 1996. *Religion: A Humanist Perspective*. London: Routledge.

Feuerbach, Ludwig. [1854] 1957. *The Essence of Christianity*. George Eliot (trs.). New York: Harper.

Hume, David. [1757] 1957. *Natural History of Religion*. H.E. Root. (ed.). Stanford: Stanford University Press.

King, Richard. 1999. *Orientalism and Religion*. New Delhi: Oxford University Press.

Kopf, David. 1979. *The Brahmo Samaj and the Shaping of the Modern Indian Mind*. Princeton, N.J.: Princeton University Press.

Kulke, Hermann. 1986. 'Max Weber's contribution to the study of "Hinduization" in India and "Indianization" in Southeast Asia'. In D. Kantowsky (ed.). *Recent Researches on Max Weber's Studies of Hinduism*. Munchen: Weltforum Verlag.

Lorenzen, David N. 1999. 'Who invented Hinduism?' *Comparative Studies in Society and History* 41, 4: 630–59.

Lukes, Steven. 1973. *Émile Durkheim: His Life and Work*. Harmondsworth: Penguin.

Madan, T.N. 2001. *Religion in the Modern World*. Bangalore: National Institute of Advanced Studies.

Marriott, McKim. 1955. 'Little communities in an indigenous civilization'. In M. Marriott (ed.). *Village India: Studies in the Little Community*. Chicago: University of Chicago Press.

Mathur, K.S. 1965. *Caste and Ritual in a Malwa Village*. Bombay: Asia Publishing House.

Michaels, Axel. 2005. *Hinduism: Past and Present*. Barbara Harshav (trs.). New Delhi: Orient Longman.

Mitzman, Arthur. 1985. *The Iron Cage: An Historical Interpretation of Max Weber*. London: Transaction.

Munshi, Surendra. 2003. 'Revisting Max Weber on India'. In H. Hartmut Lehmann and J.M. Ouedraogo (eds). *Max Webers Religionssoziologie in interkultureller Perspective*. Goettingen: Vanenhoeck & Ruprecht.

Nietzsche, Friedrich. 1974. *The Gay Science*. W. Kaufmann (trs.). New York: Anchor.

Parsons, Talcott. [1937] 1949. *The Structure of Social Action*. Glencoe, Ill., The Free Press.

Pickering, W.S.F. (ed.). 1975. *Durkheim on Religion*. London: Routledge and Kegan Paul.

Radcliffe-Brown, A.R. [1922] 1964. *The Andaman Islanders*. Glencoe, Ill: The Free Press.

————. 1952. Foreword. In M.N. Srinivas 1952, q.v.

Sachau, Edward C. (trs.) [1914] 2002. *Alberuni's India*. New Delhi: Rupa & Co.

Saran, A.K. 1962. 'Some aspects of positivism in sociology'. *Transactions of the Fifth World Congress of Sociology*. Vol. 1: 199–233, Washington DC: International Sociological Association.

————. 1963. 'The Marxian theory of social change'. *Inquiry* 6: 70–127.

————. 1964. 'A Wittgensteinian sociology?' *Ethics* 75: 195–200.

————. 1987. 'Max Weber and the end of Comtean sociology'. Paper presented at an international seminar on Marx and Weber organized by Max Mueller Bhawan, New Delhi, 8–11 October. Mimeo.

Shah, A.M. and M.N. Srinivas. 1996. 'The man and his work'. In A.M. Shah et al. (eds). *Social Structure and Social Change: An Evaluation of the Work of M.N. Srinivas*. New Delhi: Sage.

Simmel, Georg. 1997. *Essays on Religion*. Horst J. Helle (ed. and trs.). New Haven: Yale University Press.

Sinha, Surajit. 1962. 'State formation and Rajput myth in tribal central India'. *Man in India*. 42: 35–80.

Smith, William Robertson [1894] 2002. *Religion of the Semites*. Intr., Robert A. Segal. London: Transaction.

Srinivas, M.N. 1942. *Marriage and Family in Mysore*. Bombay: New Book Company.

————. 1952. *Religion and Society among the Coorgs of South India*. Oxford: Clarendon Press.

————. 1958. 'Hinduism'. *Encyclopaedia Britannica*. 11: 574–7.

————. 1966a. *Social Change in Modern India*. Berkeley: University of California Press.

————. 1966b. 'The study of one's own society'. In Srinivas 1966a.

————. 1967. 'Cohesive role of Sanskritization'. In P. Mason (ed.). *Unity and Diversity: India and Ceylon*. London: Oxford University Press.

————. 1968. See Srinivas and Shah.

————. 1973. 'Itineraries of an Indian social anthropologist'. *International Social Science Journal* 25, 1–2: 129–48.

————. 1974. 'Why I am a Hindu'. *The Illustrated Weekly of India*, 17 Nov.

————. 1976. *The Remembered Village*. New Delhi: Oxford University Press.

————. 1993. 'Towards a new philosophy'. The *Times of India*, 9 July.

Srinivas, M.N. and A.M. Shah. 1968. 'Hinduism'. *The International Encyclopaedia of Social Sciences* 6: 358–66.

Thapar, Romila. 1997. Syndicated Hinduism. In G.D. Sontheimer and H. Kulke (eds). *Hinduism Reconsidered*. New Delhi: Manohar.

Tylor, Edward [1871] 1913. *Primitive Culture*. 2 vols. London: John Murray.

Weber, Max. 1930. *The Protestant Ethic and the Spirit of Capitalism*. T. Parsons (trs.). New York: Scribner.

————. 1948. *From Max Weber: Essays in Sociology*. H.H. Gerth and C.W. Mills (trs.). London: Routledge and Kegan Paul.

————. 1949. *The Methodology of Social Sciences*. E. Shils and H. Finch (trs.). Glencoe, Ill.: The Free Press.

————. 1958. *The Religion of India*. H.H. Gerth and D. Martindale (trs.). Glencoe, Ill: The Free Press.

Weber, Marianne. 1975. *Max Weber: A Biography*. New York: John Wiley.

Winch, Peter. 1958. *The Idea of a Social Science and its Relation to Philosophy*. London: Routledge and Kegan Paul.

Part Four

Cultural Traditions and Conceptual Categories

The last part of the book goes beyond the themes of religion, secularism, and national identity. Drawing upon the notions of tradition and value that inform the discussion in the previous part, the last two chapters broach the issue of cultural/ civilizational comparison. Chapter 12 is a detailed exposition of the comparative method evolved by Louis Dumont for both intra-cultural and inter-civilizational comparisons. A sustained critique is deferred. Beginning with South India, he moved on to North India to elaborate 'hierarchy' (complementary opposition) as a major foundational principle of Indian (Hindu) civilization. Proceeding by the method of 'typification' by contrast, he focused on the ideology of individualism in the West and its national (French, German) variants. For Dumont, civilizational comparison is ultimately successful and valuable if and only if it generates critical self-awareness on both sides. Not only is no culture an absolute other, but one also gets to understand one's own culture more deeply because one gets to know it in new ways by knowing the other. What is latent becomes manifest, whether it is individualism in Hindu society or hierarchy in the Western. It is in this sense that 'the view from afar' (as Lévi-Strauss calls it) is invaluable.

The last chapter of the book is an attempt to delineate the social categories of the 'private' and the 'public' in different cultural settings, including the Indian and the Western. In this respect, the broad terms 'Indian' and 'Western' are themselves problematic because there are intra-tradition variations and historical developments within each setting. The more fine-tuned the contextualization, the richer the yield of insights. The discussion is exploratory and the conclusions are only suggestive; in the format of an essay, they could not be otherwise. The exercise is an affirmation of cultural pluralism, which is, as the readers of this volume will surely discern, one of its author's basic value orientations.

Finally, a comment on perspectives and method. Readers of the book will already have noted an oscillation of perspective between the macro (sociological) and the micro (cultural anthropological). The essays comprising the first two parts of the book address the broad macro level issues of religion, secularism, and identity. In the third part the micro level (everyday life) comes into view without the abandonment of the larger perspective in the discussion of the householder tradition, the phenomenon of death, and the Weberian and Srinivasian approaches to the study of Hinduism. Of the two essays that follow, a combination of perspectives occurs in my exposition of Louis Dumont's method (involve as it did a movement upwards from the local to the inter-civilizational focus) and in my own exploration of the categories of the 'private' and the 'public'. The foundations of my scholarly career were laid in the early 1950s at the University of Lucknow, where sociology, cultural anthropology, and economics were considered complementary rather than separate disciplines. Whether one is regarded as a sociologist or an anthropologist, one is either way committed to comparison. And, from the first chapter to the last, this book is anchored in comparison.

12

Holism and Individualism
*Louis Dumont on India and the West**

Every civilization is carried on the network of a society, and it is
impossible in practice to study a civilization and its society apart
from each other.

Arnold Toynbee
A Study of History: Reconsiderations

The India of caste and *varna* teaches [the West] hierarchy, and this
is no little lesson.

Louis Dumont
'A fundamental problem in the sociology of caste'

Modern civilization has the unique advantage of commanding a
relatively good knowledge of many other civilizations and cultures;
comparison is the fulcrum.

Louis Dumont
From Mandeville to Marx

Louis Dumont's objective in his monumental oeuvre was to treat
the social anthropological (monographic) study of particular
societies and cultures as not only an end in itself but ultimately,

* This is a revised and extended version of an article of the same title
published in the *Journal of Indian Council of Philosophical Research* 19, 1
(2002): 19–44. A much shorter version appeared in Said A. Arjomand and
Edward A. Tiryakian (eds). *Rethinking Civilizational Analysis*, London:
Sage, 2004. I would like to place on record my indebtedness to Professor
Daya Krishna whose probing queries about Louis Dumont's work
motivated me to attempt answers to some of his questions. I also thank
Said Arjomand for his interest in this exercise.

and more importantly, as a means to the sociological (generalized) understanding of the human condition. The key element of his method was comparison. The comparative method in Dumont's hands became a series of productive 'confrontations'—a dialectic—across time and space. I will try in this essay to briefly illustrate his method by outlining the course of Dumont's studies within and across civilizations. Needless to emphasize, I am surer of his position on India than of what he says about the West.

Recalling the early years of his career in the late 1930s as a clerical worker in the French section of the Musée des Arts et Traditions Populaires in Paris, he approvingly mentioned the endeavour of keeping a 'scriptureless humanity...alive in its diversity' (see Galey 1982: 13). An interest in cultural difference was at that early stage established as the foundation stone of the multi-storeyed intellectual edifice that he was to build over the following fifty years. There could hardly have been a better, more productive way of developing this interest in cultural diversity— and indeed to recognize it in the first instance—than to proclaim the comparability of local, regional, and national cultures and eventually of transnational civilizations. The concept of levels was central to this enterprise, each level of observation and study and of comparison being the 'stepping stone' (Dumont 1971: 60) to another. Moreover, along with other structuralists—Dumont came to know Lévi-Strauss's work at the Musée—he came to believe that the deeper the differences between two cultures, the greater the likelihood that comparing them would yield significant understandings of both and of social life generally. Without generalization, the task of comparison is incomplete.

In the original edition of *Homo Hierarchicus* (1967a), in which he presented a sociological model of Indian (Hindu) society—and indeed of Indian civilization generally—to the French reading public, he affirmed that, for his theoretical orientation, he was deeply indebted to the French tradition of sociology (1980: xlv). Within this tradition, the comparative approach had been employed with impressive effect by Émile Durkheim himself in his magnum opus, *The Elementary Forms of the Religious Life* (1915) and by other members of the *Année Sociologique* group. As for Dumont, he acknowledged the influence of Celestin Bouglé (1971), from whom he derived the defining principles of the caste system. It was Marcel Mauss, however, above everybody else, whom Dumont recognized as his mentor.

Dumont actually became Mauss's student in the mid-1930s. Mauss was, of course, a comparativist par excellence and a Sanskritist too (see, for example, Mauss 1970). Specifically and crucially, Dumont responded positively to Mauss's teaching that 'it is through our own culture that we can understand another, and vice versa'. Such a stance implied in the first place 'an assumption about the unity of mankind', but that by itself is rather vague and therefore further entails the 'study of differences' (Dumont 1986e: 189–90). The moot point is how a focus on difference may be prevented from producing absolute separation in effect even when the notion of the unity of mankind insures against such a slide in principle. In short, how do we connect? More about this below.

At the beginning of his anthropological journeys, Dumont also knew of the work of other comparativists such as Georges Dumézil, with whom he discussed his early interest in an Indo-European comparison of dragons (see Galey 1982: 14). This interest curiously took shape during his years as a prisoner of war in the early 1940s. These were by no means wasted years, for Dumont not only improved his knowledge of German by translating three German ethnographic studies of French folk culture into French, but also learnt Sanskrit. After the end of the war (in 1945) he also learnt Tamil and Hindi. Needless to emphasize, his interest in learning languages (he wrote in both French and English) sharpened his comparativist sensibility.

The first major field study in which Dumont engaged, while the learning of Indian languages was in progress, was that of the French folk cult of Tarascon, which he carried out on behalf of the Musée. Published as a monograph, *La Tarasque* (1951), one already sees in it his eye (and ear) for ethnographic detail and his commitment to contextualization and the holistic approach— the local Tarascon seen in relation to Mediterranean Christianity. His exploration of aspects of Indian society and culture, whether primarily based on fieldwork or on textual studies—both sources were drawn upon in complementarity rather than mere juxtaposition—continued and refined this early approach.

* * *

Dumont's cultural and educational background in France had sensitized him to the empirical presence of the individual in society and of the normative value of individualism. His preparatory studies had already readied him to encounter the salience of the group (caste) rather than of the individual in India. This difference was to create problems for the comparison of the two cultures. For a start, there was no escape from caste, and it was a South Indian subcaste, namely the Pramalai Kallar of Tamil Nadu, that he chose to study. The individual here was submerged in the group, and the local group itself was not an autonomous but an embedded entity. To quote Dumont: 'All castes of a given culture area—[such as] the Tamil language area—rest on fundamental common institutions. These institutions must be discovered under individual diversity, and they constitute, along with the caste system itself, the social morphology of the civilization in question' (1986g: 3). The aforementioned task of discovery entailed intra-civilizational comparison.[1]

The scholarly product of two years of intensive fieldwork in South India was a monograph which was completed in 1954 (Dumont 1957a). Like all good ethnography, it was local, but the comparative perspective, as we shall see below, was not absent. The experience of fieldwork had, however, obviously confirmed what Dumont had learnt from Mauss, namely that what the people being observed 'believe and think' is as important as what they are seen to be doing. In other words, what a people do must make sense to them, even if it does not to the observer. It is, therefore, the intellectual obligation of the observing anthropologist to inquire into these configurations of meaning—the internal or first order interpretations of social behaviour—without abandoning his own understanding of the observed social act.

It is obvious that a complex methodological procedure is proposed. An early and seminal statement of the same is found in Dumont's 1955 inaugural lecture at the École Pratique des Hautes Études (6th section), Paris, entitled 'For a sociology of India'. Here Durkheim's teaching is recalled, namely that 'social facts...are at once things and representations', and an adequate method for their understanding is said to be the one evolved by social anthropology, which insists that 'the observer sees things from within (as integrated in the society which he studies) and from without' (1970c: 7). Dumont acknowledged E.E. Evans-Pritchard's insight that the movement from the indigenous interpretation to the anthropological is one of 'translation', but cautioned:

> In this task it is not sufficient to translate indigenous words, for it frequently happens that the ideas which they express are related to each other by more fundamental ideas *even though these are unexpressed*. Fundamental ideas literally 'go without saying' and have no need to be distinct, that is tradition. Only their corollaries are explicit (ibid., emphasis original).

We see here the structuralist distinction between 'latent' and 'manifest' structures, and note the implication that this distinction is itself a relation. In other words, it is imperative that we recognize the fact that several interlinked levels of social facts and their understanding are involved. From the immediately observable level of social behaviour we move to its indigenous (first order) interpretation, and then derive from such interpretations the underlying but unstated assumptions, which may be assumptions about how the really existing things are (ontology) or about how they ought to be (value preferences). And yet the external (non-native) observer may find the observed phenomena elusive (alien) until he constructs his own second order interpretation of them, which is informed by prior cognitive categories derived from his culture and his discipline (social anthropology or comparative sociology). Comparison here thus involves a series of confrontations. Social action confronts and is confronted by ideology; internal understanding is confronted by the external; within the external understanding, the lay is confronted and eventually superseded by the professional, but the latter is not autonomous or unchallenged.

Let me recall here Dumont's formulation of the predicament of the Western anthropologist—the original anthropologist was of course a Westerner—in an insightful 1979 essay (Dumont 1986f). The social scientist, he wrote, is exposed to the ideologies that are prevalent in his society. In the case of the Western social scientist, an absolutely crucial ideology is that of individualism, and this is 'fundamentally opposed ... to the principle of anthropology and all sound or thorough sociology' (ibid.: 204). This principle, according to Dumont, has to be holism: 'a comparative sociology, i.e. a comparative view of any society, is holistic' (ibid.: 213). It follows that the anthropologist (and the sociologist) 'should agree to distinguish between his absolute convictions [normally derived from the "surrounding ideology", for no person invents his own personal ideology] and his specialized [professional] activity' (ibid.: 205). To distinguish between the two points of view—'man thinks by distinctions' (ibid.: 225)—entails comparison and the establishment of a relationship in terms of a grammar of values. In fact, the relationship may be conceptualized in terms of 'hierarchy', which is essentially 'the encompassing of the contrary' (ibid.: 227) and is, therefore, marked by tension.

More precisely, Dumont argues that the elevation of the individual to the status of being the bearer of value in Western society is a 'mental construct' rather than a 'physical phenomenon'—empirically the individual as an agent is of course present everywhere. Consequently, society has come to be seen as an aggregative phenomenon and its sociological study is focused on the 'interaction of individuals' (1970e: 134–5). It is in this manner that the prevalent social ideology encompasses and defines the sociologist's specialized (professional) activity. The social anthropologist's view from 'without' (outside) in relation to the natives' view from 'within', therefore, could constitute an 'impediment to comparison' if the society under study does not entertain an ideological position about the individual similar to or, at least in consonance with, the corresponding ideology of Western society. This indeed is, according to Dumont (and not him alone), true of India.

The organizing principle of Hindu society, Dumont notes, is dharma or social order, which is part and parcel of the universal order: 'in the traditional Indian view there is no separation between man and nature and the human order is realized by conforming to the universal order' (ibid.: 142). And the 'man' of Indian conception is a 'dyadic subject', because interpersonal relationships are conceived 'as internal to reality, as its core'. 'Instead of an indivisibility (the individual), the subject is a totality of opposites, empirically multiple, ontologically one' (ibid.: 141).

Given the conflict between the external and internal points of view on the nature of the 'elementary unit' for the purpose of social anthropological study, is one left with the conclusion that comparison is not possible and that inter-cultural dialogue and understanding are not available to us? Characterizing such a position as solipsistic and an invitation to domination, Dumont

emphatically declares: 'Cultures not only *can* be made to commu-
nicate, they *must*' (1970f: 161). But how? The answer is: 'the two
societies [the Western and the Indian], while so directly opposed
in their ideal[s], in reality may have much in common; there might
well be something of *dharma* in modern society, something of the
Individual in the counterpart' (1970e: 141). The individual as the
bearer of value—as the occupant of a normative role—does find
a place in Hindu (Brahmanical) thought, but as the renouncer.
The argument, as formulated by Dumont, proceeds as follows:
(i) 'the society must submit and entirely conform to the absolute
order'; (ii) 'consequently the temporal, and hence the human, will
be subordinate'; and (iii) 'while there is no room here for the
individual, whoever wants to become one may leave society
proper' (1970d: 59–60). In other words, one ceases to be a member
of a caste or a household. This does not mean, however, that the
renouncer becomes socially irrelevant. From his own point of
view, it is only his own spiritual progress, his freedom from all
social ties—from choice-making in an arena of social obligations—that matters. But from the point of view of the society that
lets him and indeed urges him to leave, he emerges as a critic,
a reformer, and a teacher—indeed a 'creator of values' (ibid.: 46).
And, therefore, 'the secret of Hinduism may be found in the
dialogue between the renouncer and the man-in-the-world' (ibid.:
37; see also Madan 1987).

The individual has been identified in both the Western and the
Indian cultures, but this does not yet mean that comparison has
been rendered unproblematic, or the contrast of the cultures
diminished. A critical difference survives: while in the West the
individual is in the world, in India he is outside it, 'at least in
principle' (1970d: 45). The West too has known the individual-
outside-society, but that is a pre-modern idea. Among 'the first
Christians', as Dumont calls them, the individual as value was
located outside the social and political domains: he was
'outworldly' in contrast to modern 'inworldly' individuals. Drawing
upon his knowledge of the Indian institution of renunciation,
Dumont argues that 'individualism could not possibly have
appeared in another form and developed otherwise from
traditional holism, and that the first centuries of the history of the
Church showed the first lineaments of the accommodation to the
world of that strange creature [the outworldly individual]' (1986c:

51). With the Reformation, which 'picks the fruit matured in the Church's lap' (ibid.: 59), and particularly with Calvin's elaboration of Luther's thesis regarding salvation, the individual, even while seeking religious merit, locates himself within the secular world and also submits to the established political authority. As Dumont puts it: 'The field is absolutely unified. *The individual is now in the world, and the individualist value rules without restriction or limitation.* The inworldly individual is before us' (ibid.: 53, original emphasis).

With the foregoing brief remarks about the comparison of three types of individuals, one Hindu and the other two Christian, and thereby of two civilizations, I have already proceeded from Dumont's methodological premises to his substantive studies— to his comparative sociology. I will now highlight selected conclusions of these studies of aspects of Indian and Western civilizations.

* * *

The Pramalai Kallar are a subcaste. Much that is true of them is true of all Kallar subcastes and some of it is also true of other castes/subcastes of Tamil Nadu that are of the same or comparable ritual and social status. Understanding is here obtained through an inside-out movement. Castes that rank higher or lower in the social hierarchy also share many values, beliefs, and practices with the Pramalai Kallar by virtue of participation in a common regional Tamil culture. Tamils themselves are one of the four major linguistic groups, each numbering millions, that together comprise the Dravidian culture of South India.

A widely shared social organizational feature of the Dravidian South is what used to be called 'consanguineal' or 'cross-cousin marriage' (marriage of a boy/man with his mother's brother's daughter). Intensive fieldwork combined with careful reading of the available ethnography and Lévi-Strauss's seminal work on 'the elementary structures of kinship' (1967), originally published in 1949, enabled Dumont to provide a new interpretation of the preferential form of marriage among the Dravidian peoples. The method was comparison within the region (at the caste/subcaste and local levels) and the substantive conclusion was that the so-called consanguines, or cross-cousins, are properly conceived of as predetermined affines. Under the prevailing regime, marriages are not merely episodic events, but enduring arrangements between wife-giving and wife-receiving lineages. Affinity (the relationship established through marriage) could thus be said to be inherited or transmitted from generation to generation and in principle permanent. Dumont (1957b) proposed therefore that marriage in South India, being of distinctive character from what it is in the West, should be called 'marriage alliance'. The contrast was further stressed later when he wrote that, in the West, 'affinity...merges into consanguinity for the next generation... [and] is *undervalued in relation to it*' (1983: vii, original emphasis).

At the time of the first publication of the relevant monograph (1957b), Dumont stated the conclusion that marriage alliance was 'the fundamental principle of South Indian kinship' (1983: 104). Absence of any reference to the character of marriage in North India was apparently due to the fact that no major studies of the subject based on fieldwork were available, although some Indological studies did exist. His own fieldwork in a North Indian village began only that year and he would not have arrived at any definite conclusions.

Dumont addressed the issue of the North–South comparison only ten years later (Dumont 1966). He then noted that although interkin marriage is not allowed, and the institution of marriage alliance is absent, other evidence is available about the relations between wife-givers and wife-takers (such as an asymmetrical flow of gifts from the former to the latter) to indicate a stress upon affinity that appears to be a pan-Indian phenomenon. This consists, he wrote, 'in the valuation, and in the consequent elaboration and ordering or patterning of affinal relationships. This valuation is, of course, consistent with the caste system insofar as...membership [in a caste] depends upon the [caste] status of both parents, and thus upon marriage' (ibid.: 113). In his discussion of South India, Dumont had earlier pointed out that the principle of alliance was also 'fundamental' in relation to caste, since endogamous marriage was its basis. Hence the conclusion: 'marriage is crucial on both levels of caste and kinship,...it constitutes in a sense their articulation' (1983: 104).

The conception of a comparative sociology and its methods are here complete. North India is first distinguished from South India through inter-regional or intra-civilizational comparison but, in the next move, both north and south are accommodated within a pan-Indian emphasis on marriage and hierarchy, even at the cost of playing down the differences between them. This emphasis serves to bring out the contrast between India and the West (inter-civilizational comparison). Thus, he finds it ironical that the equalitarian Westerners 'practice subordination—the relation between consanguinity and affinity is exactly...a *hierarchical relation*—while South Indian people, who live in a hierarchical society...make a simple, straightforward, symmetrical distinction between them' (1983: vii, emphasis original).

The idea of hierarchy—the encompassing of the contrary—lies at the very core of Dumont's most ambitious work, namely, *Homo Hierarchicus* (1967a, 1970a, 1980). As is well known, given its status as a modern classic, the book is an analysis of the caste system. The presence of castes everywhere, he had earlier said (Dumont 1970c), was a token of the civilizational unity and distinctiveness of India. *Homo Hierarchicus* opens with civilizational contrasts being placed at the very centre of the inquiry. 'The caste system is so different from our own social system in its central ideology', Dumont wrote, 'that the modern reader is doubtless rarely inclined to study it fully'. Moreover, 'the very authors who have devoted books to it have more often tried to explain the system as an anomaly than understanding it as an institution.... More is necessary: the conviction that caste has something to teach us about ourselves' (1980: 1). Put differently, this meant that caste must be taken seriously as a civilizational scheme or mode and not be treated as a product of social 'degeneracy' (see Madan 1999: 478). The question that arises here is why Western observers and thinkers have been so negative about caste. Dumont's answer is that the unquestioning acceptance of equality as an ideal is responsible for this. The bearer of the values of Western civilization knows equality or its binary opposite, inequality. He does not think in terms of hierarchy, which integrates groups rather than separates (classifies) them within the social system. Moreover, he fails to ask 'to what extent [equality] runs contrary to the general tendencies of societies, and hence how far our society is exceptional, and how difficult it is to realize this ideal' (1980: 20).

Ethnocentrism is a universal failing and scholars suffer from it no less than laypersons. The tendency is to make sense of the unfamiliar by comparing it to the familiar. Needless to emphasize, this procedure introduces category assumptions into the interpretation and may distort it. Thus, no less an intellectual than Max Weber conceived of caste, as Dumont notes, as 'a particular kind of status group (German *Stand*) or estate, in the sense of the three estates of the *Ancien Régime* of France' (ibid.: 26). The idea that 'caste is a limiting case of social class' (ibid.) is widespread. What this does is to obscure the fact that, viewed from within Hindu society, religious values are crucial to an understanding of caste in a manner that renders uncritical comparisons with modern (Western) society—and for that matter with the so-called primitive societies—misleading. In Dumont's view, the ethno-centricity of the Western observer makes him introduce considerations of power where religious values are primary; similarly, the interests and perspectives of the individual are introduced where the group and holism prevail.

An authentic effort at understanding Indian civilization through a focus on the fundamental and ubiquitous institution of caste, according to Dumont, must begin with first principles chosen by Indians themselves, but should not stop there. The dialectical method requires that the first principles, or ideology, be confronted by practice, and the view from within be confronted by the view from without. The external (Western or any other) perspective is not eliminated, but relocated in the structure of the argument as a particular possibility that might illumine other such particulars, rather than as a universal tendency. Instead of 'classification', which brings down social and cultural diversities to the level of the lowest common denominator, a more heuristically productive procedure is 'typification', which enlarges rather than narrows the framework of comparison, and produces understanding through contrasts (or controlled comparison) (see Dumont 1967b).

Following a methodological first principle that he himself had earlier enunciated—'a sociology of India lies at the point of confluence of Sociology and Indology' (1970c: 2)—Dumont focused on the notion of ritual purity, which he derived from both the Indological tradition and extant ethnography, as the point of departure for his analysis of the caste system. Others too—notably Bouglé (1971), who derived the hierarchical separation of castes and their interdependence from it—had identified this idea as crucial, but Dumont's handling of it (although indebted to Bouglé's formulation) was innovative. He disowned any interest in the search for causes: 'I do not claim that the opposition between pure and impure is the "foundation" of society except in the intellectual sense of the term: it is by implicit reference to this opposition that the society of castes appears consistent and rational to those who live in it' (1980: 44). The opposition, it must be added, is neither merely difference or simply social gradation: it is hierarchical, that is, the impure is both opposed to as well as included in the pure. Stated as a general principle, hierarchy is *'the principle by which the elements of a whole are ranked in relation to the whole,* it being understood that in the majority of societies it is religion which provides the view of the whole, and that the ranking will thus be religious in nature' (ibid.: 66, original emphasis).

Having grounded himself thus, Dumont proceeded to demonstrate that the various aspects of the caste system—marriage rules, dietary regimes, hereditary occupational roles, etc.—can be derived from the necessary and hierarchical coexistence of ritual purity and its opposite impurity. By his interpretation, caste is different from other forms of social stratification through the 'disjunction' of ritual status and secular (politico-economic) power within the social system. Secular power, although opposed in principle to ritual status, is encompassed by it.

Homo Hierarchicus is neither a historical account of the caste system nor an explanation of it in merely behavioural (interactional) terms. It is rather a logico-deductive 'experiment' (ibid.: xiii) to derive the form (or 'structure') of the 'system' from 'a single true principle' (*à la* Descartes) (ibid.: 43). Since castes exist 'from one end of the country to the other, and nowhere else', pointing to an empirical 'unity of India' (1970c: 4), the underlying ideology—'a system of ideas and values' (1980: 36)—signifies a civilizational perspective. The ideology does not explain everything, although it encompasses the social reality, nor does the observation of actual behaviour reveal everything. A 'residue' remains which can only be explained through a 'confrontation of ideology and observation' (ibid.: 77). Thus, the exclusion of power from the notion of status leaves unexplained empirical evidence of the exercise of authority. To understand it, the principle of hierarchy is held to be applicable but also incomplete: it is 'completed by dominance' (ibid.: 183). But the first principle may not be abandoned through the elevation of economics and politics to a level on par with or above religious values. Doing so would amount to 'a misconstruction of Indian civilization' (ibid.: 388). When such an equation is seen to occur in fact, Dumont maintains, it can only be termed the pretentiousness of power.

Internal comparison is thus built into Dumont's model of the caste system. External comparison also is indicated, in the assertion that castes are found in India and nowhere else, and is required for a complete understanding of the phenomenon. The argument is completed by providing an answer to the crucial question: 'Are there castes among non-Hindus and outside India?' (ibid.: 201–16). So far as communities adhering to other (non-Hindu) religions (notably Indian Muslims and Christians constituting respectively about 13 and 2 per cent of the total population) are concerned, Dumont's contention is that caste is found among them in 'more or less attenuated forms.... A non-Hindu group cannot be regarded as independent of the environment in which it is set, as really constituting a society by itself, however strongly its values push into this direction' (ibid.: 210).[2]

Carrying comparison outside the subcontinent to consider traditional Sri Lankan social organization, Dumont acknowledges the presence of 'all the characteristics of caste' but notes that 'the king has remained the centre both of group religion...and of political and economic life': 'the supremacy of the priest [standing for religious values, notably ritual purity] is an Indian fact which has remained unexportable' (ibid.: 216).

What is of deeper significance in the context of the present essay is the paradigm of inter-civilizational comparison that Dumont presents, of hierarchical Indian society versus egalitarian Western society. As he puts it, the task is to 'set the two types face to face' to show that 'explicit and valorized ideas in the one case' are 'by contrast, subordinate or unrecognized in the other'. Each type comprises the same elements, but the manner of their arrangement is different, even irreconcilable. To wit, hierarchy (separation and interdependence) as a value *is opposed to* equality (in a framework of economics and politics); holism ('society taken as a whole', 'man as society'), to individualism ('man as individual'); subordination of economic and political interests to religious value, to relegation of religion to the private domain (individual life); individualism as renunciation ('individual outside-the-world'), to holism as totalitarianism (ibid.: 232–3). To leave the characterization in the foregoing mutually exclusive form would be 'mechanical': it is important to note that 'the pole of opposition which is not valorized is none the less present, each implies the other and is supported by it'. Thus, 'the tendency to hierarchize still exists [in modern society]', although occasionally in 'ferocious and morbid' forms (for example, as racism) (ibid.: 265). It follows that if the two civilizational perspectives are reversed, hierarchical society will illumine egalitarian society and vice versa.

A significant conclusion (taken from an earlier essay included as an Appendix in *Homo Hierarchicus*) runs as follows:

> Comparative sociology requires concepts which take into account the values that different societies have, so to speak, chosen for themselves. A consequence of this choice of values is that certain aspects of social reality are clearly and consciously elaborated, whilst others are left in the dark. In order to express what a given society does not express, the sociologist…must…have recourse to societies which have expressed those same aspects. A general theory of 'inequality'…must be centred upon those societies which give it a meaning and not upon those which, while presenting certain forms of it, have chosen to disavow it. It must be a theory of hierarchy in its valorized, or simple and direct forms, as well as in its non-valorized or devalorized, or complex, hybrid, covert forms… In so doing one will of course in no way impose upon one society the values of another, but only endeavour to set mutually 'in perspective' the various types of societies. *One will try to see each society in the light not only of itself but of the others* (ibid.: 266, emphasis added).

Having started at home in Europe, Dumont set out on a voyage of discovery to India, only to return home to rediscover Europe in its own varieties of civilizational unity and diversity.

* * *

The holism and hierarchy of traditional Indian society enabled Dumont to problematize the individualism and equality of modern Western society. He queried: 'how and why has this unique development that we call "modern" occurred at all' (1977: 7)? It was, in his judgement, nothing less than a *'revolution of values'*. In all traditional (pre-modern) societies, 'the relations between men' had been 'more highly valued, than the relations between men and things. This primacy is reversed in the modern type of society, in which relations between men are subordinated to relations between men and things' (ibid.: 5). The reversal entailed, in a manner of speaking, the subversion of the whole (society) and its replacement by the parts, namely self-oriented, choice-making, rational individuals operating in compartmentalized and specialized domains of activity.

The paradigm shift had its beginnings in the late eighteenth century (Dumont suggests 1776, the year of publication of Adam Smith's *Wealth of Nations*, as a convenient date), and was consolidated throughout the nineteenth and twentieth centuries. The political and economic domains were separated from the totality through the severance of 'the link between immovable wealth and power over men', and 'movable wealth [became] autonomous'. Symbolizing the dominant role of the economy in society, 'the market and its concomitants' within the political philosophy of 'liberalism' acquired almost a 'sacrosanct role' in society. In Karl Polanyi's well-known formulation, this was indeed 'the great transformation' (ibid.: 6; see Polanyi 1957).

Focusing on the ideology underlying this transformation, Dumont describes its progression through a careful consideration of the views of several social thinkers, notably Francois Quesnay (France). John Locke (England), Bernard de Mandeville (the Netherlands), Adam Smith (Scotland), and Karl Marx (Germany), all makers of the modern ideology. It was Quesnay who introduced the idea of the economic domain as 'a consistent whole', although he believed this holism to be 'the projection on the economic plane of the general conception of the universe as an ordered whole' (Dumont 1977: 41). In other words, Quesnay's was a basically traditional position, notwithstanding the bow to the conditional autonomy of the economic domain. Locke, of course, preceded Quesnay, but he had already gone further in the direction of the separation of economics from politics, illustrated best by his conceptualization of the notion of 'property' within an individualistic framework. 'What is essential is that, with property, something that is exclusively of the individual is made central to a realm of consideration and facts that was governed by holistic, hierarchical considerations' (ibid.: 53). In Locke, Dumont writes, 'Morality and economics provide, in the "law of nature", the basis on which political society should be constructed.' In other words, 'politics as such is reduced to being an adjunct of morality' (ibid.: 54).

With Mandeville a critical transition occurred: value and fact were separated. Elsewhere, Dumont (1986f: 233) maintains that the separation of 'is' and 'ought', which begins with Kant, renders modern thought 'exceptional' and that this distinction should not be thoughtlessly imposed on other cultures. In Mandeville's *Fable of the Bees*, private vices bring about public virtue in the form of activity and prosperity, not by any internal logic but by skilful political management. From a careful examination of the import of the *Fable* and of Mandeville's views on the nature of morals and society, Dumont concludes that Mandeville disjoined hedonism from morality and established 'the primacy of the relation of man to goods over the relations between men—if not in principle, then in the actual life of a large and powerful society' (1977: 81). Material prosperity thus became a self-certified moral end.

Mandeville is important in relation to Adam Smith's curious notion of the 'Invisible Hand', of how in the economic domain the apparently selfish pursuit of particular interests by individuals unwittingly yields the common good (ibid.: 61). Crucial to Dumont's argument is Smith's 'stress on labour as a measure of value' and his 'preference for the definition of value through exchange' (ibid.: 92). The consequence of this orientation is that man is presented as the creator of wealth in relation to the material world. The full potential of value thus created by man is realized through exchange. In sum, 'we have here the elevation of the individual subject, of man as "self-loving" labouring-and-exchanging, who through his toil, his interest, and his gain works for the common good, for the wealth of nations' (ibid.: 97).

In the detailed discussion of Marx that follows, Dumont shows the logical steps by which the 'material conditions of life', already a central idea in Smith and in the burgeoning economic ideology of the West, are given explanatory value by Marx. For him production is *the* human activity par excellence: 'production in the economic sense is used here as the prototype of a much wider category that tends to encompass the whole of human life.

Relations between men are subsumed under a term that properly designates relations to things' (ibid.: 156). As Marx himself put it, 'Religion, family, state, law, morality, science, art, etc. are only *particular* modes of production and fall under its general law' (ibid.: 155). The 'paramountcy' of the economic domain, conceived of as the infrastructure in relation to the other domains, the superstructure, is explicitly asserted. Indeed, 'Marx can be said to have brought economic ideology to its accomplishment' (ibid.: 169). Economics, it will be noted, has become economic ideology and as such is irreversible—it is, in Max Weber's famous phrase, modern man's 'iron cage' (Weber 1930: 181).

From the traditional Indian perspective, this is an inversion of values, for there the moral order (dharma) encompasses the unified politico-economic domain (*artha*): value and fact remain integrated in a holistic configuration. To call it non-modern, instead of traditional, would amount to the illegitimate imposition of the categories of one ideology upon another, a procedure that Dumont rejects.

By the time Dumont completed his exploration of the genesis and triumph of economic ideology, the link between individualism and equality, implied at the commencement of his studies of Western ideology ('Individualism implies both equality *and liberty*', necessitating a distinction between its liberal and socialist versions, 1986a: 76), had begun to recede into the background. But it was really never abandoned even in the face of compelling criticism (see Béteille 1986: 127 and Dumont 1987; see also Parkin 2003: 79–80) and despite his engagement later on with an exceptional case in his last book (Dumont 1994). Further studies were devoted to the elaboration of the idea of individualism (see Dumont 1986a) and its implications for the institution of civil society and the state. In this context, he contrasts organic political theories (Plato's Republic, Hegel's State) to 'mechanical' theories (Locke's social compact). The 'global' (general, 'most common') ideology of individualism, constitutive of Western civilization, having been discussed, he finally focused on the comparison of national cultures. 'It is a fact that modern ideology takes notably different forms in the different languages or nations or, more precisely, in the different subcultures that more or less correspond to these languages and nations' (1986b: 15–16). To stress and illustrate the point, a Franco-German ideological—in fact cultural—contrast was formulated in stark and memorable terms (1986c: 130–1):

> On the French side I am a man by nature and Frenchman by accident.... [T]here is nothing but a void between the individual and the species.... On the German side...I am essentially a German, and I am a man through being a German: man is immediately acknowledged as a social being.... Therefore, while the French were content with juxtaposing nations as so many fragments of mankind, the Germans acknowledging the individuality of each nation, were preoccupied with *ordering* the nations within mankind in relation to their value— or to their might.

To paraphrase the above, French individualism is the general/ universal type and German individualism, the exceptional/particular type.

Dumont's last book, *The German Ideology* (1994), while sustaining the Franco-German contrast—in fact refining it to make room for interaction within the framework of modernity—focuses on the German variant of the modern ideology. In doing so, the method fashioned and employed in the earlier works is strongly reaffirmed as 'the fire of comparison' (ibid.: viii) and restated as follows (ibid.: 216):

> My aim here has been to elucidate an ideological configuration and some of its factual concomitants.... [I]n my view the study of such general representations requires three conditions: (1) they should be identified through comparison; (2) they should be considered in a long-range historical perspective; (3) the analysis should follow a hierarchical method, going from the global level to the local and not the reverse.

It is noteworthy that in India he had proceeded from the local to the global level: an empirical base must of necessity be established first when studying a society from the outside. But this principle is reversed in the study of one's own society (from the inside), the empirical base of which is one's home territory, as it were. In both cases the primacy of the global perspective in principle is sustained.

On the substantive side, Dumont explains that the beginnings of the divergence between the two national cultures are traceable, in significant measure, to the fact that the German version of the

Enlightenment was religious in contrast to the French which was secularist. In the setting of Lutheran Pietism and Reformation, the German variant of individualism emerged as a cultural category par excellence, distanced from the French (Western) variant, in which the socio-political domain was crucial under the influence of the Revolution. But the political category was not absent in the German ideology: the belief that the German state had a vocation to dominate the world, notwithstanding the equality of nations, took care of that. Both the variants were the outcome of the 'interaction' (or dialectic) of a 'world civilization' (universalism) and particular national cultures (ibid.: 36 et passim).

The 'idiosyncratic formula of German ideology' was the combination of 'community holism and self-cultivating individualism' (ibid.: 20). In this context, Dumont presents a detailed and insightful analysis of the ideal of 'self-cultivation' (*Bildung*) expressed through an extraordinary intellectual and artistic blossoming in Germany between 1770 and 1830, which was marked by the growth of community consciousness defined culturally (ibid.: 69–195). A problem that crops up here is that 'self-cultivation' is, by its very nature, an elitist enterprise: individualism is thus productive of inequality in the framework of the German Ideology. Formulations derived contrastively from the Indian studies were not thus always confirmed by subsequent research. But too much should not be made of the German case: as already pointed out, it is exceptional within the Western civilization. Dumont, moreover, warns the readers of his book at the very outset that whatever he has to say about the German ideology is about 'yesterday and before', and disclaims any knowledge about 'the Germans of the present day' (ibid.: 3).

From the methodological point of view, a reference back to Dumont's work on India is in order at this point: he himself stresses the continuity (ibid.: viii). As in the Indian case, the principal concern is with the articulation of ideology, and with the tension between principle and practice (actuality), but the latter is not altogether neglected. The 'preoccupation' with principles is typical of the French intellectual tradition. Thus, the predominant ideology is said to be that of the Left, but the ideological subordinate Right, although 'ideologically impotent, has been empirically powerful in the long run' (ibid.: 209). Dumont's relative lack of interest in the happenings of the present day, whether in

India or in Germany, is an expression of this preoccupation. Not that he does not consider contemporary changes in the caste system: in fact, he provides an insightful analysis in terms of a world of 'relations' and interdependence being replaced by one comprising competitive 'substances' or blocks (1980: 222). But the manner he does so—interestingly as an exercise in comparison between the past and the present—results in a devaluation of change, which is said to be confined to the ideologically subordinate politico-economic domain (ibid.: 228; see also Madan 1994a: 61–71; Madan 1999: 479).

As for the German–French contrast, it has immense philosophical import that can only be noted here. In Dumont's own words, 'How, without contradiction, can we acknowledge the diversity of cultures and at the same time maintain the universal idea of truth-value? I think it can be done by resorting to a...complex model...where truth-value would figure as a "regulative idea", in the Kantian sense' (1994: 34). Such an exercise is not, however, taken up in the book. Indeed, it ends with a rhetorical question that once more and—as it turned out—for the last time underlined Dumont's fascination for the comparative study of ideologies. He did not find it surprising that France and Germany, 'each bound to its idiosyncracy', should stand ideologically in a kind of back-to-back relationship. Not surprising, but certainly 'pathetic', for such a stance has meant that each country 'neutralize[s] its own experience in order to salvage the ideological framework in terms of which...[it] has been wont to think of itself and the world over a great length of time' (ibid.: 235).

* * *

My aim in this essay has been limited to an exposition of Dumont's approach to the study of cultures and civilizations. More precisely, I have concentrated on outlining the scope and strategies of the comparative method at his hands, using his words extensively blended with my glosses and commentary. I have tried to show that Dumont's method was clearly intended to produce results in the form of understandings, in the first place, of particular cultures through an internal or controlled comparison across social space (localities/regions) or across time. The scope of comparison was expanded in the next move to cover the civilizations comprising the local, regional, or national cultures. Throughout the effort was to enlarge and deepen understandings by focusing on distinctions (typification) rather than on common features (classification), deferring the exposition of commonalities to yet another, higher, level (generalization). Comparison of social behavioural patterns was subordinated to, or—one might say—carried out in terms of values and ideas. The data for comparison, whether of social interaction or of ideologies, were derived from ethnographical and historical sources. An evaluation, even a summarized one, of Dumont's substantive conclusions at any level (micro, meso, or macro) is beyond the scope of this essay. Such references to it as occur here are only illustrative, and pertain much more to India and the India–West comparison than to the West and the France–Germany comparison. Limitations of both my competence and space are responsible for this restriction.

There is general agreement among interested scholars about the immense importance of the questions that Dumont posed. As Edmund Leach once put it, they made him one of the most distinguished anthropologists of the twentieth century. The methodology employed and the substantive conclusions arrived at by him have been the subject of a voluminous, vigorous, and fruitful debate over the last fifty years. Critics have perhaps outnumbered supporters. Some of the main points of criticism may be mentioned here to indicate their purport.

(1) It is arguable that the emphasis upon 'value-ideas' characteristic of Dumont's method has led to a relative devaluation of 'interests' as these find expression in everyday life, and a certain distortion of the existent social reality has occurred. In the case of India, it has been complained, the preoccupation with ideology has yielded understandings that are essentially upper caste (Brahmanical) in character: the voices of the oppressed and exploited lower castes are not heard. Similarly, a preoccupation with stability and religious values respectively precludes an accurate understanding of contemporary social change and economic and political forces operative in society. The emphatic exclusion of the concerns of the Germans of today is equally problematic in the context of assessing the continuing relevance of particular 'value-ideas' in Western society. Also, as in the case

of India, internal social differentiation (notably by class) in relation to the affirmation of the dominant ideology is disregarded.

(2) In the contrastive interpretations of the value premises of the Indian and Western civilizations, the necessary relationship of hierarchy and holism is less problematic than the relationship of individualism and equality. The rhetoric of the Revolution in France may well have held both these latter values to be supremely and equally important. Societies characterized by a capitalist economy, itself an expression of individualism (opportunity, enterprise, competition, achievement, etc.), are, however, characterized by class divisions and socio-economic inequalities.

(3) The Dumontian typifications are not only over-schematized, they are also essentialist. If the 'value-ideas' of hierarchy and holism are fundamental in Indian civilization, then it does not exist independent of them. This is indeed what Dumont said about the notion of structure in the context of caste: it exists or does not exist, it does not change (1980: 219). The critics consider such characterizations as a present-day reproduction of the nineteenth century typology of the Occident and the Orient— 'ourselves' versus 'the others'.

(4) In arriving at the India–West contrast, Dumont seemingly endorses another nineteenth-century idea (associated primarily with Hegel and Marx), namely that India 'in the absence of the individual' has a past but 'no history' (1970e: 143). A consequence of this conclusion (it is really an assumption) is that history as a source of data seems to suffice in the case of Europe, but needs ethnography to complement it in India. In the event, a virtually timeless India is compared with the modern West. In the case of Germany, his assertion (noted above) that he knows 'nothing' of the 'present', only of 'yesterday' (1994: 3), does not, however, mean that his reading of German history is any broader than his reading of Indian history (see Llobera 1996).

A discussion of the foregoing and other queries directed at Dumont by his critics has to await another occasion. It is also not necessary to do so for the purpose of this essay. The fact that I consider the Dumontian approach to the study of civilizations a most valuable and novel contribution does not mean that all one has to do is to mechanically borrow his categories and procedures. He invites emulation rather than uncritical imitation. In my own study of the ideologies of secularism and fundamentalism in India

(Madan 1997), I identified 'religious traditions' within the setting of Indian civilization (Hinduism, Islam, Sikhism), and examined them with a view to finding out if they harbour ideas comparable to those of 'secularism' and 'fundamentalism' as these have been formulated in the West in the context of Christianity and modernity. The dualism of the latter, expressed in the dichotomy of the sacred and the profane (or secular), is not exactly echoed by the former. Nor is the passage of cognitive categories from one civilizational matrix to another (anticipated in the hopefulness of the Enlightenment universalism or as a historical inevitability) unproblematic. To say so does not, however, mean that cultural traditions are insulated phenomena and that inter-civilizational communication does not occur. Nor did Dumont think so. To hold otherwise would mean falling into the suffocating trap of cultural solipsism and denying what for an Indian is undeniable, namely, that India has throughout the twentieth century responded creatively, if not always thoughtfully and successfully, to the call of tradition, as well as the invitation of modernity.

To conclude: it is from the comparison of the modern and the non-modern that the vision and possibility of a common civilization takes shape. Its character could, however, come as a surprise to the hegemonic West. 'Without prejudicing the originality which one would like each culture to retain', Dumont writes (1986a: 209), *'it is clear that the non-modern cultures are going to weigh more and more heavily in the making of the common civilization of the world'* (emphasis added; also see Dumont 1975: 159). The point of departure is a unity (a common humanity); then the focus shifts to differences, primarily cultural but societal also; and finally it is envisaged that a unity of a higher (cognitive) level will be constituted by 'uniting through differences' (1986a: 233). This is the essence of Dumont's method as I understand it.

NOTES

1. Why did Dumont decide to go to South India instead of North India? He has clarified that, before he set sail for India, he believed that it was the encounter of the Aryan-speaking people of the north with the southern Dravidians (again a linguistic category) that had been responsible for the genesis of post-Vedic Hinduism and the socio-cultural configuration of classical India: a subject of considerable interest in the intellectual circles of France, Germany, and Britain.

More immediately, the principal promoter of Dumont's fieldwork in India was the Indologist Louis Renou (see Galey 1982: 14). In later years Dumont considered these early assumptions about Indian cultural history 'primitive' and excessively 'culturological', and blamed the state of scholarly opinion of the times for them. Moreover, studies of Dravidian culture were less common as compared to the Aryan, and it seemed a good idea to choose a non-Brahman caste—North India was believed to be the *locus classicus* of the Brahmans—as the point of entry into this under-explored domain (see Madan 1999: 476). Underlying the choices that were made, a consistently comparative perspective (Aryans compared to Dravidians, North India to South India, Brahman castes to non-Brahmans) is noticeable.

2. For other conceptualizations of castes or caste analogues among Muslims, see, e.g., Ahmad 1978 and Madan 1994b.

REFERENCES

Ahmad, Imtiaz (ed.). 1978. *Caste and Stratification among the Muslims in India*. New Delhi: Manohar.

Béteille, André. 1986. 'Individualism and equality'. *Current Anthropology* 27, 2: 121–34.

Bouglé, Celistin. 1971. *On the Caste System*. Cambridge: Cambridge University Press.

Dumont, Louis. 1951. *La Tarasque: essai de description d'un fait local d'un point de vue ethnographique*. Paris: Gallimard.

———. 1957a. *Une Sous-Caste de l'Inde du Sud. Organisation Sociale et Religion des Pramalai Kallar*. Paris/The Hague: Mouton.

———. 1957b. *Hierarchy and Marriage Alliance in South Indian Kinship*. London: Royal Anthropological Institute.

———. 1966. Marriage in India. The present state of the question. Part III: North India in relation to South India. *Contributions to Indian Sociology* 9: 90–114.

———. 1967a. *Homo Hierarchicus: Essai sur le systeme des castes*. Paris: Gallimard.

———. 1967b. 'Caste: A phenomenon of social structure or as an aspect of Indian culture?' In A.de Rueck and J. Knight (eds). *Caste and Race: Comparative Approaches*. London: J. and A. Churchill, pp. 28–38.

———. 1970a. *Homo Hierarchicus: The Caste System and its Implications*. Chicago: University of Chicago Press.

———. 1970b. *Religion, Politics and History in India*. Paris/The Hague: Mouton.

———. 1970c. 'For a sociology of India', in 1970b: 2–18.

Dumont, Louis. 1970d. 'World renunciation in Indian religions', in 1970b: 33–60.

————. 1970e. 'The individual as an impediment to sociological comparison', in 1970b: 133–50.

————. 1970f. 'A fundamental problem in the sociology of caste', in 1970b: 152–65.

————. 1971. 'On putative hierarchy and some allergies to it', *Contributions to Indian Sociology* 5: 58–78.

————. 1975. 'On the comparative understanding of non-modern civilizations'. *Daedalus* 104, 2: 153–72.

————. 1977. *From Mandeville to Marx: The Genesis and Triumph of Economic Ideology*. Chicago: University of Chicago Press.

————. 1980. *Homo Hierarchicus: The Caste System and its Implications*. Complete English Edition. Chicago: University of Chicago Press.

————. 1983. *Affinity as a Value: Marriage Alliance in South India with Comparative Essays on Australia*. Chicago: University of Chicago Press.

————. 1986a. *Essays on Individualism: Modern Ideology in Anthropological Perspective*. Chicago: University of Chicago Press.

————. 1986b. 'Introduction', in 1986a: 1–19.

————. 1986c. 'On modern ideology. Genesis, I: The Christian beginnings: From the outwardly individual to the individual in the world', in 1986a: 23–59.

————. 1986d. 'On modern ideology. A national variant', in 1986a: 113–32.

————. 1986e. 'Marcel Mauss: A science in process of becoming', in 1986a: 183–201.

————. 1986f. 'The anthropological community and ideology', in 1986a: 202–33.

————. 1986g. *A South Indian Subcaste: Social Organization and Religion of the Pramalai Kallar*. New Delhi: Oxford University Press.

————. 1987. 'On individualism and equality'. *Current Anthropology* 28, 5: 669–72.

————. 1994. *The German Ideology: From France to Germany and Back*. Chicago: University of Chicago Press.

Durkheim, Émile 1915. *The Elementary Forms of the Religious Life*. New York: Macmillan.

Galey, Jean-Claude 1982. 'A conversation with Louis Dumont'. In T.N. Madan (ed.). *Way of Life: King, Householder, Renouncer: Essays in Honour of Louis Dumont*. New Delhi: Vikas.

Lévi-Strauss, Claude 1967. *The Elementary Structures of Kinship*. Boston: Beacon Press.

Llobera, Joseph R. 1996. 'The French ideology: Louis Dumont and the German conception of the nation'. *Nations and Nationalism* 2, 2: 193–211.

Madan, T.N. 1987. *Non-renunciation: Themes and Interpretations of Hindu Culture*. New Delhi: Oxford University Press.

————. 1994a. *Pathways: Approaches to the Study of Indian Society*. New Delhi: Oxford University Press.

————. 1994b. 'The construction of social identities in rural Kashmir'. In T.N. Madan, *Pathways: Approaches to the Study of Indian Society*. New Delhi: Oxford University Press.

————. 1997. *Modern Myths, Locked Minds: Secularism and Fundamentalism in India*. New Delhi: Oxford University Press.

————. 1999. 'Louis Dumont: A memoir'. *Contributions to Indian Sociology* 33 (3): 473–501.

Mauss, Marcel. 1970. *The Gift: Forms and Functions of Exchange in Archaic Societies*. London: Cohen and West.

Parkin, Robert. 2003. *Louis Dumont and Hierarchical Opposition*. New York: Berghahn.

Polanyi, Karl 1957. *The Great Transformation*. Boston: Beacon Press.

Toynbee, Arnold 1961. *A Study of History*, volume xii, *Reconsiderations*. London: Oxford University Press.

Weber, Max. 1930. *The Protestant Ethic and the Spirit of Capitalism*. London: Allen and Unwin.

Annex to Chapter 12

Toynbee, Kroeber, Weber

A quotation from the concluding volume of Arnold Toynbee's *A Study of History* occurs first among the epigraphs of this essay. I chose it, not because there is any significant similarity between Toynbee's and Dumont's approaches, but primarily because, as a sociologist, I consider it an imperative point of departure. Moreover, my interest in the comparative study of civilizations was awakened when I discovered the first six volumes of Toynbee's *History* during my days of studentship at the University of Lucknow in the early 1950s.

As a matter of fact, Toynbee's and Dumont's approaches have hardly anything in common that is significant. In spite of the claims to be a historian with a scientific approach, Toynbee was more a religious visionary and a prophet than a historian. His method was eclectic and, it seems to me, inspirational, illustrating through selective evidence conclusions promulgated at the very beginning of the project, rather than arrived at the end of it from a critical examination of the available data. It is interesting to note here that at least one of Dumont's critics maintains that 'his ideas are not the result of the comparison, but rather the other way round' (Llobera 1996: 203). Such a criticism, I think, may be more convincingly directed at Toynbee than at Dumont. He was a system builder receptive to criticism in respect of points of detail rather than the essentials of his *a priori* argument. (Volumes VII to X do mark a major shift, however. See Geyl 1962.) But there was great erudition in the books combined with brilliance of style, a fascination for literary classics, and vast knowledge of anthropology, all of which made for instructive and pleasurable reading. Whatever Toynbee wrote about the Indic civilization—and this was considerable—served only to illustrate the general pattern of 'genesis', 'growth', 'breakdown', etc., and did not probe deep into the sociological character of Hinduism or Buddhism. In many ways, however, my prior acquaintance with Toynbee's work prepared me for my encounter with and appreciation of Dumont's contributions, although I have found no reference to it in them.

* * *

If the comparison of civilizations is the subject, and considering that Dumont was a cultural-social anthropologist, it may well be asked, as indeed the distinguished philosopher Daya Krishna has (in a personal communication), 'What about Alfred Kroeber?' Some similarities with Dumont (and of course Toynbee; see Sorokin 1952) are at once apparent. He too began locally (all good ethnography is local), among the Zuni Indians studying kinship and clanship among them. He spread his inquiries wider in course of fieldwork time to write about the cultural and natural areas of native north America. He engaged in ethnographic and archaeological fieldwork in the Philippines and Peru respectively. For our present concern, Kroeber's magnum opus is *Configurations of Culture Growth* (1944).

The focus of *Configurations* is what Kroeber called 'high cultures', how these change and grow, and the role 'creative geniuses' play in this process. This reads very much like Toynbee with his concepts of 'civilization' and 'creative minority'. Also, he too conceptualizes high cultures in terms of beginnings, developments, peaks, declines, and freezes (his terms). It should be noted that Kroeber completed his book in 1939, by when the first three volumes of Toynbee's *Study* had been available for some years.

In the specific and, for us, the most immediate context of India, Kroeber and Dumont are poles apart in terms of principal interest, method, and conclusions. Kroeber did write about caste (see Kroeber 1930), but not with much insight, defining caste as a special form (closed) of social class. This was the very approach (of seeing institutions everywhere in terms of comparable Western institutions) that Dumont was to repudiate. In *Configurations*, Kroeber is primarily concerned with the intellectual and artistic aspects of creativity, but also with its material and practical dimensions. Alongside the Indian, he considered what he called the Greek, Christian, and Occidental high cultures as also the Arab-Muslim and the Chinese.

Apart from the vagueness of his key concepts (most notably 'high-value culture pattern') and an explicit Eurocentric bias, Kroeber's knowledge of India was derived entirely from secondary sources in Western languages. His conclusions often are highly debatable if not bizarre. To give but one example: 'Since 1200, little of a very high cultural order has been accomplished in India' (1944: 648). And whatever was achieved earlier was either borrowed (mathematics from the Greeks) or inferior to European achievements (Gupta art 'unrelieved by Mediterranean strains') (ibid.: 179, 257, et passim). Kroeber's contribution lay in bringing literate cultures, or civilizations, within the purview of anthropological inquiry.

Much later contributions by American anthropologists to the development of appropriate concepts and methods for the study of Hindu culture, which have mainly come out of the University of Chicago, most notably from McKim Marriott and his students (see Marriott 1990), owe a great deal to Dumont's warning against category assumptions and his emphasis upon the importance of native categories of thought. Like Dumont's own work, these studies are based on solid ethnography and an acquaintance with the textual tradition. They have, however, gone far beyond his theoretical framework and approach to cast a suspicious eye on his own Western assumptions and rationalist/intellectualist methodology. Whether these contributions carry the comparison of civilizations forward to a higher level of abstraction by focusing on difference rather than similarity (for example, Hindu thought is said to lack the notion of the 'bounded individual' and, instead, elaborates the idea of the 'permeable *dividual*'), or postpone it to a future time when the pretensions of Western social science will have been corrected, is a subject of current debate in Indianist studies, and obviously beyond the scope of the present essay (Madan 1994: 85–107).

* * *

It would surely be more worthwhile in the context of the present discussion to attempt a comparison of the methodologies of Dumont and Max Weber for the study of civilizations, but that is a major undertaking in itself and would extend this discussion beyond reasonable limits. I will confine myself, therefore, to a few preliminary observations of a general nature to indicate the scope of such an exercise. The methodologies of both Dumont and Weber (1930, 1958) are characterized by a deep interest in the role of ideas and values in the making of society at the macro level as also of particular social phenomena such as caste and capitalism. More specifically, both scholars recognize the importance of the concerns and commitments of the ideologically valorized individual in the making and maintenance of modern Western civilization as of its Christian underpinnings. In acknowledgement of Weber's insights into this issue, Dumont noted at the very beginning of *Homo Hierarchicus* that Weber, although dissatisfied with the notion of individualism, considered it a promising subject for exploration (1980: 8).

As for the study of caste, Dumont draws attention (as already noted) to Weber's distinction between class (unequal distribution of power) and status group (gradation of honour and prestige reflected in social intercourse), and his characterization of caste as 'a particular kind of status group' (closed) or 'estate in the sense of the three estates of the *Ancien Regime* in France' (ibid.: 26, 241, 248). He also observes that this analytical distinction has found wide acceptance in social science literature (ibid.: 248). We have mentioned above its adoption by Kroeber: Dumont too notes this (ibid.: 26 et passim).

But Dumont's own approach (which is, as noted earlier, typificatory rather than classificatory, focusing on the richness of differences between cultures rather than exclusively on their common factors or features), could hardly be expected to be at ease with the Weberian formulation. Dumont considered Weber's study of caste and its underlying religious values to be of great importance, but he bypassed it. In his studies of Western civilization also, Dumont hardly makes any use of Weber's work. Why should this be so? One reason, and a crucial one, would be that, in terms of Dumont's approach to the comparison of civilizations, Weber did not really ask what India could teach Europe about itself. If he had done so, he might have seen differently than he did the implications of the self-conscious individual—creating meanings, bestowing significances, and sharing them—at the very centre of Western society. Weber's methodological *individualism* cannot but be an obstacle from the perspective of the methodological *holism* favoured by Dumont. For the latter, parts (individuals) derive their significance from the whole (society), which is the matrix of value.

Another major methodological tool in the making of Weber's project of inter-civilizational comparison was the concept of 'ideal type' (Weber 1949: 95ff.). Its scope and limitations have been the subject of extensive discussion in sociological literature. Suffice it to note here, ideal types are heuristic categories abstracted from social phenomena. They are employed to mediate between the complexity of historical/sociocultural reality and its interpretations and to valorize the internal logic or rationality of aspects of social life by simplifying its structure. In other words, ideal types are neither mirror images nor preferred (ideal) versions of social reality, but instruments of meaningful ordering of data and their analysis in order to render the reality intelligible. Within the setting of the processes of rationalization that he considered typical of modern European history, Weber discussed the emergence of various economic and political institutions. Thus, after establishing an internal relationship between the Christian (Calvinist) idea of 'calling' and the 'spirit' of capitalism (Weber 1930), he undertook explorations of the relationship of religion, economy, and society in India, China, and ancient Palestine. The initial focus of his study of Hinduism (Weber 1958) was on how caste, the characteristic social institution of Hindu society, and the related Brahmanical ideas of karma (retribution) and *samsāra* (reincarnation) had produced a stern fatalism ('the most consistent theodicy ever produced by history', ibid.: 121) and a concomitant unchanging socio-economic organization. Karma and *samsāra* acquire their significance in the context of Weber's emphasis on selfhood and his preoccupation with human fate: they, alongside the notion of caste dharma, are the key to the 'spirit' of the caste system. (See Chapter 11 above for a more detailed discussion.)

Religious values are also of crucial importance in Dumont's paradigm of caste, but he steers clear of the ultramundane metaphysical notions of karma and *samsāra*, and does not at all engage with the question of theodicy that lies at the core of Weber's sociology of religion. Dumont is interested not in religion as a differentiated domain but in society— in religious ideas as determinants (not necessarily exclusive) of inter-group relations and, at a higher level of abstraction, in relations between relations. He thus focuses, as some others (S.V. Ketkar, M.N. Srinivas) had done earlier, on ritual purity/pollution, but Weber does not consider these notions. Weber cites Upanishadic (Vedantic) literature fairly extensively, and discusses at some length the 'unsurpassed' inner-worldly ethic of the *Bhagavadgītā*, according to which all ethical and soteriological commandments are relativized (1958: 190). In this, as I have noted earlier (in Chapter 11), he is mistaken, but that is another matter. Dumont leaves these texts alone except in a solitary reference to Upanishadic speculations (1980: 186). For him the most relevant classical text is the worldly *Manusmriti* (over a dozen references), which Weber passingly mentions in a couple of footnotes. Nor is Dumont interested in the cosmological premises of the Hindu social order beyond the concept of dharma. To reiterate, what matters to him is the logic of social relations.

Dumont pays a rich tribute to Weber's study of Hinduism, calling it 'the richest and most fine-drawn comparison between the Western and the Hindu universe' (ibid.: 30), and praises the 'brilliant historical reconstructions'—for example, in respect of the category of the Vaishyas— but is sceptical of the manner in which Weber erects 'hypotheses' on the available data, which gives them a rather 'fictitious' character. The basic fault of Weber's approach in Dumont's judgement is that these data are interpreted 'within the framework of general ideas taken from the West' (ibid.: 394), vitiating the objective of genuine comparison. In view of the foregoing, any hasty conclusion that the interest of Dumont and of Weber in the role of ideas in social and cultural histories may be expected to produce convergences in their comparative sociologies is unwarranted.

The contrast between the Weberian and Dumontian approaches to civilizational comparison is perhaps best illustrated by recalling their respective visions of the future. Taking his stand as a 'product' (legatee) of 'modern European civilization', Weber writes at the very outset of his Protestant ethic book that 'cultural phenomena' that have appeared in Western civilization alone may yet be seen to be 'in a line of development having *universal* significance and value' (Weber 1930: 13) or, as an Indian sociologist prefers to translate the concluding phrase, '*universal* significance and validity' (Munshi 2003: 53). I take this to mean that the historical process of rationalization that started in the West, but not elsewhere, including India, because of the peculiarities of culture and social structure, foretold the future course of events everywhere.

Dumont thought differently. Writing of the comparative study of modern and non-modern civilizations half a century after Weber's death, he observed (1975: 159):

> The interaction between civilizations increases powerfully every day, and it should now be obvious to all that a future state of the common civilization of the world cannot be imagined as a mere extrapolation from our own 'development', but rather as a point of convergence of different evolutions resulting from the interaction between various traditions.

Even such a cursory description of the two approaches as outlined above, and in the light of what has been written in the main text of this essay, Dumont's approach to the Europe–India comparison is both methodologically and substantively different from Weber's. Underlying his analysis is the objective of establishing significant relationships: drawing upon what is manifest (above the level of consciousness) in one society to 'decipher' what is latent in the other (1980: 254). As Dumont himself puts it, comparison between the two civilizations should not focus on absolute (mutually exclusive) opposition but on '*difference in the distribution and emphasis of the* [constituent] *parts*' (ibid.: 186, original emphasis). Hence the search for 'holism' and 'hierarchy' in the West, and for 'individualism' and 'egalitarianism' in India.

References

Dumont, Louis. 1975. 'On the comparative understanding of non-modern civilizations'. *Daedalus* 104, 2: 153–72.

———. 1980. *Homo Hierarchicus: The Caste System and its Implications*. Chicago: University of Chicago Press.

Geyl, Peter. 1962. *Debates with Historians*. London: Fontana.

Kroeber, A.L. 1930. 'Caste'. *Encyclopaedia of Social Sciences*, III: 254b–257a.

———. 1944. *Configurations of Culture Growth*. Berkeley: University of California Press.

Llobera, Joseph R. 1996. 'The French ideology: Louis Dumont and the German conception of nation'. *Nations and Nationalism* 2, 2: 193–211.

Madan, T.N. 1994. *Pathways: Approaches to the Study of Indian Society*. New Delhi: Oxford University Press.

Marriott, McKim (ed.). 1990. *India through Hindu Categories*, New Delhi: Sage.

Munshi, Surendra. 2003. 'Revisiting Max Weber'. Hartmut Lehman and Jean Martin Ouedrago (eds). *Max Webers Religionssoziologie in Interkultureller Perspective*. Goettingen: Vandenhoeck & Ruprecht, pp. 53–68.

Sorokin, Pitrim. 1952. *Social Philosophies of an Age of Crisis*. London: A.&C. Black.

Toynbee, Arnold. 1961. *A Study of History*, Vol. XII, *Reconsiderations*. London: Oxford University Press.

Weber, Max. 1930. *The Protestant Ethic and the Spirit of Capitalism*. Talcott Parsons (trs.). London: Allen & Unwin.

——. 1949. *The Methodology of the Social Sciences*. Edward Shils and Henry Finch (trs.). Glencoe, Ill: The Free Press.

——. 1958. *The Religion of India*. H.H. Gerth and Don Martindale (trs.). Glencoe, Ill: The Free Press.

13

The Private and the Public
Considerations of Cultural Context*

Concepts lead us to make investigations; [they] are the expression of our interest, and direct our interest.

Wittgenstein
Philosophical Investigations

You can translate a word by a word, but behind the word is an idea, the thing which the word denotes, and this idea you cannot translate, if it does not exist among the people in whose language you are translating.

Bankimchandra Chattopadhyay
Bankim Rachanābalī

* * *

Private a. & *n.* 1. (Of person) not holding public office or official position. 2. kept or removed from public knowledge or observation. 3. not open to public. 4. one's own. 5. confidential. 6. (Of place) retired, secluded.

* This is a revised and expanded version of an article published earlier (Madan 2003). The present version was presented as the First T.G. Vaidyanathan Memorial Lecture at Bangalore in August 2003.

I am grateful to Gurpreet Mahajan, Helmut Reifeld, and Margrit Pernau for their encouragement. Sudhir Chandra put me in his debt by reading and correcting the first draft. I would also like to place on record my deep appreciation of Lakshmi Kumar's invitation to me to join in paying tributes to the memory of Vaidyanathan. None of them, nor indeed the authors cited here, are of course responsible for my formulations and conclusions.

Public a. & n. 1. *a.* of or concerning people as a whole. 2. done by or for, representing, the people. 3. open to or shared by all the people. 4. open to general observation, done or existing in public. 5. of or engaged in the affairs or service of the people. 6. *n.* the community in general.

The Concise Oxford Dictionary

WORDS AND IDEAS

Conceptual categories are by definition context-sensitive, the context being an intellectual tradition or, more broadly, a cultural tradition. This is particularly true of *clinical* concepts, generated from the effort to make sense of the flow of everyday life in a particular place at a particular time, rather than of *theoretical* constructs arrived at deductively. Concepts of either type can creatively serve as cues in the exploration of social life across cultural boundaries so long as one is careful to avoid uncritical category assumptions or premature generalizations. Such transfers of ideas from one tradition to another are problematic as satisfactory translations may not be easy to achieve for the reason identified by Bankimchandra Chattopadhyay (see the first epigraph above) and others; but they need not be abandoned altogether either. The procedure has its uses if handled with care.

The foregoing remarks are offered here to introduce the following discussion of the social categories 'private' and 'public' derived from the Western intellectual tradition. They respectively represent not only social institutions (for example, the family and the state), or entities (for example, the individual and the crowd), but may also denote a relationship of mutual implication among them as binary opposites. In other words, each category *usually* acquires its full significance in contradistinction to the other, and does not exist by itself or make sense on its own. Needless to emphasize, contradistinction is a particular kind of relationship, not its absence.

The opposition between the 'private' and the 'public' in Western thought can be (like so much else) traced back to the Greeks. For Aristotle, the domestic domain (*oikos*), where the will of the head of the household held sway, existed in contrast to the political domain (*polis*), where the collective judgement of the citizenry (a restricted category) prevailed. 'The rule of a household is monarchy, for every household is under one head, whereas constitutional rule is a government of freemen and equals' (see Book I, Chapters 3 and 7 of *Politics*). This contrast may not be pushed too far, however, for it is virtually absent in Aristotelian ethics, in which the balancing of the demands of public duties and personal preferences—of manners and morals—is the ideal.[1]

Onward in time, the social teachings of the Christian (Roman Catholic) Church stressed universal love and compassion and the ecclesiastical unity of civilization (the universal Church). In the gospel according to John we read: 'A new commandment I give to you, that you love one another; even as I have loved you, that you also will love one another' (John 13: 34). And in Matthew (10.37) we have an elaboration: 'He that loveth his father or mother more than me is not worthy of me; and he that loveth his son or daughter more than me is not worthy of me.' Such biblical exhortations not only blurred the distinction between 'self' and 'neighbour', but actually privileged the broad ties of the community of faith over the narrow bonds of the family. Generally, the Church did not interfere with the existing social conditions, but considered it imperative to 'transform' the structure of family relations since it was seen as a possible site of resistance (see Troeltsch 1981: 129–32). Altogether, the dichotomy of the categories under discussion had an uncertain passage during the Middle Ages until it gained prominence in the context of the Reformation in the sixteenth century, with the contrast between the privacy of the individual Christian's quest for salvation and the externality of the Church as a public institution. We will return to this theme below.

Moving from religious to secular thought, we find Machiavelli, early in the sixteenth century, maintain with typical brevity and firmness that the values of private morality, given their absolute character and lack of concern for consequences, can hardly be a guide to public conduct, which must needs be expedient and consequentialist in orientation. The point was not which was better—each was right in its own context—but that the two were incompatible. While cruelty, deceit, and falsehood in the private sphere were reprehensible, they were sometimes necessary in the relations between the rulers and the ruled and between states. Thus, Machiavelli advised that 'a ruler who wishes to maintain his power must be prepared to act immorally when this becomes necessary;' and that 'there is nothing that is so self-consuming as generosity: the more you practice it, the less you will be able to practise it;' and so on (Machiavelli 1988: 55, 59).

Subsequently, in the seventeenth century, at the dawn of modernity in the West, the Enlightenment *philosophes* exalted the empire of human reason, and derivatively the objectivity of collective will (public opinion), placing it on a higher plane than the domain of emotions centred in the family. Kant had opened the way with his call for 'the public use of one's reason such as that of a public scholar before the reading public'; this was contrasted with 'private use' in circumscribed civil posts or offices, to conclude, in his famous essay 'What is Enlightenment?', that public use 'alone can bring about enlightenment among men' (Kant 1991). Later, Hegel postulated a qualified conceptual opposition between the family (the domain of privacy in the present discussion), on the one hand, and the nation (the ultimate public domain), on the other. This was done in terms of gradations of the ethical principle which Hegel considered 'intrinsically universal': 'as the *immediate* being of the ethical order, [the family] stands over against the order which shapes and maintains itself by working for the universal'. The individual as a family member is at best 'only an unreal impotent shadow' compared to the citizen, 'because it is only as a citizen that he is actual and substantial' (Hegel 1977: 268–70).

Marx's identification of class conflict as the engine of societal development bestowed a unique significance on the public arena, relegating the domain of kinship to the determined epiphenomenal superstructure. The relations of production that obviously spill over into extra-domestic space in all but the most primitive societies were, it was argued, the determining forces of social formations. In the Marxist utopia, following the abolition of private property, the family would be ultimately shorn of its social (public) relevance and retreat into the innermost recesses of privacy.

Around the middle of the nineteenth century, John Stuart Mill, liberal political philosopher and contemporary of Karl Marx, while discussing 'the limits of the authority of society over the individual' (*On Liberty*, chapter 4), made a 'distinction' that, he warned, 'many persons [would refuse] to admit', between the part of a person's life which concerns only himself and that which concerns others, particularly when his actions could cause 'damage' to others (whether 'an individual' or 'the public'). The former (private) domain, Mill argued, should be exempt from the constraints of public opinion; but the situations in which others are implicated in one's actions should be 'taken out of the province of liberty and placed in that of morality or law'. Mill's search, as is well known, was for the right balance between the rights of the individual (the private domain) and the power of the state.

The foregoing distinction made an emphatic entry into nascent sociological theory soon afterwards in the work of Ferdinand Tönnies. He wrote of, on the one hand, 'home life' at the very core of the community (*Gemeinschaft*), with its underlying values of free will, sharing and organic unity and, on the other, of the association (*Gesellschaft*) and the state, where enlightened public opinion acts as the cement of social life and as a basis of 'what laws the state will decree or maintain' (Tönnies 1955: 60–74, 255–7, et passim). Echoes of the Aristotelian categorization are all too audible. A hundred years on, Edmund Leach spoke of the isolation of 'the domestic household' in English society, its 'narrow privacy and tawdry secrets', its fall from grace as 'the basis of the good society', and indeed its transformation into 'the source of all our discontents' (1967: 44).

More recently, Jürgen Habermas (1991) in his masterfully written, multi-dimensional study of the emergence of a bourgeois public sphere in the West in the setting of a market economy, has discussed its 'fundamental separation' from the private sphere. This was much more than merely the 'disengagement of elements of social reproduction and political power, which…[earlier] were welded together' (ibid.: 141). As a defining feature of modern society, the liberal public sphere—where public opinion against the ruling powers is shaped—stands out (ibid.: 27). One of Habermas's major concerns in this study was whether we can today reinvent the public sphere which has undergone a social-structural transformation—but that must not detain us here. Suffice to reiterate that, the antinomy of the social categories of the private and the public has for well over a century enjoyed paradigmatic status in social theory, although the values attached to each have changed with time, reflecting mostly changes within Western society. As for the philosophical roots of the dichotomy of the public and the private, these have, as hinted above, a long history, although it has not been a simple straightforward story.

A comparative perspective reveals, however, that these or similar social categories may or may not be present in non-Western societies and, if they are, their mutual relationship may be of a different kind than that characteristic of Western society. It follows that the manner in which they are seen to operate in particular arenas, such as culture or politics, or contexts, such as ritual performances or democratic citizenship, varies from case to case. In what follows, I explore some of these variations and, at the same time, suggest some patterns among them to overcome the familiar phenomenon of ethnographic dazzle.

BRINGING INDIA INTO CONSIDERATION

As a first and rather simplistic illustration of the differences of connotation of the terms under consideration, we may consider dictionary meanings. The *Chambers English–Hindi Dictionary* (Awasthi and Awasthi 1985) renders 'private' as *ashāskīya* (non-governmental), *asārvajanika* (non-collective), *nijī* (personal), *vyaktigata* (individual), *gopnīya* (secret), and so on. In contrast, 'public' connotes *shāskīya* (governmental), *sāmūhika* (collective), *prakata* (explicit), etc. Some of these terms (such as *nijī* or *prakata*) appear to be original words in Hindi but others (notably *ashāskīya* or *asārvajanika*) may well be lexical fabrications in the setting of cultural and linguistic contact. Examination of Hindi literary texts suggests that the English terms have significations—in Trilling's words 'a culture's hum and buzz of implication' (1951: 206)—that literal translation fails to capture. This obviously is the reason why many Hindi litterateurs reproduce phonetically the original English words 'private' and 'public' in their compositions: thereby they represent sensibilities that are a product of inter-linguistic communication and cultural hybridization.

Let me illustrate the foregoing point. In an insightful address on the novel in comparative perspective, the distinguished Hindi prose writer Nirmal Verma (2000) observes that it was inside a nineteenth-century preserved house in Bergen (Norway) that he had the inspiration (*ilhām*, 'revelation') to conclude that it must have been inside such homes that the European novel had its birth. Contrasting the openness and wholeness of the epic poem to the enclosed and fragmentary character of the novel, he dwells upon 'privacy'—the English word is written in Nagri script—and its correlate, the individual, in their interrelatedness—'*vyakti kī praivasy*', the individual's privacy (Verma 2000: 60)—as the critical condition for the genesis of the novel. He conceptually links the epic to relatively open spaces and collectivities, such as audience halls, battlefields and domestic compounds, and employs *sārvajanik* as the generic Hindi term for them, but apparently does not feel the need to use the English word 'public'.

More to the point, Verma denies the contradistinction of the private and individual, on the one hand, and the open and collective, on the other, in the context of the novel in the non-Western world. In it the private and the collective are not 'separate' but 'mirror images' of each other. The novel here is said to acquire its form in the space between the mythological epic and the European novel. He writes that it is not itself an epic or a replica of the original novel, but is inspired by *collective* mythic rituals and constructed from *inter-individual* relationships (ibid.: 61). Verma's elaboration of the foregoing argument does not concern me here. The point I wanted to make about the significance of cultural difference in the use of words like 'private' and 'public' is, I trust, clear enough.

One may, of course, abandon these words altogether, and opt for analogous but culturally rooted terms that might facilitate a more nuanced presentation of Indian perspectives on the distinctions under consideration. One could, for instance, invoke the distinction employed in early classical Tamil poetry (*ca.* 100 BC–AD 250) between *akam* and *puram* poems. The former pertain to, in A.K. Ramanujan's felicitous phrase, 'the interior landscape', and the latter are about the 'exterior', or the external domain. The former are about personal experience, more precisely about romantic love. The latter are about action, most notably about war. The *puram* poems may not be said to be wholly lacking in the subjective dimension, but the action, particularly when it ends in heroic death, is unlike the lovers' tryst, for everyone to see and admire (see Ramanujan 1985). It is noteworthy that while Ramanujan considers 'public' an acceptable denotation of the word *puram*, he does not render *akam* as 'private'. What Nirmal Verma found in the old Bergen house, we might well say, was the interior landscape, not privacy but interiority.

A word of caution is in order here. The contrast to which Ramanujan draws our attention should not be overgeneralized. Mattison Mines, an anthropologist, writing on the basis of over two decades of intermittent fieldwork in recent years among the very same Tamils, observes that, in the articulation of individuality, there is 'no clear separation' between its private and public aspects (Mines 1994: 12–13). This characterization finds echoes in other parts of India. Thus, another anthropologist, Marzia Balzani, describes how the Maharaja of Jodhpur (in north-western India) stepped out of the privacy of his sprawling palace in 1986 to go on a pilgrimage in collective (not personal) interest and interacted 'publicly with those of his realm'. As she puts it, 'no absolute lines can be drawn between private and public when dealing with kings and kingship' (2003: 123). What is true of commoners and South Indians, then, seems to be also true of kings and North Indians too. In short, contexts define the concepts under consideration: cross-culturally valid usages may be difficult to establish.[2]

DISCONTINUITIES AND CONTINUITIES: INDIA AND JAPAN

Let me turn to my own ethnography for further elaboration. In the course of fieldwork in a cluster of villages in south-eastern Kashmir in the 1950s and 1960s, I heard both the terms 'private' and 'public' in everyday Kashmiri speech, but with denotations that were rather different from those in a standard English dictionary. Of the two terms, 'private' (often pronounced *'pray-vut*, *'vut'* as in 'but') was not generally used, but when employed it referred to matters of household concern rather than those of individual interest. Privacy lay in the rooms that a household occupied inside a house which often was lived in by another household or other (never more than three) households (see Madan 1975: 138–41; 1989). Houses of agnatically related kin were usually located around a commonly owned compound, which was a kind of public (as opposed to private) space, but the term 'public' was not used to refer to it. Nor was it used to refer to more widely shared and utilized intra-religious (Hindu or Muslim) or inter-religious (Hindu–Muslim) community spaces, such as Hindu cremation grounds, Muslim graveyards, or pasture lands available to everybody. In fact, religious and village gatherings, marked by highly valued and enduring common interests and emotional bonds, were not even remotely regarded as 'public', nor deemed to have dimensions that could be legitimately called public by the villagers. Collective (*ralith-milith*, 'mixed together') and focused activities of various kinds inside the village were, however, contrasted with the 'goings on' in the nearby town of Anantnag and the remoter city of Srinagar, which the villagers visited from time to time to meet relatives, make purchases, attend law courts, or seek medical treatment.

Since the 1930s, a new and important element had entered into the lives of Kashmiris, namely, agitational politics aimed at securing economic and political rights from the autocratic government of the Maharaja and the feudal families associated with or created by the ruling family from 1846 onwards, when it came into the possession of the territories jointly designated as the State of Jammu and Kashmir (see Rai 2004 and Chapter 9 above). The people of the State were formally identified as the 'subjects' of the Maharaja: they had no citizenship rights as such and the only thing they could pray and hope for were kingly favours. These were arbitrary and discriminatory.

It was against this state of affairs that the community-based political organizations, the Muslim Conference and the Sanatan Dharma Yuvak Sabha, and the secular National Conference, came into existence in the Kashmir Valley. Given the high incidence of illiteracy, particularly among the Muslims, the most viable modes of political education and mobilization of the masses were public meetings (*jalsa*), at which leaders gave speeches (*takrīr*), and processions (*julūs*). By the time of the initial period of my fieldwork (1957–8), radical political changes had occurred: the Maharaja's government had been replaced by a people's government (so-called), formed by the National Conference, which had introduced sweeping land reforms (see Madan 1966). Political mobilization had been put into high gear: the political meeting and the procession were still the principal vehicles of securing people's support, although radio broadcasting too had appeared on the scene. It was to such gatherings that the villagers applied the term 'public' (pronounced as in standard English speech), sometimes derogatorily. In other words, the 'public' was constituted by political discourse, and comprised political leaders speaking in a park, on the roadside, or some such place, and their audience.[3]

Participation in political meetings and processions in Kashmir was voluntary and intentional for some, externally induced for others, and fortuitous for still others. For the villagers, it was mostly fortuitous: one listened to the speakers, or watched the processionists, if one happened to be in the town. The public gatherings were considered unstable and occasional: they formed, dissolved, and reformed with never exactly the same people participating on successive occasions. They had important consequences, gradually arousing interest in the people's citizenship rights, but many villagers did not take them seriously, considering them mere spectacles (*tamāsha*). Occasionally I even heard them characterized as nuisances because of noise, crowding, traffic jams, pressure on transport (people travelled mostly by tongas but motor buses also connected some villages to the towns), disturbance of normal market activities, and other inconveniences.

In sum, the notions of the 'private' and 'public' had entered the Kashmiri villagers' consciousness and speech, but they were contextually unrelated and carried different loads of signification. They and the phenomena they referred to existed independent of each other. They could not be meaningfully said to be opposites of each other, or mutually implicated.

* * *

Ethnographic and historical evidence from non-Western societies indicates that even when the 'private' and the 'public' are present as comparable social categories, their relationship and significance may not be similarly comparable to what these primarily are in the West. Thus, in traditional Japanese society, the public was continuous with rather than in contradistinction to the private. This holds good even now in a variety of contexts. An illustration is the manner in which the concept or ideology of the household, *ie*, which is a private, corporate, residential group, 'penetrates every nook and corner of the society' (Nakane 1972: 4). A variety of traditional and modern groups are modelled on and legitimized by the ethic of the *ie*. This is as true of the traditional word for one's work place (*uchi-no*) as of the medieval *ichizoku-roto* (a family group and its retainers), or the modern usage of *kokutetsu-ikka* (literally 'one railway family') to designate the Japanese National Railways.

What is noteworthy in this context is that, although the *ie* as an institution is said to be weakening, the ethic associated with it survives in extra-familial, public settings, such as factories or offices. Like the *ie*, these are vertically structured on the lines of the parent (*oya*)–child (*ko*) relationship. One's employer, superior, or boss is said to enjoy the status of a parent: he is the caring *oyabun*. Reciprocally, filial obedience is expected from the *kobun* (one in a position comparable to that of the child).

The continuity of the domestic and extra-domestic domains may well be a source of both strength and weakness in Japanese society. While the harmony that obtains in the work place may have been a major factor in the rapid post-World War II recovery of a shattered economy, it has also been asserted that there is 'a serious dearth of the type of public spirit that transcends both individual and group' (Doi 1977: 42) and is characteristic of Western society. Indeed, what I have described as the continuity of the private and the public has been characterized as 'confusion' or 'conflation' of the two social categories, resulting in such aberrations as the private use of public property (ibid.: 43).

The concern for the evolution of an appropriately conceptualized public spirit, characteristic of democratic citizenship in the West, is paradoxically expressed through the use of the term *oyake*, which stands for the notion of the 'public' and its extensions such as the 'public sector'. The paradox arises from the fact that, traditionally, *oyake* referred to the Japanese imperial family and, as such, had a very restricted or private connotation. A positive consequence of this conflation has been the characteristic behaviour of disgruntled factory workers who will resort to over-production to cause losses of profit to the owners but never damage the plant. The flexibility of the social categories under discussion—the fuzziness of their boundaries—may not be in consonance with explicit distinctions made in other contexts, such as that between the notions of the 'inner' and the 'outer', which is regarded as relevant mainly to the individual. But in this context too, discrepancies and stresses are glossed over. In short, the Japanese do not seemingly subscribe to the logic of binary oppositions in the manner of the Western or even Indian mentalities.

CONTRADISTINCTIONS, OVERLAPS, MERGERS:
INDIA, GERMANY, CLASSICAL GREECE

In the context of the ethnography of rural Kashmir, I tried to show above that the connotations of the borrowed words 'private' and 'public' were discontinuous: not only were the corresponding domains different, there was no obvious relation between them, not even that of contradistinction. Instances of the presence of such a relationship are, however, available in India too, emphasizing the bounded character of the two categories and defining the limits of their transgression. The case that I will now present is marked by the confrontation of traditional Hindu custom and modern Western law, and illustrates the reaching out of the domestic (private) sphere into the jural (extra-domestic) for succour. The situation could also be looked upon as an intrusion of the public domain (law courts, newspapers) into the privacy of the home.

Rukhmabai, an eleven-year-old school girl was married in 1873 by her parents (mother and stepfather) to a young man about eight years older than her. She was not, however, sent to live with him pending the attainment of puberty, and the acquisition by her husband of sufficient education to enable him to earn a living and assume the responsibilities of a householder. Early marriage and the postponement of its consummation were common occurrences of the time in Hindu society. The husband turned out to be not only sickly but also an indolent person of bad habits. He was averse to being educated and remained a dependent member of his maternal uncle's household. He eventually hoped to live on his wife's patrimonial inheritance. Although Rukhmabai was withdrawn from school, her informal education continued at her parental home.

Eleven years after her marriage, Rukhmabai was still with her parents, and her husband decided to initiate legal proceedings for the 'restitution of conjugal rights' under Anglo-Hindu law. Soon thereafter she herself resorted to another public forum, namely, the press, by pseudonymously writing letters in a newspaper (*Times of India*) about the low social status of Hindu women and the inequities of child marriage and enforced widowhood. Her views were endorsed editorially by the English-owned newspaper and by other persons of socially progressive views, but criticized by the defenders of orthodoxy. The debate in the press (involving English language and vernacular newspapers in such far flung cities as Bombay, Lahore, Allahabad, and Calcutta) bearing upon a wide range of issues concerning Hindu women's duties and rights (or lack of rights) raged throughout 1885 and the following years.

Meanwhile, Rukhmabai's husband's plea for judicial intervention for the restitution of his conjugal rights was heard by a single judge of the Bombay High Court, an Englishman. He decided against the husband even without hearing Rukhmabai's defence, saying that she could not be forced to take up cohabitation with her husband against her wishes. He recognized that accumulated case law would favour the husband, but maintained that since conjugal relations had not been instituted in this case, the notion of restitution was inapplicable. His judgement was more in consonance with Western notions of privacy, and of the rights and dignity of the individual, than Hindu notions of wifely duties and family solidarity.

The case was heard again (in 1886) by a two-member appellate bench of the same court on the husband's prayer. The judges (both of them Englishmen) reversed the earlier judgement, holding the view that a wife's proper place was in her husband's home. The distinction between the notions of institution and restitution of conjugal rights was, they held, not good in law. The case then came up for trial, again before a single judge (and again an Englishman), who decreed (in 1887) that Rukhmabai should go to live with her husband. There was another appeal for review, this time by Rukhmabai. The matter, however, came to an anticlimactic end (in 1888) through a compromise decree issued by the court the terms of which were worked out by the two parties: while Rukhmabai agreed to pay her husband a monetary compensation for the expenses incurred by him in seeking legal remedy, he in return agreed not to demand cohabitation from her. Incidentally, Rukhmabai went on to become the first qualified Indian woman practitioner of modern (allopathic) medicine.

The Rukhmabai case may be viewed in terms of the contrasting as well as overlapping orders of the private and the public and an evolving notion of citizenship rights. Sudhir Chandra, on whose monograph *Enslaved Daughters* (1988) I have depended for the basic facts, notes that the antagonists in the case partook of both the private world of domesticity, centred around marriage and family, and the public world comprising the relations between the rulers and the ruled. 'Ironically, those most vocal in opposing the extension of colonial authority into their socio-religious affairs were the keenest...to utilize the colonial legal system and its alien practices' (ibid.: 2).

The private domain was the locus of tradition, and Rukhmabai wanted it overturned—because it was discriminatory against women—by public debate and eventually by legislative intervention, both of them modern devices. In other words, she invited the intrusion of public institutions into the privacy of a Hindu home. Her husband also appealed to a major public institution, the law court, to uphold that same world of tradition as perceived at that time by some sections of public opinion. As for the judges, the one who favoured Rukhmabai did so (as already stated) in terms of Western notions of individual choice and dignity, confronting one conception of the private, namely the Hindu home, by another, namely the Western type individual, through the medium of the public court of law established by the state. The judges who favoured Rukhmabai's husband also confirmed the legitimacy of the law court sitting in judgement over disputed positions within the domestic domain, but in the name of Hindu tradition. In deciding that the wife was obliged to live with her husband, they refrained from defining cohabitation in terms of both coresidence and sexual intercourse, leaving the latter component to the privacy of the bedroom, a kind of an inner sanctum within the private world.[4]

The issues comprising the Rukhmabai case did not end in the Bombay High Court. They were ultimately selectively debated in the Imperial Legislative Council, which decided to freeze the intervention of the organs of the state in the private domain of conjugal relations at the limits already attained by it. Needless to emphasize that within a colonial setting the unavailability of citizenship rights to the ruled subjects, except within a very limited compass, flowed from the character of the state: it was a restrictive rather than expansive relationship.

The foregoing discussion underscores the point that the private and the public are best understood not in substantive terms (as insulated, cross-culturally valid entities) but interactionally (as open, relatively complex, context-sensitive bundles of relations).

* * *

The interpenetration or merging of the private and the public, it should be pointed out, is not confined to non-Western cultural settings although it is these on which the foregoing observations have been based. Even in the Western society itself, while the opposition of the categories, and the underlying dualistic logic of classification, are firmly established, there are occasions and situations when social reality becomes fully comprehensible only through their complementarity. Albert Hirschman (1998) has pointed out that one of the basic distinctions in economic analysis is that between private and public goods. The former are most simply and accurately represented by the loaf of bread and the latter by public (that is, state-sponsored) health and education. The consumption of private goods, which are limited in normal circumstances, is marked by the clash of individual interests. The number of loaves of bread available to each individual depends upon the total number of loaves and of consumers: if someone gets a loaf more than the others, then someone else must get a loaf less. Such a limitation obviously does not affect the consumption of public goods. A further dimension of this distinction is that while the provision of private goods may be left to the market, the production of public goods must be concurrently provided by the state in discharge of its obligations to the citizens. In such dichoto-mization, Hirschman observes, 'Little attention was paid to goods that would somehow be intermediate between the private and the public category [sic] or would belong to both' (ibid.: 17).

To illustrate the melding of the two categories, Hirschman cites an insightful essay by the German sociologist Georg Simmel on the sociology of the meal (*Mahlzeit*). Anticipating the later distinction by economists noted above, Simmel argued that eating (and drinking) are 'most self-centred', since 'what is eaten by a single person can under no circumstances be eaten by anyone else'. People however normally eat together: 'thus arises the sociological construct of the meal—it turns the exclusive self-seeking of eating into the frequent experience of being together and into the habit of joining in a common purpose' (quoted in Hirschman ibid.: 18).

In an interesting extension of the argument, Hirschman points out that in classical Greece (fifth century), the ancient institution of the banquet (which was, by definition, collective and public) emerged redefined as an obligatory act on the part of the citizens who represented the city of Athens after the democratic reforms of Kleisthenes: it became 'institutionalized as a symbol of the permanence of political power in a democracy'. In the post-classical (Hellenistic) period, banquets fostered and reinforced 'social and citizen relationships': they occupied 'a key position connecting...the religious, the public and the private spheres': they became 'the preeminent expression of what we like to call today "civil society"'. Hirschman feels persuaded to suggest the plausibility of 'a direct link...between the banquet and the emergence of Athenian democracy' (ibid.: 22–3). Examples of commensality linked to socially disruptive activities also are, however, noted by him (see ibid.: 25–8). Hirschman concludes: 'From the purely biological point of view, there is no doubt that eating has a straightforward relationship to individual welfare. But once they are done in *common*, eating and drinking normally go hand in hand with a remarkably diverse set of public or collective activities', for good or for bad (ibid.: 28–9).

* * *

To reiterate the importance of the oppositional conceptualization of the categories of the private and the public in Western culture, and the possible relevance of the same to other (non-Western) cultural settings, I would like to draw attention to the notion of privatization of religion. As is well known, the idea had two sources, one religious (the Reformation) and the other secular (the Enlightenment). Among the many strands that comprised the religious reform movements of the sixteenth century, which are collectively referred to as the Protestant Reformation, mention may here be made of lay piety and practice, scholarly debate about the true character and import of the teachings of Jesus Christ, and an abiding concern with the redemption of the individual sinner and an erring humanity. In all these expressions, the Reformation set itself against any mediatory role for the Church and its priesthood between the believer, whose sole justification was said to lie in faith, and God.

The Christian faith, it was asserted, required of the believer acknowledgement of the sovereignty of God and the supremacy of scripture. No other guidance was necessary. Martin Luther and other reformers were accused by their critics of providing unrestricted scope for individual or private interpretations of the scripture (see Bainton 1956). For the present purpose, an examination of the merits of the new formulations and of their critiques is not relevant. The main point is to draw attention to the arrival of the this-worldly individual in the midst of Christian society and the privatization of the religious endeavour (see Dumont 1986). This does not of course mean that the Reformation did not have social and cultural consequences, or that it was unrelated to public activity, such as the establishment of schools, for the promotion of particular versions of it. Moreover, Luther maintained that the Christian as citizen must submit to secular authority.

By repudiating the claims of the Church to speak for all of a Christian's concerns, the Reformation opened the way for secularization and the legitimization of the rights of both the political community and the individual citizen. This process of differentiation—of the carving out of secular areas of activity from a holistic design of living—was reinforced by the rise of the Age of Reason and the Enlightenment (17th–18th centuries). By its very nature, the Enlightenment, in its own various versions, included a critique of religion as a world view centred in the idea of God and as an institutional structure. It called upon human beings to 'dare to know' (Kant's admonition *sapere aude!*) whatever there is to be known through observation and the exercise of reason. Religion was admissible but only 'within the limits of reason' (Cassirer 1968: 163). Human intelligence was deemed adequate for achieving the goal of the perfection of social institutions. The notion of the reasons of the state (originally formulated by Machiavelli), rather than private religious values, were to be the means of and the justification for an ordered political domain.

In short, religion as faith was relegated to the innermost recesses of private life. In Max Weber's well known words, a result of secularization ('rationalization and intellectualization') has been not only the ending of magic, miracles, and mysteries ('disenchantment'), but also the 'retreat' of 'the ultimate and most sublime values' from 'public life either into the transcendental realm of the mystic life or into the brotherliness of direct and personal human relations' (1948: 155). This is as clear a statement of the antinomy of the private and the public as any other that is possible.

The opposition of the two categories has further implications in Weber's sociology that are of interest here. To mention but one of these, there is his typological distinction between patrimonialism (and feudalism), on the one hand, and the institutions of the modern state on the other. This could also be represented as the contrast between the private and the public. Patrimonial rule (domination) rests on the *personal* loyalty that the ruler receives from his household, entourage, administrative corps, and military force. The modern state is centrally governed, and its economy is regulated by an *impersonally recruited* and *rationally oriented* bureaucracy. It is in the social space that can only be called public that the modern ideas of rational law, legal domination, legislative regulation, legitimate force, citizenship rights, etc., can possibly arise (see Weber 1947 and 1948). The antinomy of the categories remains a central strand of Weber's thinking. And yet, on occasion, he drops it, in nostalgia as it were, as when he said that politics 'was not a product of the head alone', that 'an ethic of ultimate ends and an ethic of responsibility are not absolute contrasts but rather supplements' (1948: 127).

SUMMARY AND CONCLUDING REMARKS

It should be clear by now that I have been concerned in this exercise mainly with conceptual clarification, and not at all with the kinds of policy issues that are the staple of political controversy these days in India, whether focused on the relationship of the private and public sectors of the economy, or on the duties of the state vis-à-vis the religious communities. I have suggested that the social categories of the private and the public may not only be empirically found to be interrelated in different ways— contradistinction, discontinuity, continuity, overlapping, melding— in a variety of sociocultural settings, analytically too attentiveness to their interaction may be as productive of understandings of aspects of social reality as a focus on their contradistinction. Thus, a novelist may well consider privacy, or withdrawal from a surfeit of social interaction, an essential condition of his creativity; some have actually gone into hiding. Commenting on the award to him of the Nobel Prize for literature (in 1954), Ernest Hemingway was reported to have said that it was a good thing that public recognition rarely came the way of a great artist, for he or she must live alone in order to be able to face eternity and resist seizure by society. But we must not forget—as surely Hemingway did not—that, ultimately, the novelist writes for the reading public. The book is published, that is it is made public, sometimes ceremonially, sold in bookstores, and reviewed in journals. In short, the private makes way for the public. What is true of the writer is of course also true of the painter and the sculptor.[5]

Similarly, a villager, who has known only subjecthood under an autocratic-feudal regime, may well consider public political gatherings unfamiliar, impermanent, amorphous, and even inconvenient phenomena. But, eventually, he finds his individuality redefined, even without his cooperation by such events; he is made aware of his citizenship rights under democratic governance. Such rights not only promote and protect his civil rights, and entail political (public) participation in various forms as a duty, they may also embrace aspects of family (private) life. The relationship of the private and public domains, as evident from the Rukhmabai case, is an evolving (expanding, contracting) one.

Private life in any form should not be, however, regarded as something passive, a field for arbitrary public intervention or imposition from the outside. As the brief reference to some Japanese conceptualizations of the relationship of the two categories shows, public life may in fact be sustained by values that have their origin in private life and are therefore legitimized by it. These values are not static but might occasionally change in significant ways without a total rupture of roots as a result of broad politico-economic and social changes.

Now, there are situations in which the separation of the private and the public may be deemed politically expedient and socially beneficial. A good and familiar example is the identification of certain areas of economic activity (the social sector) that may not be left to the caprices of the market (private sector), but must be controlled directly or indirectly by the state (public sector), so that the interests of the under-privileged sections of the population, and thereby of the society at large, may be served. Similarly, privatization of religion (secularization) may be defended on the ground that public or state religions could threaten significant individual rights such as the freedom of conscience (to choose and profess a religion of one's choice or to opt for agnosticism). But the public sector has been known to be inefficient and corrupt with a tendency to invade areas where private enterprise serves the community better. On the contrary, the last quarter of the twentieth century has provided ample evidence from Latin America, East Europe, and elsewhere of the positive role of public religion (the Catholic Church) in the promotion of citizenship rights against dictatorial regimes (see Casanova 1994).

In short, experience and deeper reflection reveal that policies of mutual exclusion of domains defined as private and public may produce public (political, economic, social) gains, but they could also have public costs. The interests of the community in general rather than rigid ideological positions would seem to be the obvious guide to collective action, but this is more easily said than done. Moreover, it may be noted, that the melding of the private and the public may not always follow from consciously pursued policies; it may rather be an unintended consequence of indirectly related decisions or fortuitous developments.

Apart from contradistinction or overlapping and merging, the private represented by the family, and the public, by the state, frame a middle ground, a social space for citizen initiatives and action that is designated as civil society. Needless to emphasize, this, too, is a public sphere and, like the political community, may be viewed as a structure of mediation between the state and the society at large. Here the citizens may assert their rights as individuals or corporations against one another or against the state. Civil society is in the foregoing perspective an arena *par excellence* for the dialectic of the private and the public.

To conclude. One of the several possible ways of concluding an exploratory essay like this one is to go back to where one began. In the present case, this was Nirmal Verma's idea of how a constructed, architectural space, namely, the inside of an old European house, could be considered to have been the psychological, private, space for the birth of a particular genre of literary creativity in a manner public spaces could not have. The inspirations, or vibrations, in the two settings are different. It is arguable, however, that unresolved conceptual oppositions call for resolution through a radical relativization or by moving to a higher level to dissipate the tension.

Let me persist with the example of built-over spaces. Normally, no house anywhere stands in a state of total isolation nor is it internally entirely undifferentiated. In a study of nineteenth-century Delhi, Margrit Pernau argues how a bazar, the urban public space *par excellence*, received customers and vendors through feeder lanes which could have been considered private in relation to it. These lanes, in turn, were public pathways in relation to the various residential quarters built alongside or beyond them. Within such quarters each house was the domain of privacy. And each home had its grades of privacy, the women's rooms being the most private. The demarcating lines are utterly fluid. They varied 'not only according to space and time, but also at any given moment within the same cultural setting, according to the point of view' (Pernau 2003: 122).

The foregoing represents contextual diffusion without an alteration of levels. Dissolution of the opposite categories through their synthesis at a higher level, or transcendence, is the last of the series of relationships I would like to consider here. Charles Correa, one of India's most distinguished contemporary architects, has written that private and public spaces can indeed merge into a third type at a level other (higher) than their own. I will illustrate the point by taking the example of a Hindu home, with its courtyard walled in from outside, public spaces. Make a *kolam/rangoli* (a graphic floral-cum-geometric floor design using coloured powder)—an auspicious sign of domestic well-being in South/North India (in Correa's words this is a 'sacred gesture')—and the space becomes sacred. Its private character is not abolished but temporarily recedes into the background, as it were. Not every traditional Hindu home has a courtyard, however. Colourful *kolams/rangolis* are made, nevertheless, in front of the house—even if a humble one—in the quasi-public lane (or narrow street). The people who go by—whether acquaintances or strangers—do not normally trample over it, for this bit of public space is generally acknowledged as sacred by everybody. To consider it privatized—the encroachment of the private on the public domain—would be a misreading of the gesture.

All cultures have procedures of such setting apart of domestic or extra-domestic spaces, temporarily or permanently. Some do this more than the others. Sacred spaces thus created are the third transcendental category, besides the private and the public. Correa puts it succinctly: 'To the Japanese Mount Fuji is sacred; to the Swiss Mont Blanc is just a high mountain. This difference is decisive to their architecture and to their lives' (1989: 94). The point, then, is not whether the West knows only of the relationship of contradistinction, although it privileges the same, or that non-Western societies do not know it, for they obviously do, but that the latter societies and cultures know it in other ways. Our search is for the many ways in which the private and the public are contextually related, not in some mindless quest for diversity, but in the conviction that one sees the particular better in the light of the many rather than under the shadow of its own torch alone.

NOTES

1. One could go back a step and recall that Plato wanted the 'guardians' to be free of 'excessive' family bonds of 'joys and sorrows' that make one take 'whatever he can get for himself into a private home', militating against a regime of 'fellow feeling'. It should be emphasized, however, that he did not consider such a state of affairs reasonable for the community as a whole (*The Republic* V. 463–4).
2. Let me get one false cue out of the way straightaway. Laxity in the use of terms, which is common enough, may create the impression that the private–public dichotomy prevails widely across cultures in essentially the same form. Closer attention to the precise connotations of words readily dispels the error. This may be illustrated by citing the case of the Vedic performances known as *shrauta* (from *shruti*, revealed knowledge) rituals, which are contrasted to *grihya* (domestic) rituals, and generally described as public (in contrast to private) by Indologists. The correct distinction is that the *shrauta* ritual is extra-domestic, with wider concerns, but not wholly separate from domestic rites, one of its three fires being that of the householder (see Flood 1996: 42–3, 54–5, et passim). It is by no means open to public participation: everyone allowed to be present is a qualified participant. There are no spectators who may come and go as they please.
3. After the above had been written, I came across the following observation in a historical study:

   The fact that 1931 was the beginning of anti-Dogra political activity in Kashmir is highly overstated. Despite the fact that the public arena was severely proscribed in the state prior to 1932, *the Kashmiri Muslim leadership had crafted and laid claim to a public space in which they defined their political agenda as well as the contours of their community identity* (Zutshi 2003: 211, emphasis added).

The significance or otherwise of the events of the early 1930s is arguable, but my interest here is in the convergence in the use of the term 'public' in people's speech and a historian's text.

4. It is obvious that the location of a cultural practice within an appropriate domain—public or private—must have seemed immensely problematic to the British in the discharge of their administrative and judicial responsibilities, because of the lack of fit between English (Western) and Indian conceptual categories. Indeed, it has been suggested that 'the adjudication of competing claims among groups over rights to use public areas' was quite strenuous, and the hope that there might be no real Indian concept of the 'public' must have been fondly entertained. Thus, English missionaries regarded customary practices such as 'hookswinging' or sati in the open as 'public profanation of space' that colonial rulers should forbid. 'Public opinion', according to Dirks (2002: 152–3), 'seemed to the British a quality of civil society that in India was vastly underdeveloped [in the late nineteenth century], and yet the public domain, which was believed to exist in the most tenuous ways, was seen for the most part as a site of immense danger.' This insight should be developed further.

5. On this complex point Naipaul (2003: 182) quoted Marcel Proust in his Nobel Lecture with obvious admiration:

> In fact, it is the secretions of one's innermost self, written in solitude and for oneself alone, that one gives to the public. What one bestows on private life—in conversation... or in those drawing room essays that are scarcely more than conversation in print— is the product of a quite superficial self, not of the innermost self which one can only recover by putting aside the world and the self that frequents the world.

References

Aristotle. 1943. *Politics*. Benjamin Jowett (trs.). New York: Walter J. Black.

Awasthi, Suresh and Induja Awasthi. 1985. *Chambers English–Hindi Dictionary*, New Delhi: Allied.

Bainton, Roland H. 1956. *The Reformation of the Sixteenth Century*. Boston: Beacon Press.

Balzani, Marzia. 2003. *Modern Indian Kingship: Tradition, Legitimacy & Power in Rajasthan*. Oxford: James Currey.

Casanova, José. 1994. *Public Religions in the Modern World*. Chicago: University of Chicago Press.

Cassirer, Ernst. 1968. *The Philosophy of the Enlightenment*. Princeton, N.J.: University of Princeton Press.

Chattopadhyay, Bankimchandra. 1969. *Bankim Rachanābali (English Works)*, by Jogesh Chandra Bagal (ed.). Calcutta: Sahitya Samsad.

Correa, Charles. 1989. 'The public, the private, and the sacred'. *Daedalus* 118(4): 93–114.

Dirks, Nicholas B. 2002. *Castes of Mind: Colonialism and the Making of British India*. New Delhi: Permanent Black.

Doi, Takeo. 1977. *The Anatomy of Dependence*. Tokyo: Kodansha.

Dumont, Louis. 1986. *Essays on Individualism*. Chicago: University of Chicago Press.

Flood, Gavin. 1996. *An Introduction to Hinduism*. Cambridge: Cambridge University Press.

Habermas, Jürgen. 1989. *The Structural Transformation of the Public Sphere: An Inquiry into a Category of Bourgeois Society*. Cambridge: MIT Press.

Hegel, G.W.F. 1977 [1807]. *Phenomenology of Spirit*. A.V. Miller (trs.). New York: Oxford University Press.

Hirschman, Albert. 1998. *Crossing Boundaries: Selected Writings*. New York: Zed Books.

Kant, Immanuel. 1991. *Political Writings*, 2nd edn. Hans Reiss (ed.), H.B. Nisbet (trs.). Cambridge: Cambridge University Press.

Leach, Edmund. 1967. *A Runaway World*? London: Oxford University Press.

Machiavelli. 1988. [1513]. *The Prince*. Quentin Skinner and Russell Price (eds). Cambridge: Cambridge University Press.

Madan, T.N. 1966. 'Politico-economic change and organizational adjustment in a Kashmiri village'. *The Journal of Karnatak University (Social Sciences)* 2: 20–34.

————. 1975. 'On living intimately with strangers'. In André Béteille and T.N. Madan (eds). *Encounter and Experience. Personal Accounts of Fieldwork*. New Delhi: Vikas.

————. 1989. *Family and Kinship. A Study of the Pandits of Rural Kashmir*. Second Enlarged Edition. Delhi: Oxford University Press.

————. 2003. 'Of the social categories 'private' and 'public': Considerations of cultural context'. In Mahajan (q.v.).

Mahajan, Gurpreet (ed.). 2003. *The Public and the Private: Issues of Democratic Citizenship*. New Delhi: Sage Publications.

Mill, John Stuart. 1982. *On Liberty*. Gertrude Himmelfarb (ed.). Harmondsworth: Penguin.

Mines, Mattison. 1994. *Public Faces, Private Voices: Community and Individuality in South India*. New Delhi: Oxford University Press.

Nakane, Chie. 1972. *Japanese Society*. Berkeley: University of California Press.

————. 1978. Personal communication.

Naipaul, V.S. 2003. *Literary Occasions: Essays*. New York: Alfred Knopf.

Pernau, Margrit. 2003. 'From a "private" public to a "public" private sphere: Old Delhi and the north Indian Muslims in comparative perspective'. In Mahajan (q.v.).

Plato. 1945. *The Republic*. F.M. Cornford (trs.). New York: Oxford University Press.

Rai, Mridu. 2004. *Hindu Rulers, Muslim Subjects*. New Delhi: Permanent Black.

Ramanujan, A.K. (trs.). 1985. *Poems of Love and War*. New Delhi: Oxford University Press.

Sudhir Chandra. 1998. *Enslaved Daughters: Colonialism, Law and Women's Rights*. New Delhi: Oxford University Press.

Tönnies, Ferdinand. 1955. *Community and Association*. London: Routledge and Kegan Paul.

Trilling, Lionel. 1951. *The Liberal Imagination*. London: Secker and Warburg.

Troeltsch, Ernst. 1981. *The Social Teaching of the Christian Churches*. Vol. 1. Chicago: University of Chicago Press.

Verma, Nirmal. 2000. 'Upanyas ki parti parikatha' (in Hindi). *Bahuvachan*, 2, 2: 60–67. New Delhi: Mahatma Gandhi International University.

Weber, Max. 1947. *The Theory of Economic and Social Organization*. New York: Oxford University Press.

―――. 1948. *From Max Weber: Essays in Sociology* by H.H. Gerth and C.W. Mills (eds and trs.). London: Routledge and Kegan Paul.

Wittgenstein, Ludwig. 1953. *Philosophical Investigations*. G.E.M. Anscombe. (trs.). New York: Macmillan.

Zutshi, Chitralekha. 2003. *Languages of Belonging*. New Delhi: Permanent Black.

Index

Razdan, K., 258
reform/reform movements/
  reformist sects, 120, 161, 169,
  191, 207
Reformation, 31, 32, 65, 328, 339,
  356, 369, 370; *See also* Protestant
  Reformation
Rehman, F., 64
reincarnation, 285, 288
relativism, 133, 214, 215
religion/religiosity, ix, x, 1–9, 13,
  14, 17, 19–25, 33, 36, 40, 42,
  48, 52, 56, 58, 61, 63–5, 68–71,
  77–87, 92, 93, 101–4, 105nn2, 3,
  108nn14, 16, 17, 113–24, 128,
  129, 134, 136, 138, 140, 149,
  154–61, 163, 168–70, 188, 190,
  191, 193, 200, 207, 209, 211,
  211n, 212, 213, 227, 230, 232,
  234–7, 251, 296, 297, 299, 301,
  302, 309, 312–15, 314nn2, 4,
  315nn6, 7, 8, 9, 319, 332, 333,
  337, 350, 351, 370, 372;
  privatization of, 65, 128, 134,
  136, 237, 369, 370, 372
*Religion and Society among the
  Coorgs of South India* (Srinivas),
  21, 209, 294, 296, 297, 311
Religion of India, The (Weber), 305,
  306, 309, 311
Religion of the Semites (Smith), 303
religious activity/beliefs/
  doctrines/practices, 4, 5, 7, 29,
  34–7, 43–5, 47, 51, 59, 60, 68, 79,
  84, 87, 105n3, 113, 122, 125, 135,
  140, 151, 158, 159, 160, 162, 179,
  182, 198, 199, 207, 208, 211, 213,
  221, 224, 226–8, 231, 232, 234,
  244, 247, 248, 255, 256, 302, 303,
  309, 313, 315nn7, 8, 369, 371;
  boundaries, 36, 170;
  brotherhood, 93; communities,
  56, 92, 93, 115, 117, 128, 134,
  141, 147, 151, 152, 159, 213;
  conflict, 69, 84, 201;
  consciousness, 15; freedom, 17;

fundamentalism, 1, 17, 57,
  76, 101, 134, 154, 207, 211;
  identity, x, 36, 38, 44, 45, 48,
  55, 68, 94, 115, 147, 166, 199,
  235; institutions, 5, 57, 71, 119,
  133; intolerance, 88, 113;
  language, 161; liberty, 31, 32,
  34, 40, 50, 102; merit, 328;
  minorities, 38, 46, 52n, 57, 90,
  91, 130; movements, 15, 143n8;
  nationalism, 121, 147, 169, 171;
  piety/pietists, 77; pluralism, x,
  1, 30, 48, 50, 86, 87, 103, 104,
  124, 135, 137, 234, 299;
  revitalization, 160; symbolism,
  234; syncretism, 50, 102, 228,
  229, 232; terrorism, 19; thought,
  356; tolerance/toleration, 51,
  120, 121, 127, 129, 182; tradition,
  15, 18, 24, 29, 48, 49, 51, 64–6,
  76, 122, 130, 142n6, 177, 207,
  208, 213, 229, 230, 231, 233, 343;
  values, 12, 94, 105n2, 147, 151,
  207, 212, 331, 350, 351; worship
  29, 34, 51
Remembered Village, The (Srinivas),
  302, 322
Renou, L., 344n1
renouncer/renunciation, 158, 186,
  215, 216, 223, 234, 246, 247, 251,
  252, 258–61, 262n5, 272, 288,
  327, 334; *See also sannyāsa/
  sannyāsī*
Republic (Plato), 337
revealed religion, 102, 229, 359
revivalism, 15, 58, 59, 71, 120,
  136, 207, 213, 237
Ricouer, P., 140
Rig Veda, 62, 211, 247
Ripon, Lord, 93
Rishi(s), doctrines of, 178, 185,
  186, 187, 190, 198, 201
rita/rituchakra, 266
rites/rituals, 81, 101, 218, 220,
  221, 223, 231, 243, 246, 248,
  249, 250, 252, 253, 256, 258, 259,